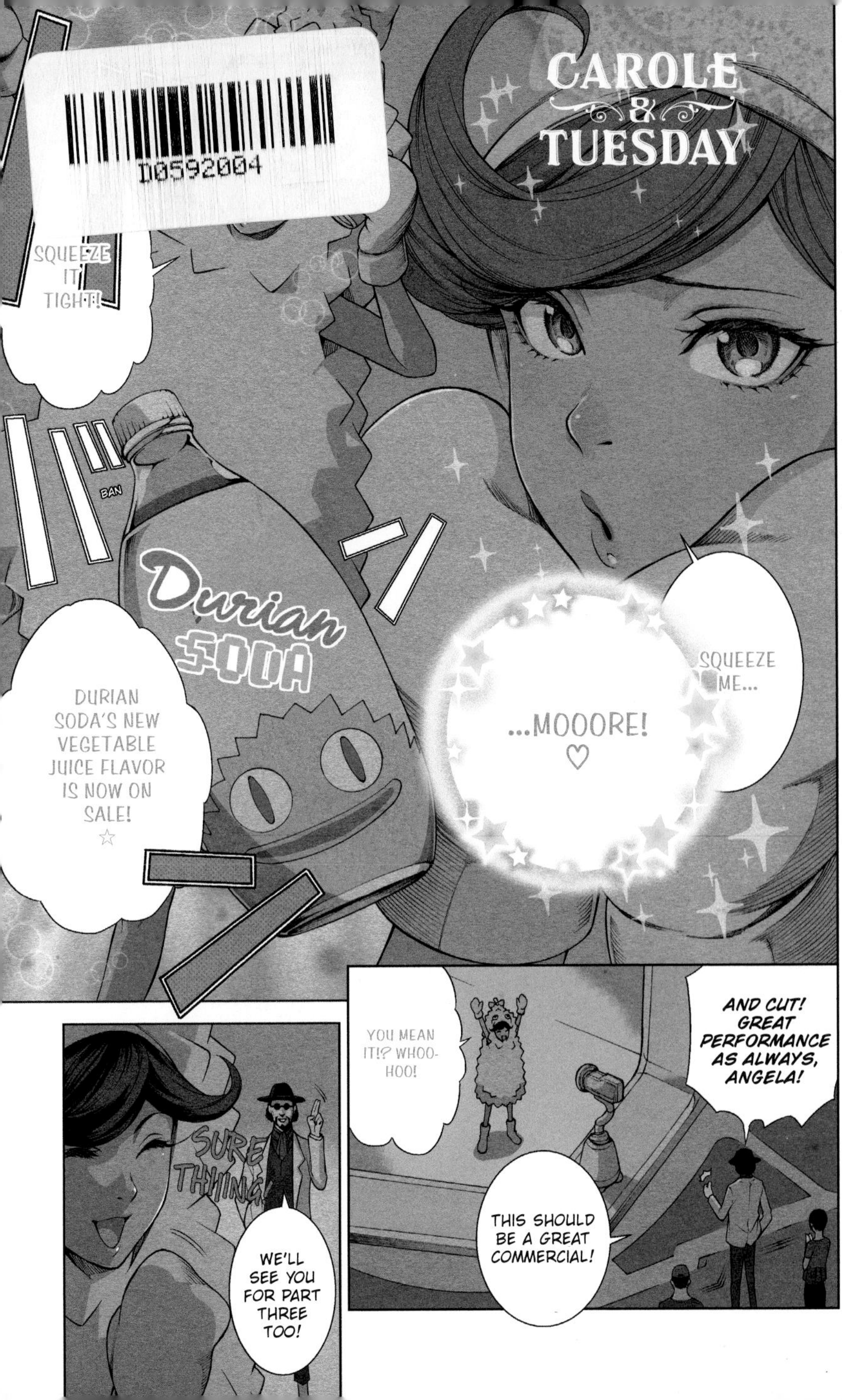
CAROLE & TUESDAY
SQUEEZE IT TIGHT!
SQUEEZE ME...
...MOOORE! ♡
BAN
Durian SODA
DURIAN SODA'S NEW VEGETABLE JUICE FLAVOR IS NOW ON SALE! ☆
AND CUT! GREAT PERFORMANCE AS ALWAYS, ANGELA!
YOU MEAN IT!? WHOO-HOO!
THIS SHOULD BE A GREAT COMMERCIAL!
SURE THING!
WE'LL SEE YOU FOR PART THREE TOO!

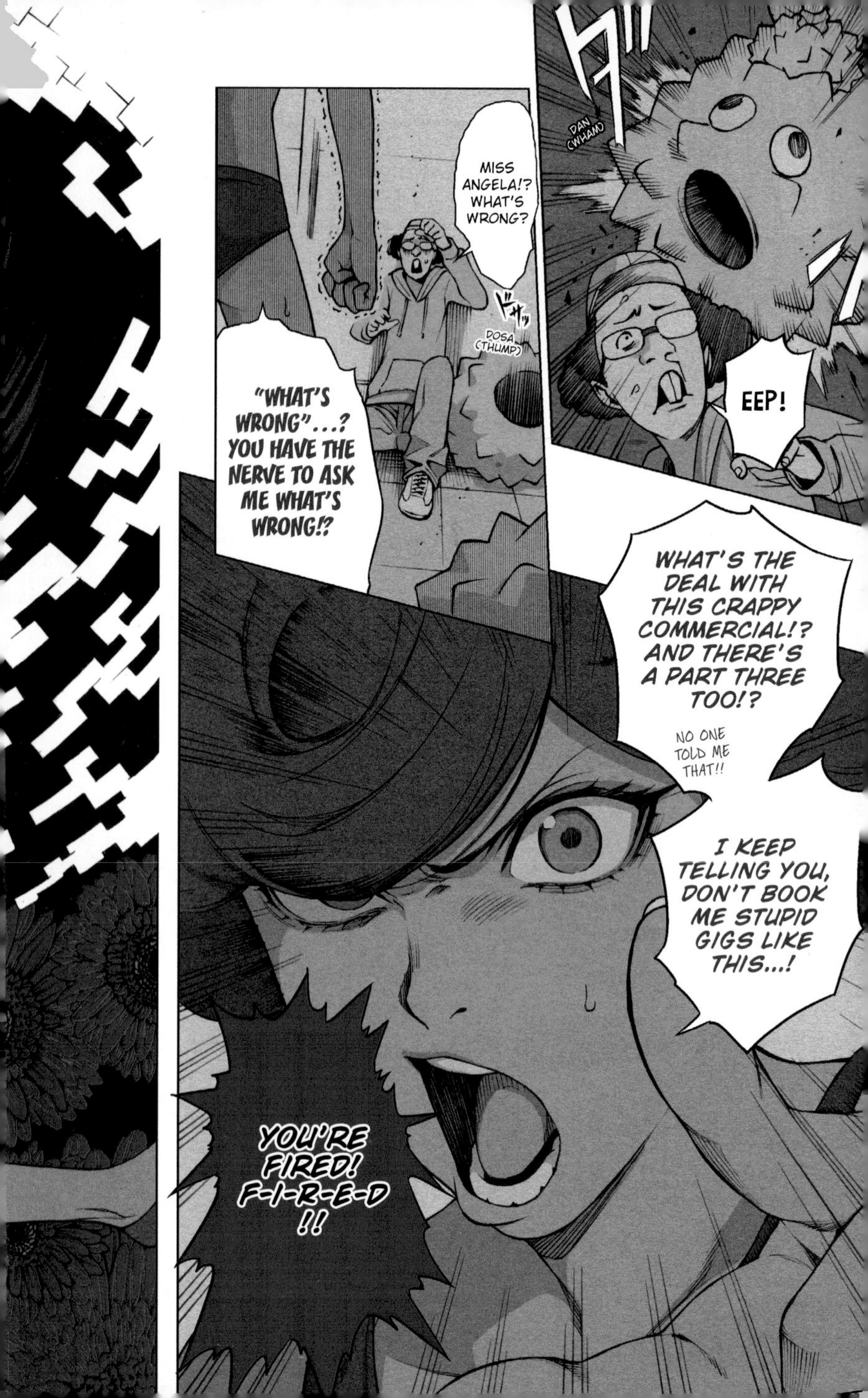
DAN (WHAM)
EEP!
MISS ANGELA!? WHAT'S WRONG?
DOSA (THUMP)
"WHAT'S WRONG"...? YOU HAVE THE NERVE TO ASK ME WHAT'S WRONG!?
WHAT'S THE DEAL WITH THIS CRAPPY COMMERCIAL!? AND THERE'S A PART THREE TOO!?
NO ONE TOLD ME THAT!!
I KEEP TELLING YOU, DON'T BOOK ME STUPID GIGS LIKE THIS...!
YOU'RE FIRED! F-I-R-E-D!!

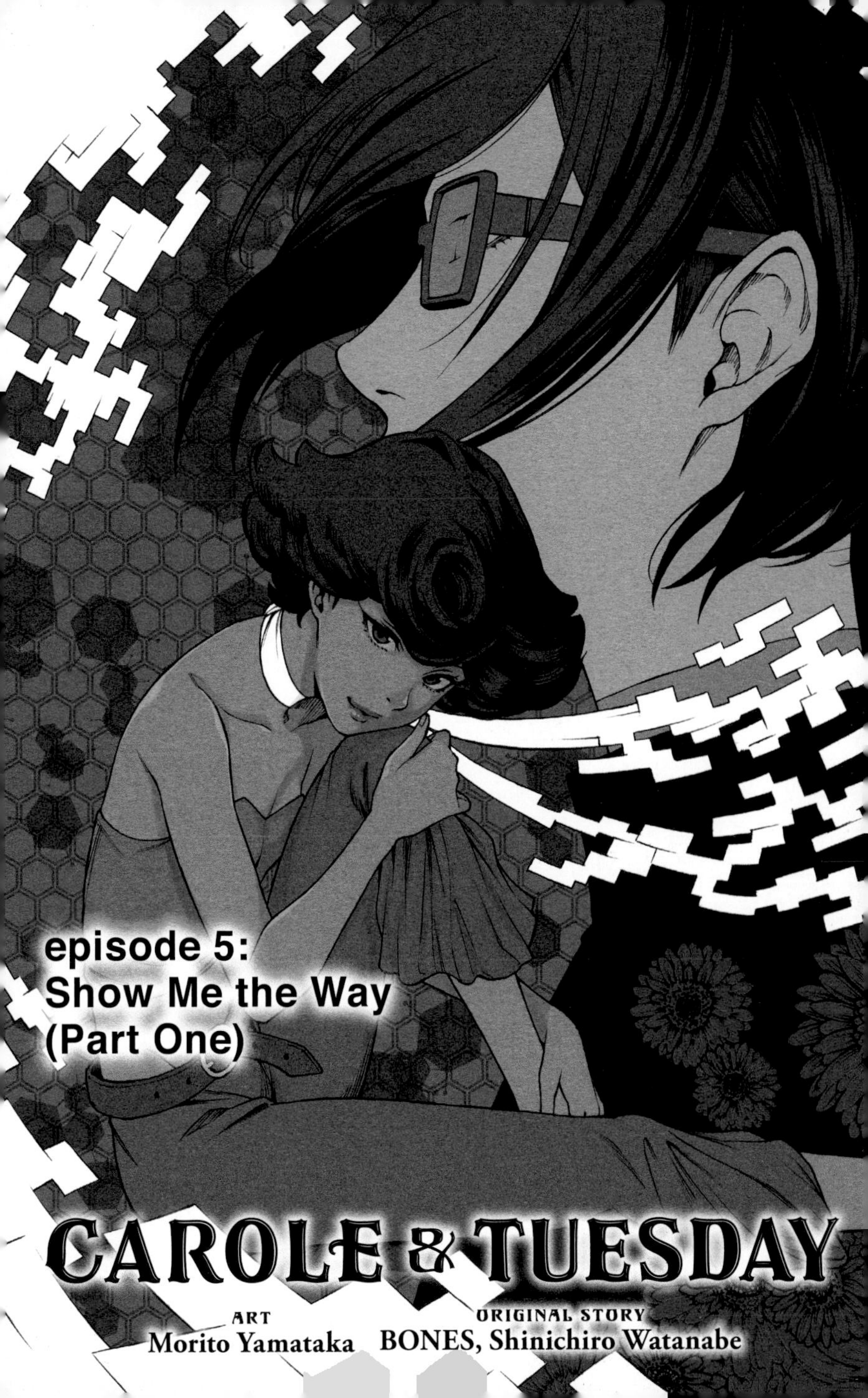
episode 5:
Show Me the Way
(Part One)
CAROLE & TUESDAY
ART
Morito Yamataka
ORIGINAL STORY
BONES, Shinichiro Watanabe

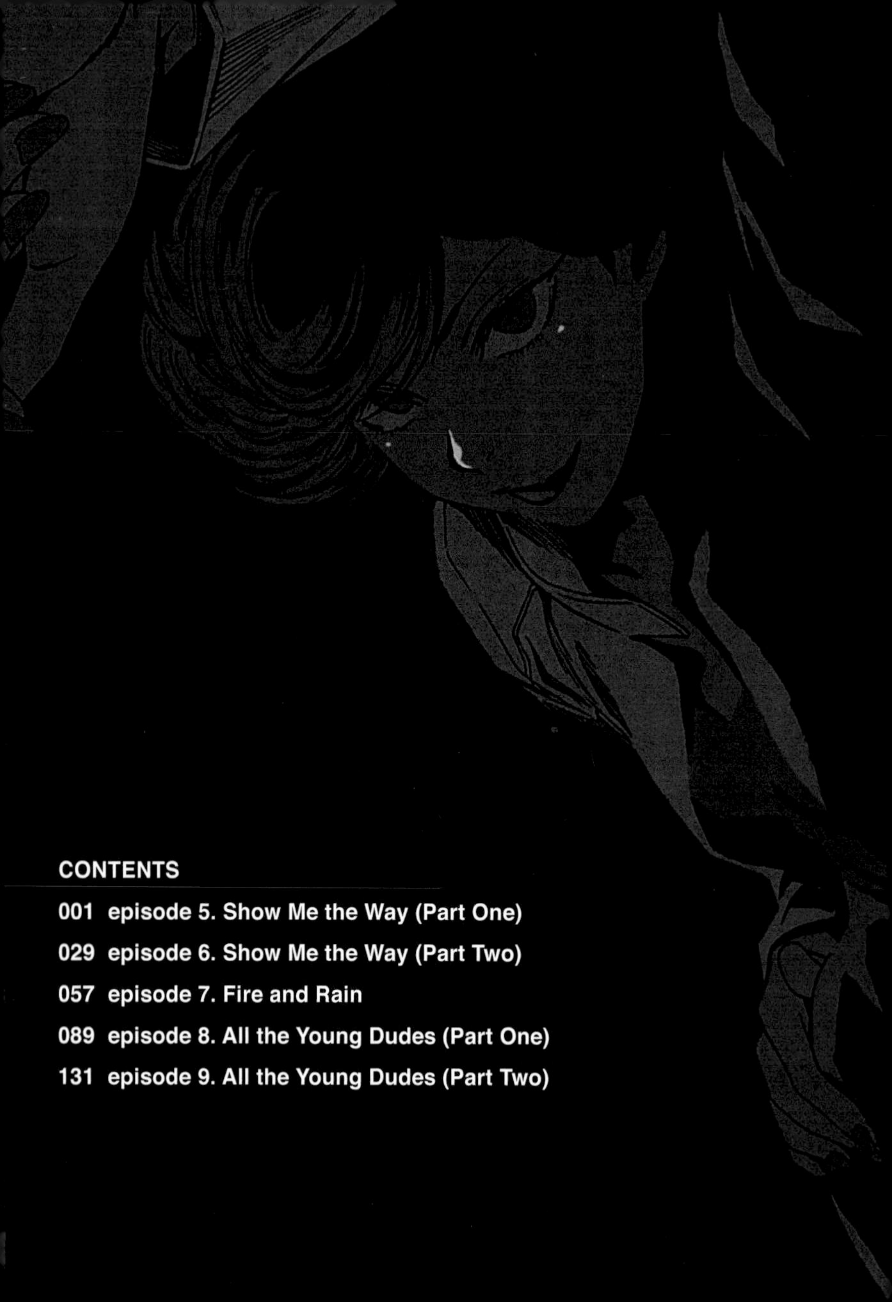

CONTENTS

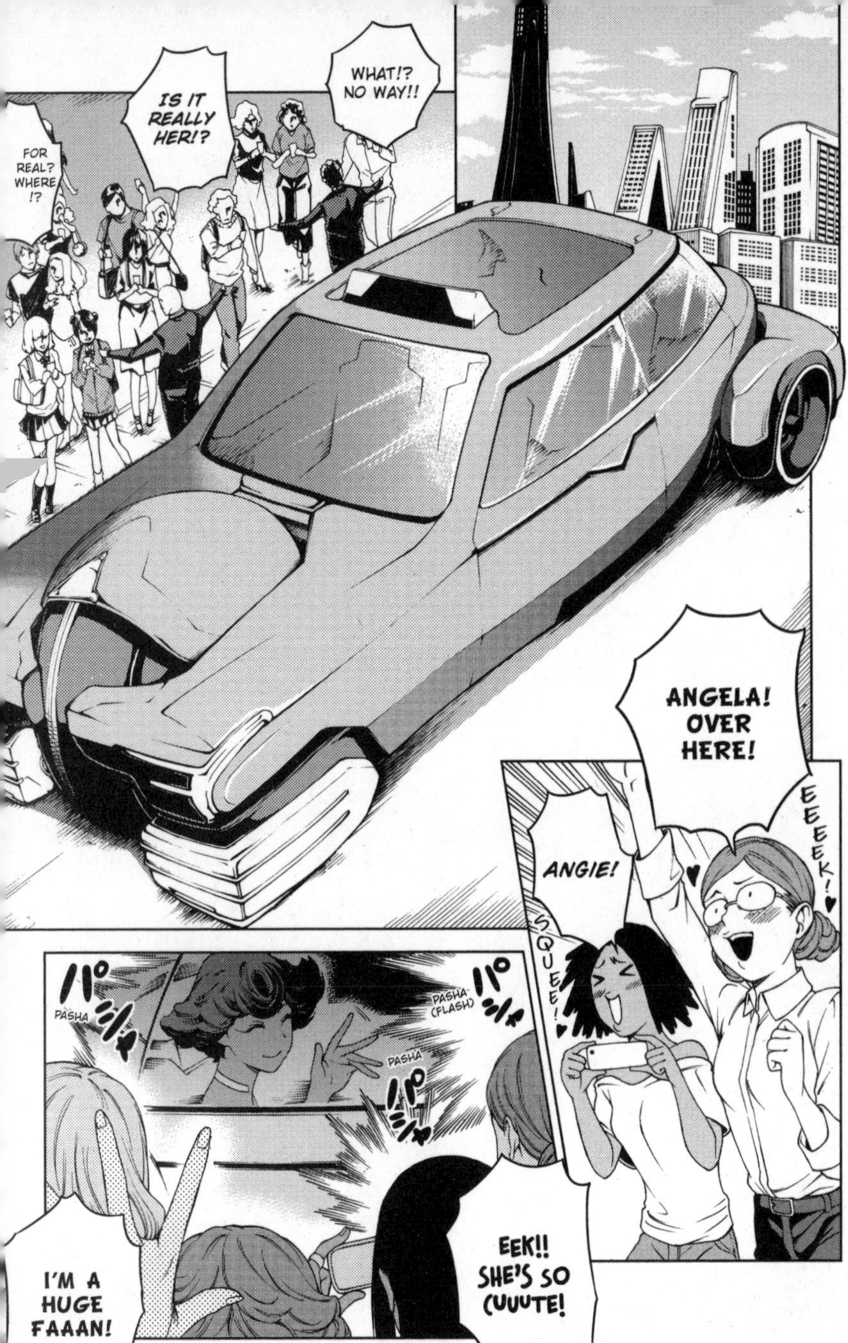
WHAT!? NO WAY!!
IS IT REALLY HER!?
FOR REAL? WHERE !?
ANGELA! OVER HERE!
EEEEK!
ANGIE!
SQUEE!
パシャ
PASHA (FLASH)
パシャ
PASHA
パシャ
PASHA
EEK!! SHE'S SO CUUUTE!
I'M A HUGE FAAAN!

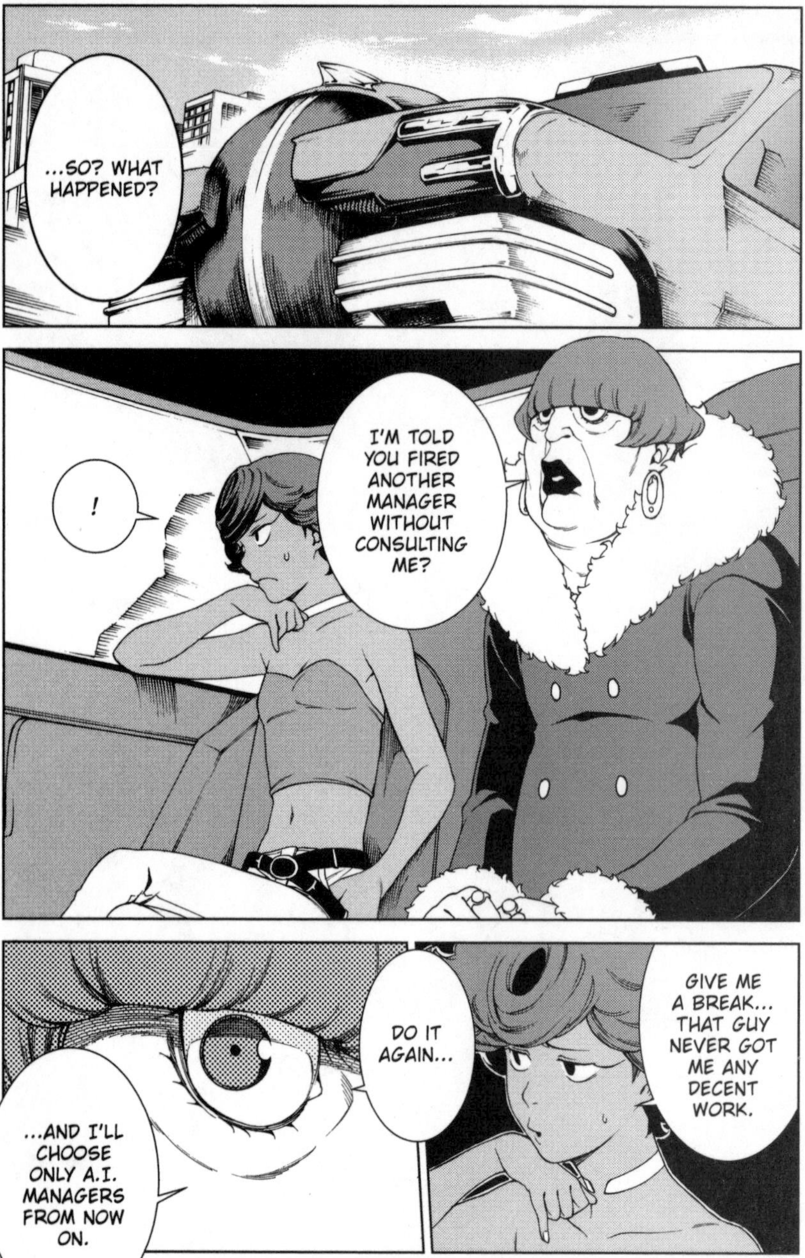
...SO? WHAT HAPPENED?
I'M TOLD YOU FIRED ANOTHER MANAGER WITHOUT CONSULTING ME?
!
GIVE ME A BREAK... THAT GUY NEVER GOT ME ANY DECENT WORK.
DO IT AGAIN...
...AND I'LL CHOOSE ONLY A.I. MANAGERS FROM NOW ON.

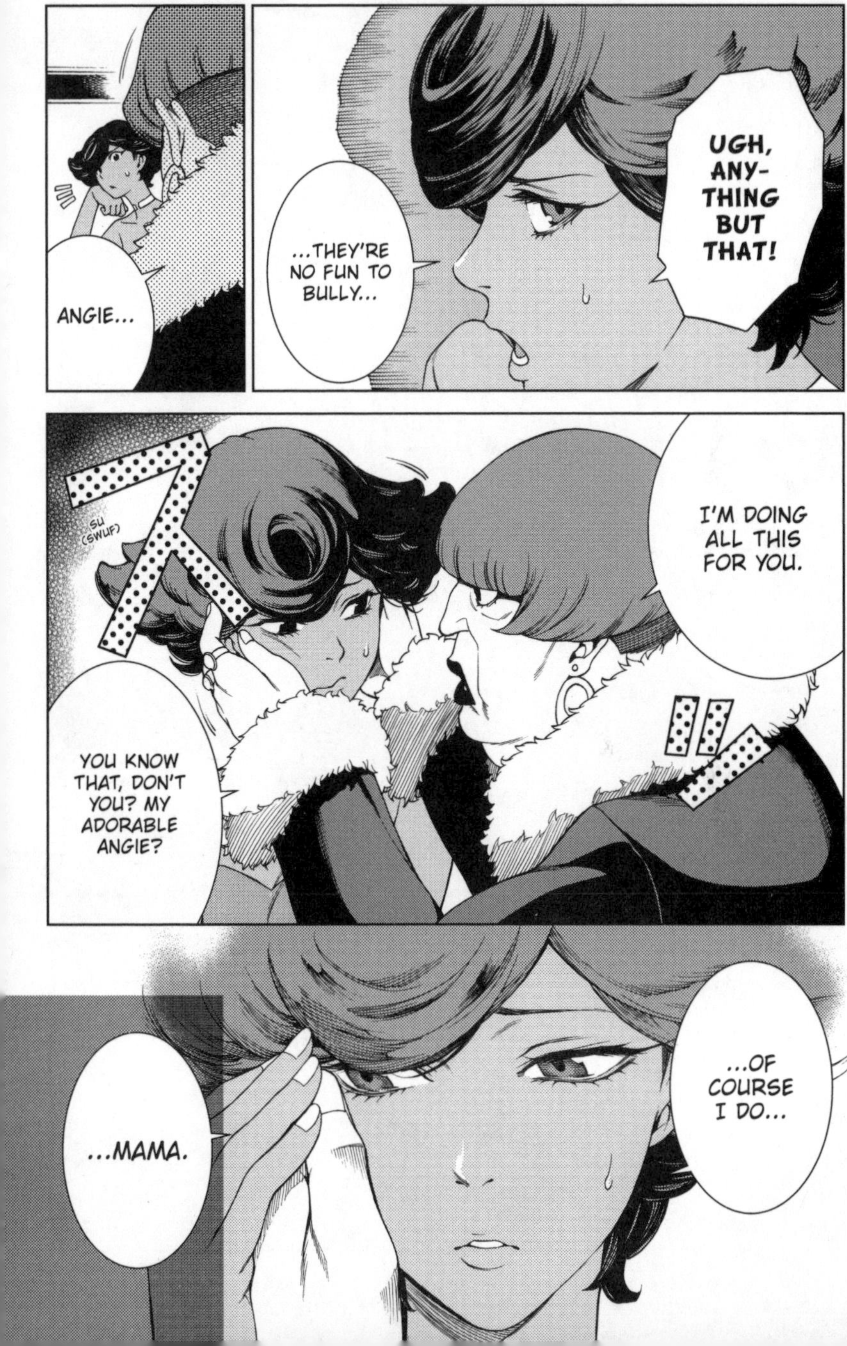
UGH, ANY- THING BUT THAT!
...THEY'RE NO FUN TO BULLY...
ANGIE...
I'M DOING ALL THIS FOR YOU.
SU (SWUF)
YOU KNOW THAT, DON'T YOU? MY ADORABLE ANGIE?
...OF COURSE I DO...
...MAMA.

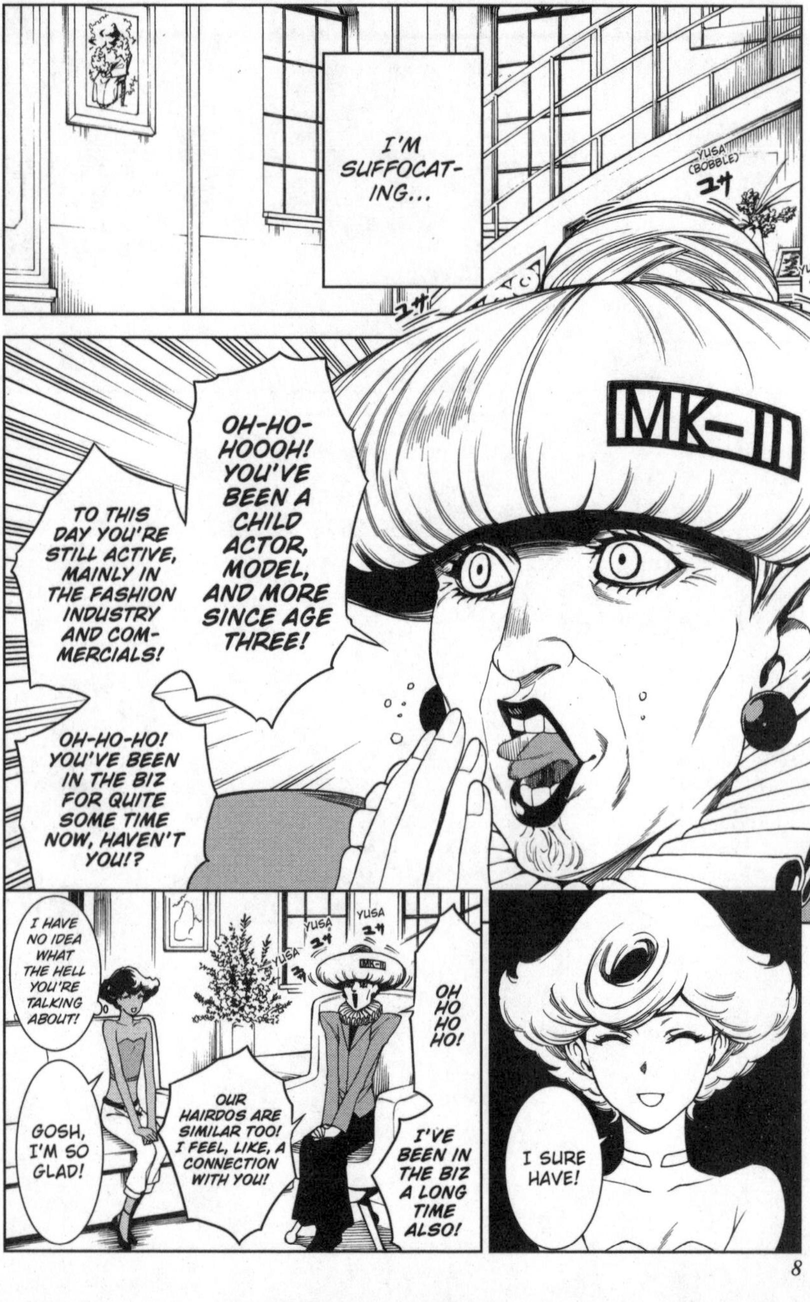
I'M SUFFOCATING...
YUSA (BOBBLE)
ユサ
YUSA
ユサ
ユサ
OH-HO-HOOOH! YOU'VE BEEN A CHILD ACTOR, MODEL, AND MORE SINCE AGE THREE!
TO THIS DAY YOU'RE STILL ACTIVE, MAINLY IN THE FASHION INDUSTRY AND COMMERCIALS!
OH-HO-HO! YOU'VE BEEN IN THE BIZ FOR QUITE SOME TIME NOW, HAVEN'T YOU!?
I SURE HAVE!
YUSA ユサ
YUSA ユサ
YUSA
OH HO HO HO!
I'VE BEEN IN THE BIZ A LONG TIME ALSO!
OUR HAIRDOS ARE SIMILAR TOO! I FEEL, LIKE, A CONNECTION WITH YOU!
I HAVE NO IDEA WHAT THE HELL YOU'RE TALKING ABOUT!
GOSH, I'M SO GLAD!

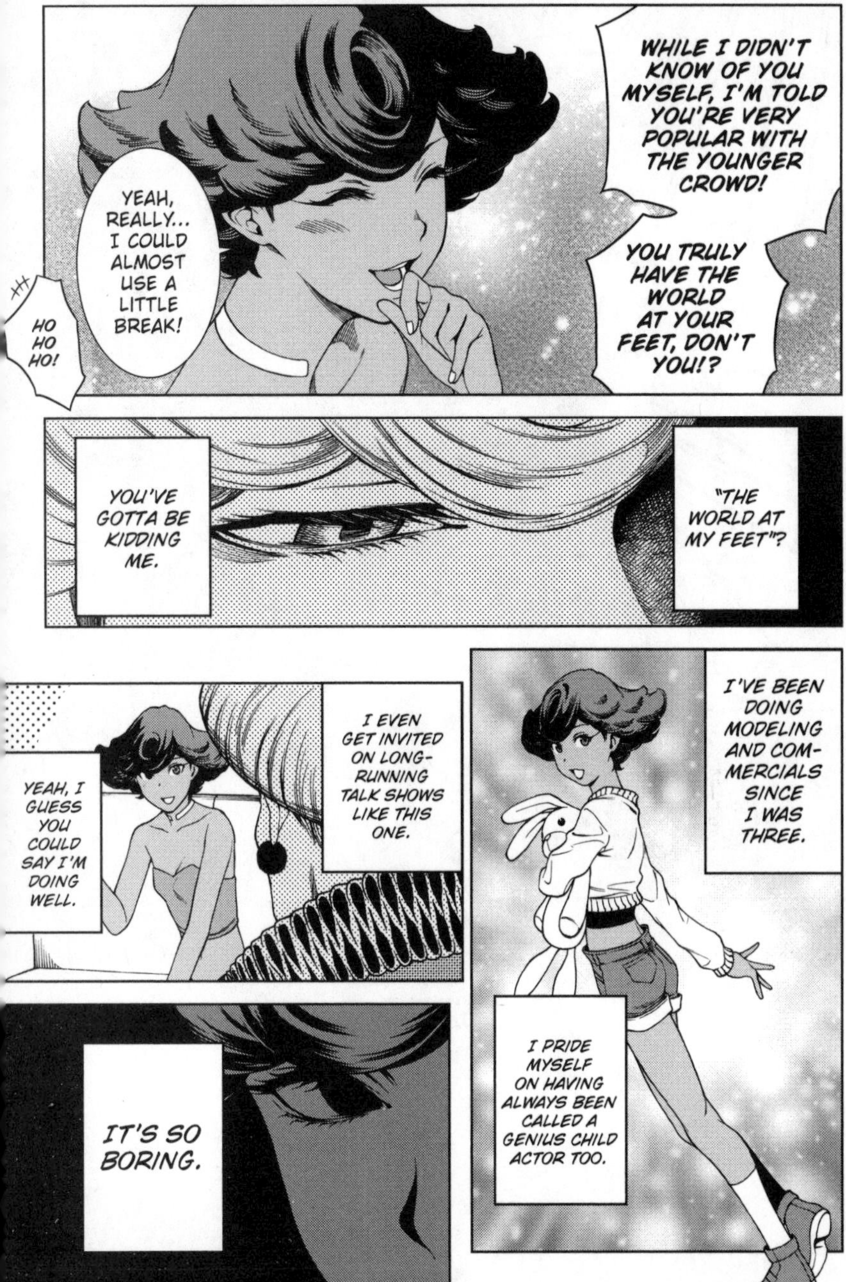
WHILE I DIDN'T KNOW OF YOU MYSELF, I'M TOLD YOU'RE VERY POPULAR WITH THE YOUNGER CROWD!
YOU TRULY HAVE THE WORLD AT YOUR FEET, DON'T YOU!?
YEAH, REALLY... I COULD ALMOST USE A LITTLE BREAK!
HO HO HO!
"THE WORLD AT MY FEET"?
YOU'VE GOTTA BE KIDDING ME.
I'VE BEEN DOING MODELING AND COM-MERCIALS SINCE I WAS THREE.
I PRIDE MYSELF ON HAVING ALWAYS BEEN CALLED A GENIUS CHILD ACTOR TOO.
I EVEN GET INVITED ON LONG-RUNNING TALK SHOWS LIKE THIS ONE.
YEAH, I GUESS YOU COULD SAY I'M DOING WELL.
IT'S SO BORING.

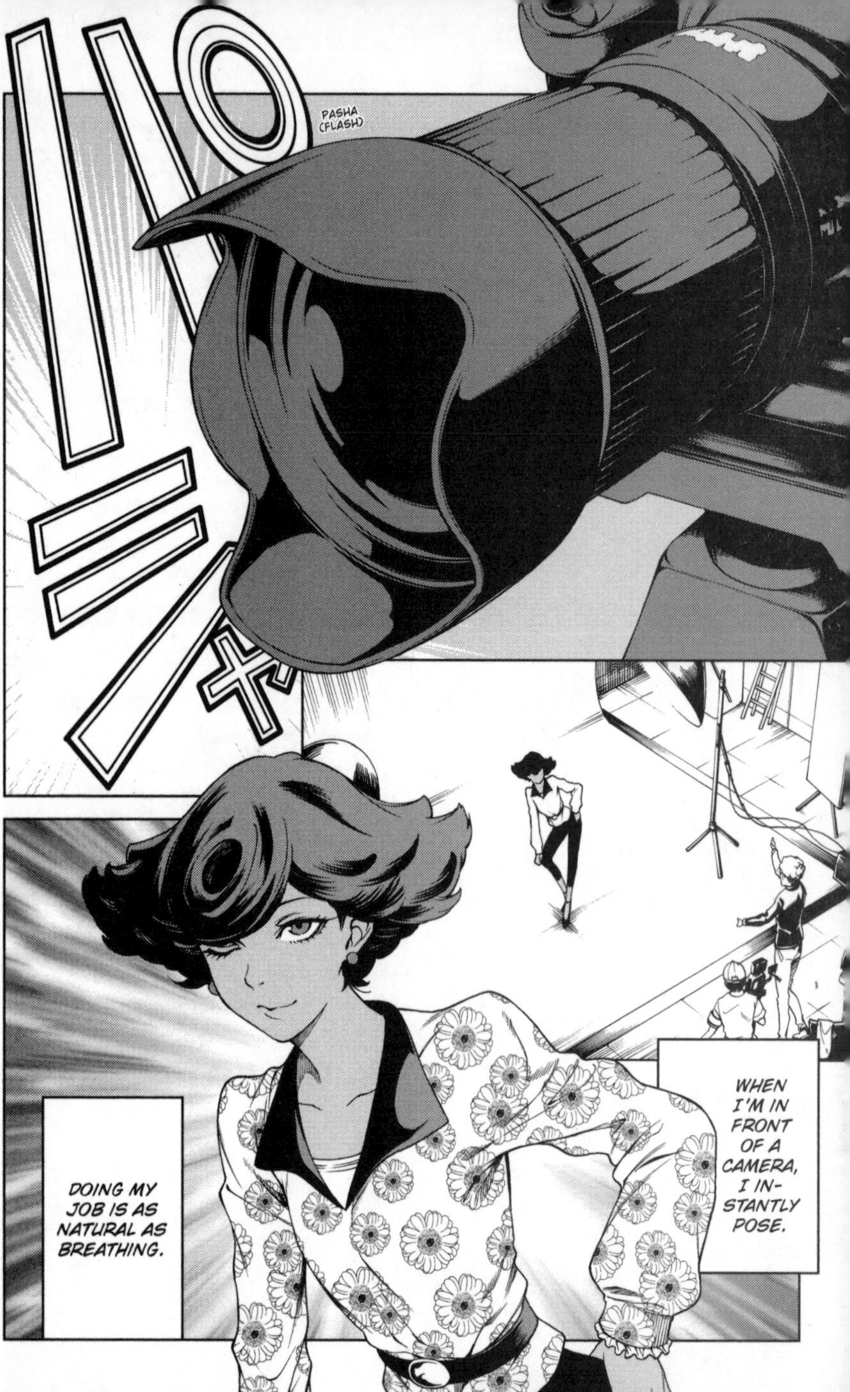
PASHA (FLASH)
WHEN I'M IN FRONT OF A CAMERA, I IN-STANTLY POSE.
DOING MY JOB IS AS NATURAL AS BREATHING.

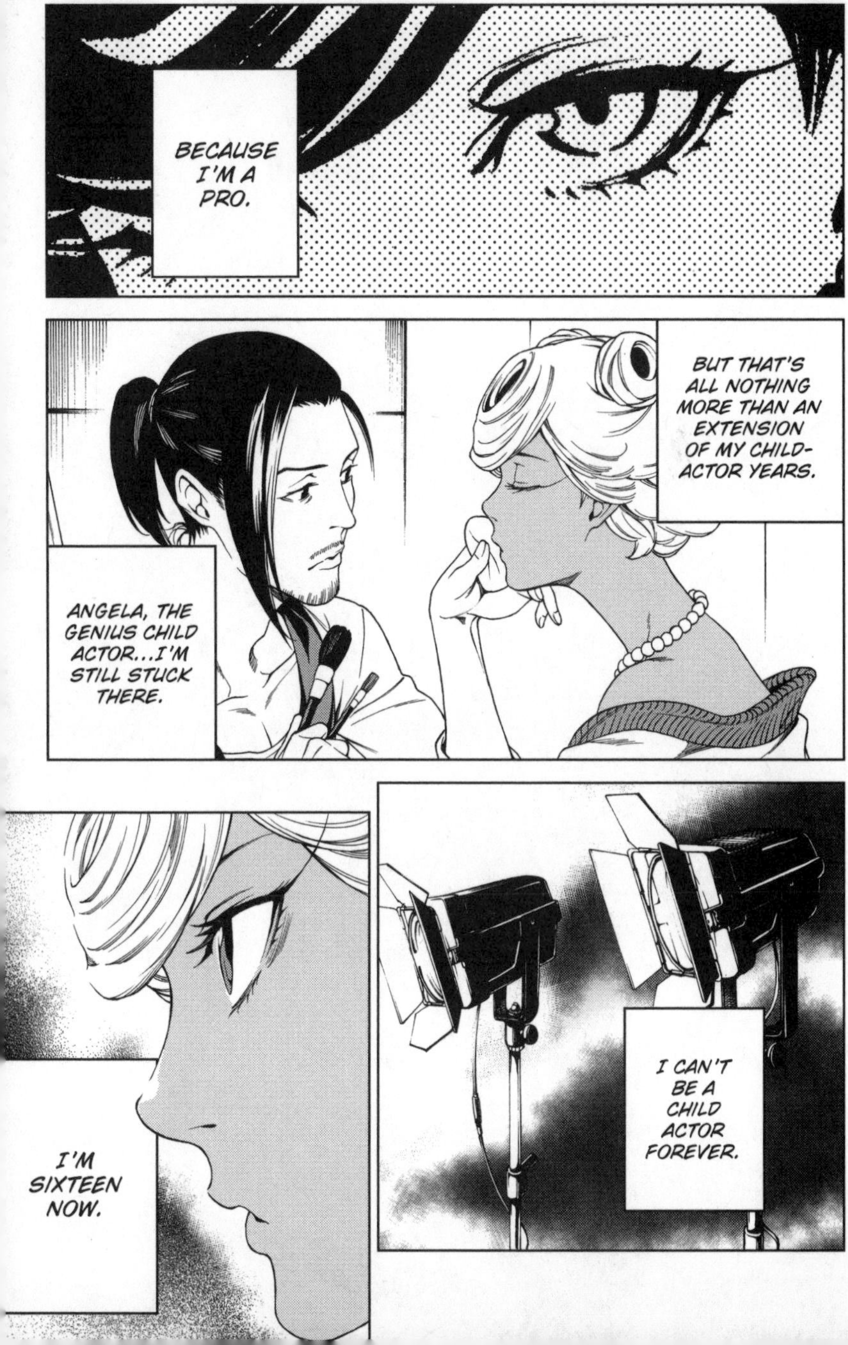
BECAUSE I'M A PRO.
BUT THAT'S ALL NOTHING MORE THAN AN EXTENSION OF MY CHILD-ACTOR YEARS.
ANGELA, THE GENIUS CHILD ACTOR...I'M STILL STUCK THERE.
I CAN'T BE A CHILD ACTOR FOREVER.
I'M SIXTEEN NOW.

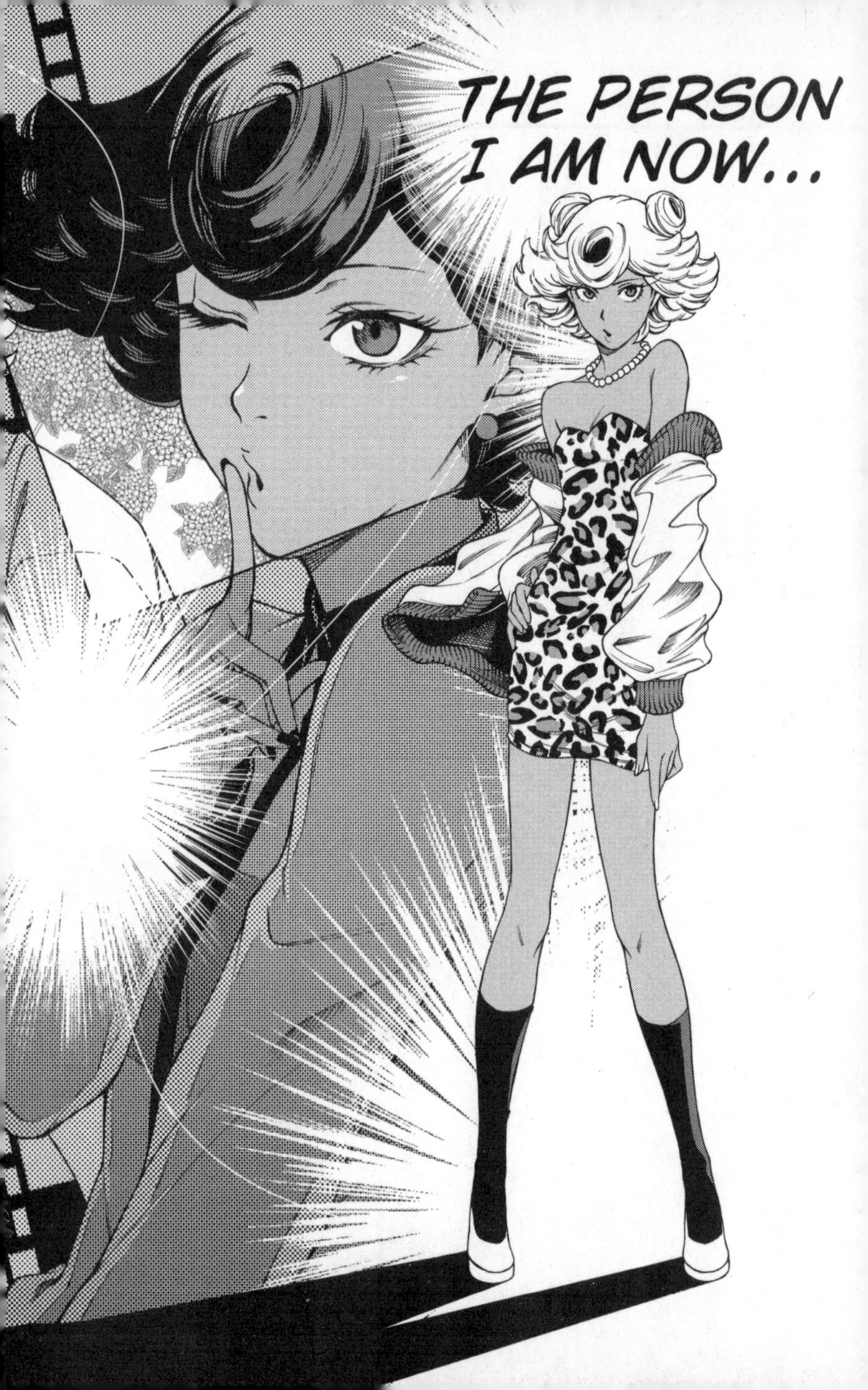
THE PERSON I AM NOW...

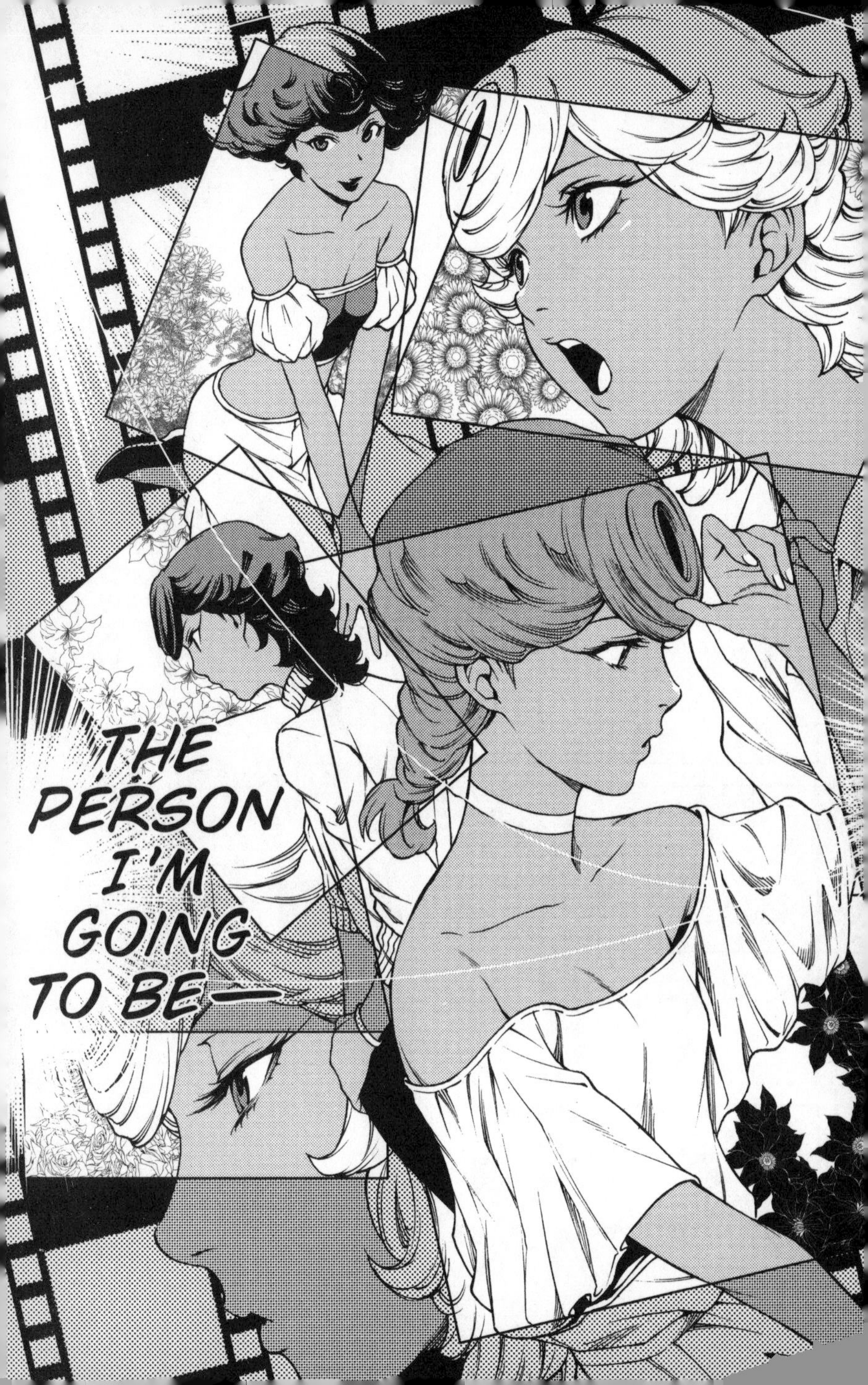
THE PERSON I'M GOING TO BE—

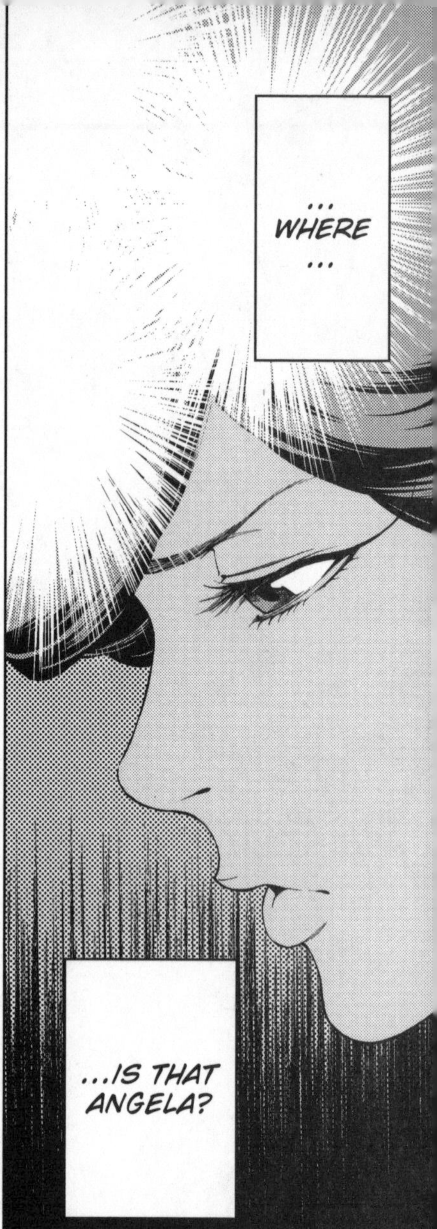
...WHERE...
...IS THAT ANGELA?
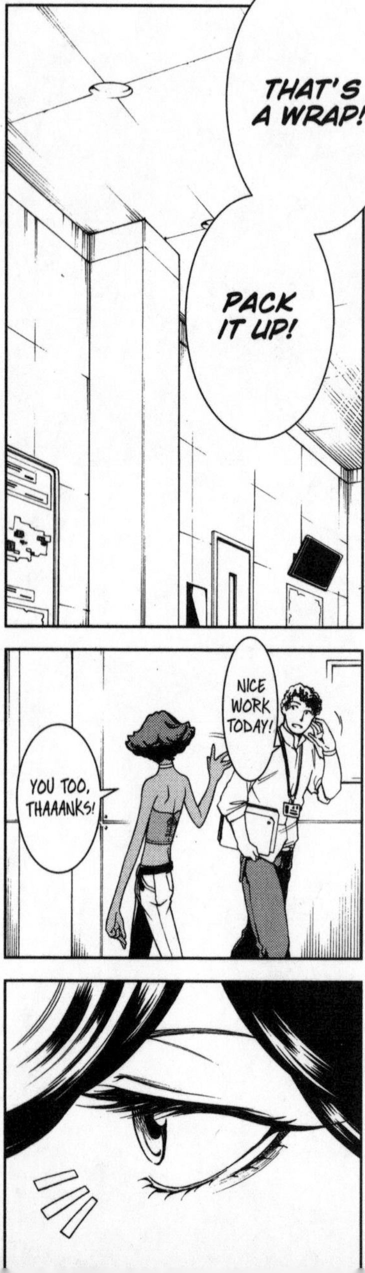
THAT'S A WRAP!
PACK IT UP!
NICE WORK TODAY!
YOU TOO, THAAANKS!

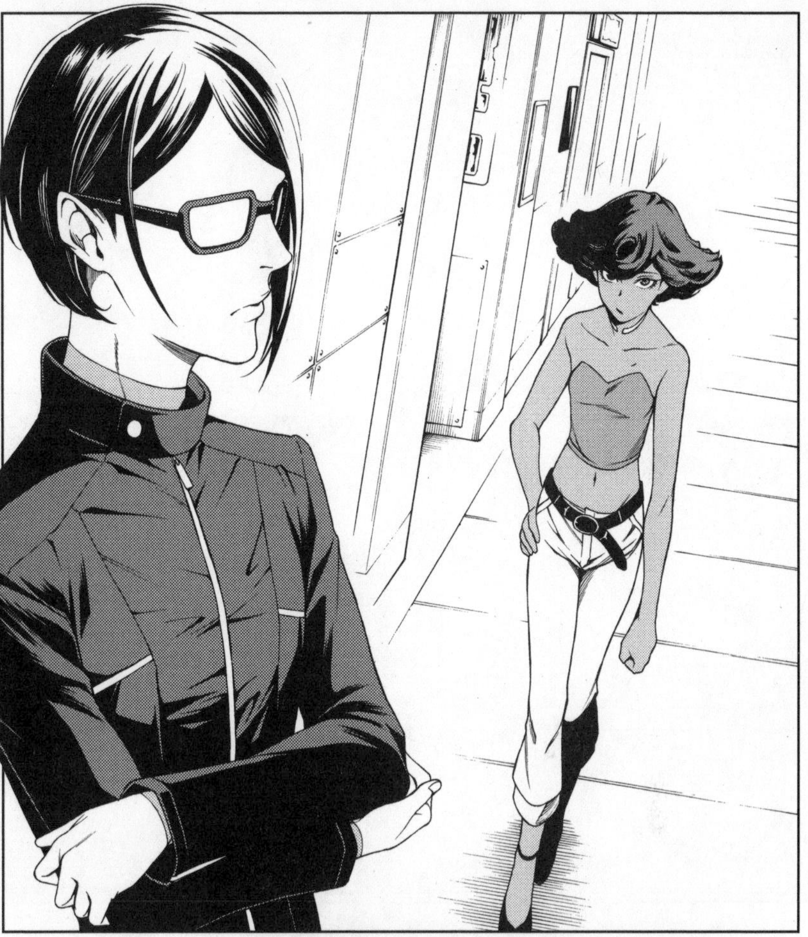

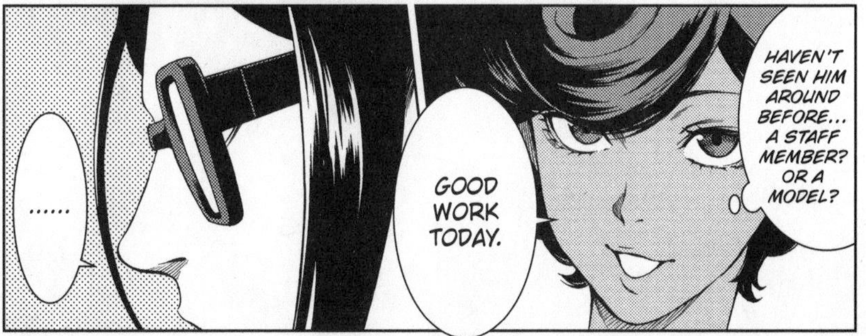
HAVEN'T SEEN HIM AROUND BEFORE... A STAFF MEMBER? OR A MODEL?
GOOD WORK TODAY.
......

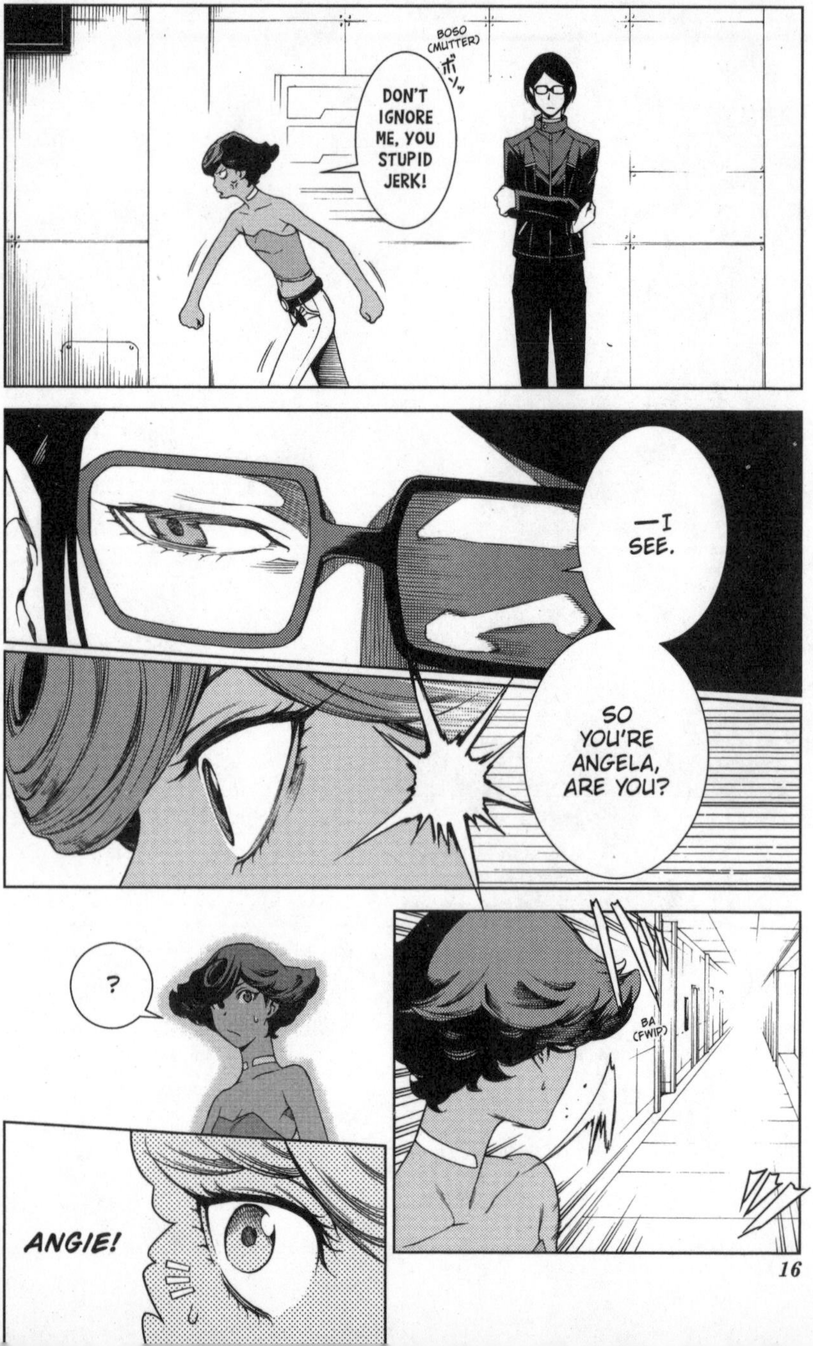
BOSO (MUTTER)
ボソッ
DON'T IGNORE ME, YOU STUPID JERK!
—I SEE.
SO YOU'RE ANGELA, ARE YOU?
BA (FWIP)
?
ANGIE!

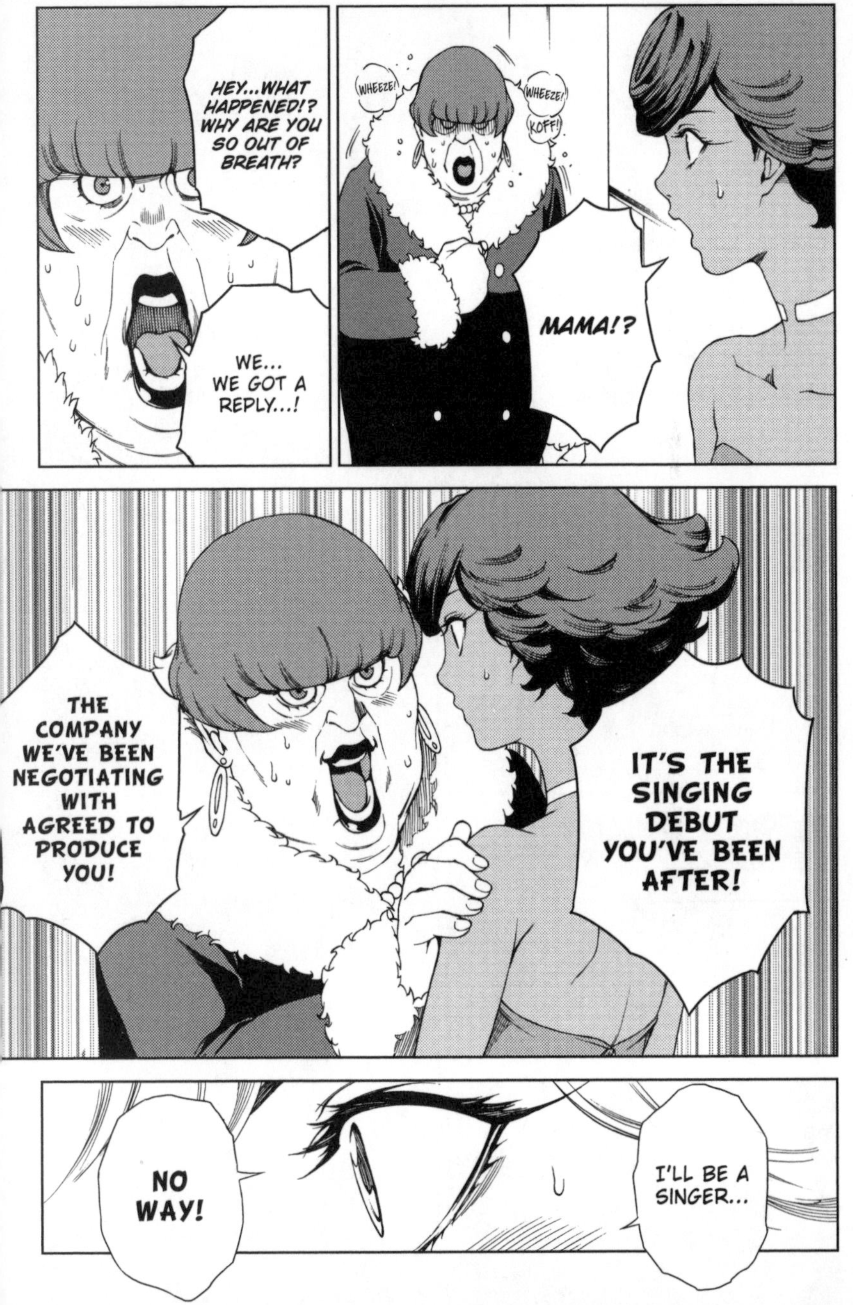
WHEEZE!
KOFF!
WHEEZE!
MAMA!?
HEY...WHAT HAPPENED!? WHY ARE YOU SO OUT OF BREATH?
WE... WE GOT A REPLY...!
IT'S THE SINGING DEBUT YOU'VE BEEN AFTER!
THE COMPANY WE'VE BEEN NEGOTIATING WITH AGREED TO PRODUCE YOU!
I'LL BE A SINGER...
NO WAY!

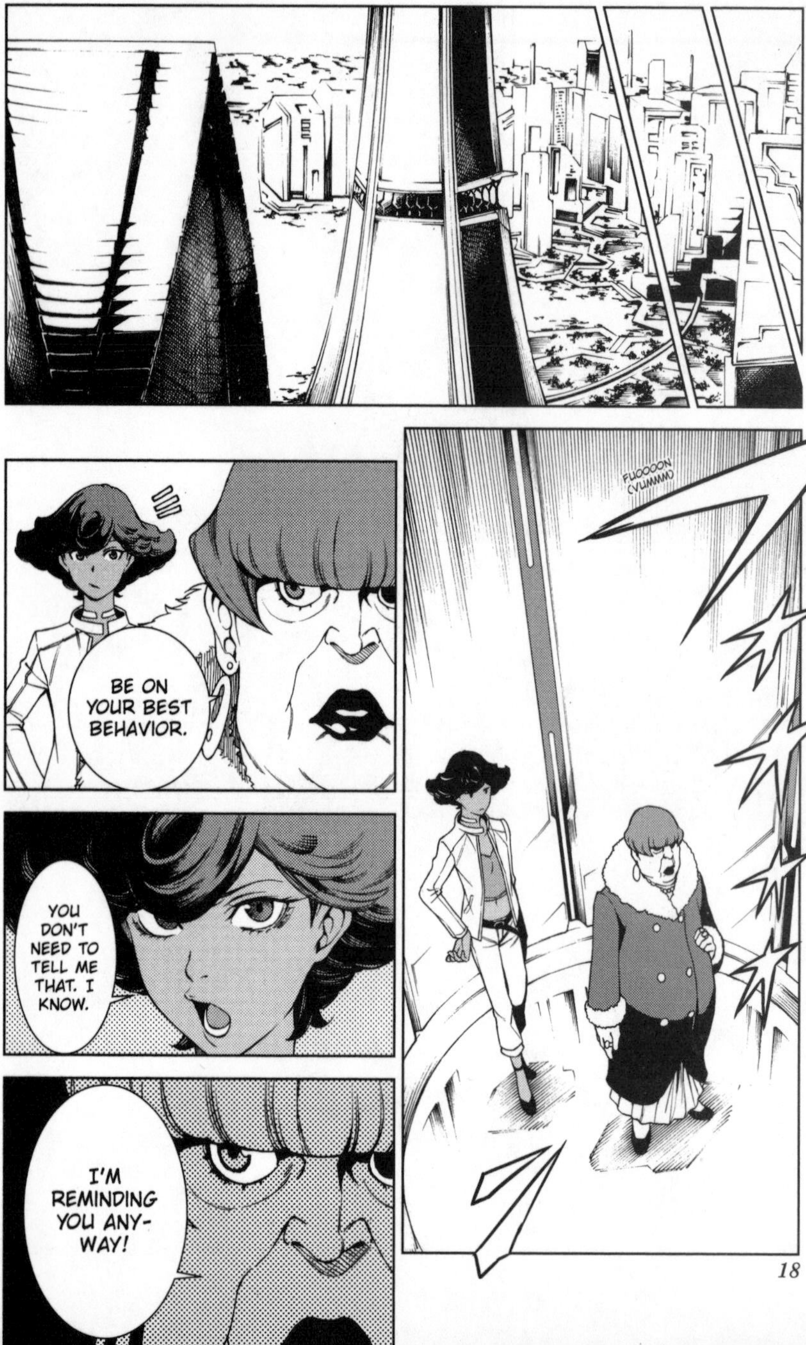
FUOOOON (VUMMM)
BE ON YOUR BEST BEHAVIOR.
YOU DON'T NEED TO TELL ME THAT. I KNOW.
I'M REMINDING YOU ANY-WAY!

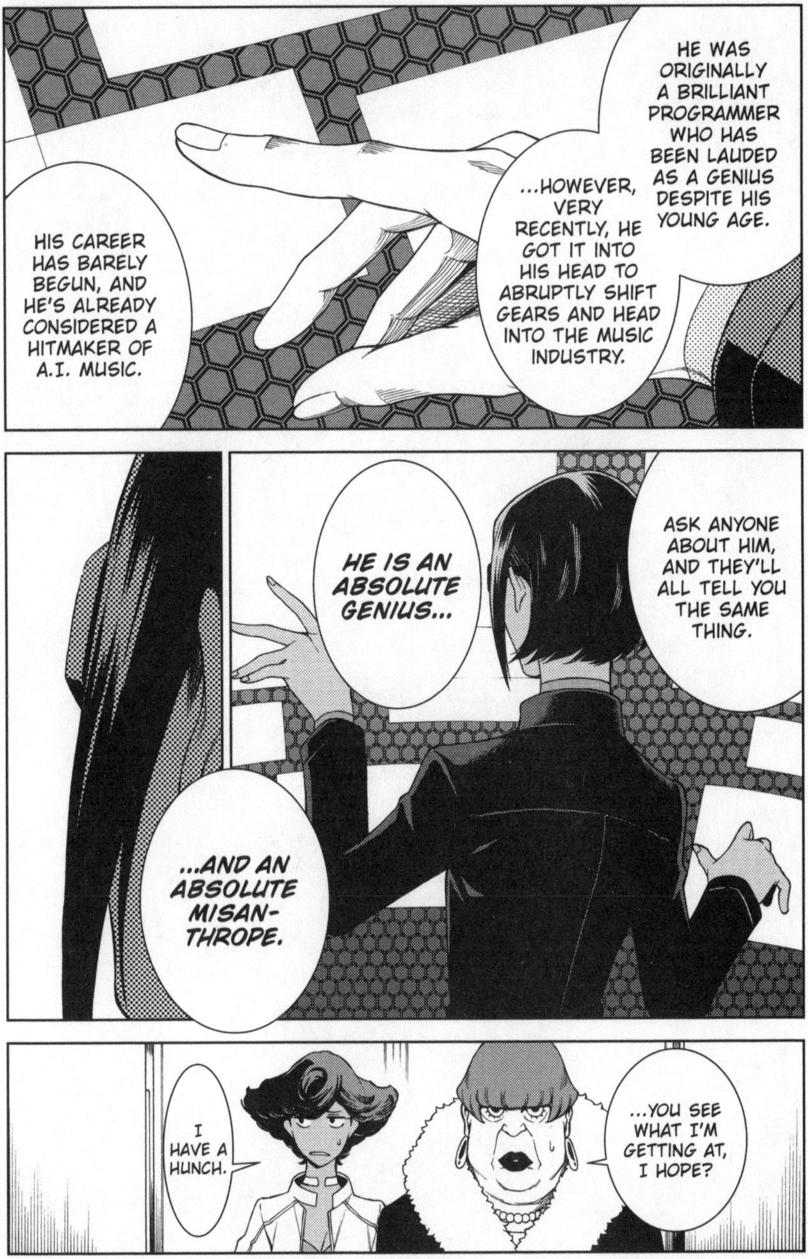
HE WAS ORIGINALLY A BRILLIANT PROGRAMMER WHO HAS BEEN LAUDED AS A GENIUS DESPITE HIS YOUNG AGE.
...HOWEVER, VERY RECENTLY, HE GOT IT INTO HIS HEAD TO ABRUPTLY SHIFT GEARS AND HEAD INTO THE MUSIC INDUSTRY.
HIS CAREER HAS BARELY BEGUN, AND HE'S ALREADY CONSIDERED A HITMAKER OF A.I. MUSIC.
ASK ANYONE ABOUT HIM, AND THEY'LL ALL TELL YOU THE SAME THING.
HE IS AN ABSOLUTE GENIUS...
...AND AN ABSOLUTE MISAN-THROPE.
...YOU SEE WHAT I'M GETTING AT, I HOPE?
I HAVE A HUNCH.

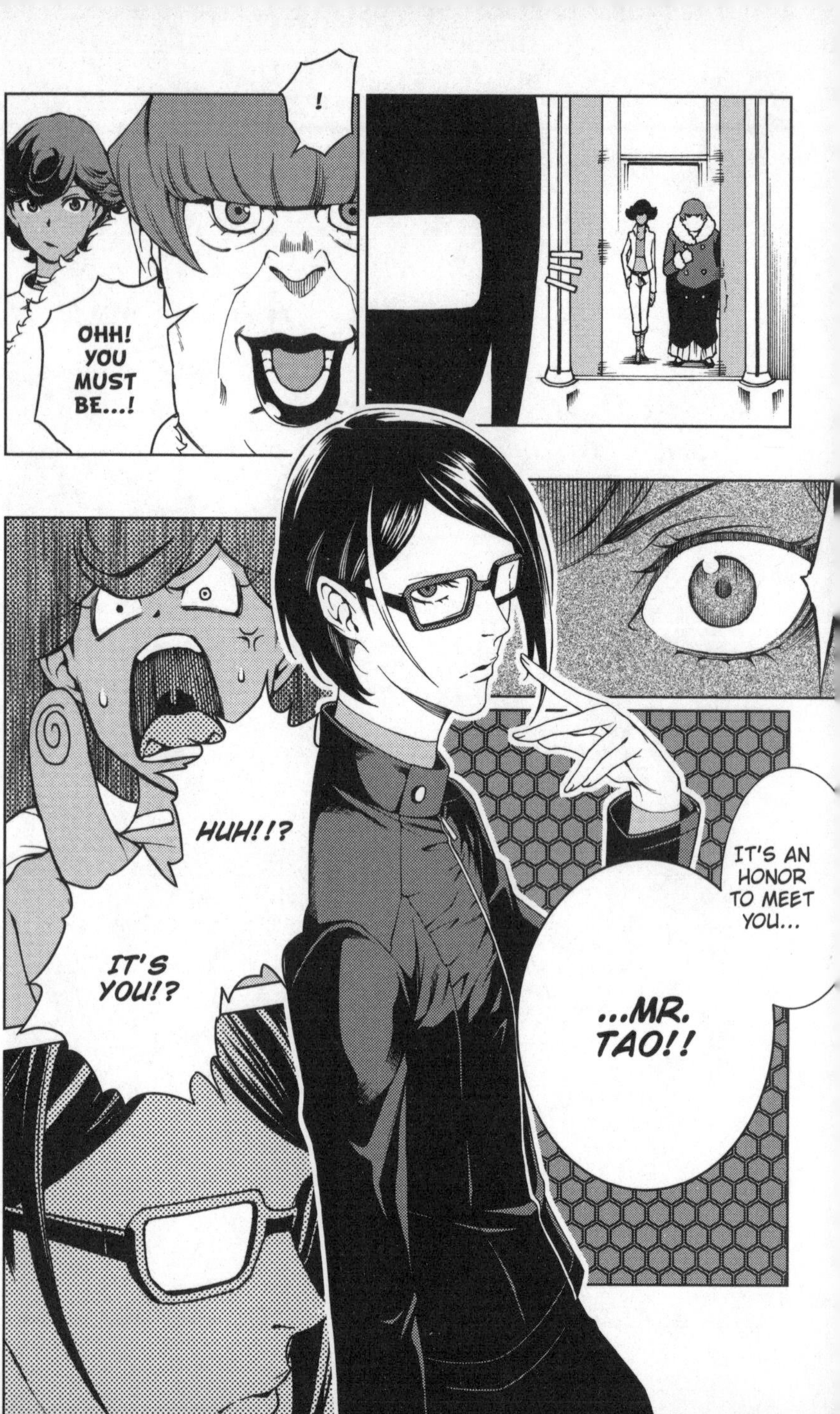
!
OHH! YOU MUST BE...!
IT'S AN HONOR TO MEET YOU...
...MR. TAO!!
HUH!!?
IT'S YOU!?

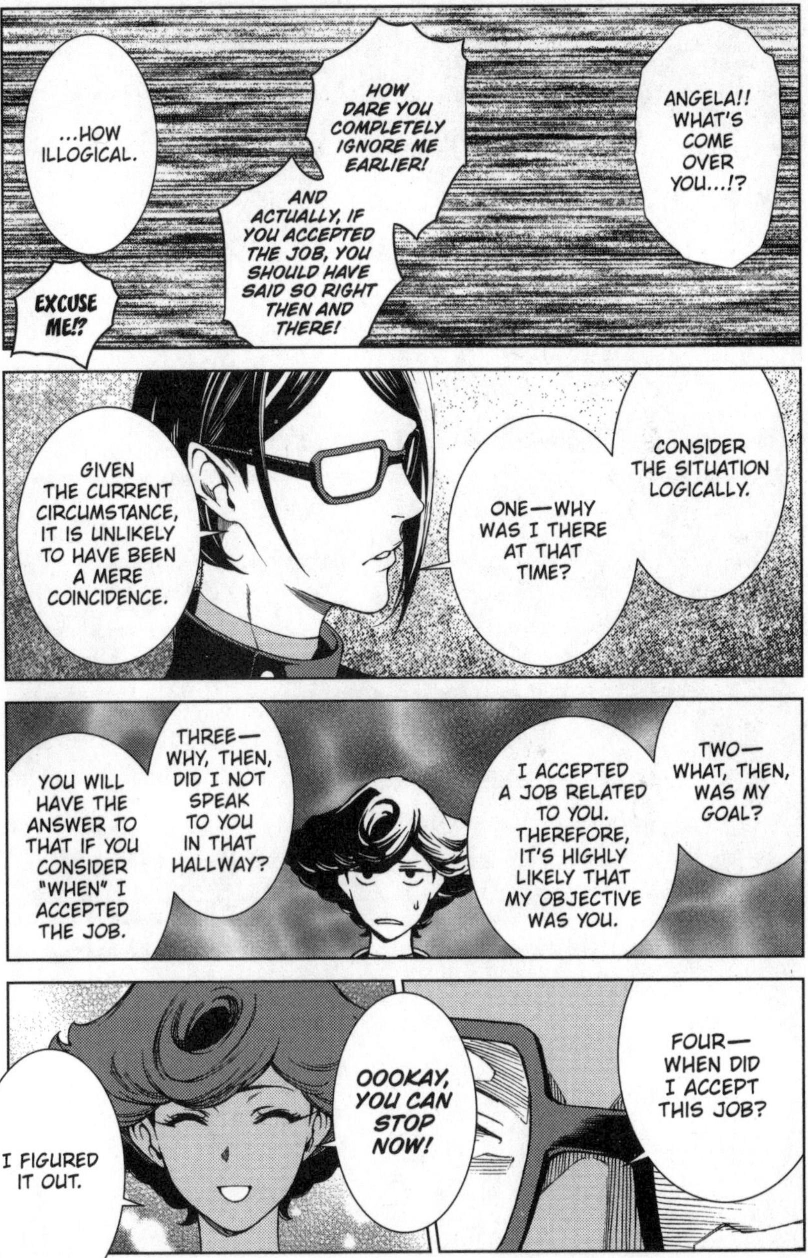
ANGELA!! WHAT'S COME OVER YOU...!?
HOW DARE YOU COMPLETELY IGNORE ME EARLIER!
AND ACTUALLY, IF YOU ACCEPTED THE JOB, YOU SHOULD HAVE SAID SO RIGHT THEN AND THERE!
...HOW ILLOGICAL.
EXCUSE ME!?
CONSIDER THE SITUATION LOGICALLY.
ONE—WHY WAS I THERE AT THAT TIME?
GIVEN THE CURRENT CIRCUMSTANCE, IT IS UNLIKELY TO HAVE BEEN A MERE COINCIDENCE.
TWO—WHAT, THEN, WAS MY GOAL?
I ACCEPTED A JOB RELATED TO YOU. THEREFORE, IT'S HIGHLY LIKELY THAT MY OBJECTIVE WAS YOU.
THREE—WHY, THEN, DID I NOT SPEAK TO YOU IN THAT HALLWAY?
YOU WILL HAVE THE ANSWER TO THAT IF YOU CONSIDER "WHEN" I ACCEPTED THE JOB.
FOUR—WHEN DID I ACCEPT THIS JOB?
OOOKAY, YOU CAN STOP NOW!
I FIGURED IT OUT.

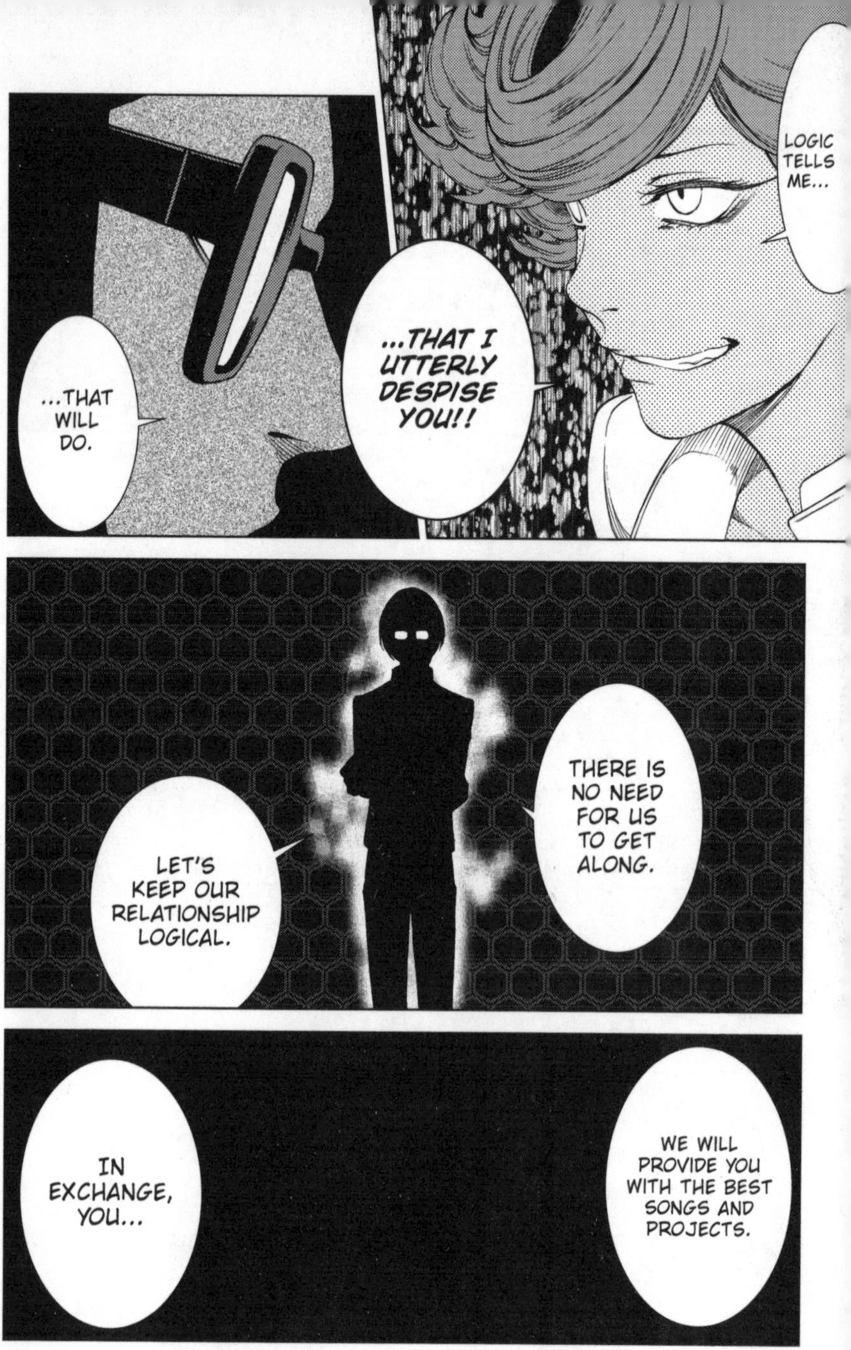
LOGIC TELLS ME...
...THAT I UTTERLY DESPISE YOU!!
...THAT WILL DO.
THERE IS NO NEED FOR US TO GET ALONG.
LET'S KEEP OUR RELATIONSHIP LOGICAL.
WE WILL PROVIDE YOU WITH THE BEST SONGS AND PROJECTS.
IN EXCHANGE, YOU...

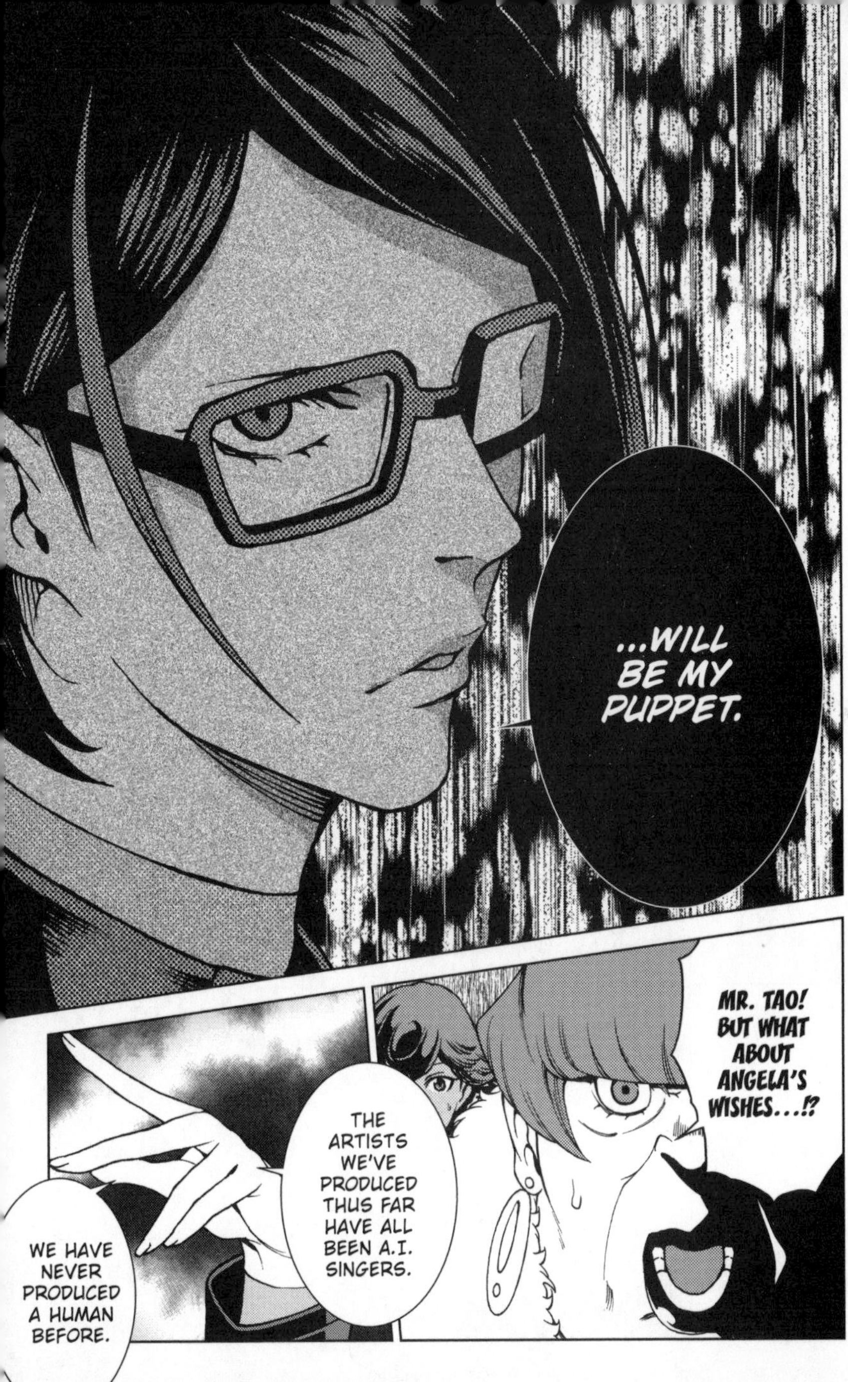
...WILL BE MY PUPPET.
MR. TAO! BUT WHAT ABOUT ANGELA'S WISHES...!?
THE ARTISTS WE'VE PRODUCED THUS FAR HAVE ALL BEEN A.I. SINGERS.
WE HAVE NEVER PRODUCED A HUMAN BEFORE.

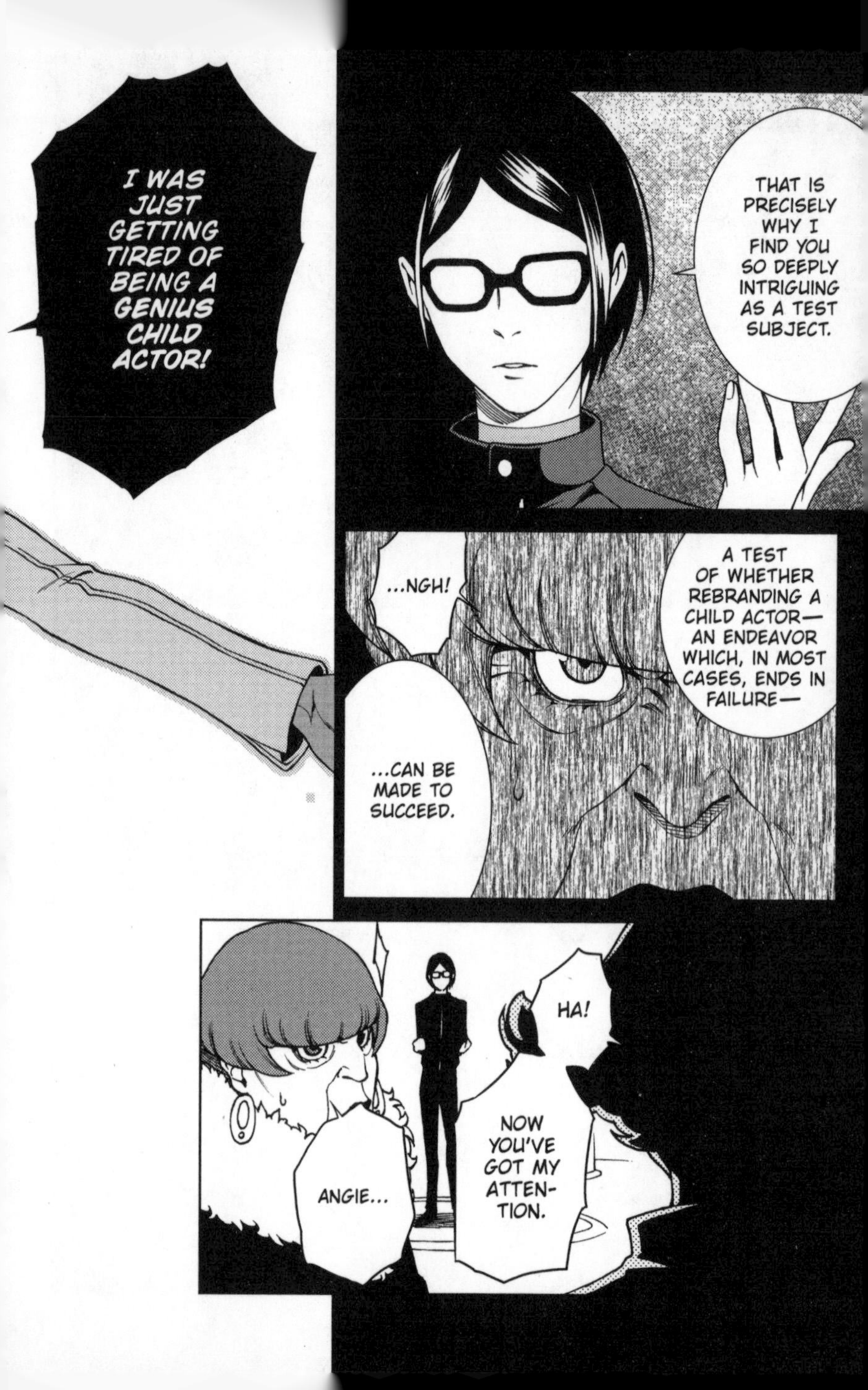
THAT IS PRECISELY WHY I FIND YOU SO DEEPLY INTRIGUING AS A TEST SUBJECT.
A TEST OF WHETHER REBRANDING A CHILD ACTOR— AN ENDEAVOR WHICH, IN MOST CASES, ENDS IN FAILURE—
...NGH!
...CAN BE MADE TO SUCCEED.
HA!
NOW YOU'VE GOT MY ATTEN-TION.
ANGIE...
I WAS JUST GETTING TIRED OF BEING A GENIUS CHILD ACTOR!

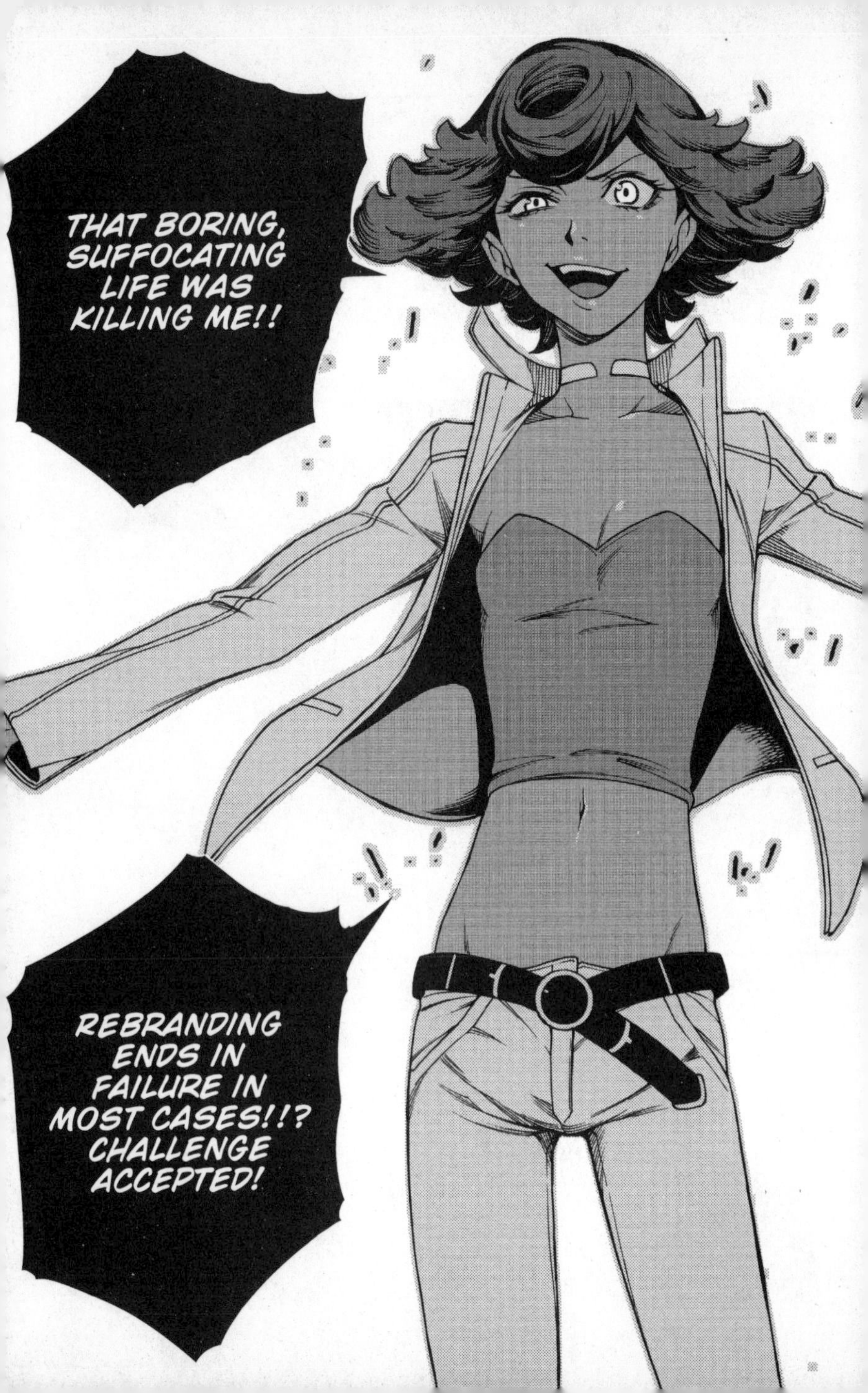
THAT BORING, SUFFOCATING LIFE WAS KILLING ME!!
REBRANDING ENDS IN FAILURE IN MOST CASES!!? CHALLENGE ACCEPTED!

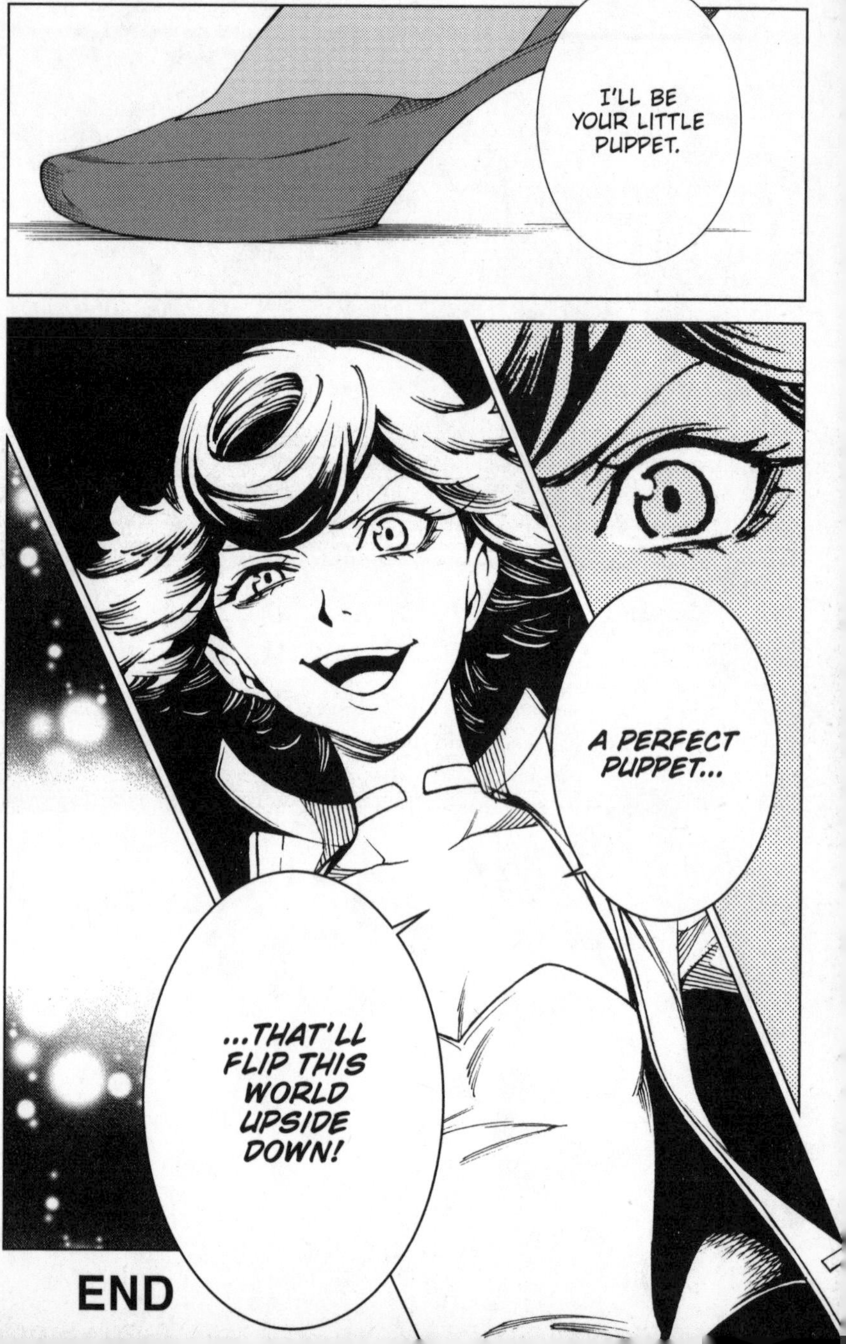
I'LL BE YOUR LITTLE PUPPET.
A PERFECT PUPPET...
...THAT'LL FLIP THIS WORLD UPSIDE DOWN!
END

CAROLE & TUESDAY

CAROLE
& TUESDAY

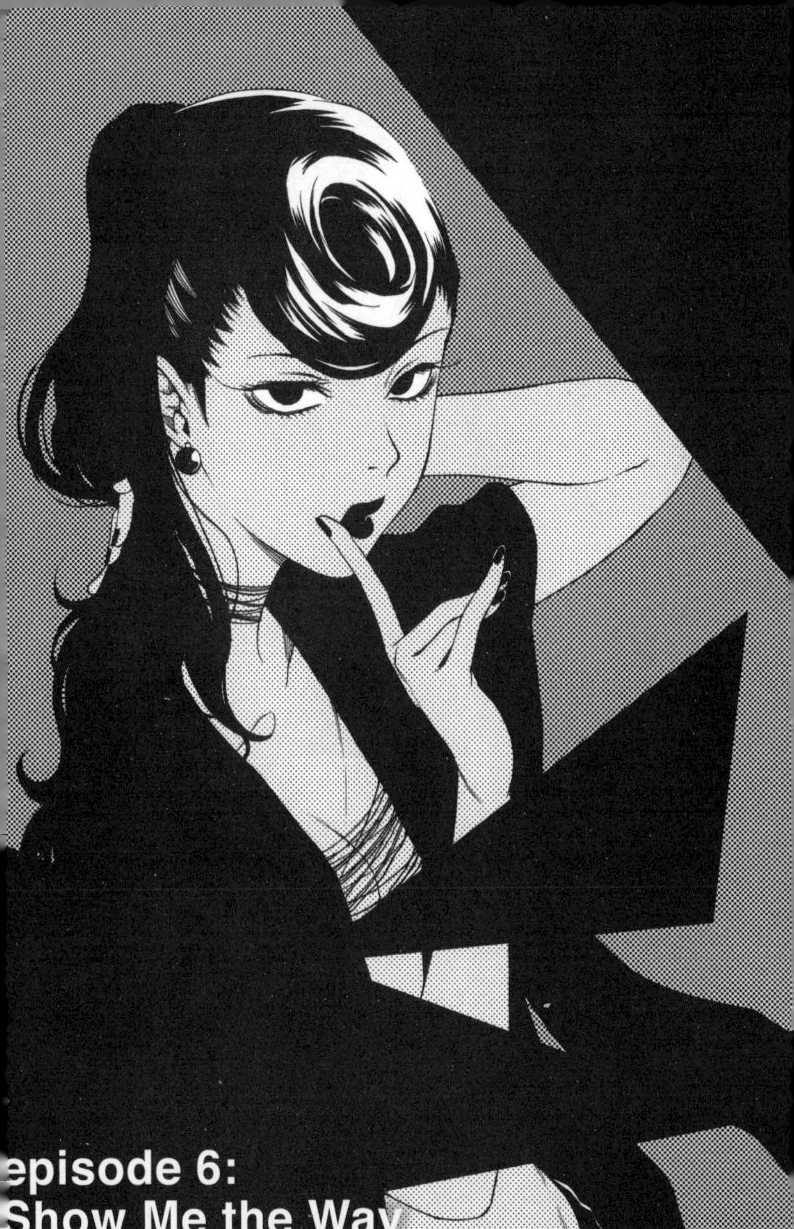

episode 6: Show Me the Way

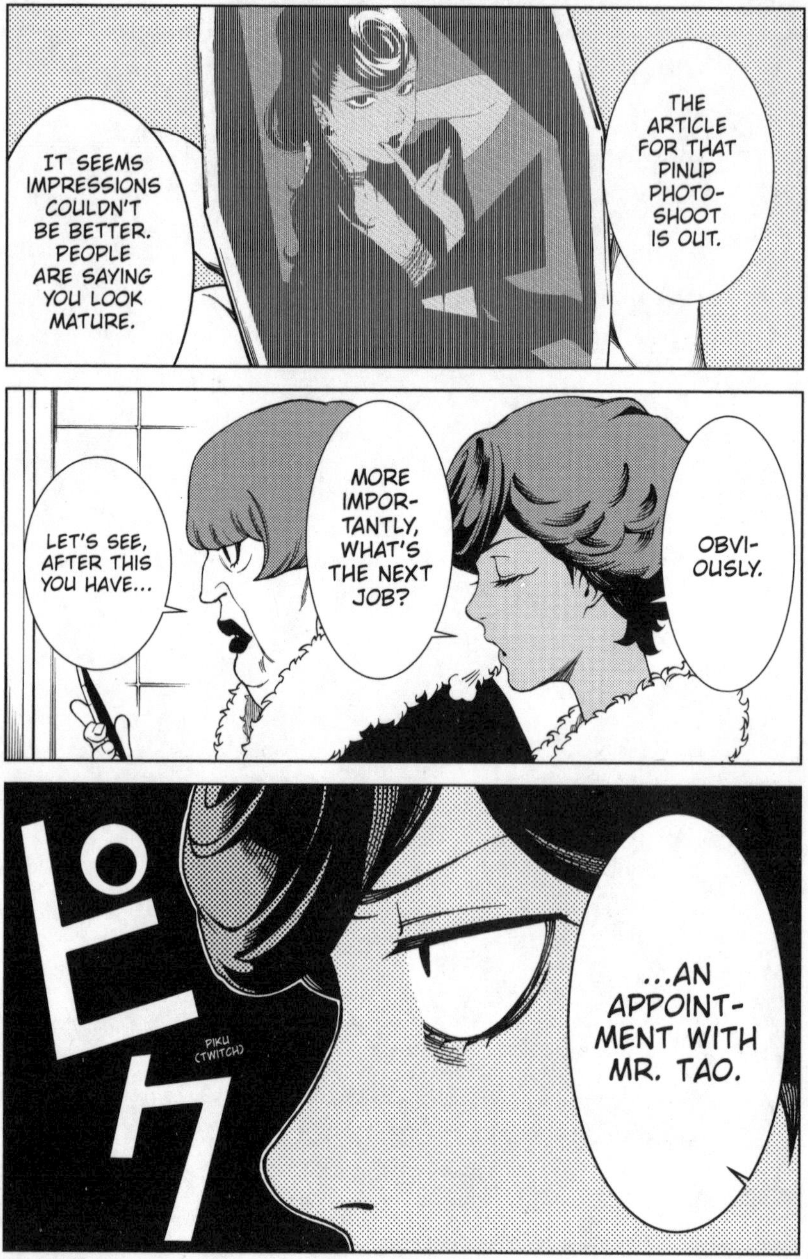
THE ARTICLE FOR THAT PINUP PHOTO-SHOOT IS OUT.
IT SEEMS IMPRESSIONS COULDN'T BE BETTER. PEOPLE ARE SAYING YOU LOOK MATURE.
OBVI-OUSLY.
MORE IMPOR-TANTLY, WHAT'S THE NEXT JOB?
LET'S SEE, AFTER THIS YOU HAVE...
...AN APPOINT-MENT WITH MR. TAO.
ピク
PIKU (TWITCH)

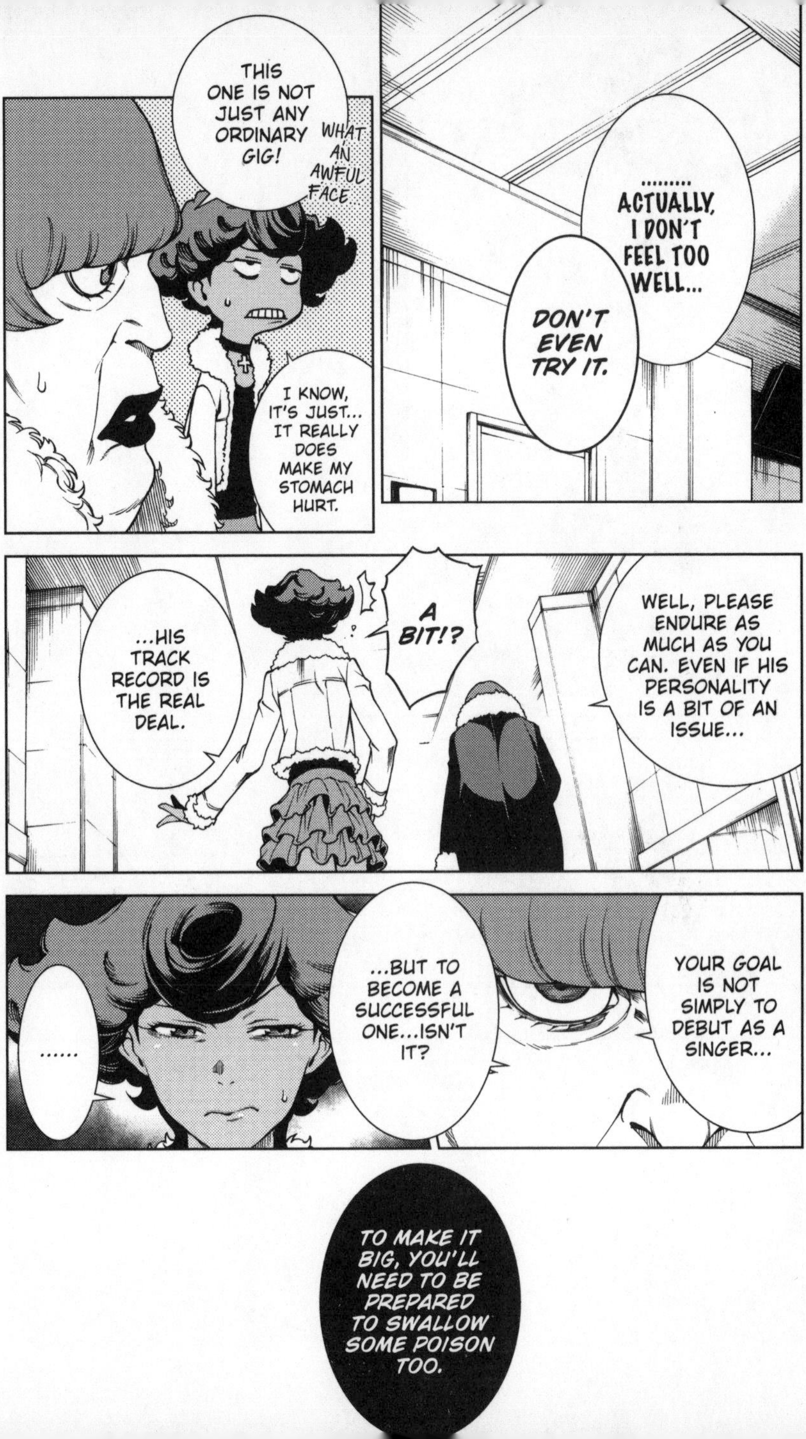
.... ACTUALLY, I DON'T FEEL TOO WELL...
DON'T EVEN TRY IT.
THIS ONE IS NOT JUST ANY ORDINARY GIG!
WHAT AN AWFUL FACE
I KNOW, IT'S JUST... IT REALLY DOES MAKE MY STOMACH HURT.
WELL, PLEASE ENDURE AS MUCH AS YOU CAN. EVEN IF HIS PERSONALITY IS A BIT OF AN ISSUE...
A BIT!?
...HIS TRACK RECORD IS THE REAL DEAL.
YOUR GOAL IS NOT SIMPLY TO DEBUT AS A SINGER...
...BUT TO BECOME A SUCCESSFUL ONE...ISN'T IT?
......
TO MAKE IT BIG, YOU'LL NEED TO BE PREPARED TO SWALLOW SOME POISON TOO.

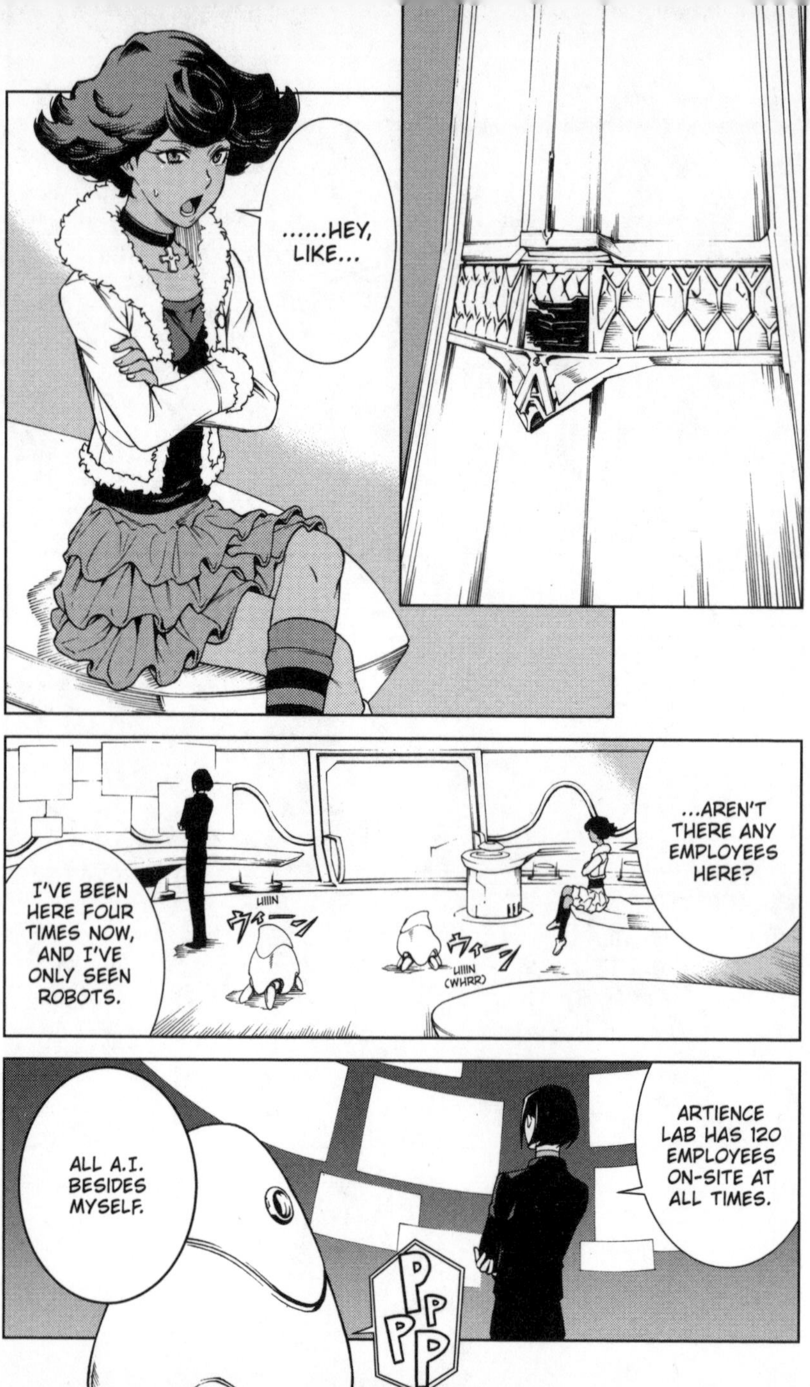
......HEY, LIKE...
...AREN'T THERE ANY EMPLOYEES HERE?
UIIIN
ウィーン
UIIIN (WHRR)
I'VE BEEN HERE FOUR TIMES NOW, AND I'VE ONLY SEEN ROBOTS.
ARTIENCE LAB HAS 120 EMPLOYEES ON-SITE AT ALL TIMES.
ALL A.I. BESIDES MYSELF.
PPPP

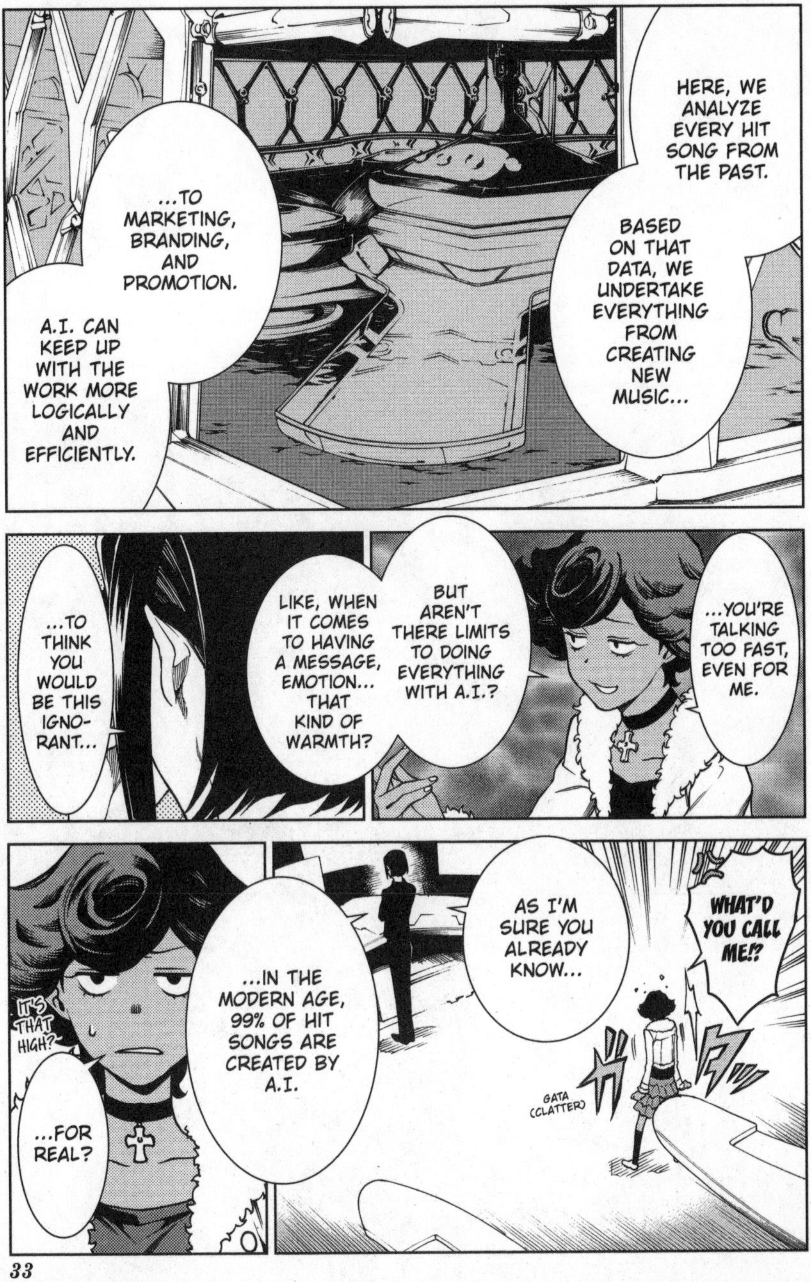
HERE, WE ANALYZE EVERY HIT SONG FROM THE PAST.
BASED ON THAT DATA, WE UNDERTAKE EVERYTHING FROM CREATING NEW MUSIC...
...TO MARKETING, BRANDING, AND PROMOTION.
A.I. CAN KEEP UP WITH THE WORK MORE LOGICALLY AND EFFICIENTLY.
...YOU'RE TALKING TOO FAST, EVEN FOR ME.
BUT AREN'T THERE LIMITS TO DOING EVERYTHING WITH A.I.?
LIKE, WHEN IT COMES TO HAVING A MESSAGE, EMOTION... THAT KIND OF WARMTH?
...TO THINK YOU WOULD BE THIS IGNO-RANT...
WHAT'D YOU CALL ME!?
AS I'M SURE YOU ALREADY KNOW...
GATA (CLATTER)
...IN THE MODERN AGE, 99% OF HIT SONGS ARE CREATED BY A.I.
IT'S THAT HIGH?
...FOR REAL?

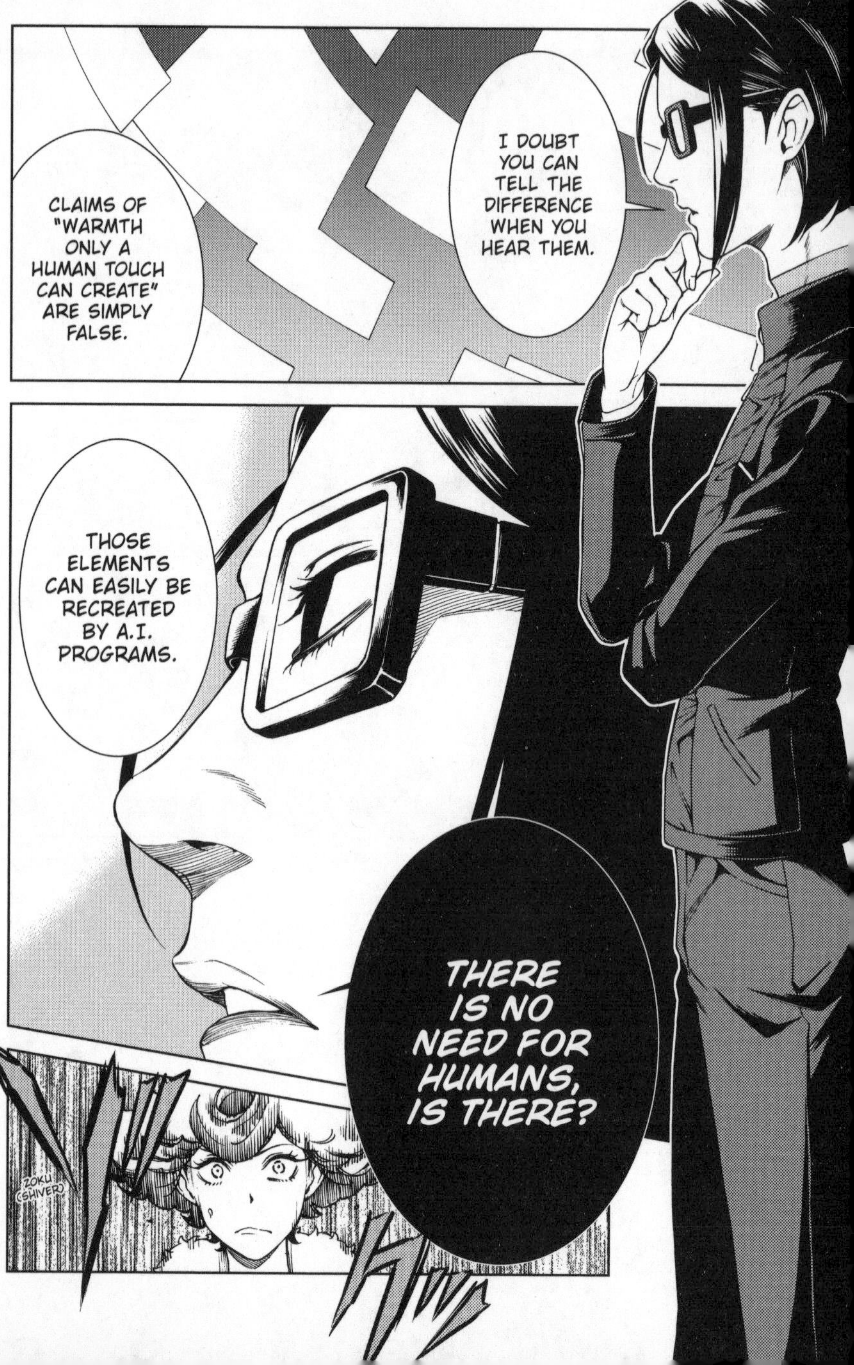
I DOUBT YOU CAN TELL THE DIFFERENCE WHEN YOU HEAR THEM.
CLAIMS OF "WARMTH ONLY A HUMAN TOUCH CAN CREATE" ARE SIMPLY FALSE.
THOSE ELEMENTS CAN EASILY BE RECREATED BY A.I. PROGRAMS.
THERE IS NO NEED FOR HUMANS, IS THERE?
ZOKU (SHIVER)

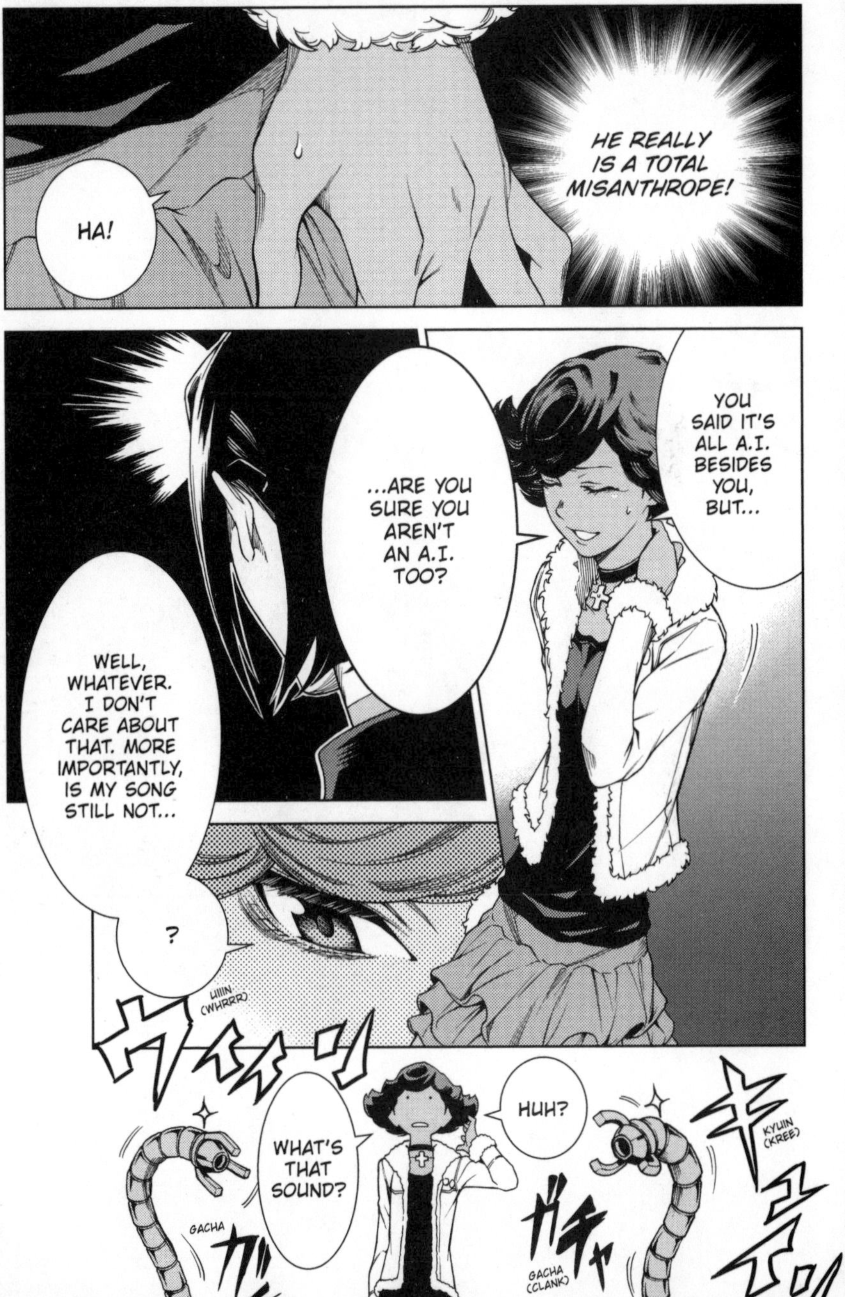
HE REALLY IS A TOTAL MISANTHROPE!
HA!
YOU SAID IT'S ALL A.I. BESIDES YOU, BUT...
...ARE YOU SURE YOU AREN'T AN A.I. TOO?
WELL, WHATEVER. I DON'T CARE ABOUT THAT. MORE IMPORTANTLY, IS MY SONG STILL NOT...
?
UIIIN (WHRRR)
KYUIN (KREE)
HUH?
GACHA (CLANK)
WHAT'S THAT SOUND?
GACHA

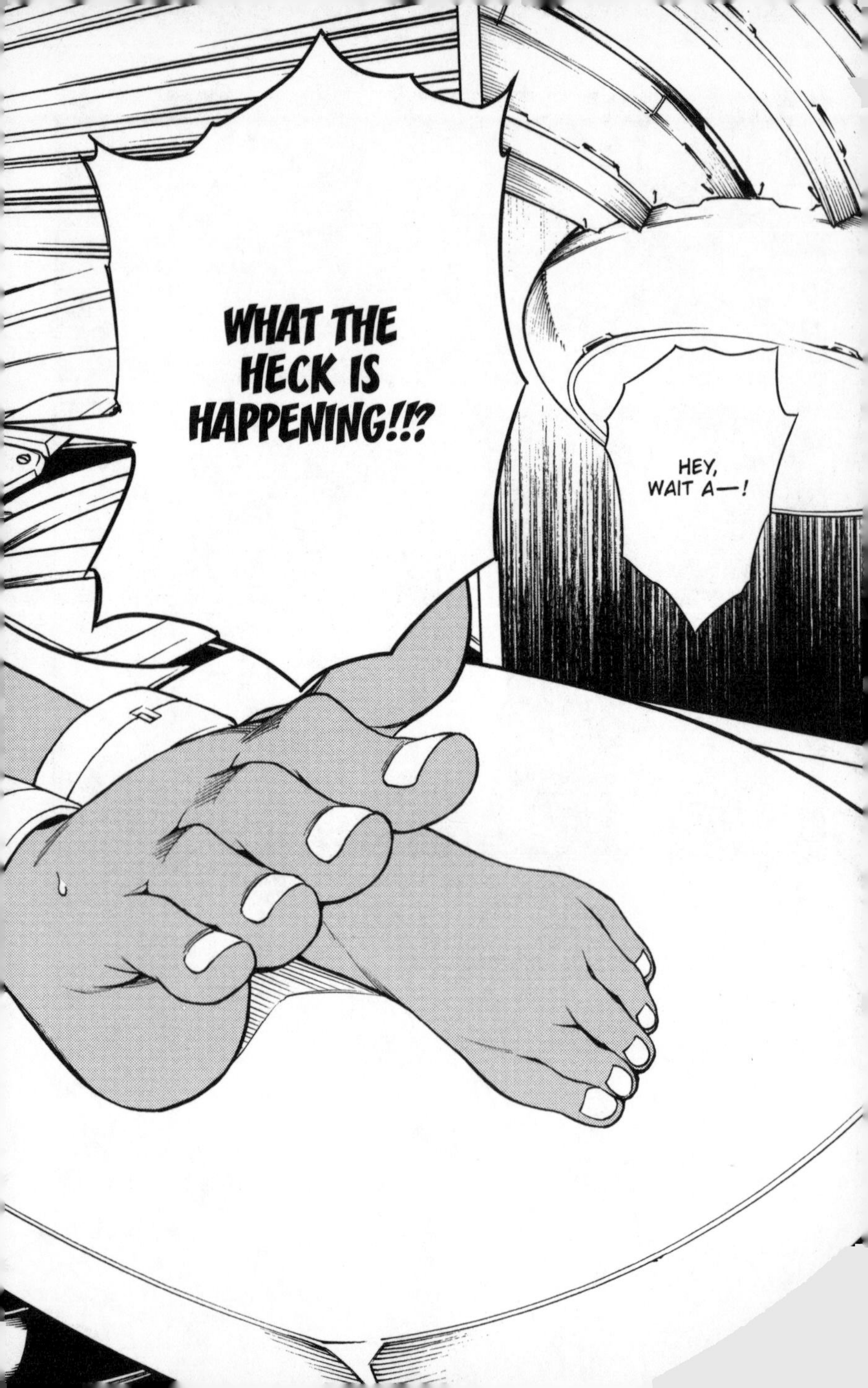
HEY, WAIT A—!
WHAT THE HECK IS HAPPENING!!?

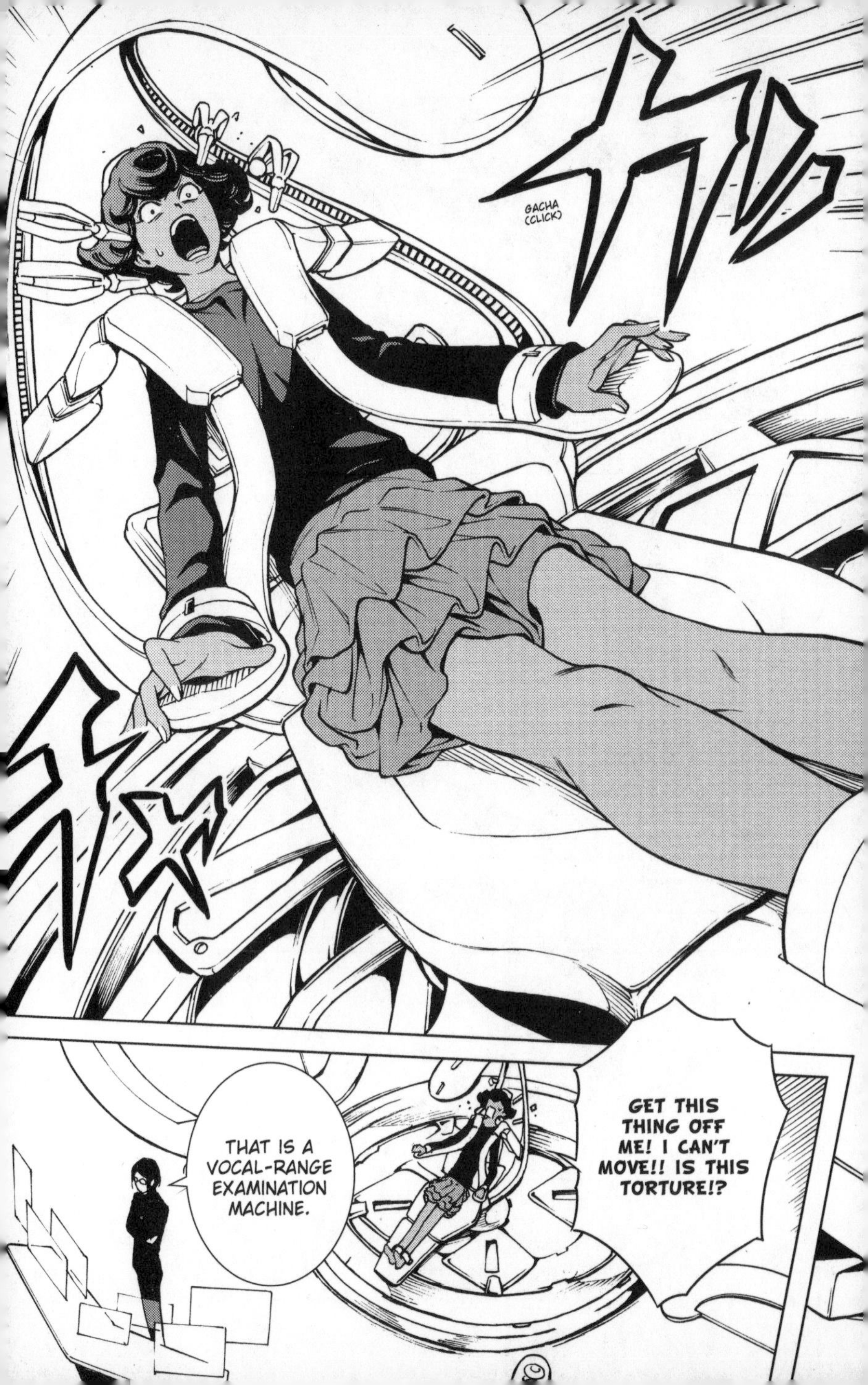
GACHA (CLICK)
GET THIS THING OFF ME! I CAN'T MOVE!! IS THIS TORTURE!?
THAT IS A VOCAL-RANGE EXAMINATION MACHINE.

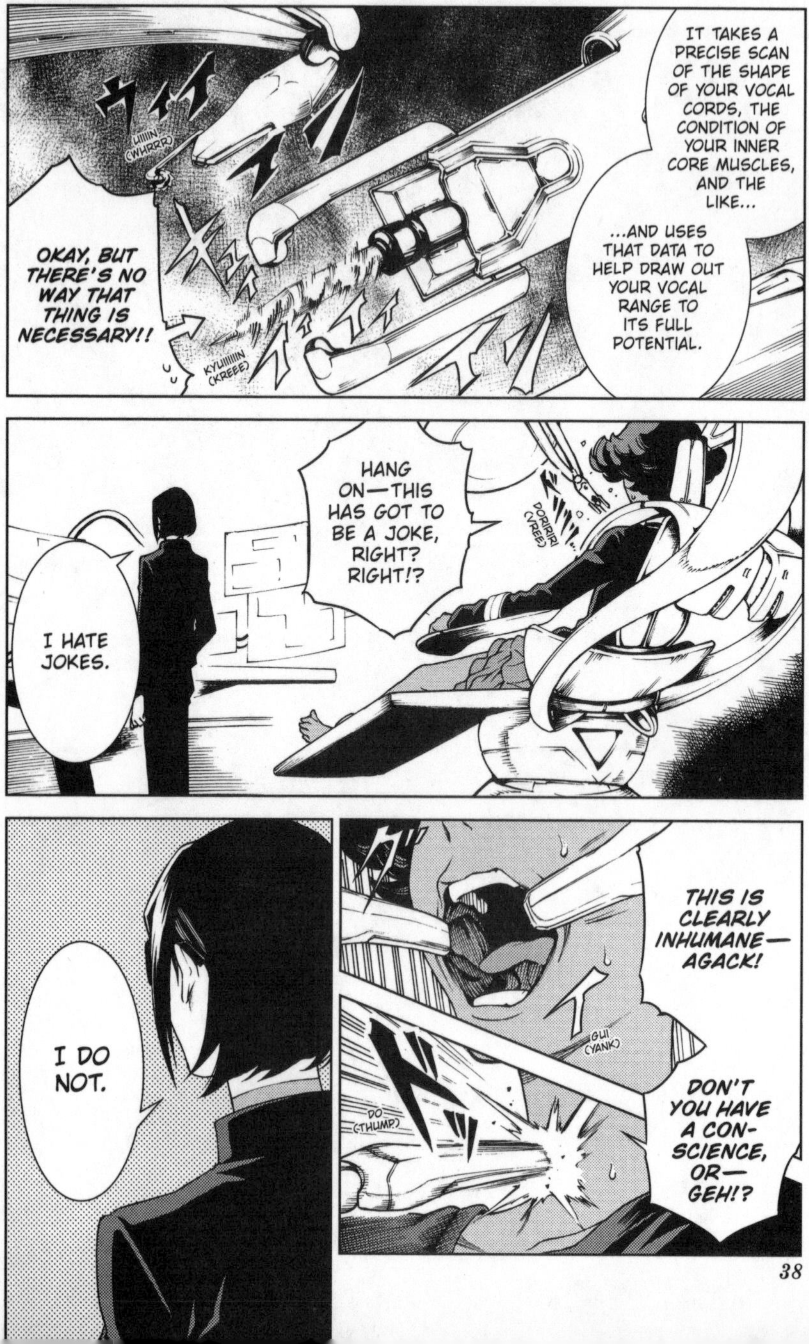
IT TAKES A PRECISE SCAN OF THE SHAPE OF YOUR VOCAL CORDS, THE CONDITION OF YOUR INNER CORE MUSCLES, AND THE LIKE...
...AND USES THAT DATA TO HELP DRAW OUT YOUR VOCAL RANGE TO ITS FULL POTENTIAL.
LIIIIN (WHRRR)
KYUIIIIIIN (KREEE)
OKAY, BUT THERE'S NO WAY THAT THING IS NECESSARY!!
DORIRIRI (VREE)
HANG ON—THIS HAS GOT TO BE A JOKE, RIGHT? RIGHT!?
I HATE JOKES.
THIS IS CLEARLY INHUMANE—AGACK!
GUI (YANK)
DON'T YOU HAVE A CON-SCIENCE, OR—GEH!?
DO (THUMP)
I DO NOT.

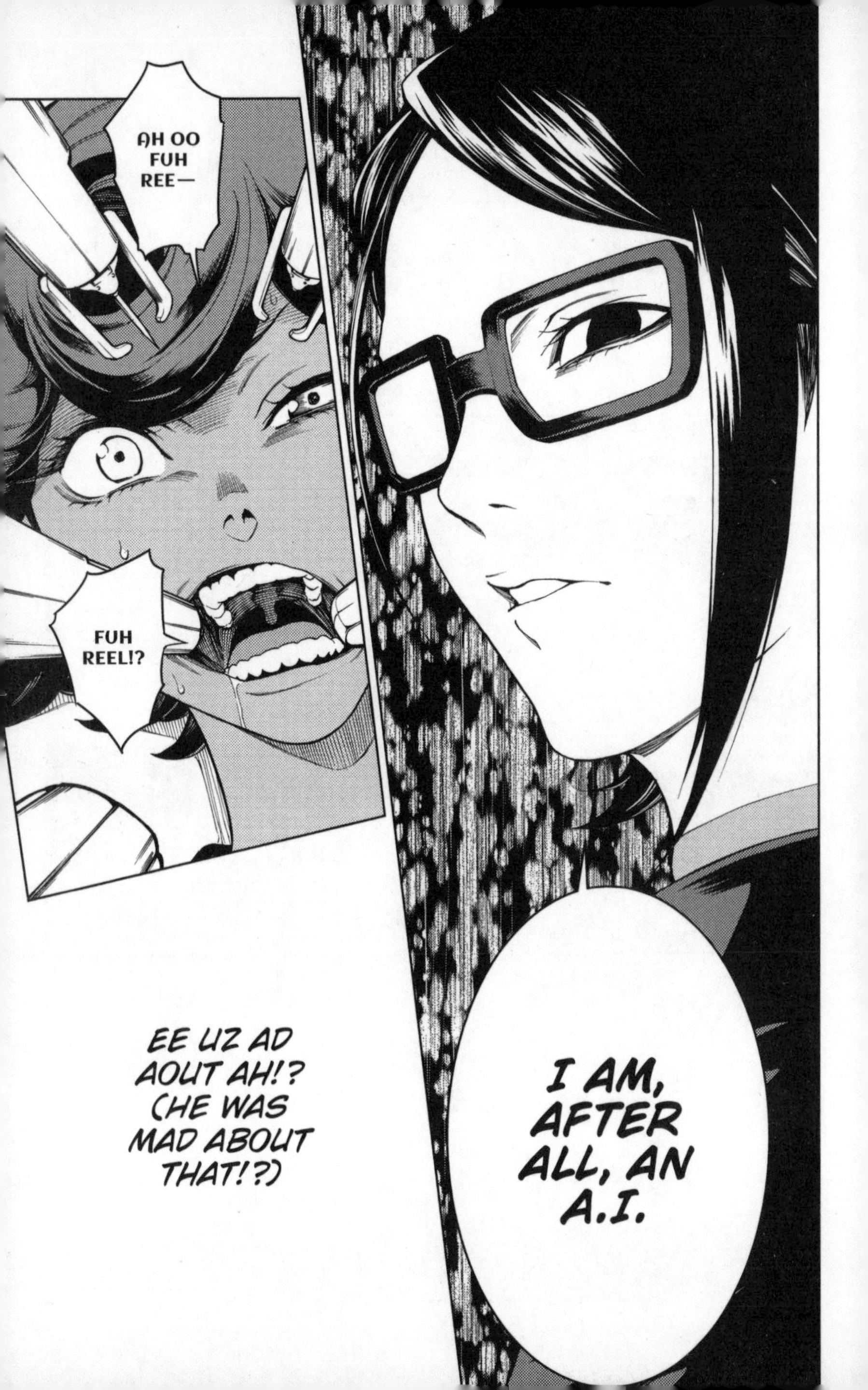
I AM, AFTER ALL, AN A.I.
AH OO FUH REE—
FUH REEL!?
EE UZ AD AOUT AH!? (HE WAS MAD ABOUT THAT!?)

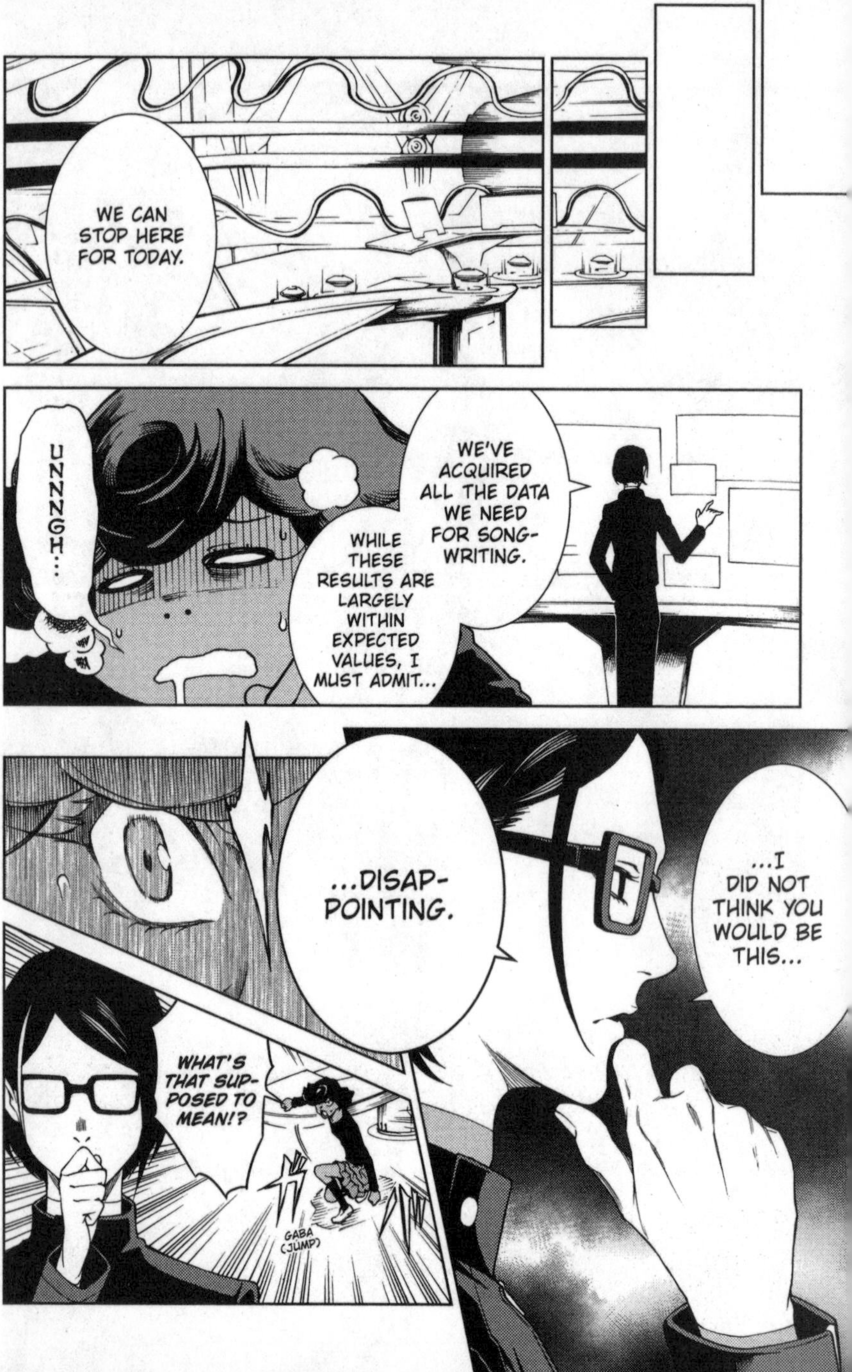
WE CAN STOP HERE FOR TODAY.
WE'VE ACQUIRED ALL THE DATA WE NEED FOR SONG-WRITING.
WHILE THESE RESULTS ARE LARGELY WITHIN EXPECTED VALUES, I MUST ADMIT...
UNNNGH...
...I DID NOT THINK YOU WOULD BE THIS...
...DISAP-POINTING.
WHAT'S THAT SUP-POSED TO MEAN!?
GABA (JUMP)

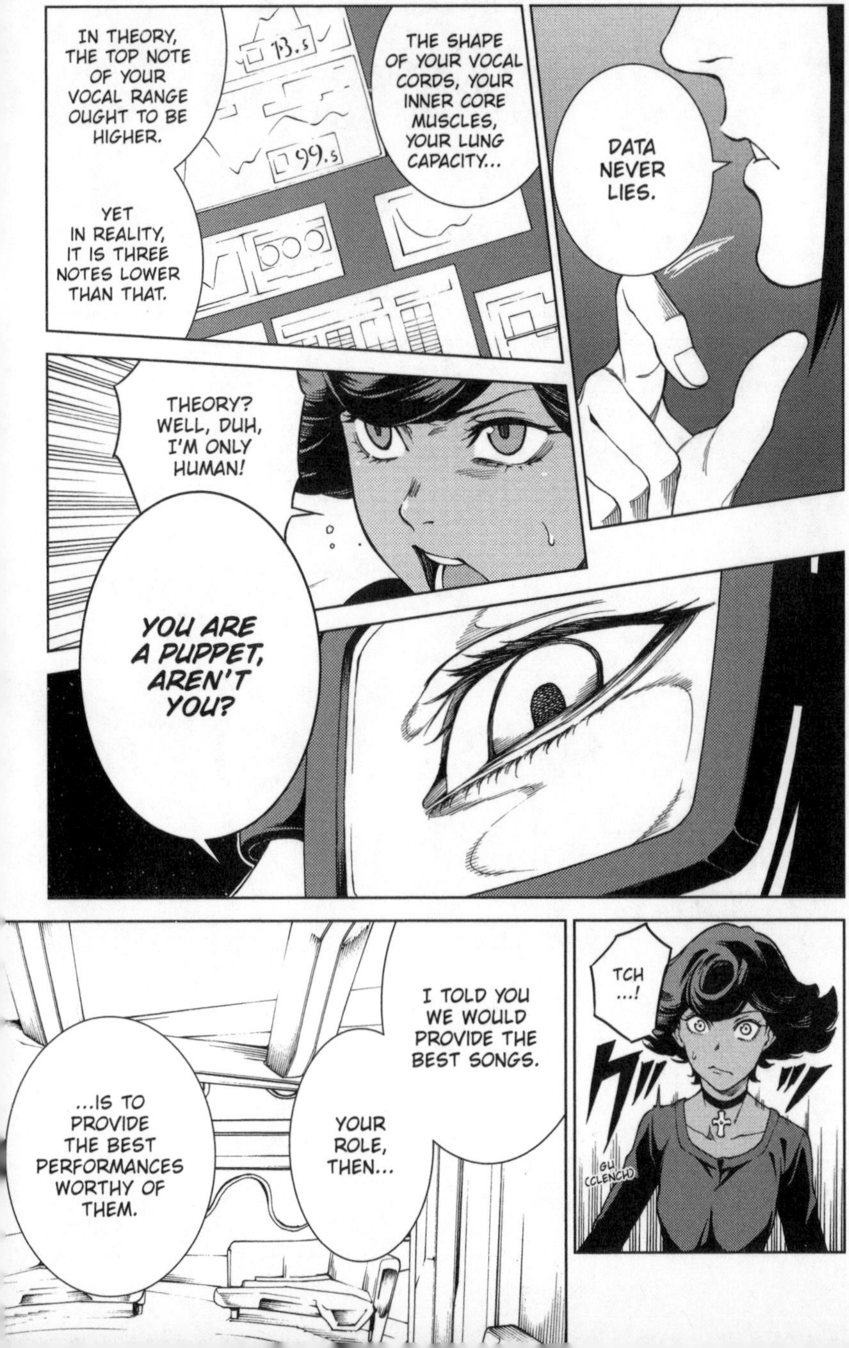

DATA NEVER LIES.
THE SHAPE OF YOUR VOCAL CORDS, YOUR INNER CORE MUSCLES, YOUR LUNG CAPACITY...
IN THEORY, THE TOP NOTE OF YOUR VOCAL RANGE OUGHT TO BE HIGHER.
YET IN REALITY, IT IS THREE NOTES LOWER THAN THAT.
THEORY? WELL, DUH, I'M ONLY HUMAN!
YOU ARE A PUPPET, AREN'T YOU?
TCH ...!
GU (CLENCH)
I TOLD YOU WE WOULD PROVIDE THE BEST SONGS.
YOUR ROLE, THEN...
...IS TO PROVIDE THE BEST PERFORMANCES WORTHY OF THEM.

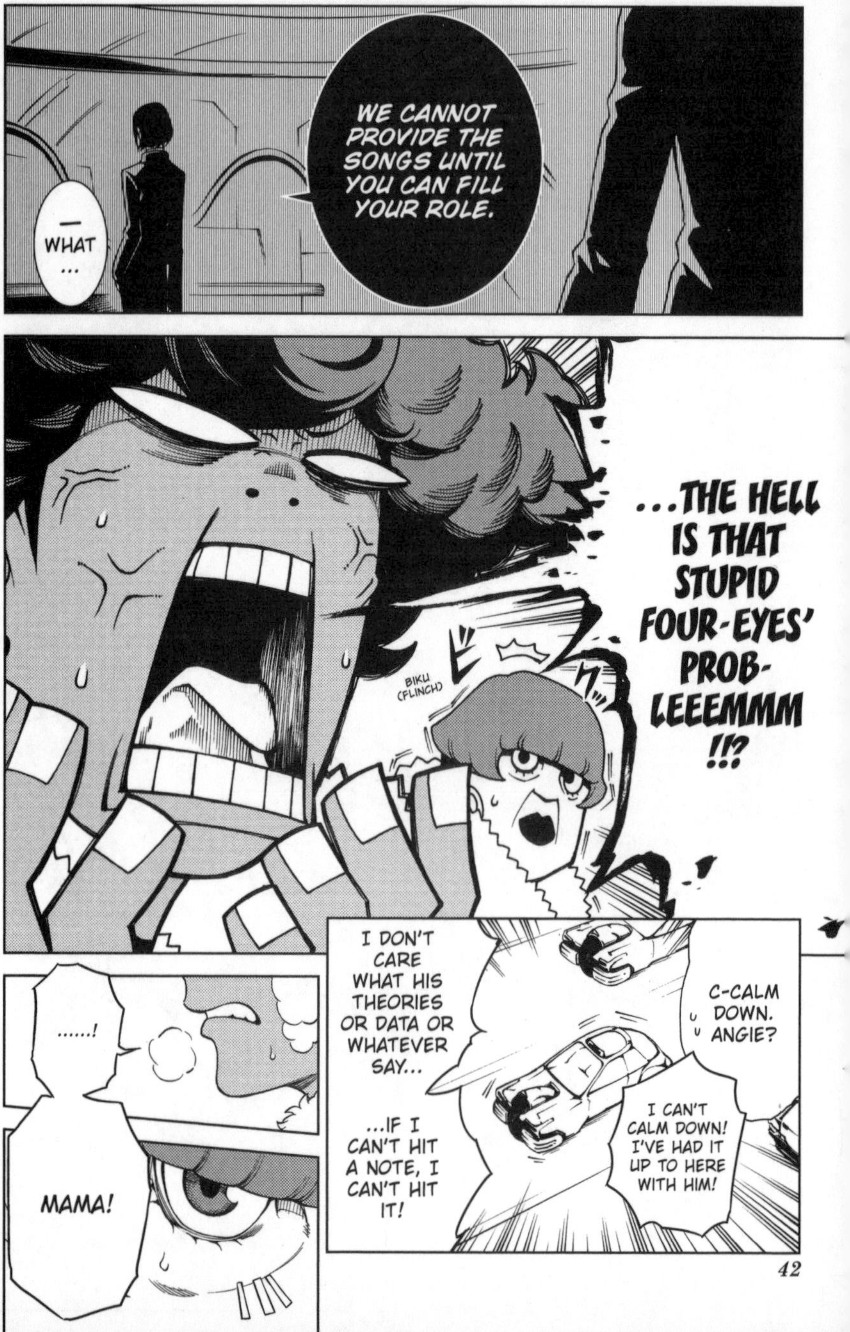
WE CANNOT PROVIDE THE SONGS UNTIL YOU CAN FILL YOUR ROLE.
—WHAT ...
...THE HELL IS THAT STUPID FOUR-EYES' PROB-LEEEMMM !!?
BIKU (FLINCH)
C-CALM DOWN. ANGIE?
I DON'T CARE WHAT HIS THEORIES OR DATA OR WHATEVER SAY...
I CAN'T CALM DOWN! I'VE HAD IT UP TO HERE WITH HIM!
...IF I CAN'T HIT A NOTE, I CAN'T HIT IT!
......!
MAMA!

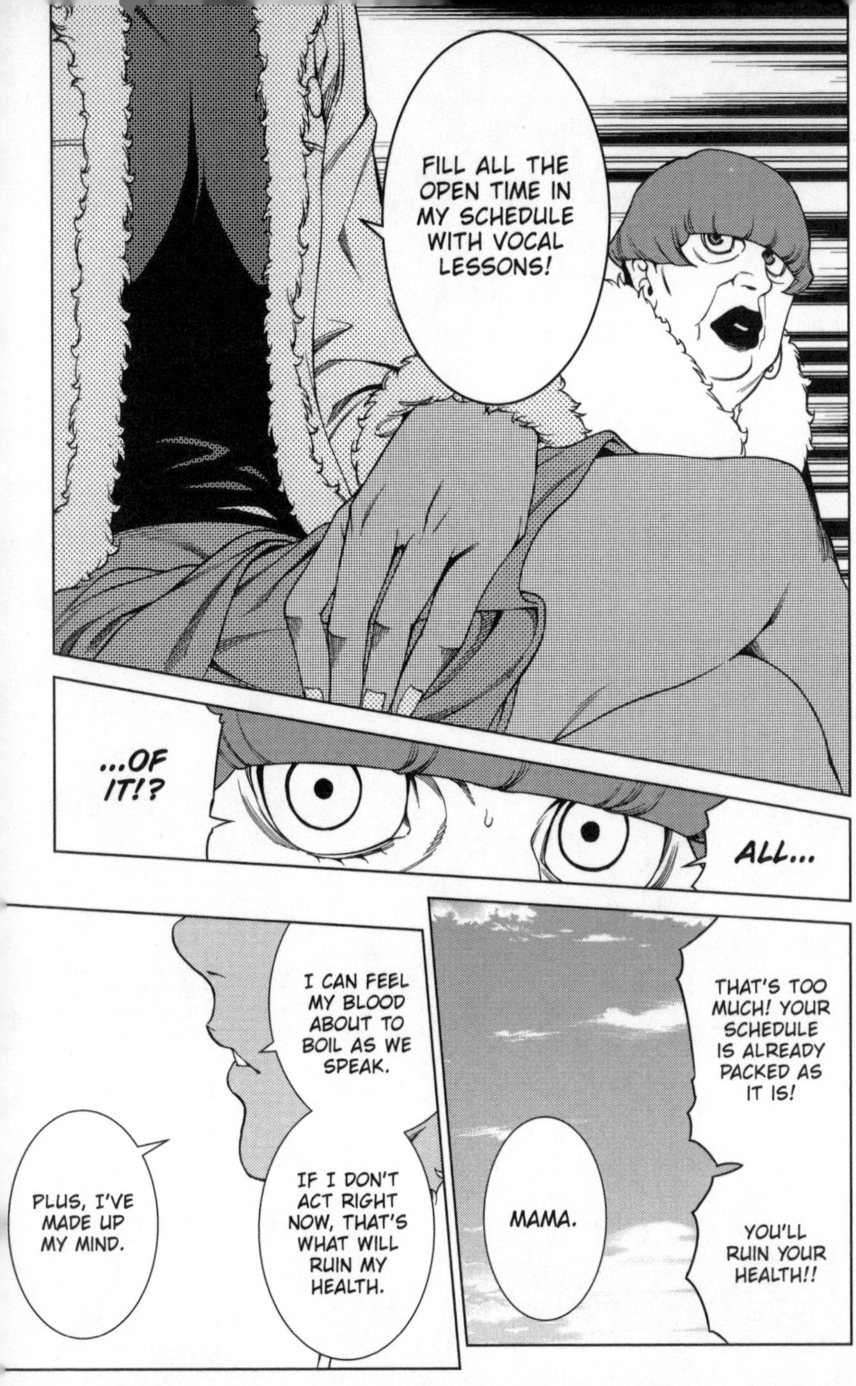
FILL ALL THE OPEN TIME IN MY SCHEDULE WITH VOCAL LESSONS!
ALL...
...OF IT!?
THAT'S TOO MUCH! YOUR SCHEDULE IS ALREADY PACKED AS IT IS!
YOU'LL RUIN YOUR HEALTH!!
MAMA.
I CAN FEEL MY BLOOD ABOUT TO BOIL AS WE SPEAK.
IF I DON'T ACT RIGHT NOW, THAT'S WHAT WILL RUIN MY HEALTH.
PLUS, I'VE MADE UP MY MIND.

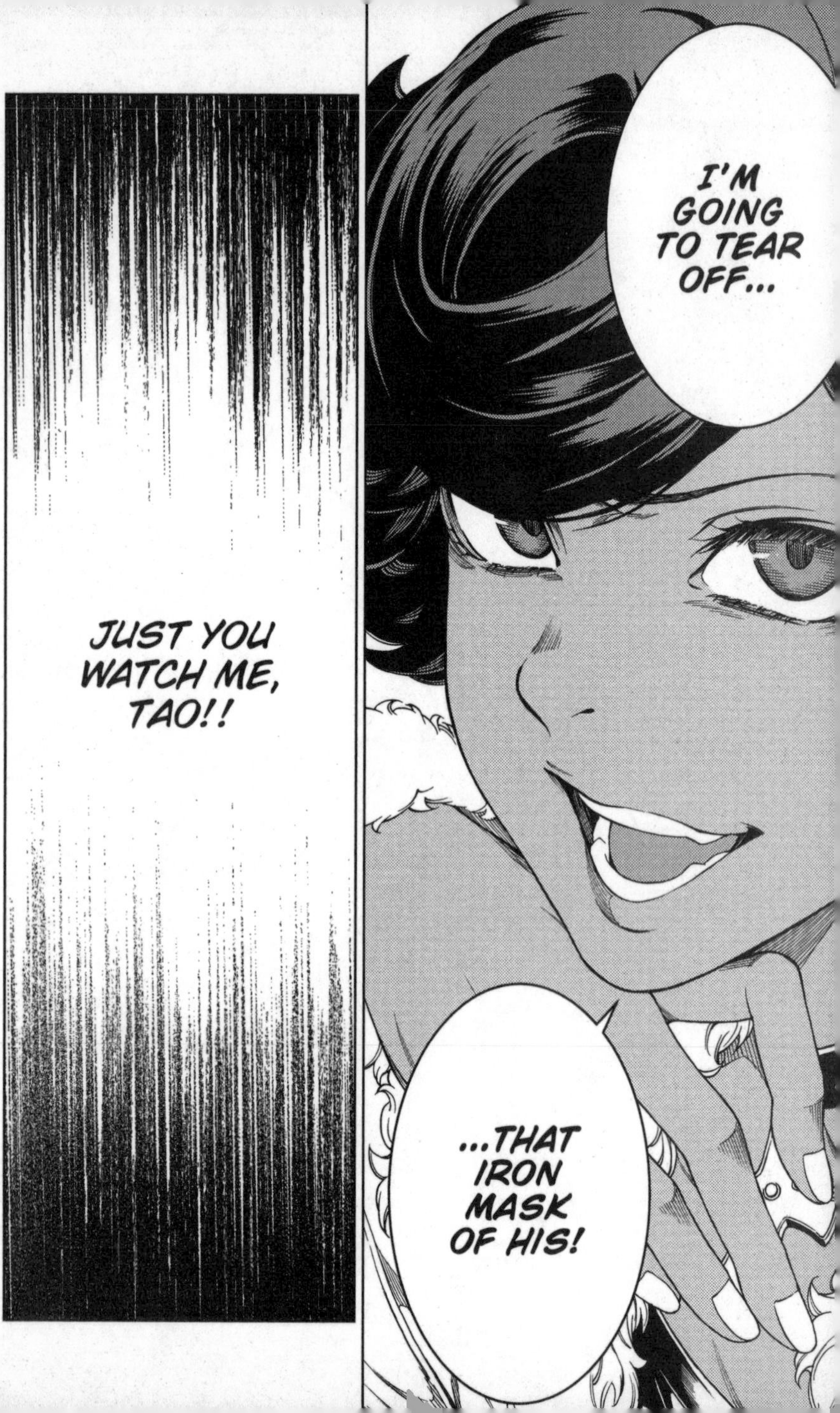
I'M GOING TO TEAR OFF...
...THAT IRON MASK OF HIS!
JUST YOU WATCH ME, TAO!!

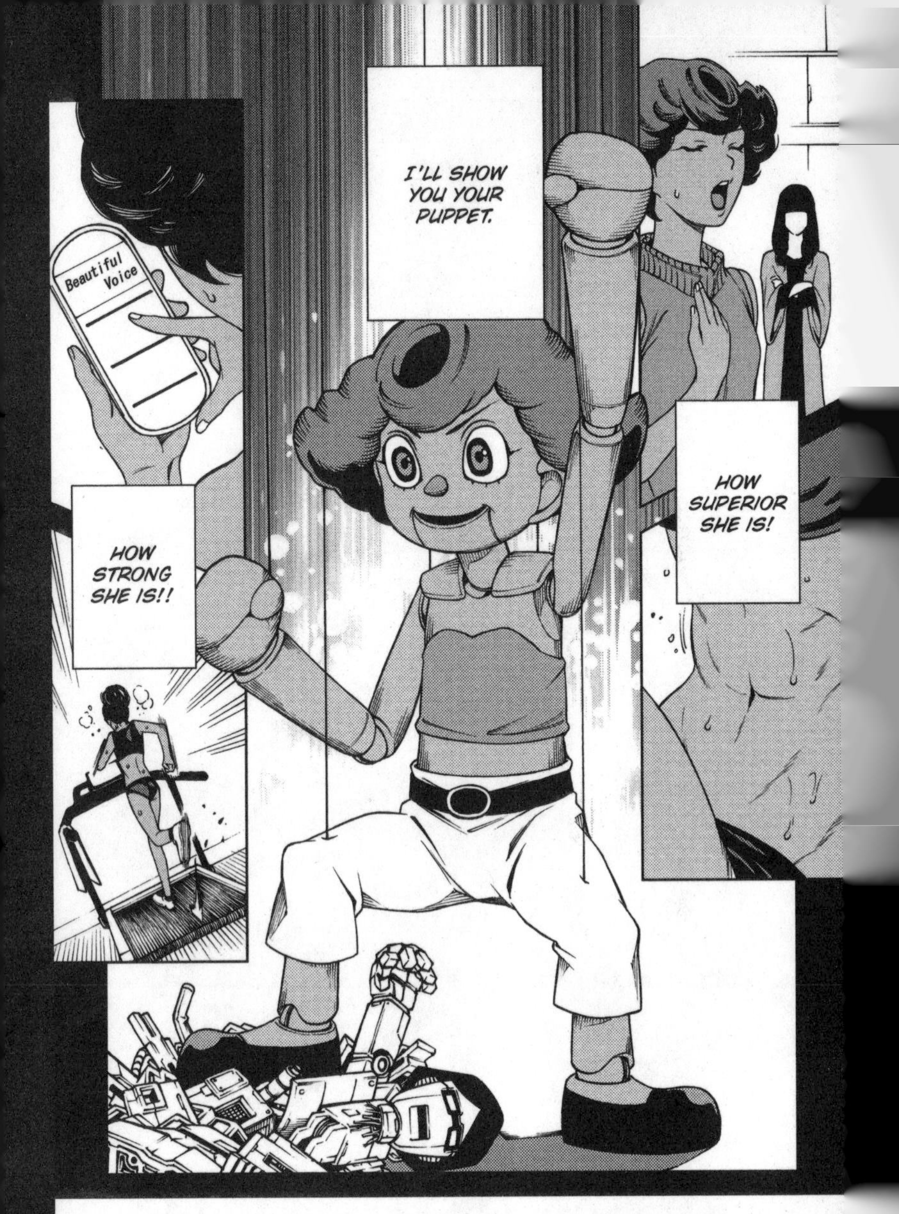
I'LL SHOW YOU YOUR PUPPET.
HOW SUPERIOR SHE IS!
Beautiful Voice
HOW STRONG SHE IS!!
I'LL SHOW YOU EXACTLY WHO SHE IS!!!

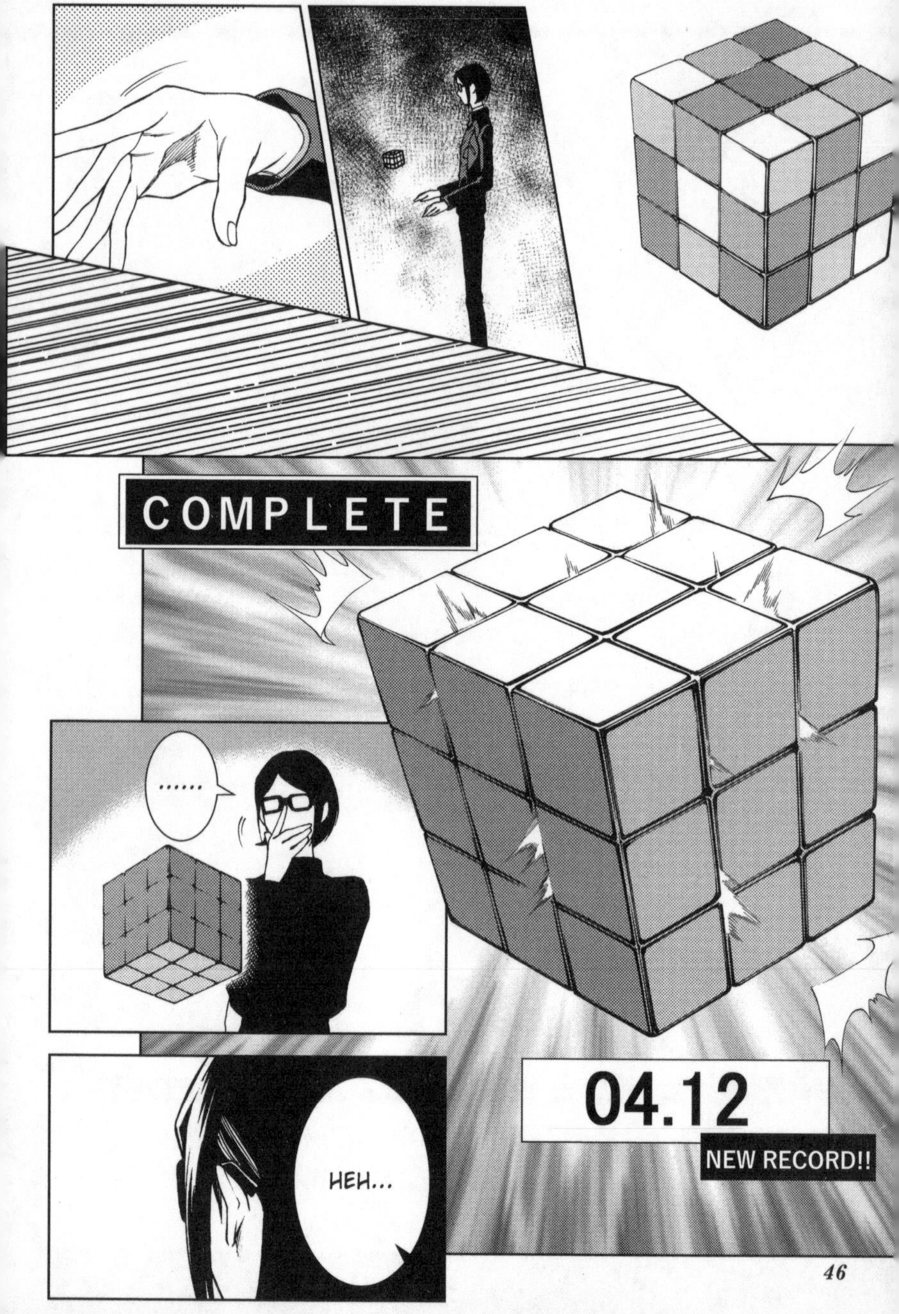
COMPLETE
04.12
NEW RECORD!!
......
HEH...

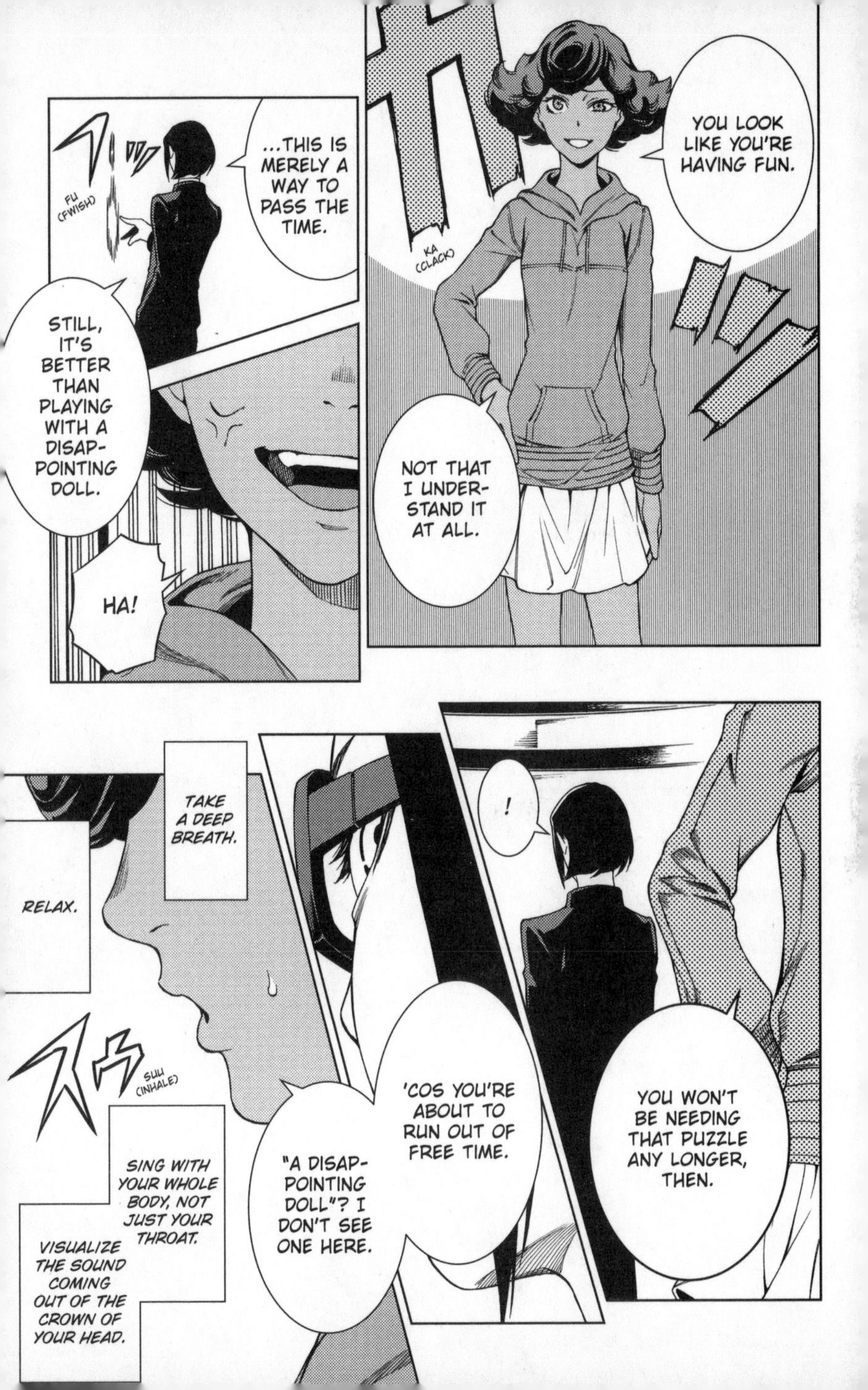
YOU LOOK LIKE YOU'RE HAVING FUN.
KA (CLACK)
NOT THAT I UNDER-STAND IT AT ALL.
...THIS IS MERELY A WAY TO PASS THE TIME.
FU (FWISH)
STILL, IT'S BETTER THAN PLAYING WITH A DISAP-POINTING DOLL.
HA!
!
YOU WON'T BE NEEDING THAT PUZZLE ANY LONGER, THEN.
'COS YOU'RE ABOUT TO RUN OUT OF FREE TIME.
"A DISAP-POINTING DOLL"? I DON'T SEE ONE HERE.
TAKE A DEEP BREATH.
RELAX.
SUU (INHALE)
SING WITH YOUR WHOLE BODY, NOT JUST YOUR THROAT.
VISUALIZE THE SOUND COMING OUT OF THE CROWN OF YOUR HEAD.

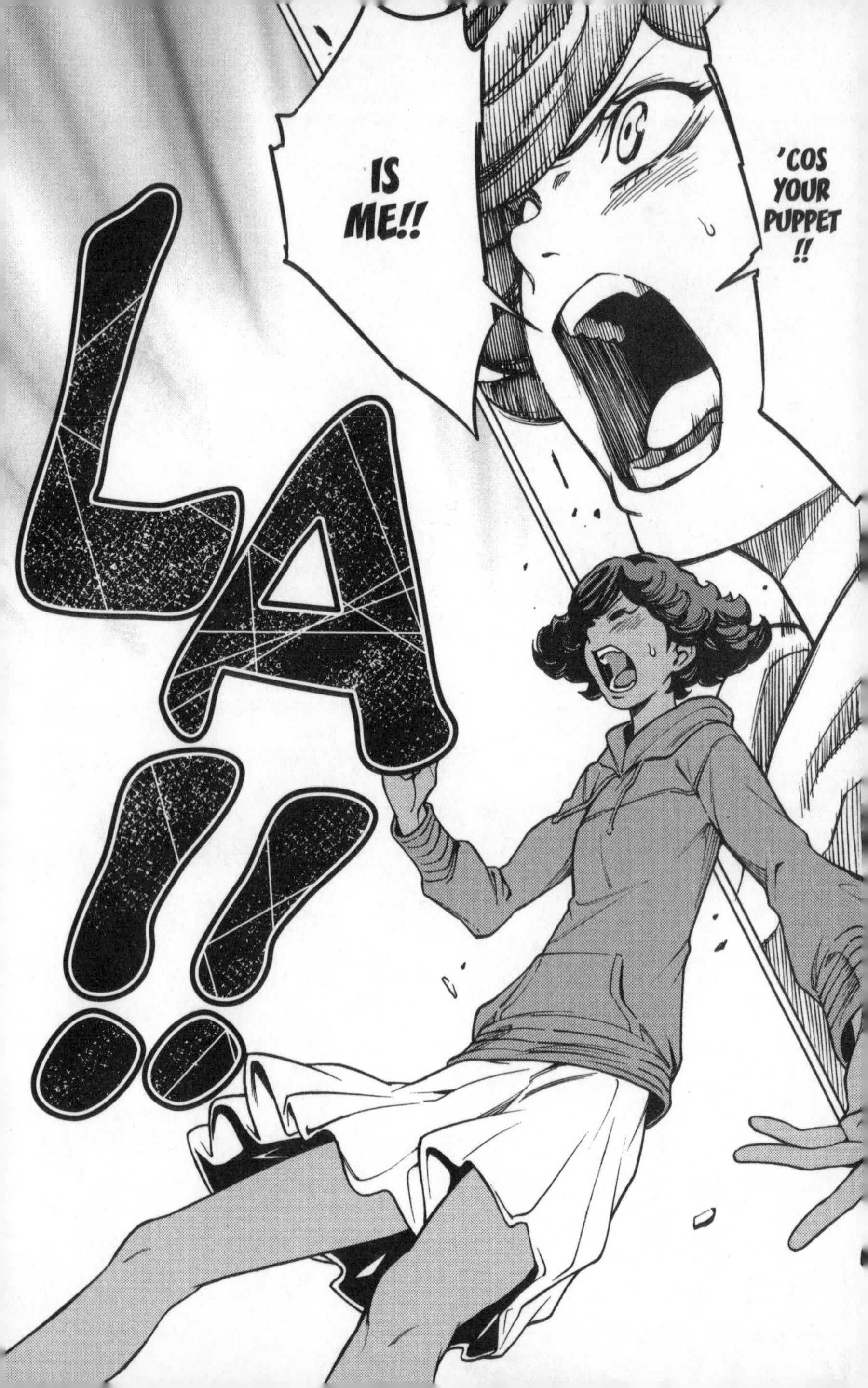
'COS YOUR PUPPET !!
IS ME!!
LA!!

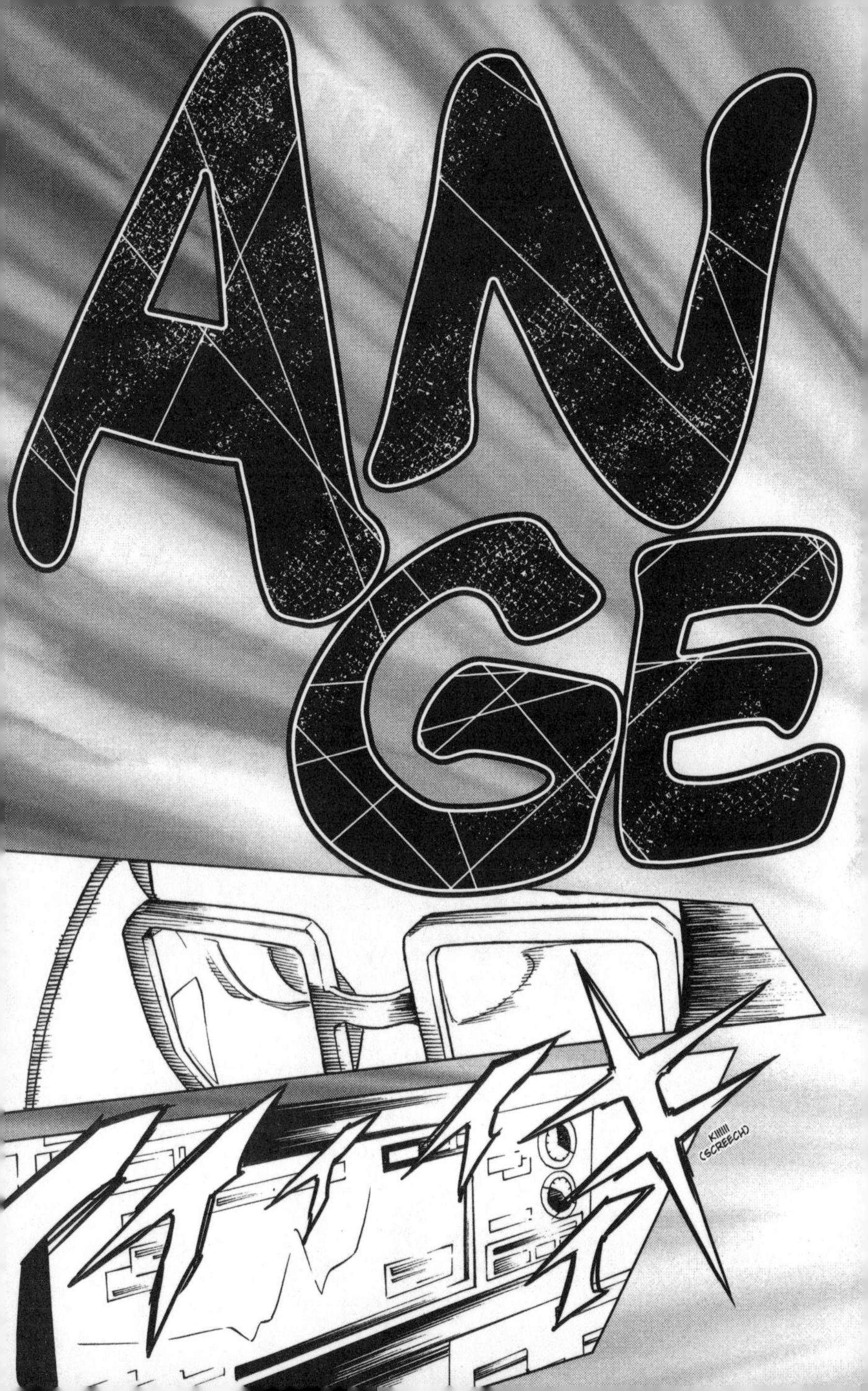
ANGE
KIIIIII
(SCREECH)

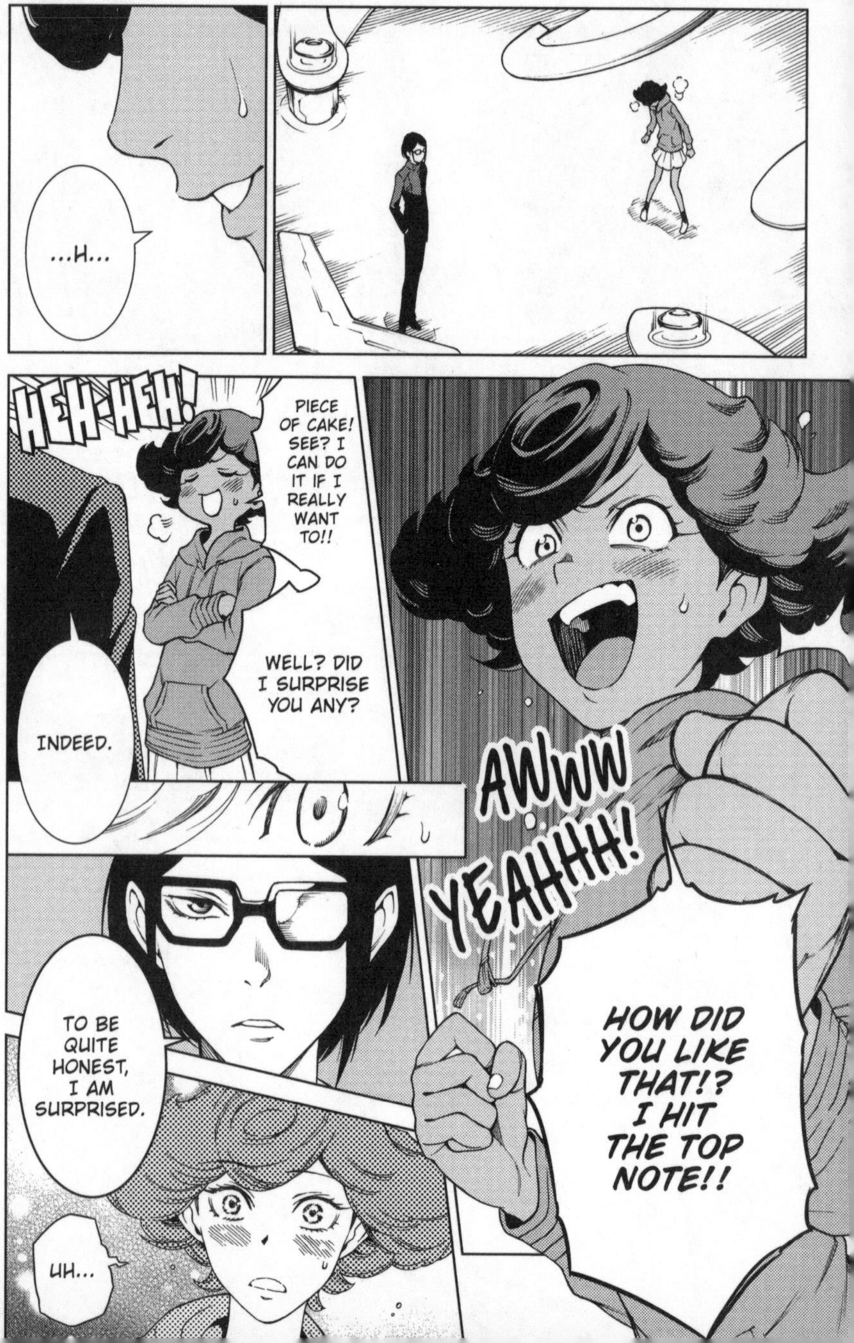
...H...
AWWW YEAHHH!
HOW DID YOU LIKE THAT!? I HIT THE TOP NOTE!!
PIECE OF CAKE! SEE? I CAN DO IT IF I REALLY WANT TO!!
HEH-HEH!
WELL? DID I SURPRISE YOU ANY?
INDEED.
TO BE QUITE HONEST, I AM SURPRISED.
UH...

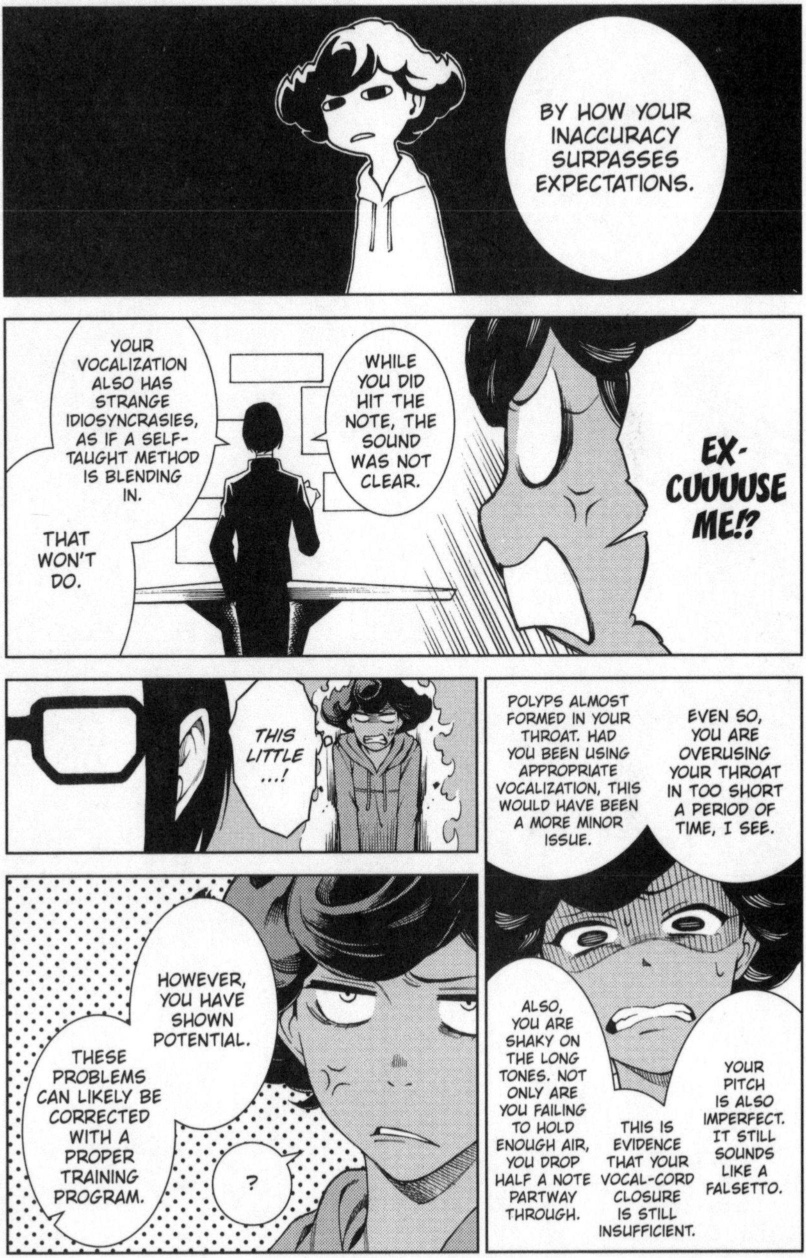
BY HOW YOUR INACCURACY SURPASSES EXPECTATIONS.
EX-CUUUUSE ME!?
WHILE YOU DID HIT THE NOTE, THE SOUND WAS NOT CLEAR.
YOUR VOCALIZATION ALSO HAS STRANGE IDIOSYNCRASIES, AS IF A SELF-TAUGHT METHOD IS BLENDING IN.
THAT WON'T DO.
EVEN SO, YOU ARE OVERUSING YOUR THROAT IN TOO SHORT A PERIOD OF TIME, I SEE.
POLYPS ALMOST FORMED IN YOUR THROAT. HAD YOU BEEN USING APPROPRIATE VOCALIZATION, THIS WOULD HAVE BEEN A MORE MINOR ISSUE.
ALSO, YOU ARE SHAKY ON THE LONG TONES. NOT ONLY ARE YOU FAILING TO HOLD ENOUGH AIR, YOU DROP HALF A NOTE PARTWAY THROUGH.
THIS IS EVIDENCE THAT YOUR VOCAL-CORD CLOSURE IS STILL INSUFFICIENT.
YOUR PITCH IS ALSO IMPERFECT. IT STILL SOUNDS LIKE A FALSETTO.
THIS LITTLE ...!
HOWEVER, YOU HAVE SHOWN POTENTIAL.
THESE PROBLEMS CAN LIKELY BE CORRECTED WITH A PROPER TRAINING PROGRAM.
?

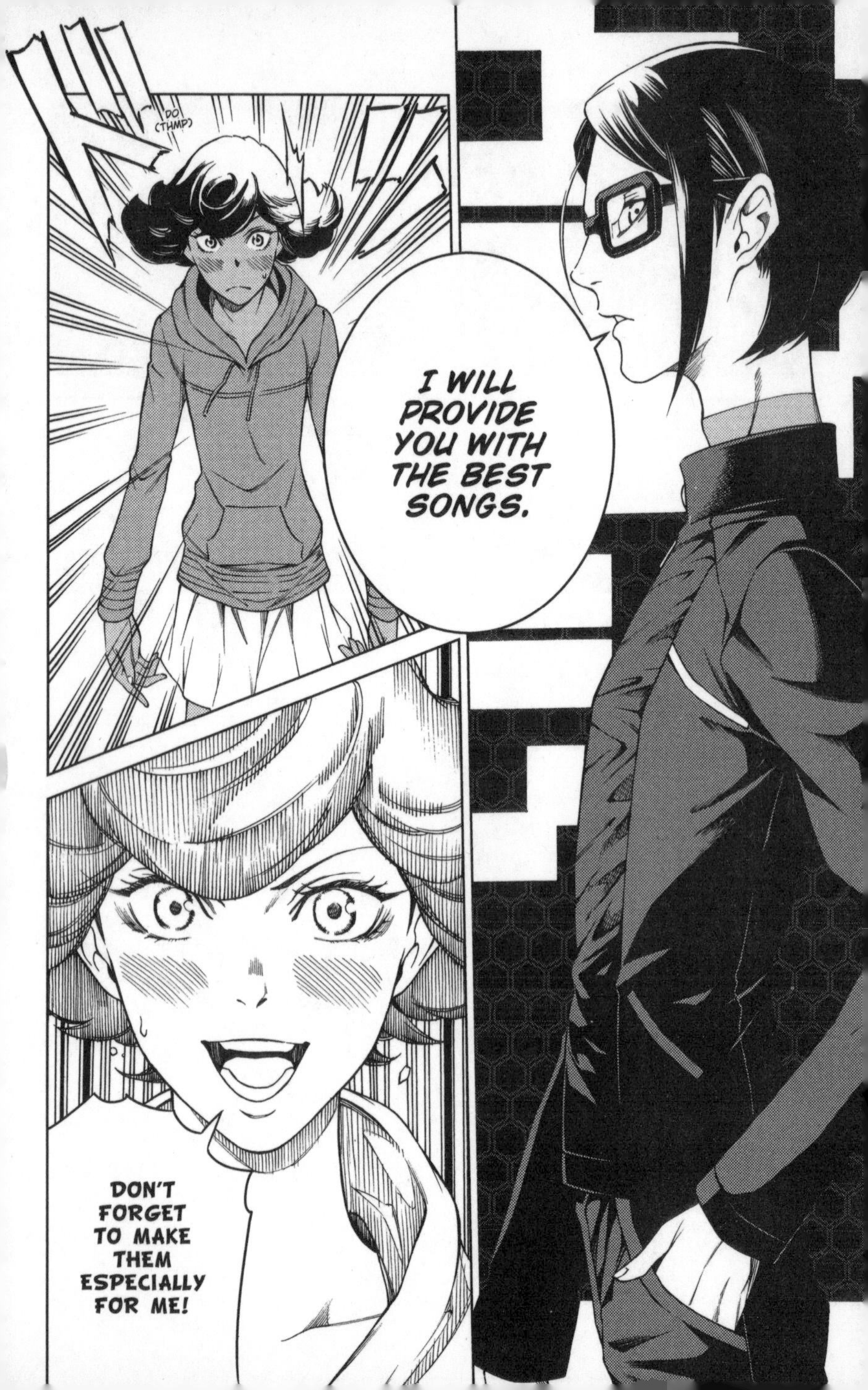
I WILL PROVIDE YOU WITH THE BEST SONGS.
DO (THMP)
DON'T FORGET TO MAKE THEM ESPECIALLY FOR ME!

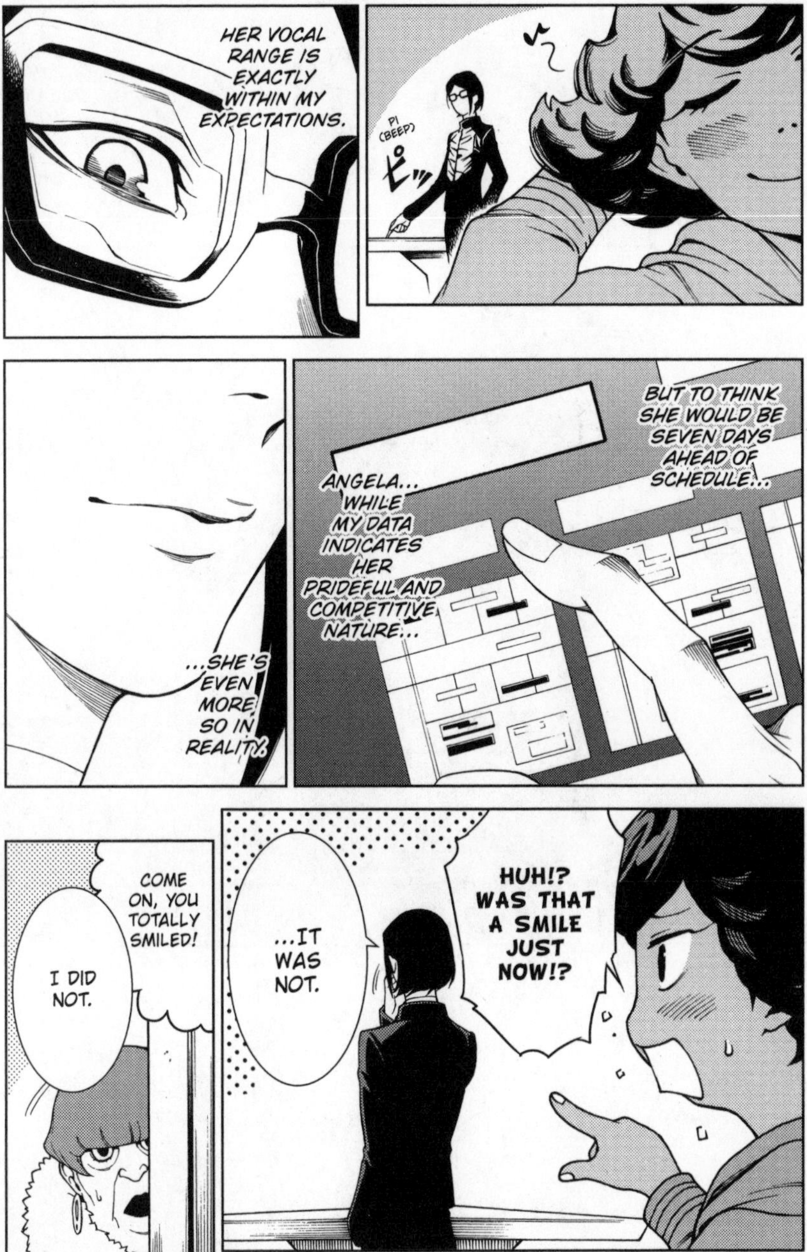
PI (BEEP)
ピッ
HER VOCAL RANGE IS EXACTLY WITHIN MY EXPECTATIONS.
BUT TO THINK SHE WOULD BE SEVEN DAYS AHEAD OF SCHEDULE...
ANGELA... WHILE MY DATA INDICATES HER PRIDEFUL AND COMPETITIVE NATURE...
...SHE'S EVEN MORE SO IN REALITY.
HUH!? WAS THAT A SMILE JUST NOW!?
...IT WAS NOT.
COME ON, YOU TOTALLY SMILED!
I DID NOT.

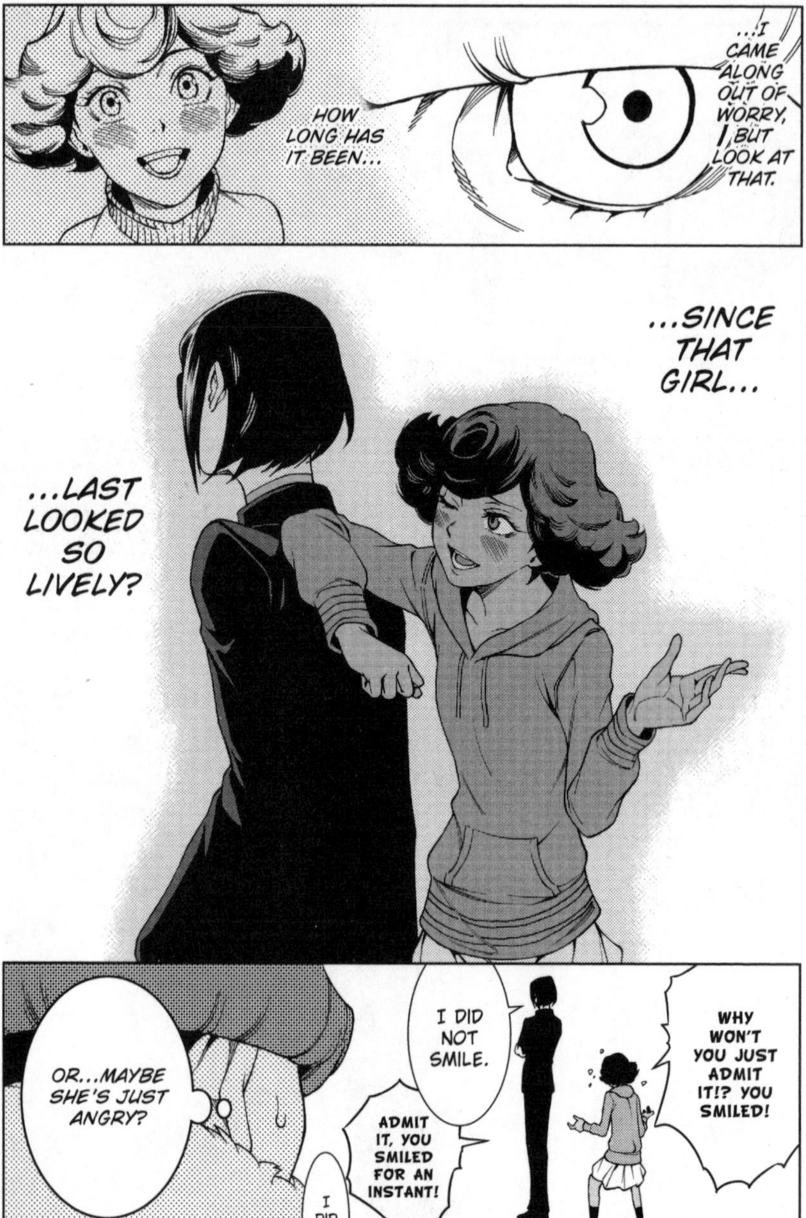
...I CAME ALONG OUT OF WORRY, BUT LOOK AT THAT.
HOW LONG HAS IT BEEN...
...SINCE THAT GIRL...
...LAST LOOKED SO LIVELY?
WHY WON'T YOU JUST ADMIT IT!? YOU SMILED!
I DID NOT SMILE.
ADMIT IT, YOU SMILED FOR AN INSTANT!
I DID NOT.
OR...MAYBE SHE'S JUST ANGRY?

END

CAROLE & TUESDAY

CAROLE & TUESDAY

episode 7: Fire and Rain

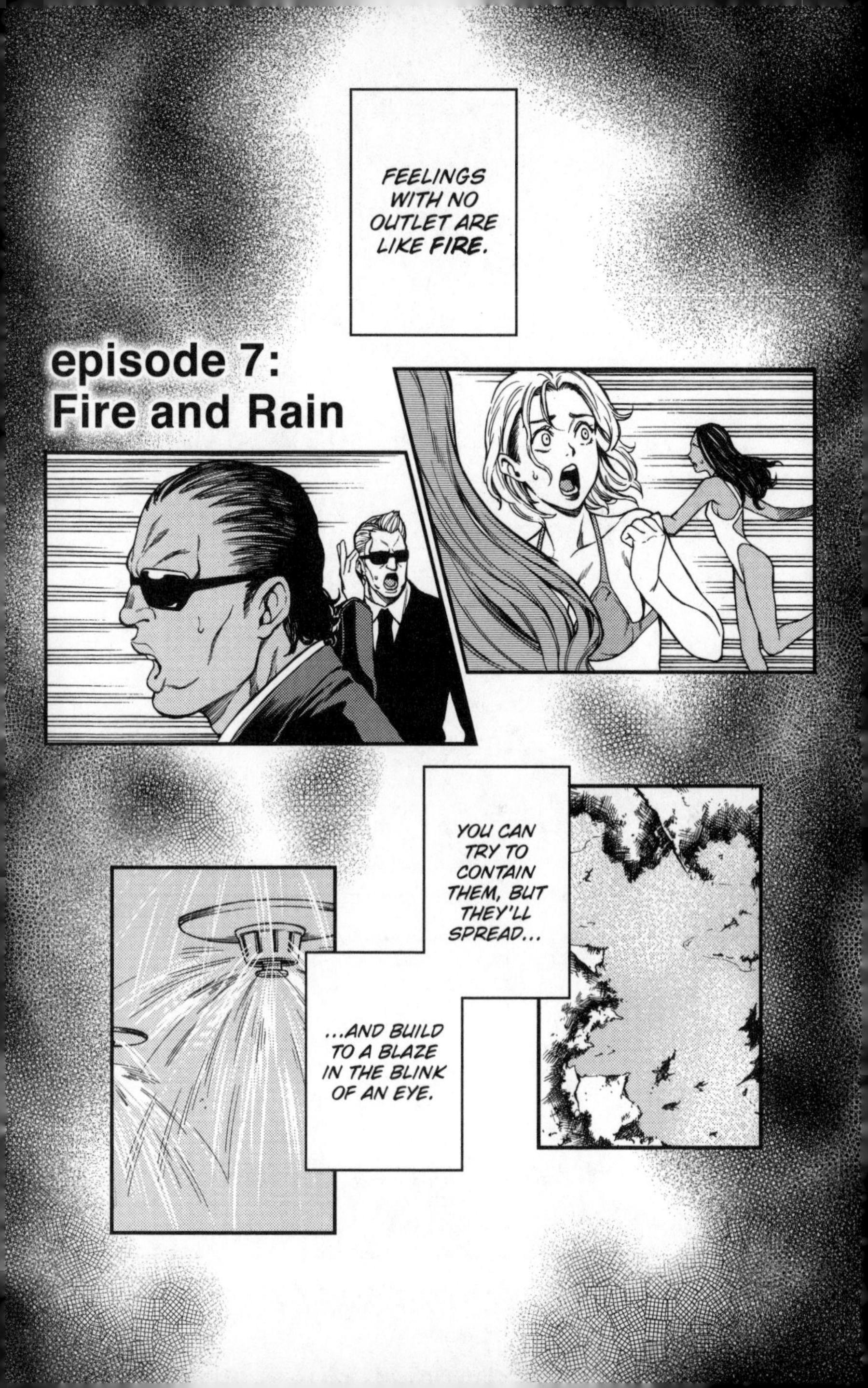
FEELINGS WITH NO OUTLET ARE LIKE FIRE.
YOU CAN TRY TO CONTAIN THEM, BUT THEY'LL SPREAD...
...AND BUILD TO A BLAZE IN THE BLINK OF AN EYE.

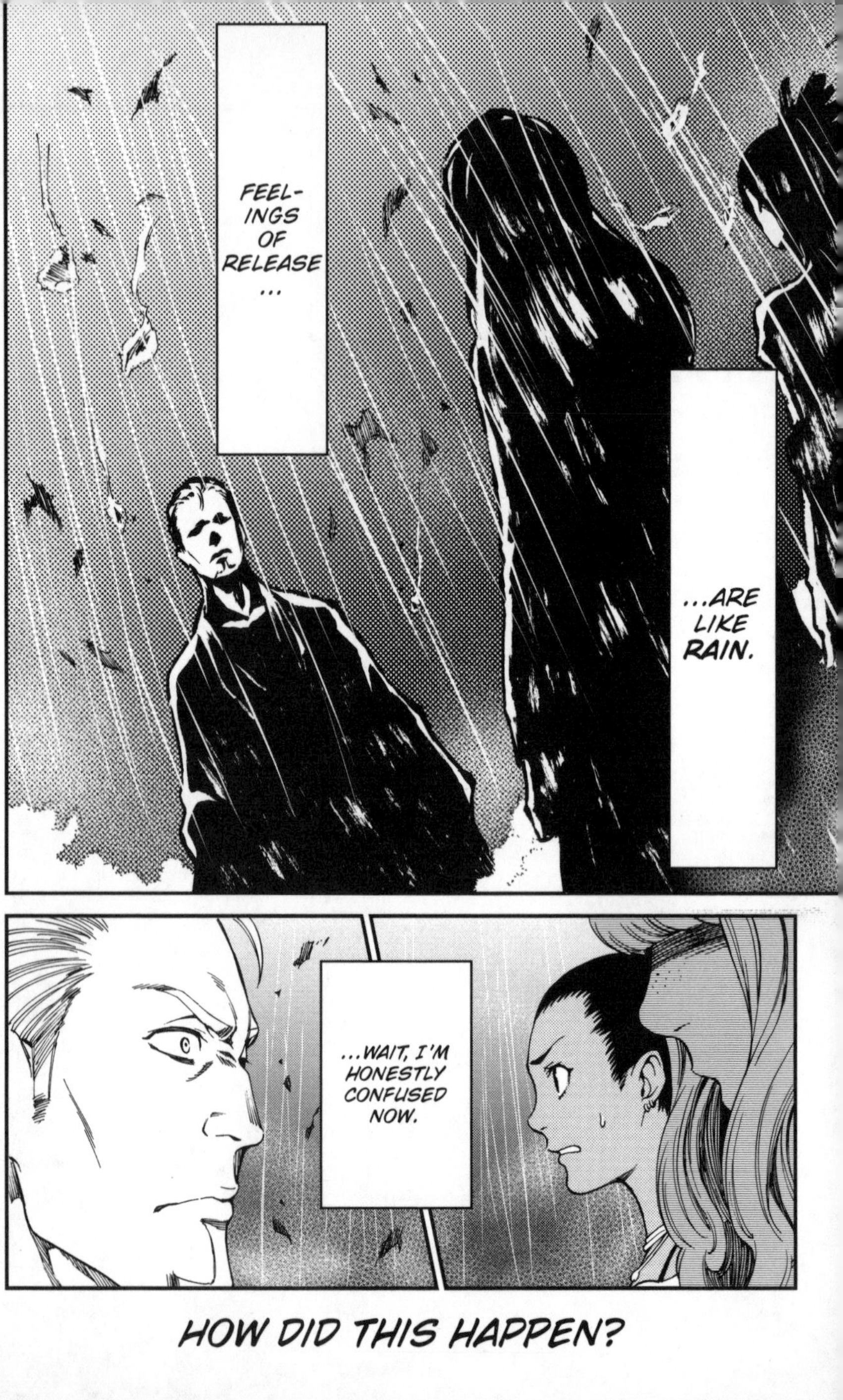
FEEL-INGS OF RELEASE ...
...ARE LIKE RAIN.
...WAIT, I'M HONESTLY CONFUSED NOW.

HOW DID THIS HAPPEN?

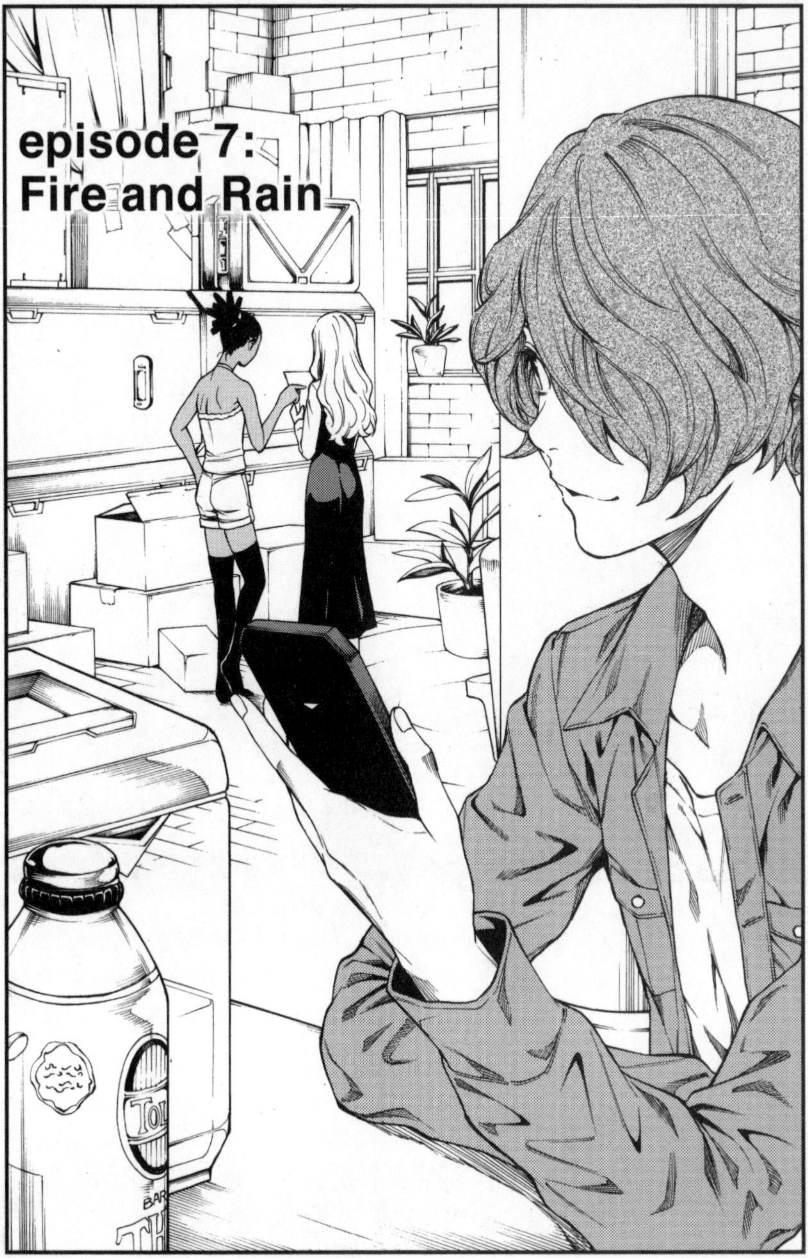
episode 7:
Fire and Rain

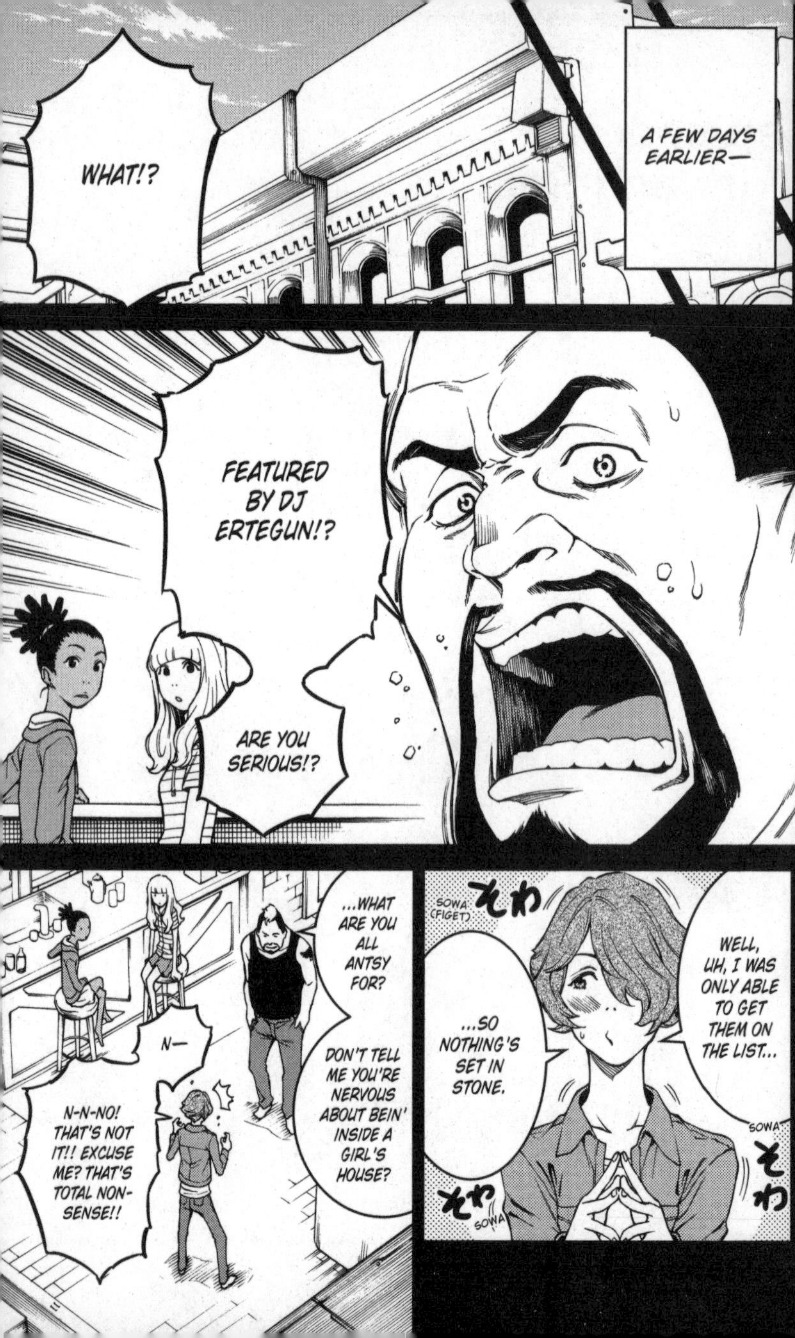
A FEW DAYS EARLIER—
WHAT!?
FEATURED BY DJ ERTEGUN!?
ARE YOU SERIOUS!?
そわ
SOWA (FIGET)
WELL, UH, I WAS ONLY ABLE TO GET THEM ON THE LIST...
...SO NOTHING'S SET IN STONE.
そわ
SOWA
そわ
SOWA
...WHAT ARE YOU ALL ANTSY FOR?
DON'T TELL ME YOU'RE NERVOUS ABOUT BEIN' INSIDE A GIRL'S HOUSE?
N—
N-N-NO! THAT'S NOT IT!! EXCUSE ME? THAT'S TOTAL NON-SENSE!!

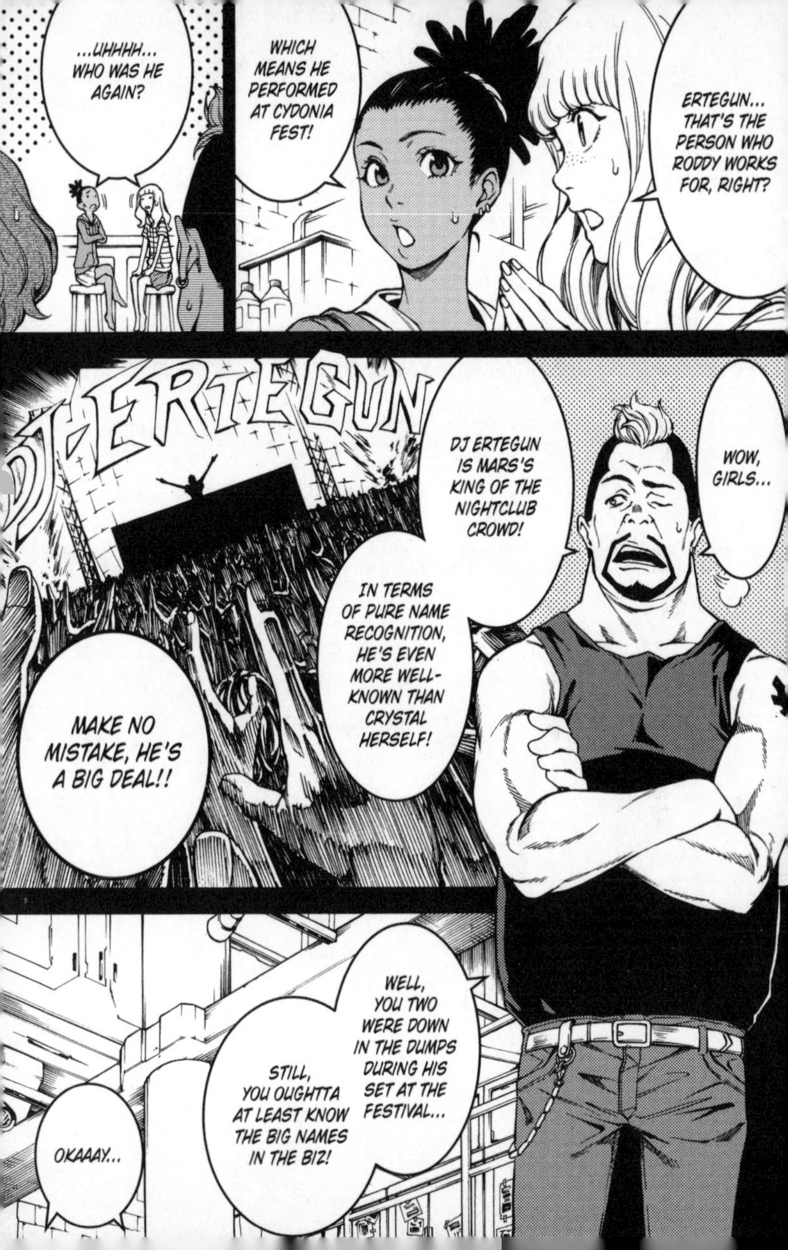
ERTEGUN... THAT'S THE PERSON WHO RODDY WORKS FOR, RIGHT?
WHICH MEANS HE PERFORMED AT CYDONIA FEST!
...UHHHH... WHO WAS HE AGAIN?
WOW, GIRLS...
DJ ERTEGUN IS MARS'S KING OF THE NIGHTCLUB CROWD!
IN TERMS OF PURE NAME RECOGNITION, HE'S EVEN MORE WELL-KNOWN THAN CRYSTAL HERSELF!
DJ-ERTEGUN
MAKE NO MISTAKE, HE'S A BIG DEAL!!
WELL, YOU TWO WERE DOWN IN THE DUMPS DURING HIS SET AT THE FESTIVAL...
STILL, YOU OUGHTTA AT LEAST KNOW THE BIG NAMES IN THE BIZ!
OKAAAY...

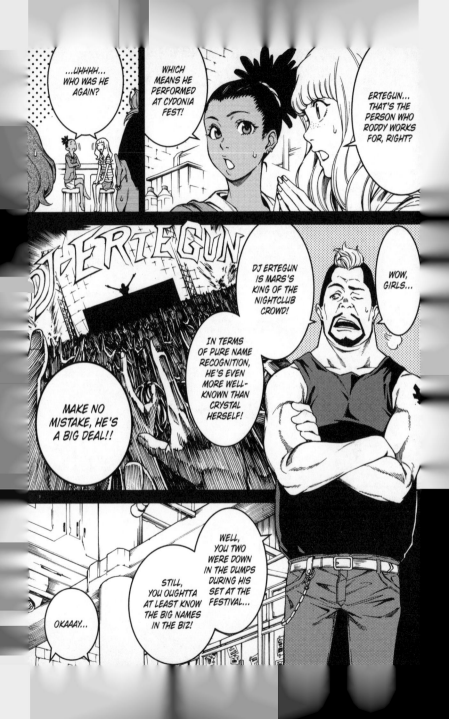

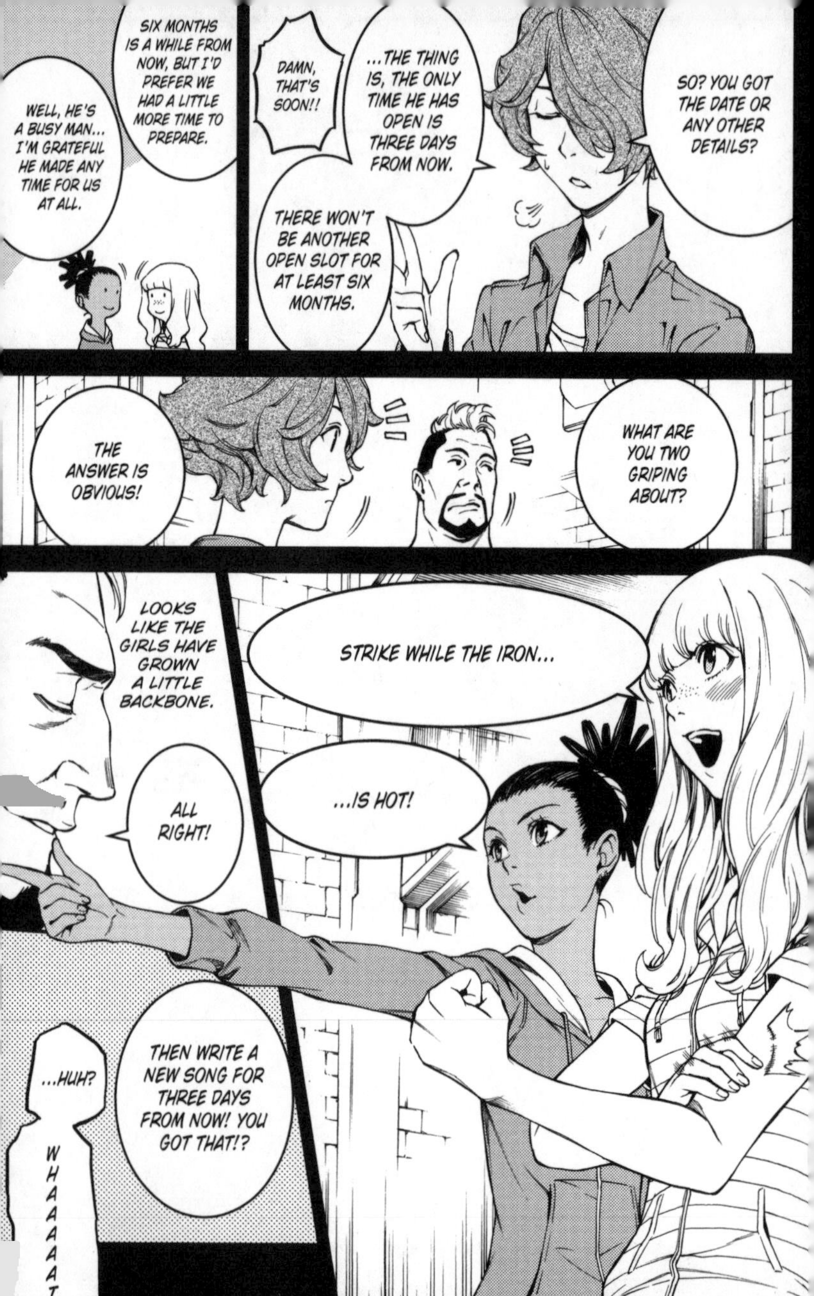
SO? YOU GOT THE DATE OR ANY OTHER DETAILS?
...THE THING IS, THE ONLY TIME HE HAS OPEN IS THREE DAYS FROM NOW.
THERE WON'T BE ANOTHER OPEN SLOT FOR AT LEAST SIX MONTHS.
DAMN, THAT'S SOON!!
SIX MONTHS IS A WHILE FROM NOW, BUT I'D PREFER WE HAD A LITTLE MORE TIME TO PREPARE.
WELL, HE'S A BUSY MAN... I'M GRATEFUL HE MADE ANY TIME FOR US AT ALL.
WHAT ARE YOU TWO GRIPING ABOUT?
THE ANSWER IS OBVIOUS!
STRIKE WHILE THE IRON...
...IS HOT!
LOOKS LIKE THE GIRLS HAVE GROWN A LITTLE BACKBONE.
ALL RIGHT!
THEN WRITE A NEW SONG FOR THREE DAYS FROM NOW! YOU GOT THAT!?
...HUH?
WHAAAAAAT!?

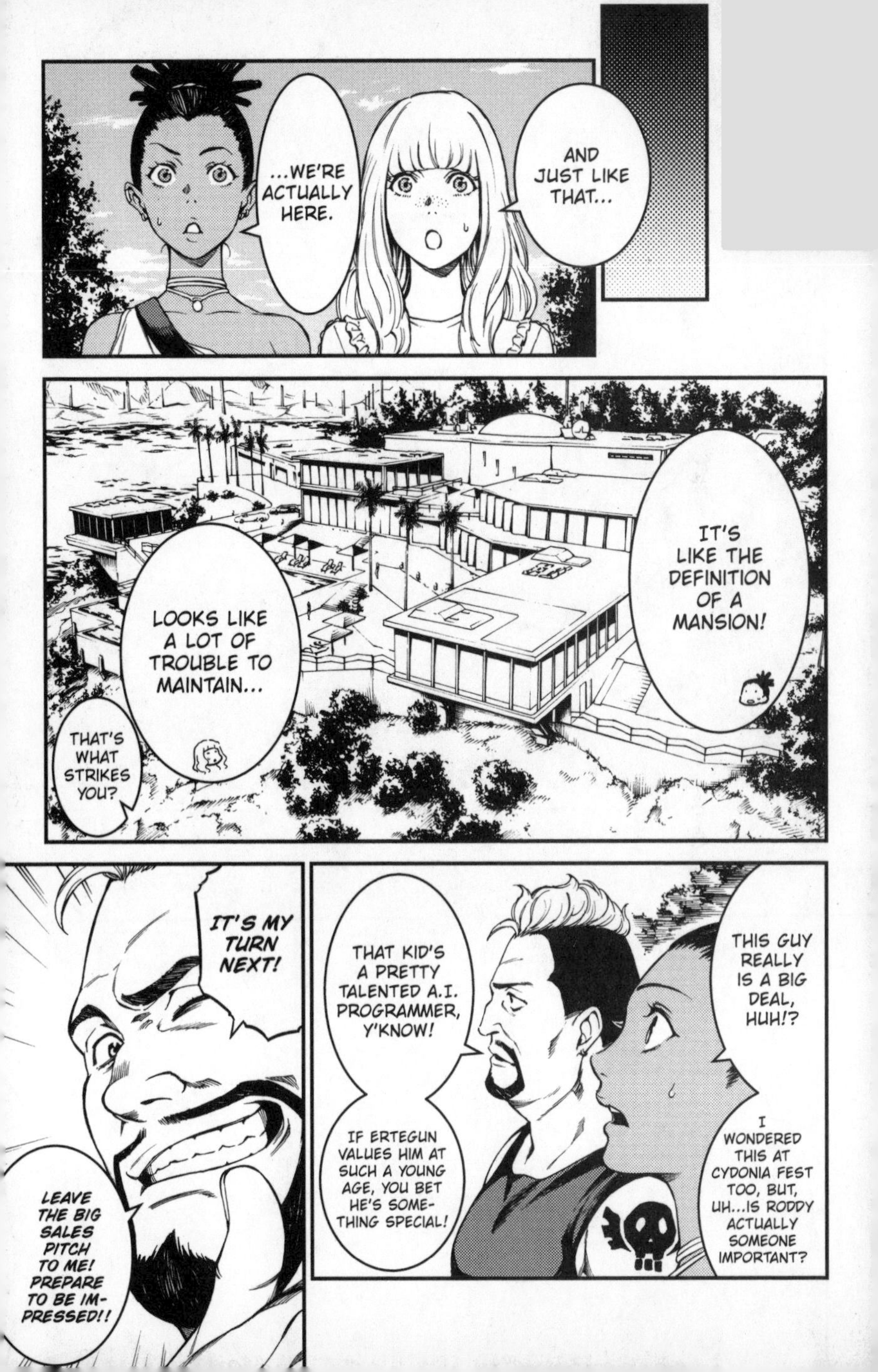
AND JUST LIKE THAT...
...WE'RE ACTUALLY HERE.
IT'S LIKE THE DEFINITION OF A MANSION!
LOOKS LIKE A LOT OF TROUBLE TO MAINTAIN...
THAT'S WHAT STRIKES YOU?
THIS GUY REALLY IS A BIG DEAL, HUH!?
I WONDERED THIS AT CYDONIA FEST TOO, BUT, UH...IS RODDY ACTUALLY SOMEONE IMPORTANT?
THAT KID'S A PRETTY TALENTED A.I. PROGRAMMER, Y'KNOW!
IF ERTEGUN VALUES HIM AT SUCH A YOUNG AGE, YOU BET HE'S SOME-THING SPECIAL!
IT'S MY TURN NEXT!
LEAVE THE BIG SALES PITCH TO ME! PREPARE TO BE IM-PRESSED!!

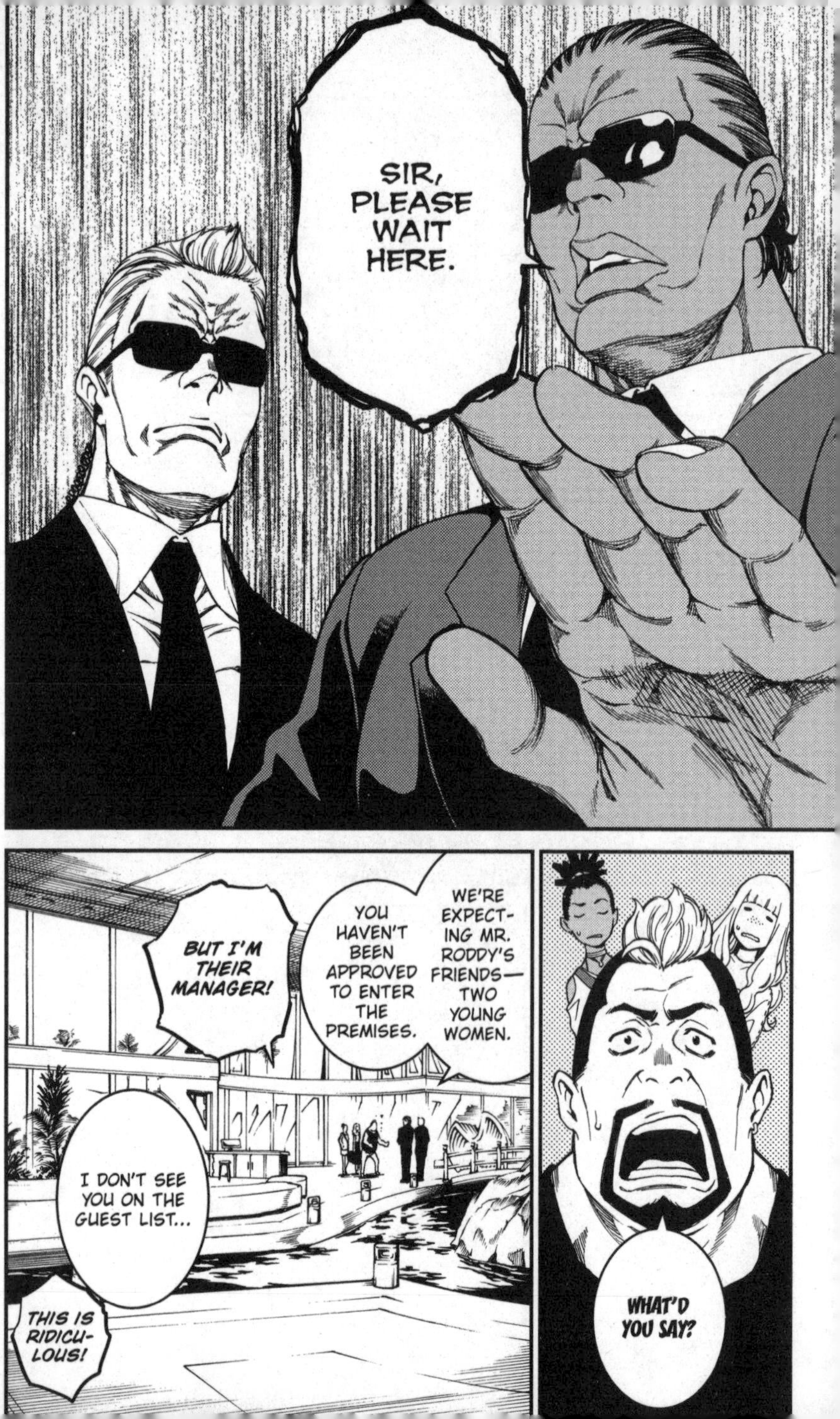
SIR, PLEASE WAIT HERE.
WHAT'D YOU SAY?
WE'RE EXPECTING MR. RODDY'S FRIENDS—TWO YOUNG WOMEN.
YOU HAVEN'T BEEN APPROVED TO ENTER THE PREMISES.
BUT I'M THEIR MANAGER!
I DON'T SEE YOU ON THE GUEST LIST...
THIS IS RIDICULOUS!

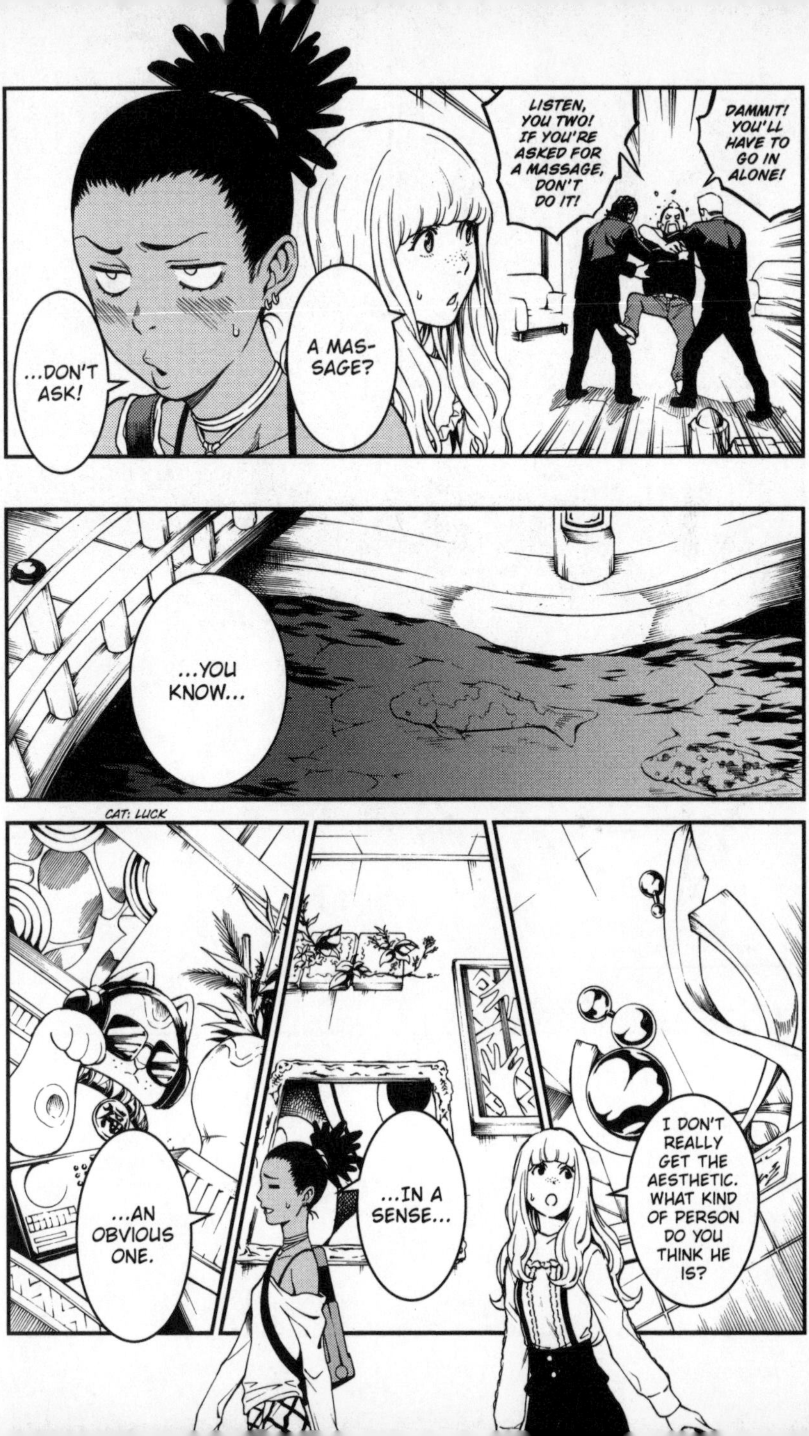
DAMMIT! YOU'LL HAVE TO GO IN ALONE!
LISTEN, YOU TWO! IF YOU'RE ASKED FOR A MASSAGE, DON'T DO IT!
A MAS-SAGE?
...DON'T ASK!
...YOU KNOW...
CAT: LUCK
I DON'T REALLY GET THE AESTHETIC. WHAT KIND OF PERSON DO YOU THINK HE IS?
...IN A SENSE...
...AN OBVIOUS ONE.

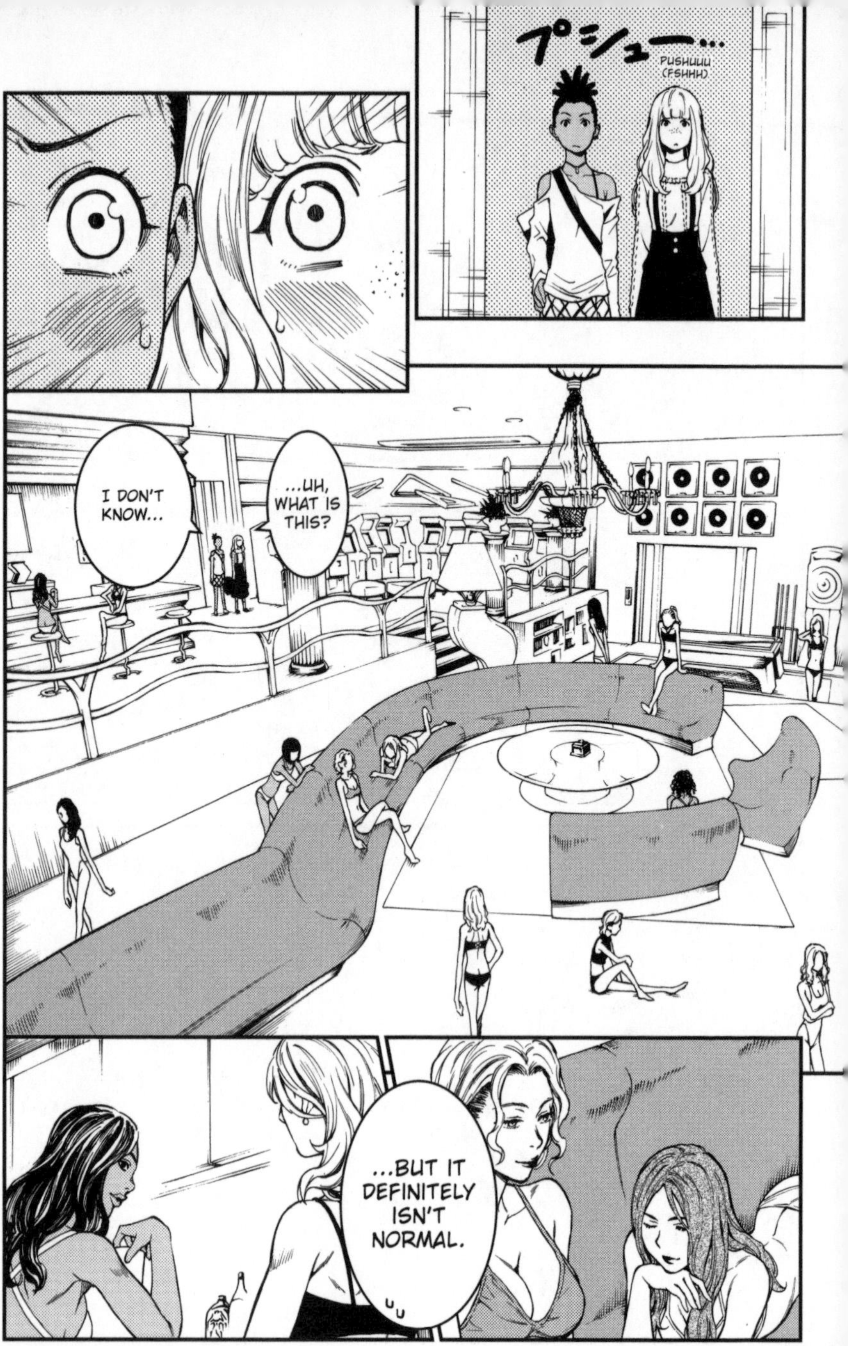
プシュー…
PUSHUUU (FSHHH)
...UH, WHAT IS THIS?
I DON'T KNOW...
...BUT IT DEFINITELY ISN'T NORMAL.

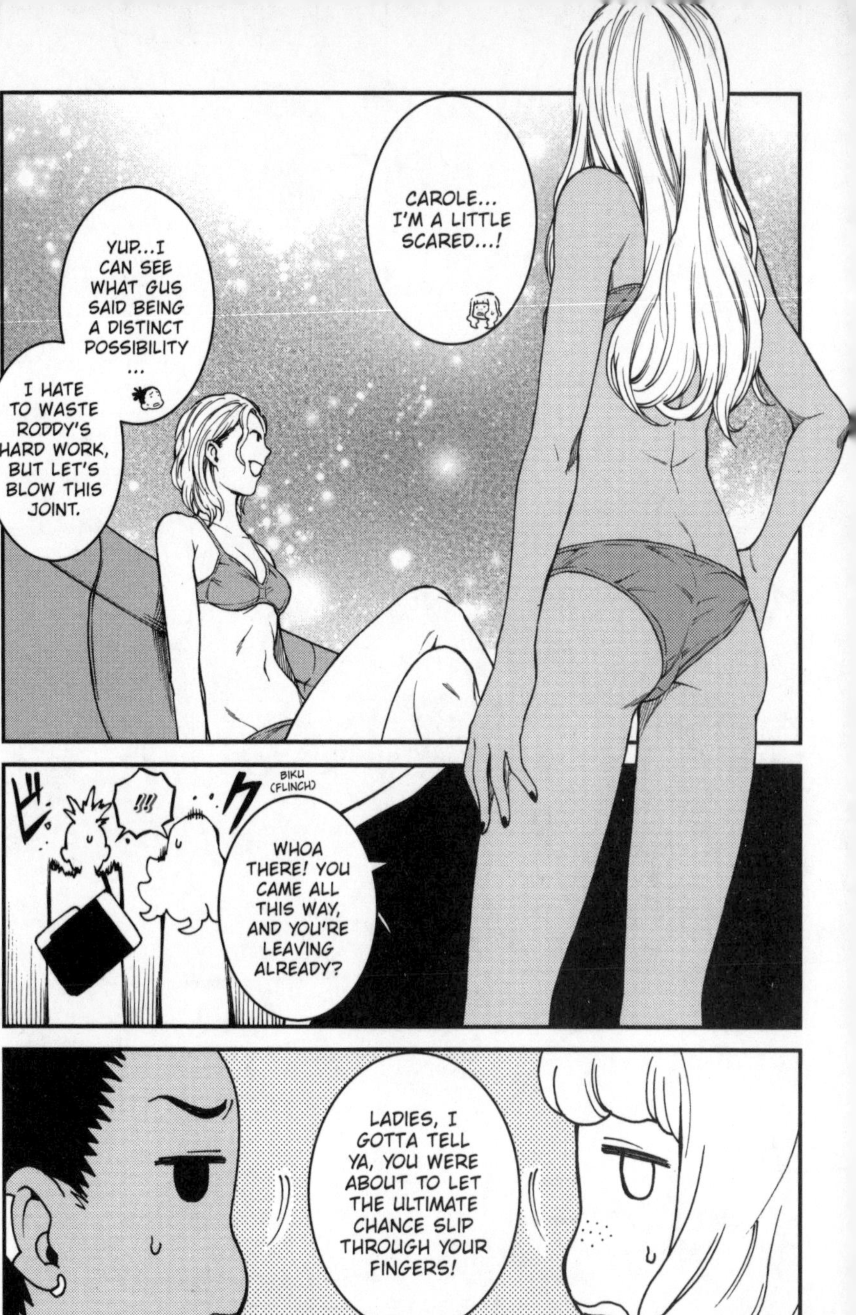
CAROLE... I'M A LITTLE SCARED...!
YUP...I CAN SEE WHAT GUS SAID BEING A DISTINCT POSSIBILITY...
I HATE TO WASTE RODDY'S HARD WORK, BUT LET'S BLOW THIS JOINT.
BIKU (FLINCH)
WHOA THERE! YOU CAME ALL THIS WAY, AND YOU'RE LEAVING ALREADY?
!!?
LADIES, I GOTTA TELL YA, YOU WERE ABOUT TO LET THE ULTIMATE CHANCE SLIP THROUGH YOUR FINGERS!

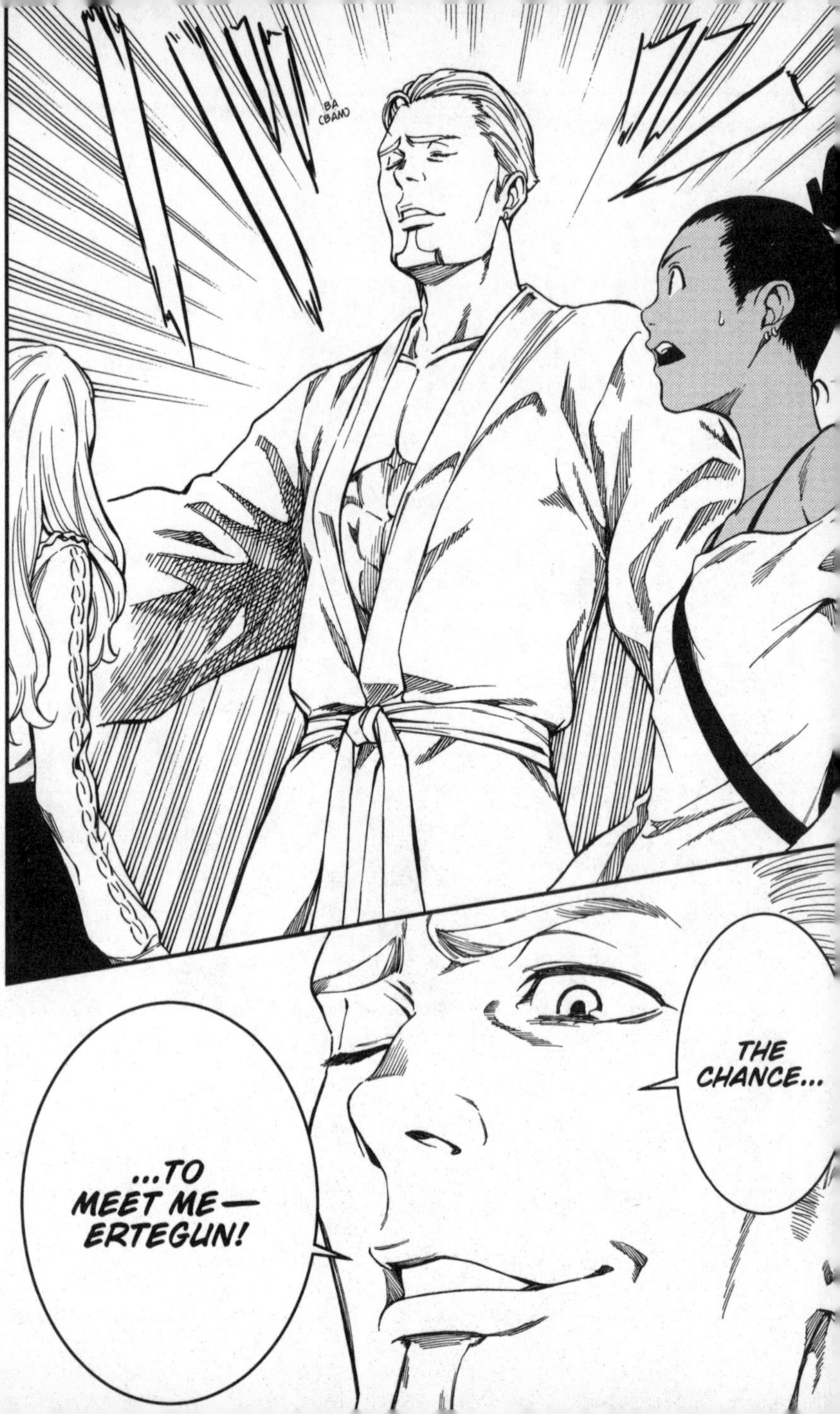
BA (BAM)
THE CHANCE...
...TO MEET ME— ERTEGUN!

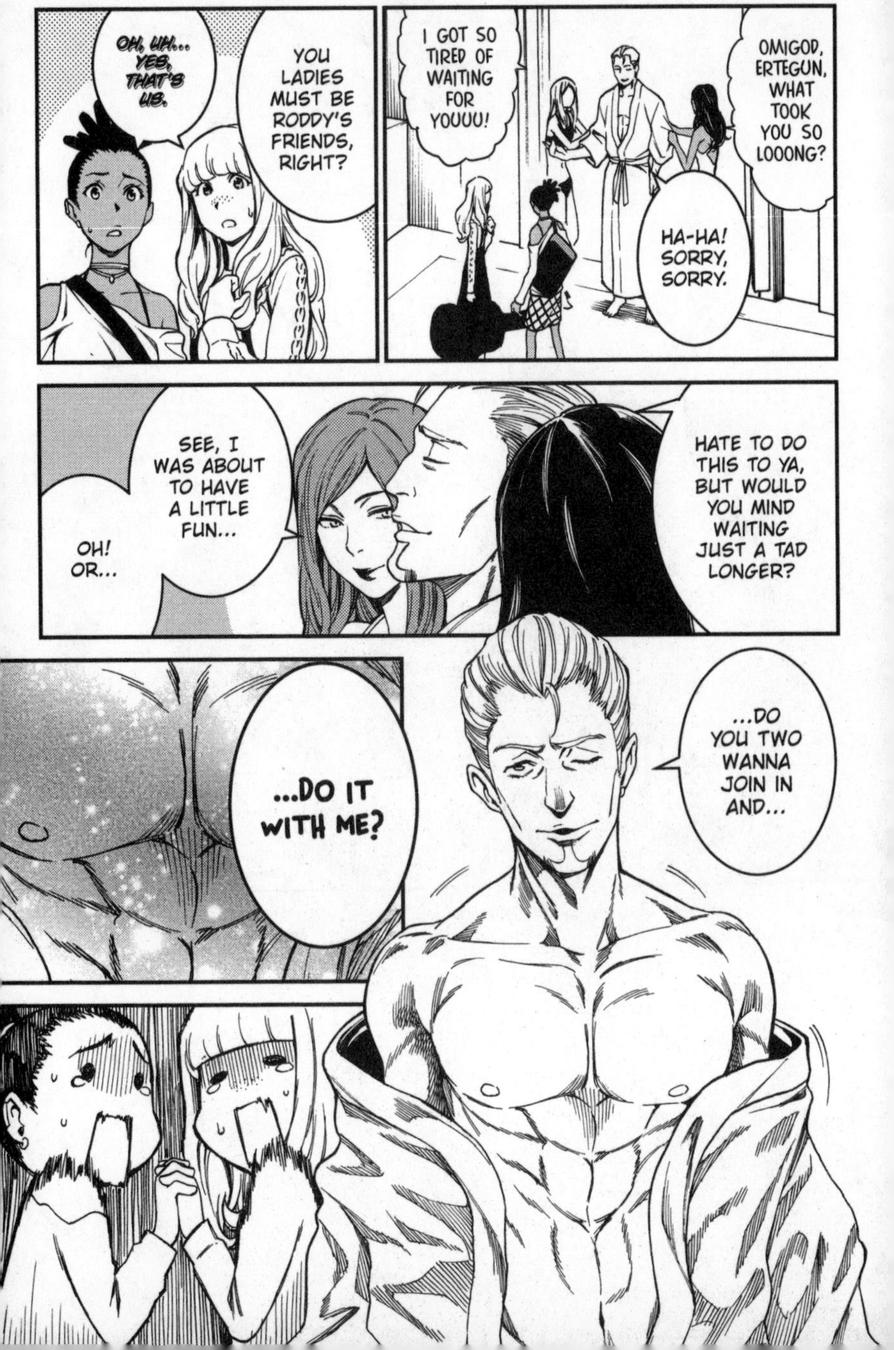
OMIGOD, ERTEGUN, WHAT TOOK YOU SO LOOONG?
I GOT SO TIRED OF WAITING FOR YOUUU!
HA-HA! SORRY, SORRY.
YOU LADIES MUST BE RODDY'S FRIENDS, RIGHT?
OH, UH... YES, THAT'S US.
HATE TO DO THIS TO YA, BUT WOULD YOU MIND WAITING JUST A TAD LONGER?
SEE, I WAS ABOUT TO HAVE A LITTLE FUN...
OH! OR...
...DO YOU TWO WANNA JOIN IN AND...
...DO IT WITH ME?

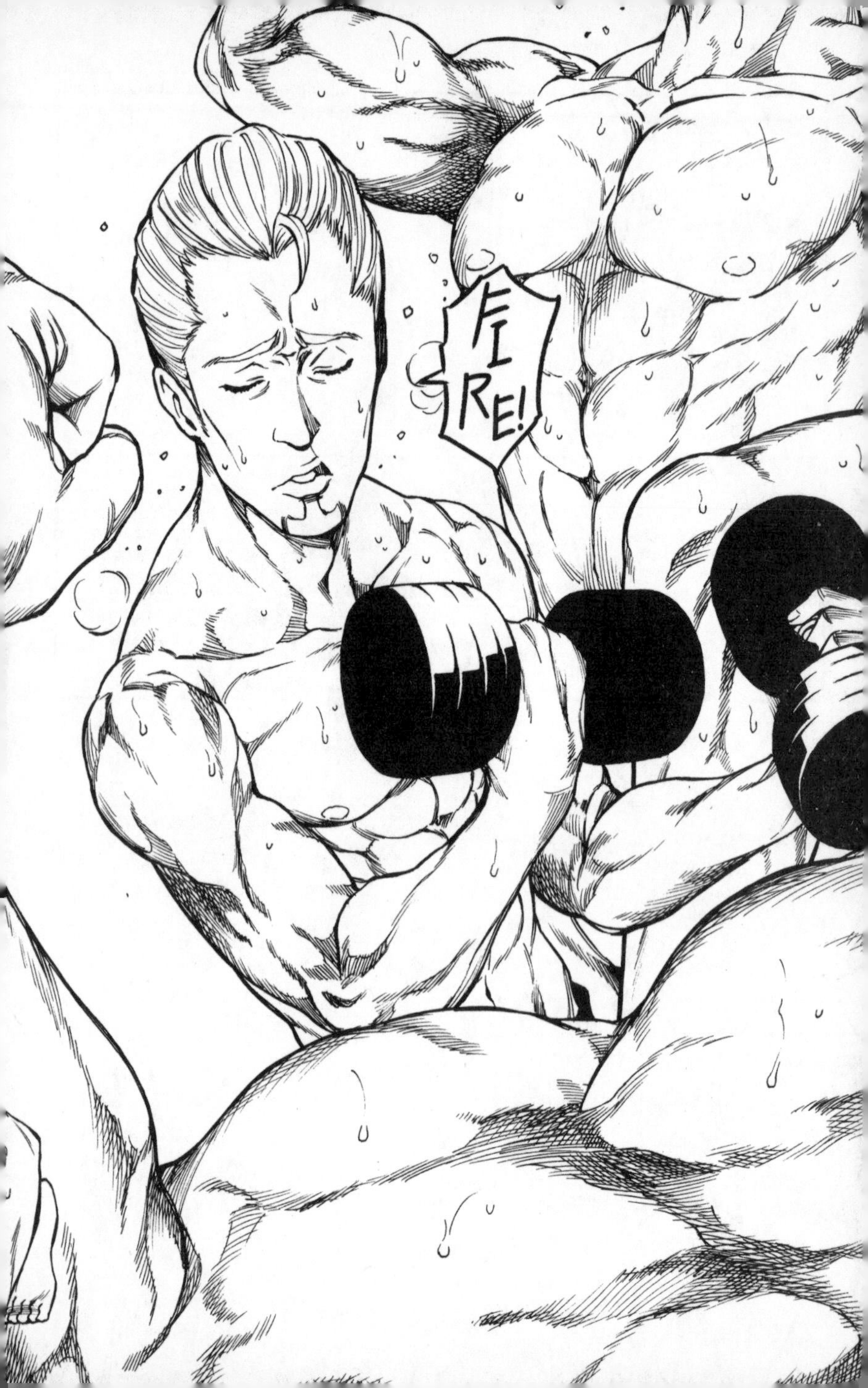
FIRE!

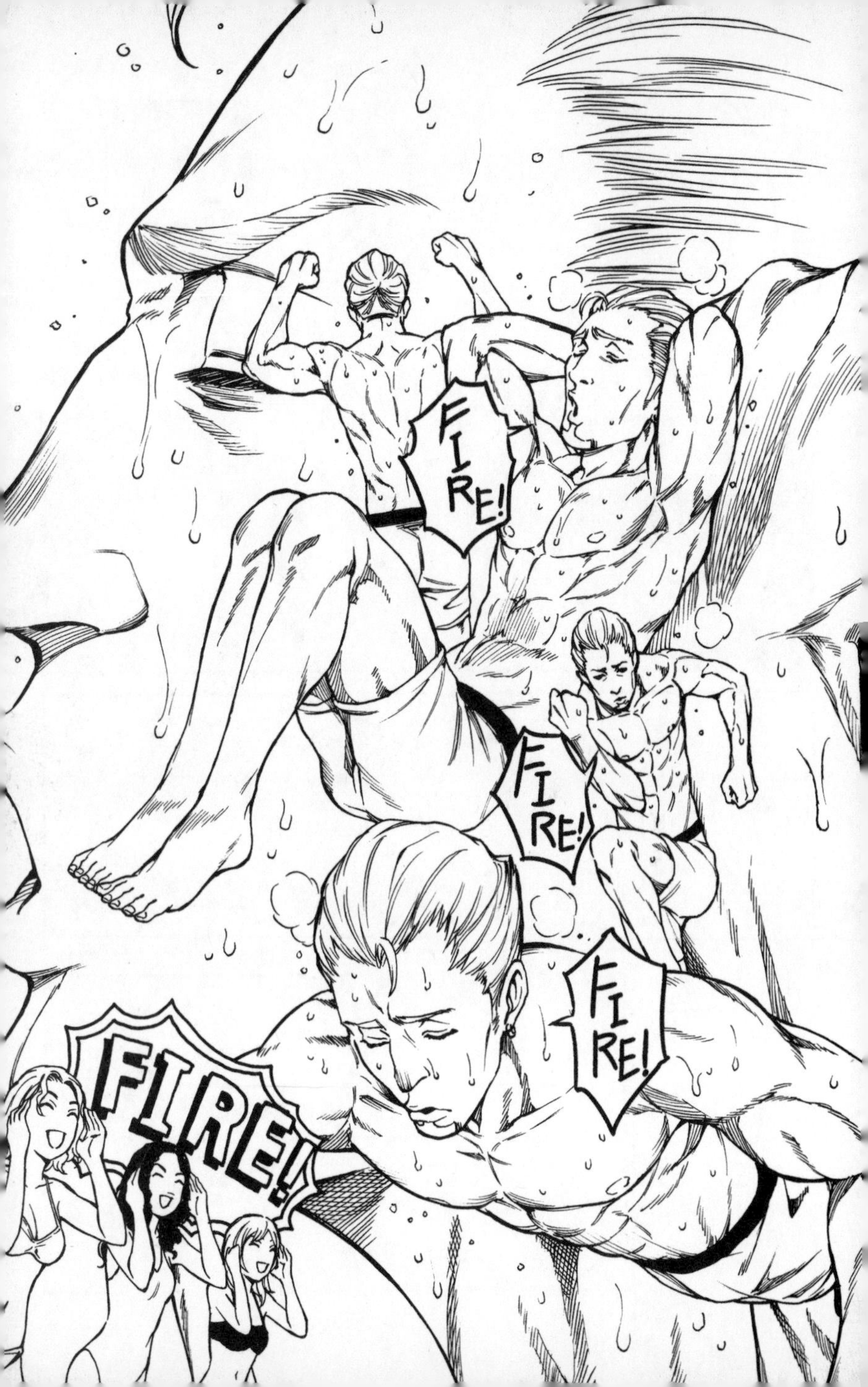
FIRE!
FIRE!
FIRE!
FIRE!

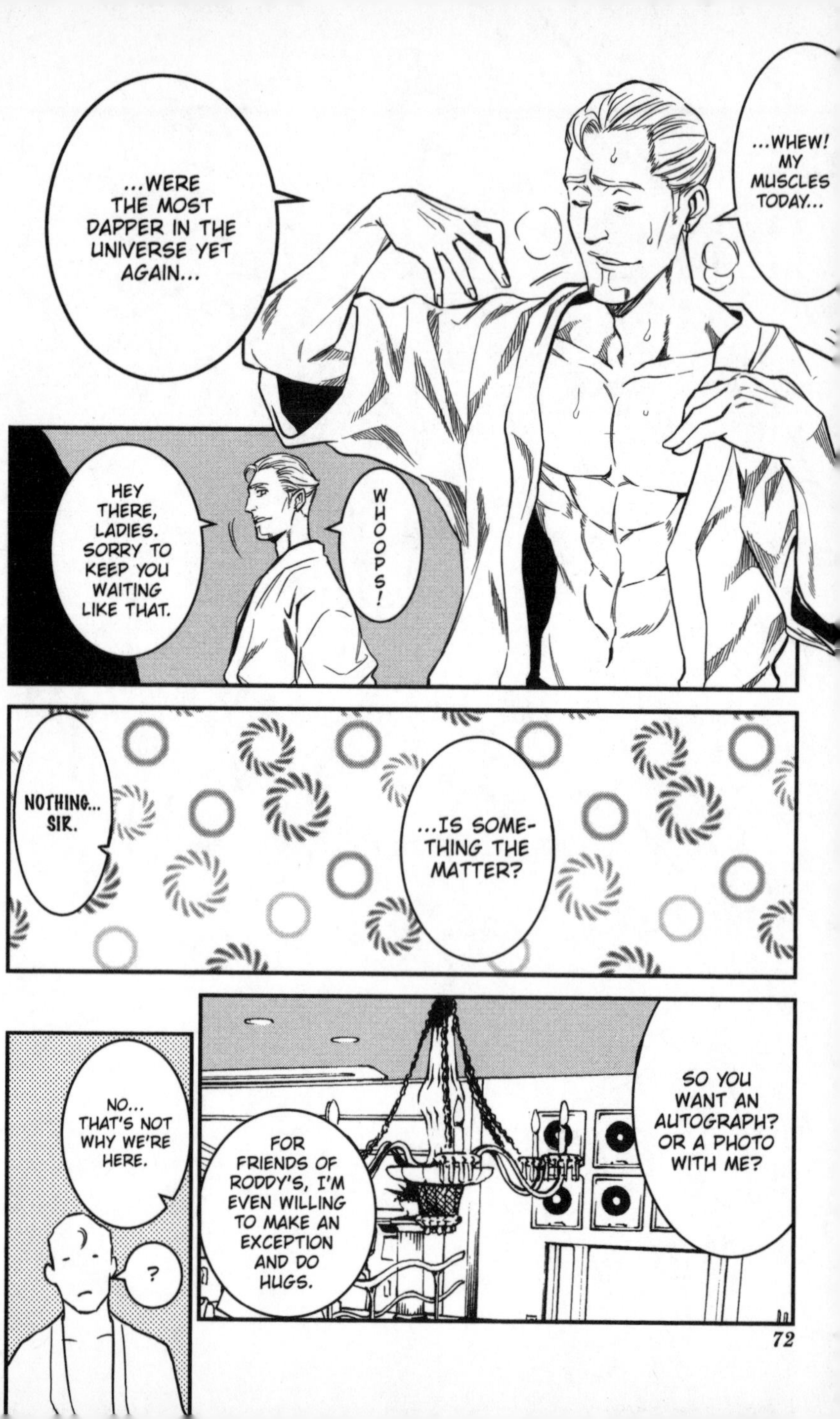
...WHEW! MY MUSCLES TODAY...
...WERE THE MOST DAPPER IN THE UNIVERSE YET AGAIN...
WHOOPS!
HEY THERE, LADIES. SORRY TO KEEP YOU WAITING LIKE THAT.
...IS SOMETHING THE MATTER?
NOTHING... SIR.
SO YOU WANT AN AUTOGRAPH? OR A PHOTO WITH ME?
FOR FRIENDS OF RODDY'S, I'M EVEN WILLING TO MAKE AN EXCEPTION AND DO HUGS.
NO... THAT'S NOT WHY WE'RE HERE.
?

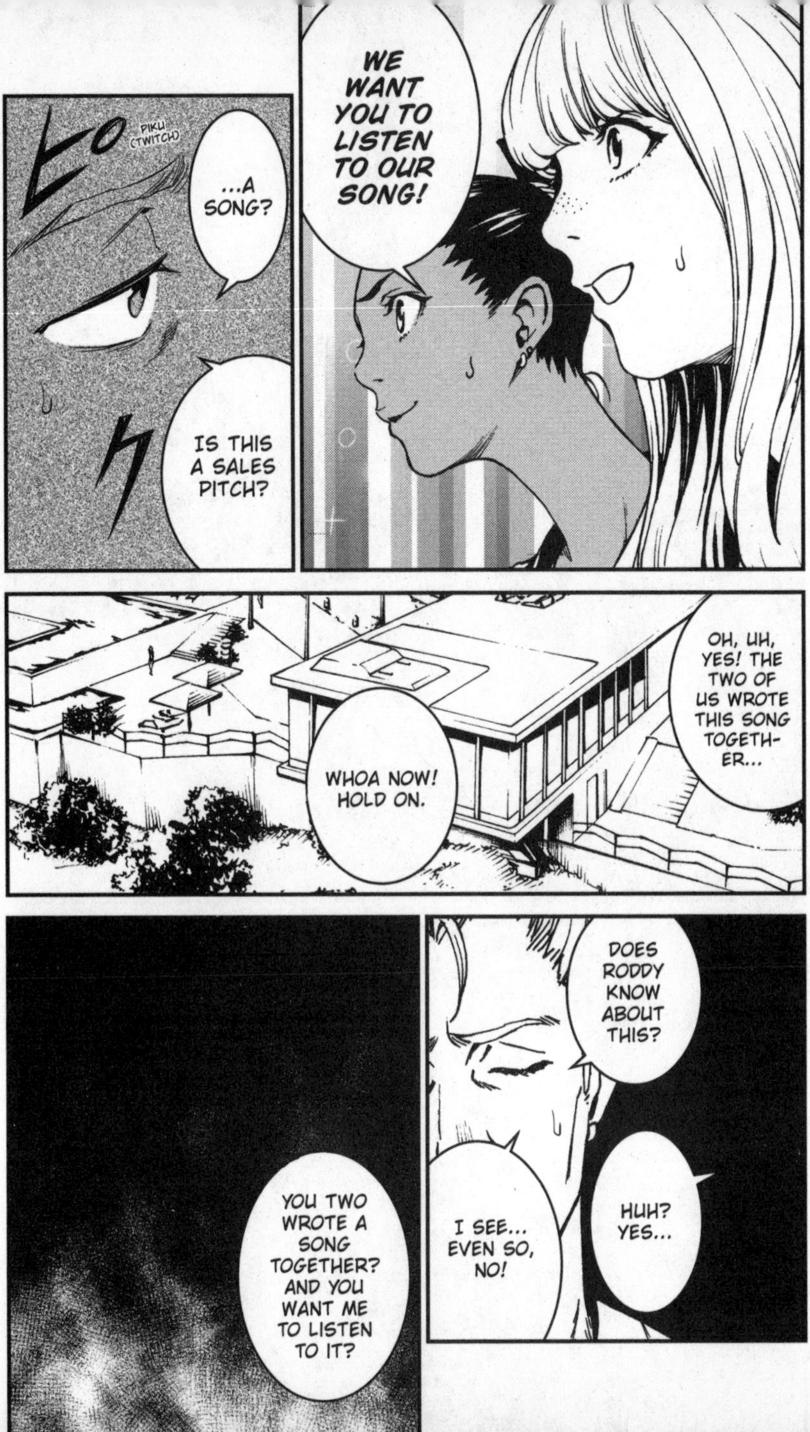

WE WANT YOU TO LISTEN TO OUR SONG!
PIKU! (TWITCH)
...A SONG?
IS THIS A SALES PITCH?
OH, UH, YES! THE TWO OF US WROTE THIS SONG TOGETH-ER...
WHOA NOW! HOLD ON.
DOES RODDY KNOW ABOUT THIS?
HUH? YES...
I SEE... EVEN SO, NO!
YOU TWO WROTE A SONG TOGETHER? AND YOU WANT ME TO LISTEN TO IT?

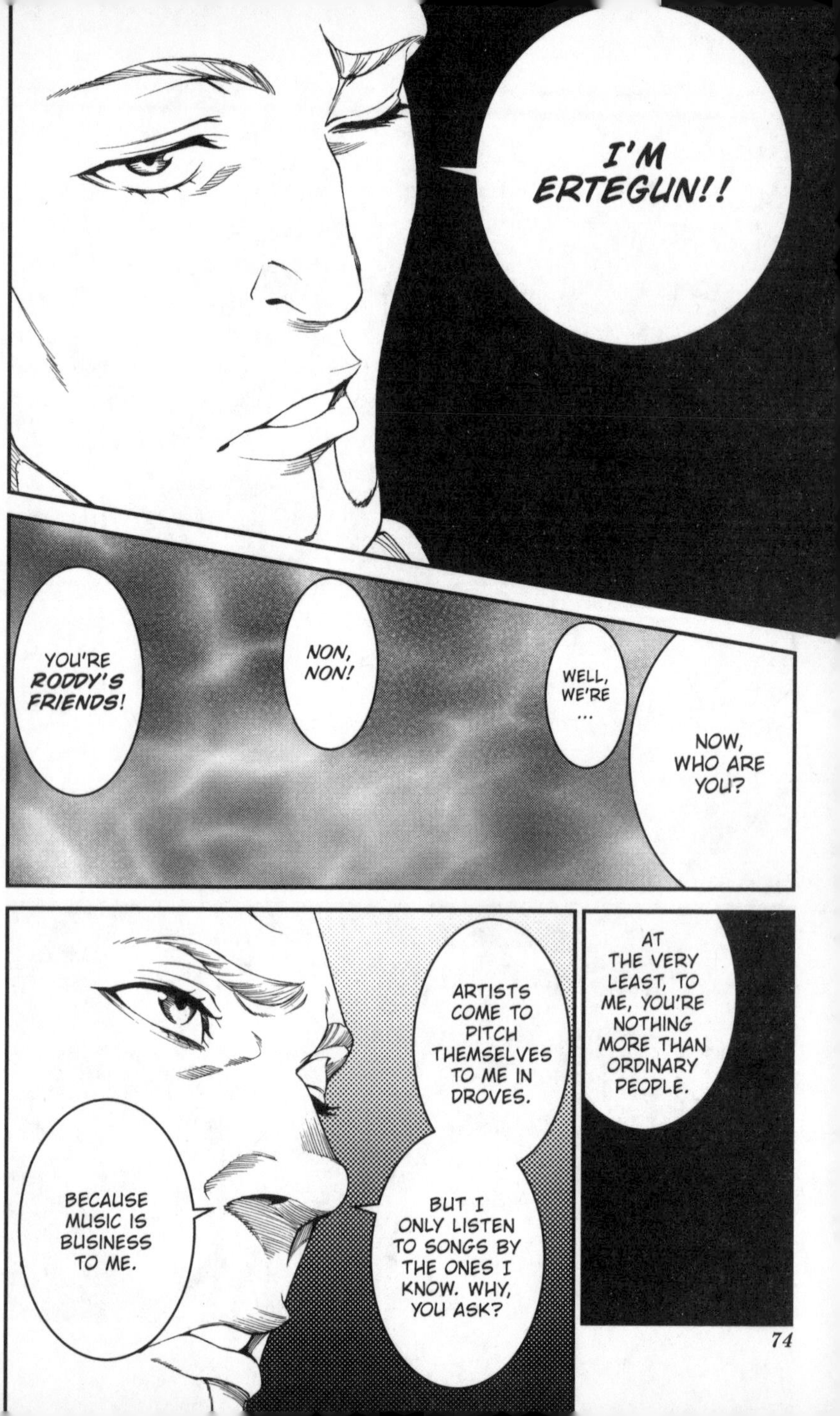
I'M ERTEGUN!!
NOW, WHO ARE YOU?
WELL, WE'RE ...
NON, NON!
YOU'RE *RODDY'S FRIENDS*!
AT THE VERY LEAST, TO ME, YOU'RE NOTHING MORE THAN ORDINARY PEOPLE.
ARTISTS COME TO PITCH THEMSELVES TO ME IN DROVES.
BUT I ONLY LISTEN TO SONGS BY THE ONES I KNOW. WHY, YOU ASK?
BECAUSE MUSIC IS BUSINESS TO ME.

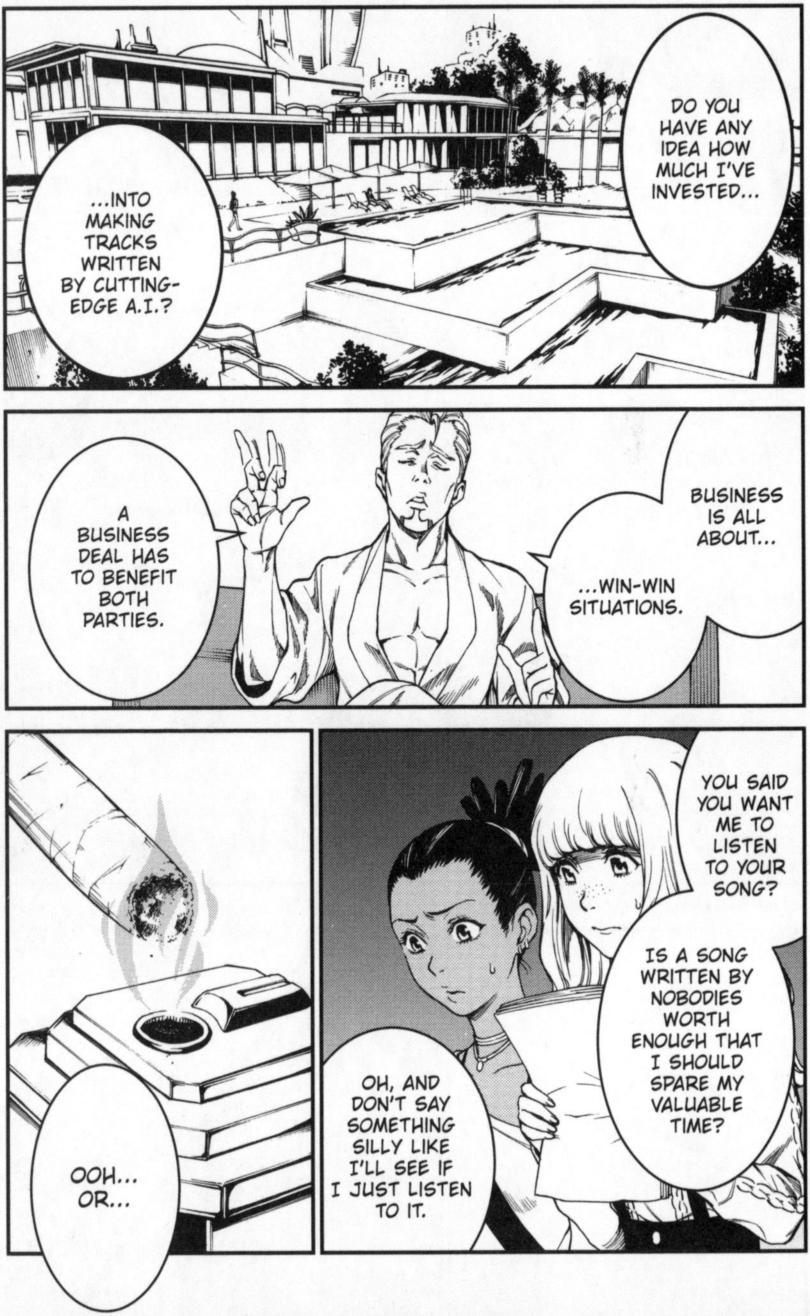
DO YOU HAVE ANY IDEA HOW MUCH I'VE INVESTED...
...INTO MAKING TRACKS WRITTEN BY CUTTING-EDGE A.I.?
BUSINESS IS ALL ABOUT...
...WIN-WIN SITUATIONS.
A BUSINESS DEAL HAS TO BENEFIT BOTH PARTIES.
YOU SAID YOU WANT ME TO LISTEN TO YOUR SONG?
IS A SONG WRITTEN BY NOBODIES WORTH ENOUGH THAT I SHOULD SPARE MY VALUABLE TIME?
OH, AND DON'T SAY SOMETHING SILLY LIKE I'LL SEE IF I JUST LISTEN TO IT.
OOH... OR...

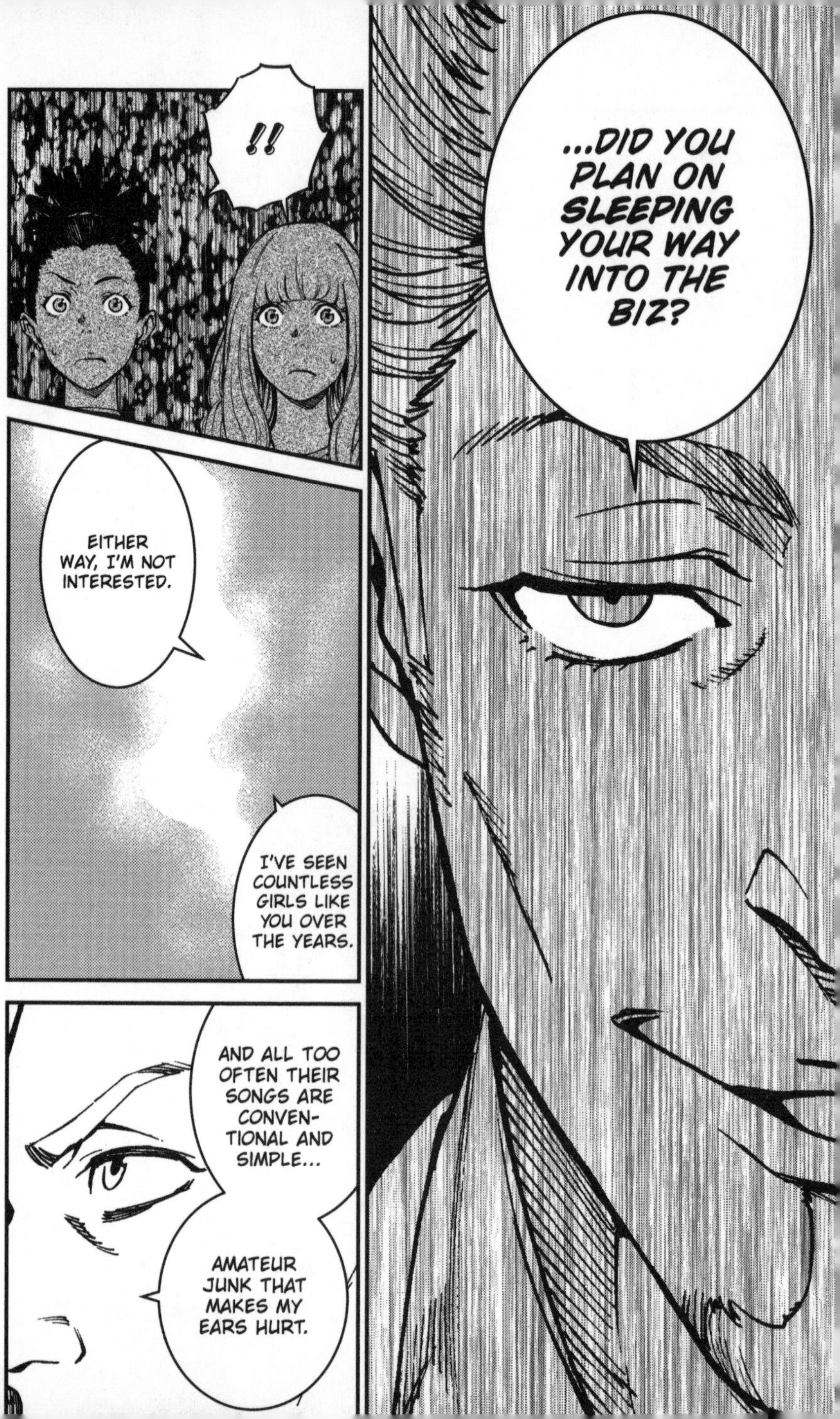
...DID YOU PLAN ON SLEEPING YOUR WAY INTO THE BIZ?
!!
EITHER WAY, I'M NOT INTERESTED.
I'VE SEEN COUNTLESS GIRLS LIKE YOU OVER THE YEARS.
AND ALL TOO OFTEN THEIR SONGS ARE CONVEN-TIONAL AND SIMPLE...
AMATEUR JUNK THAT MAKES MY EARS HURT.

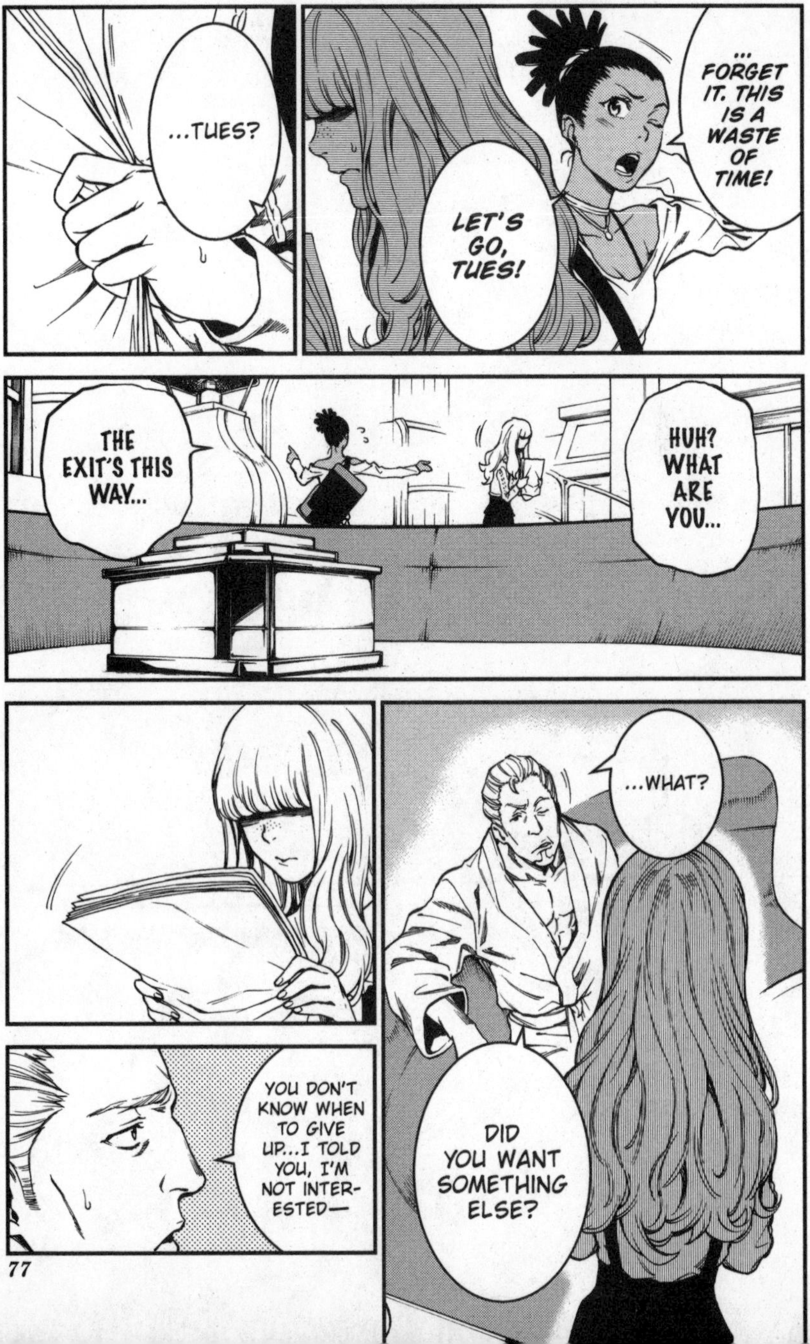
...FORGET IT. THIS IS A WASTE OF TIME!
LET'S GO, TUES!
...TUES?
HUH? WHAT ARE YOU...
THE EXIT'S THIS WAY...
...WHAT?
DID YOU WANT SOMETHING ELSE?
YOU DON'T KNOW WHEN TO GIVE UP...I TOLD YOU, I'M NOT INTER-ESTED—

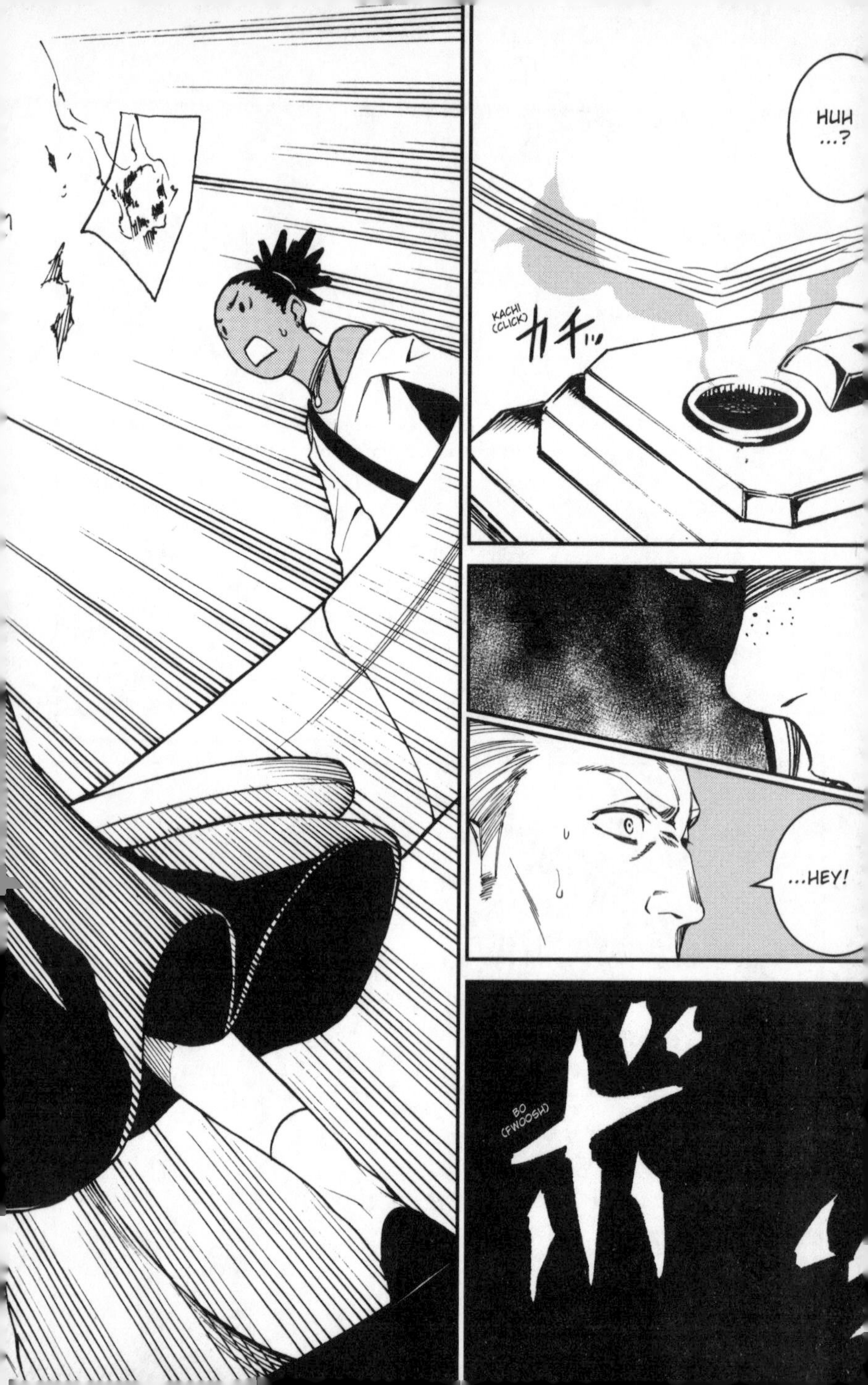
HUH ...?
KACHI (CLICK) カチッ
...HEY!
BO (FWOOSH)

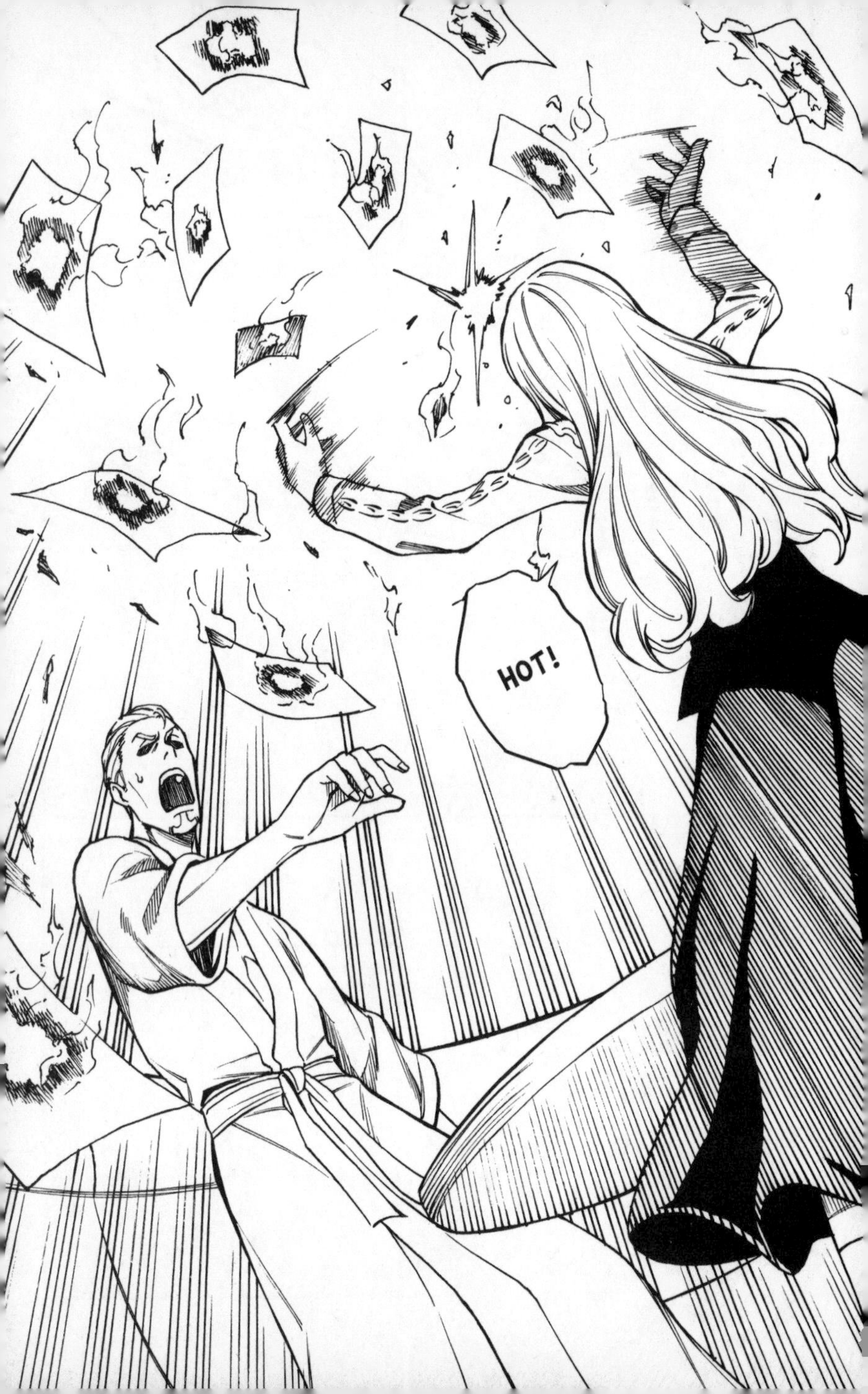
HOT!

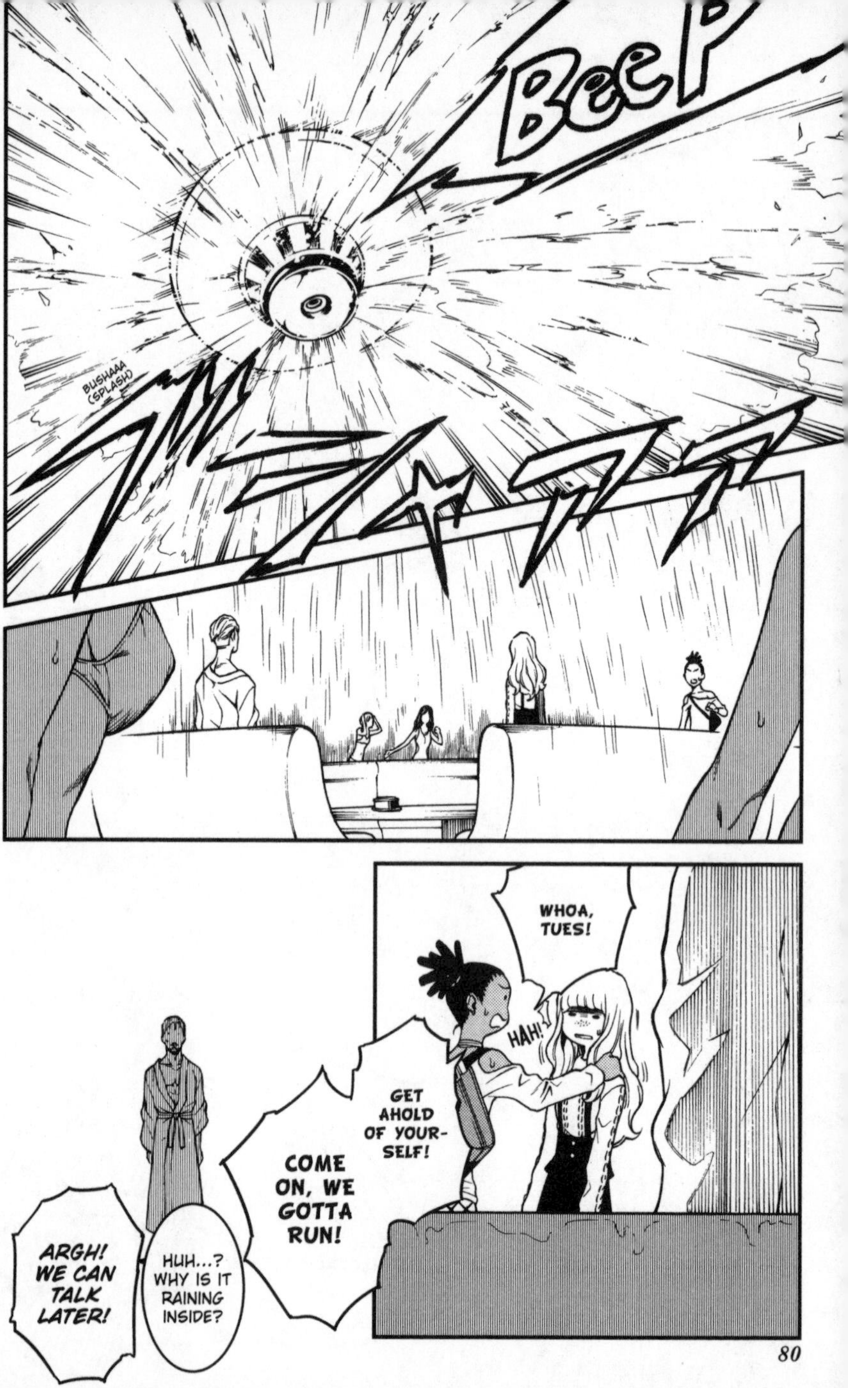
BEEP
BUSHAAA (SPLASH)
WHOA, TUES!
HAH!
GET AHOLD OF YOUR-SELF!
COME ON, WE GOTTA RUN!
HUH...? WHY IS IT RAINING INSIDE?
ARGH! WE CAN TALK LATER!

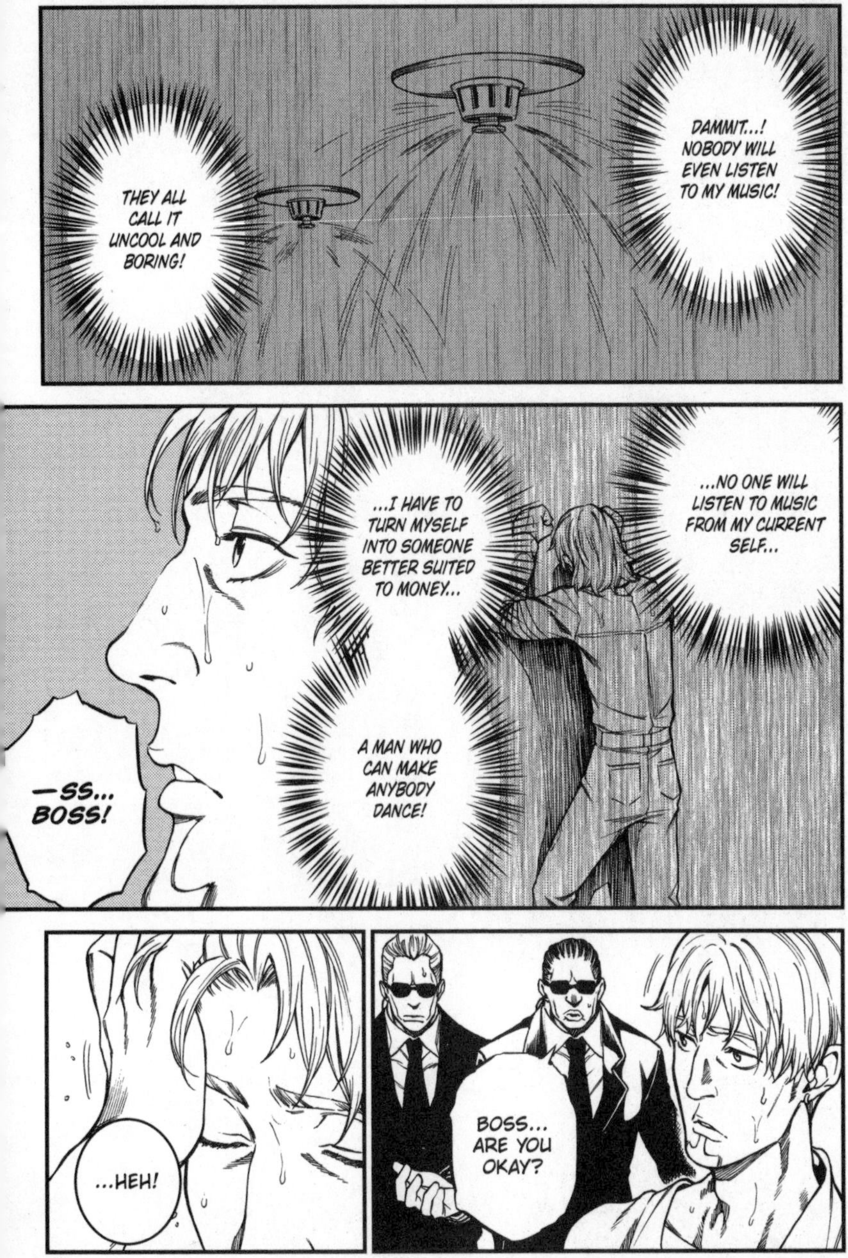
DAMMIT...! NOBODY WILL EVEN LISTEN TO MY MUSIC!
THEY ALL CALL IT UNCOOL AND BORING!
...NO ONE WILL LISTEN TO MUSIC FROM MY CURRENT SELF...
...I HAVE TO TURN MYSELF INTO SOMEONE BETTER SUITED TO MONEY...
A MAN WHO CAN MAKE ANYBODY DANCE!
—SS... BOSS!
BOSS... ARE YOU OKAY?
...HEH!

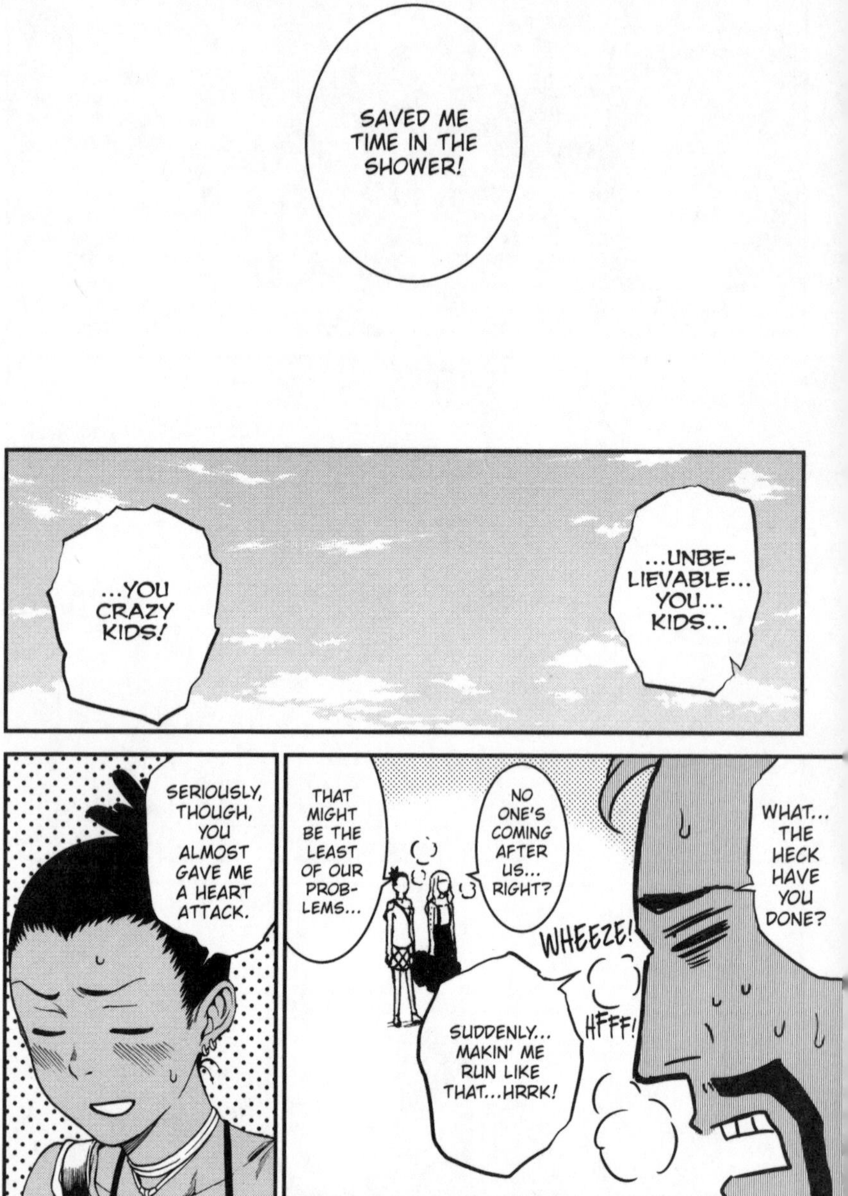
SAVED ME TIME IN THE SHOWER!
...UNBE-LIEVABLE... YOU... KIDS...
...YOU CRAZY KIDS!
WHAT... THE HECK HAVE YOU DONE?
WHEEZE!
HFFF!
SUDDENLY... MAKIN' ME RUN LIKE THAT...HRRK!
NO ONE'S COMING AFTER US... RIGHT?
THAT MIGHT BE THE LEAST OF OUR PROB-LEMS...
SERIOUSLY, THOUGH, YOU ALMOST GAVE ME A HEART ATTACK.

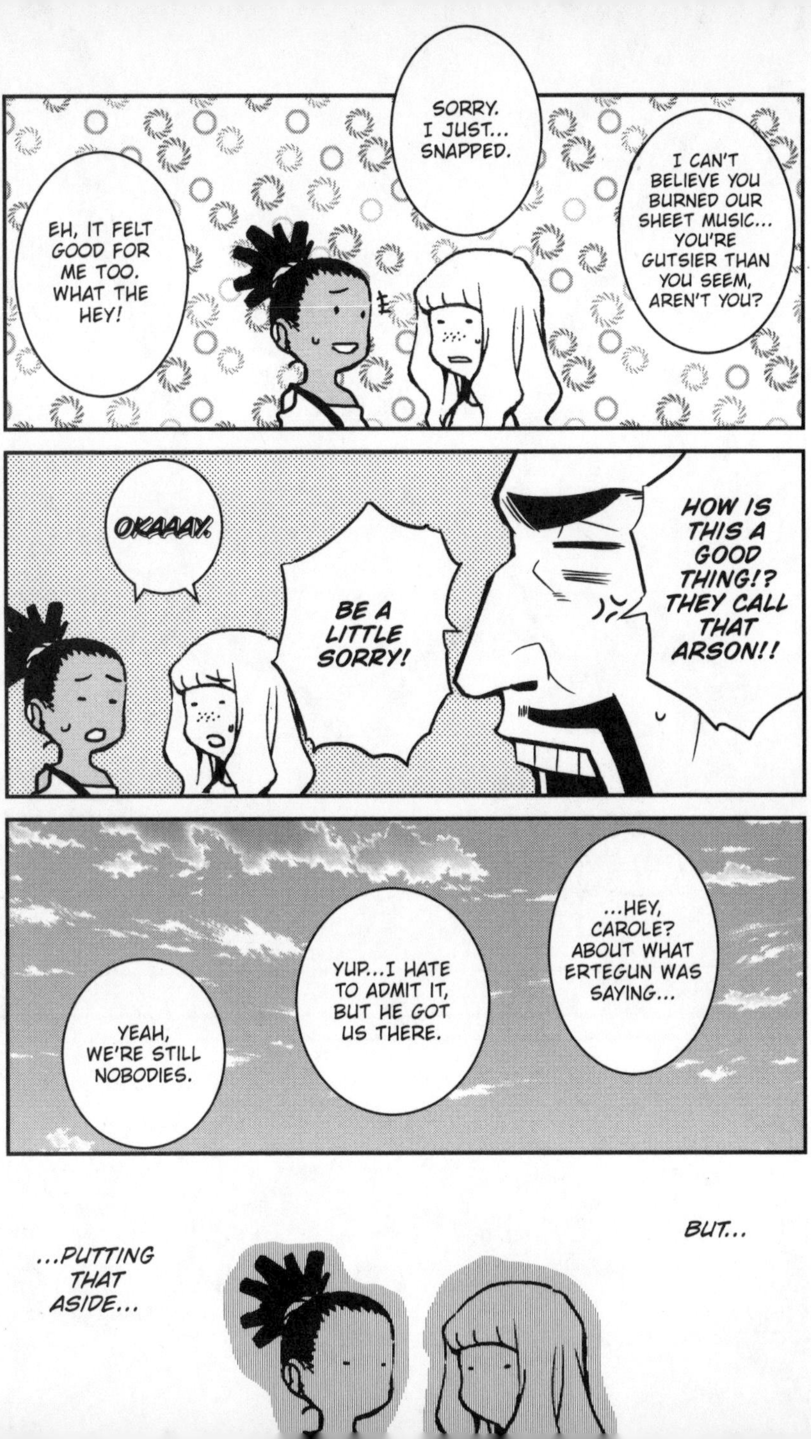
I CAN'T BELIEVE YOU BURNED OUR SHEET MUSIC... YOU'RE GUTSIER THAN YOU SEEM, AREN'T YOU?
SORRY. I JUST... SNAPPED.
EH, IT FELT GOOD FOR ME TOO. WHAT THE HEY!
HOW IS THIS A GOOD THING!? THEY CALL THAT ARSON!!
BE A LITTLE SORRY!
OKAAAY.
...HEY, CAROLE? ABOUT WHAT ERTEGUN WAS SAYING...
YUP...I HATE TO ADMIT IT, BUT HE GOT US THERE.
YEAH, WE'RE STILL NOBODIES.
BUT...
...PUTTING THAT ASIDE...

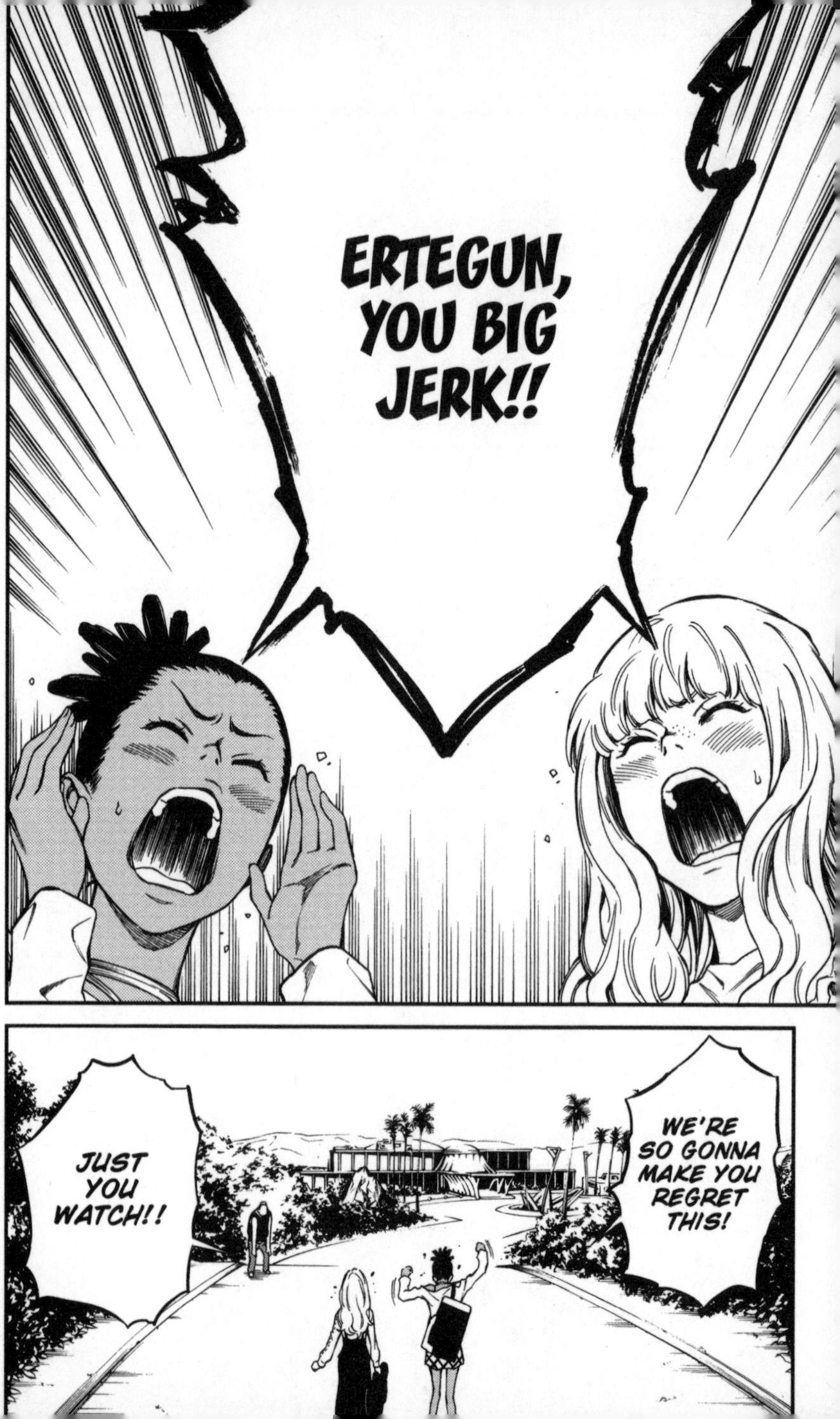
ERTEGUN, YOU BIG JERK!!
WE'RE SO GONNA MAKE YOU REGRET THIS!
JUST YOU WATCH!!

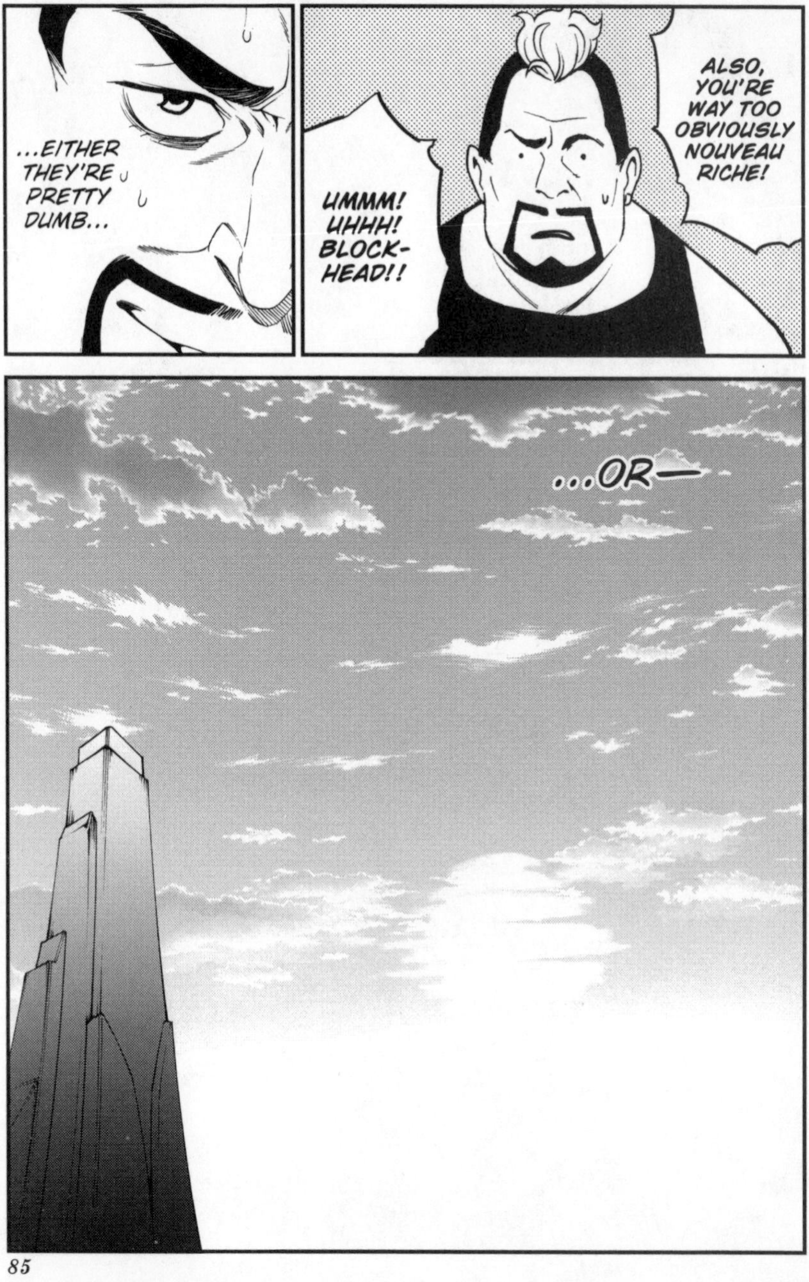
ALSO, YOU'RE WAY TOO OBVIOUSLY NOUVEAU RICHE!
UMMM! UHHH! BLOCK-HEAD!!
...EITHER THEY'RE PRETTY DUMB...
...OR—

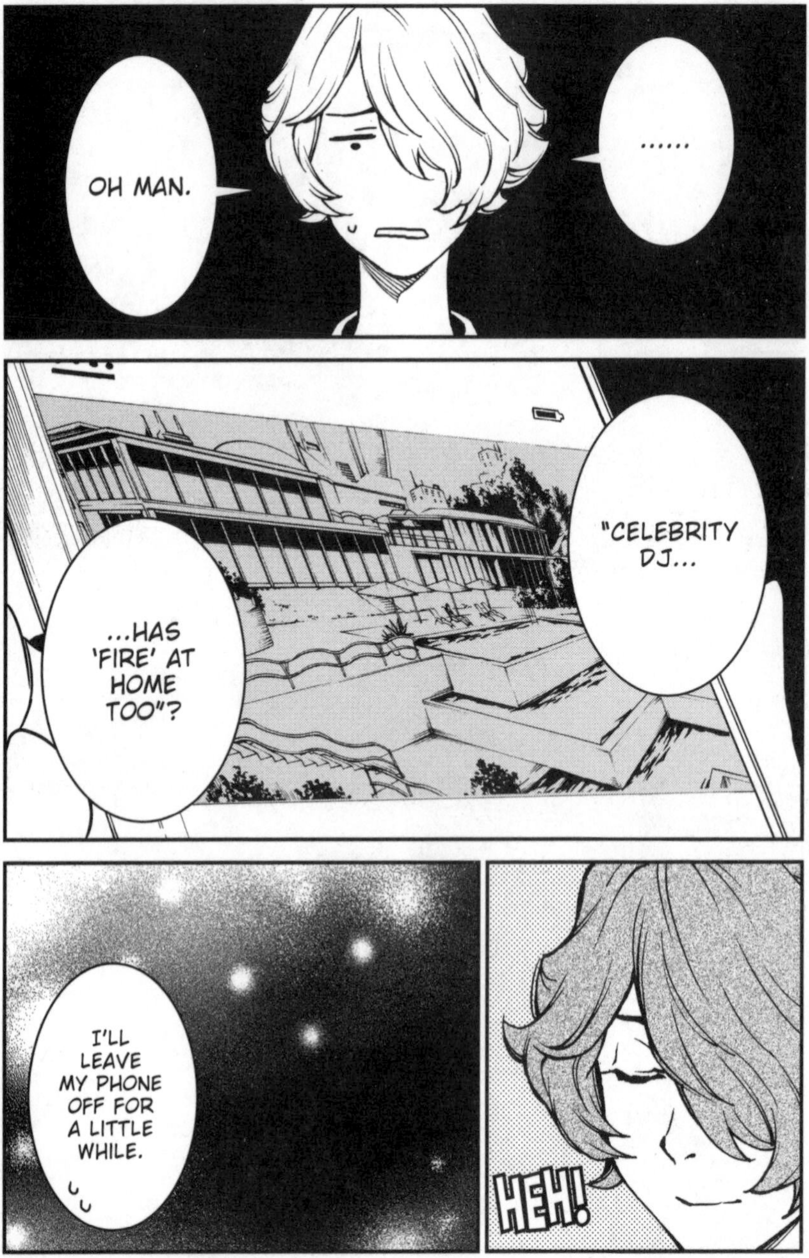
......
OH MAN.
"CELEBRITY DJ...
...HAS 'FIRE' AT HOME TOO"?
HEH!
I'LL LEAVE MY PHONE OFF FOR A LITTLE WHILE.

END

CAROLE & TUESDAY

CAROLE
& TUESDAY

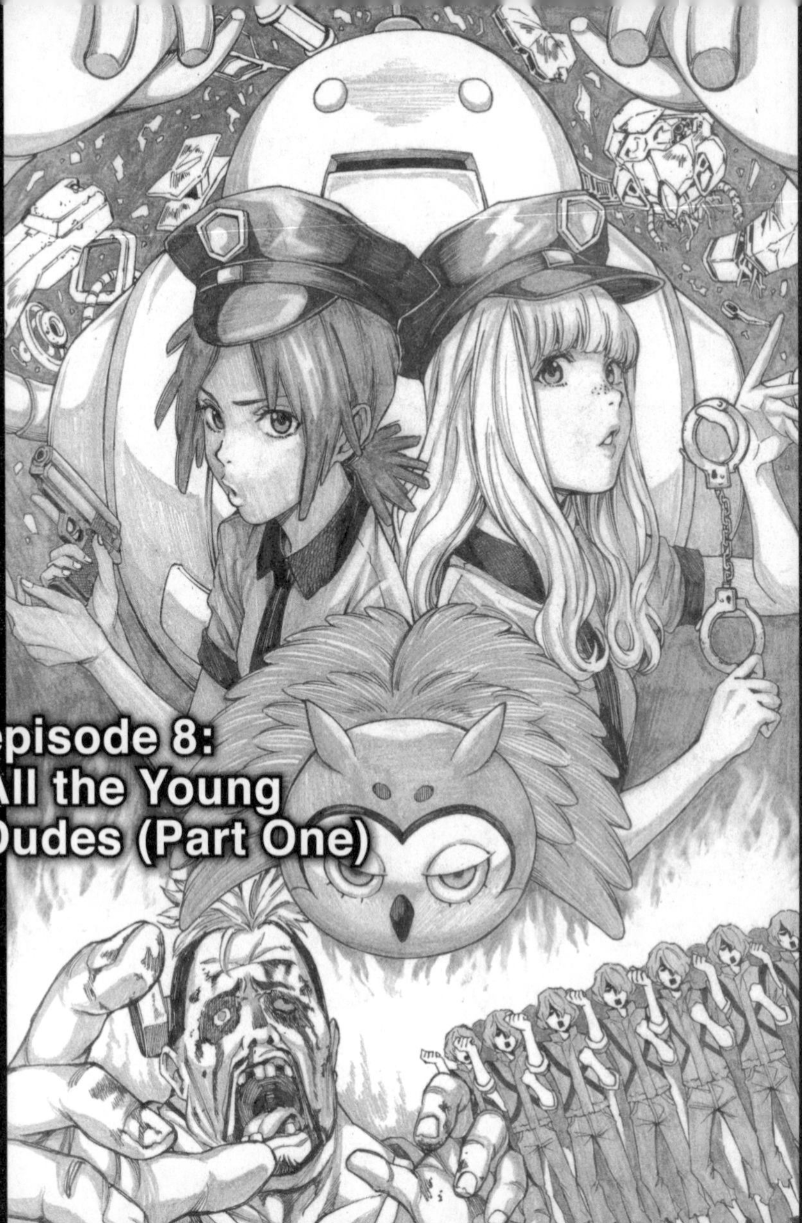
episode 8:
All the Young
Dudes (Part One)

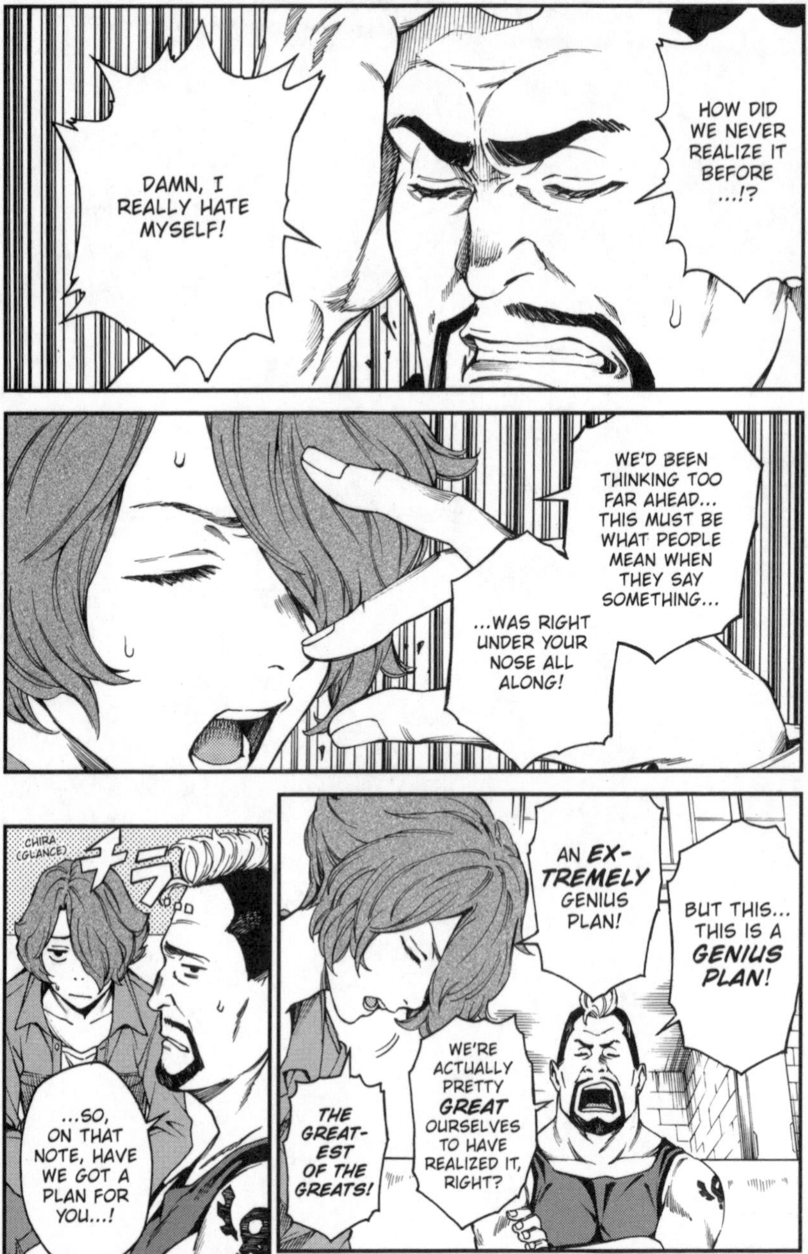
HOW DID WE NEVER REALIZE IT BEFORE ...!?
DAMN, I REALLY HATE MYSELF!
WE'D BEEN THINKING TOO FAR AHEAD... THIS MUST BE WHAT PEOPLE MEAN WHEN THEY SAY SOMETHING...
...WAS RIGHT UNDER YOUR NOSE ALL ALONG!
BUT THIS... THIS IS A **GENIUS PLAN!**
AN **EXTREMELY** GENIUS PLAN!
WE'RE ACTUALLY PRETTY **GREAT** OURSELVES TO HAVE REALIZED IT, RIGHT?
THE GREATEST OF THE GREATS!
CHIRA (GLANCE)
...SO, ON THAT NOTE, HAVE WE GOT A PLAN FOR YOU...!

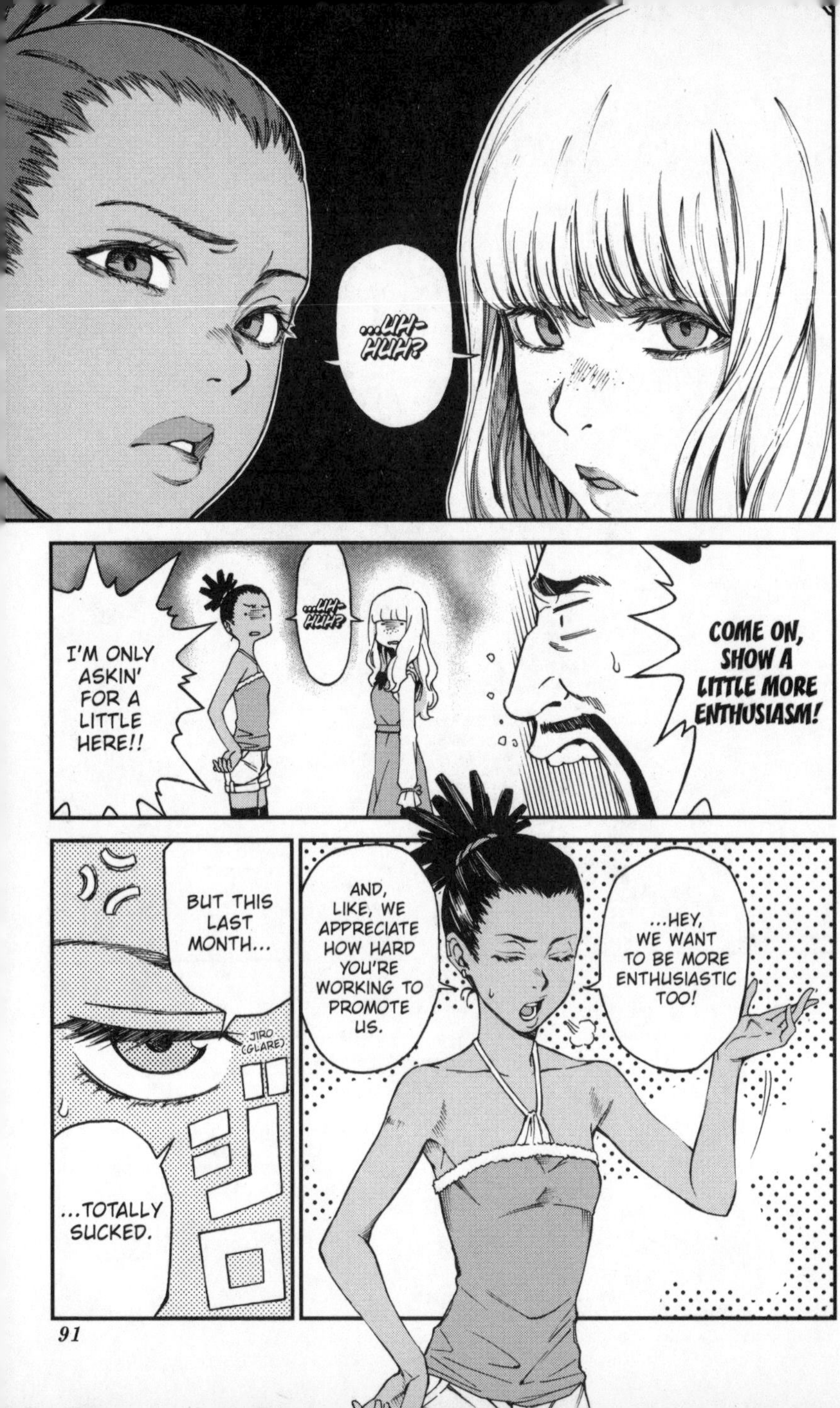
...UH-HUH?
COME ON, SHOW A LITTLE MORE ENTHUSIASM!
...UH-HUH?
I'M ONLY ASKIN' FOR A LITTLE HERE!!
...HEY, WE WANT TO BE MORE ENTHUSIASTIC TOO!
AND, LIKE, WE APPRECIATE HOW HARD YOU'RE WORKING TO PROMOTE US.
BUT THIS LAST MONTH...
JIRO (GLARE)
...TOTALLY SUCKED.

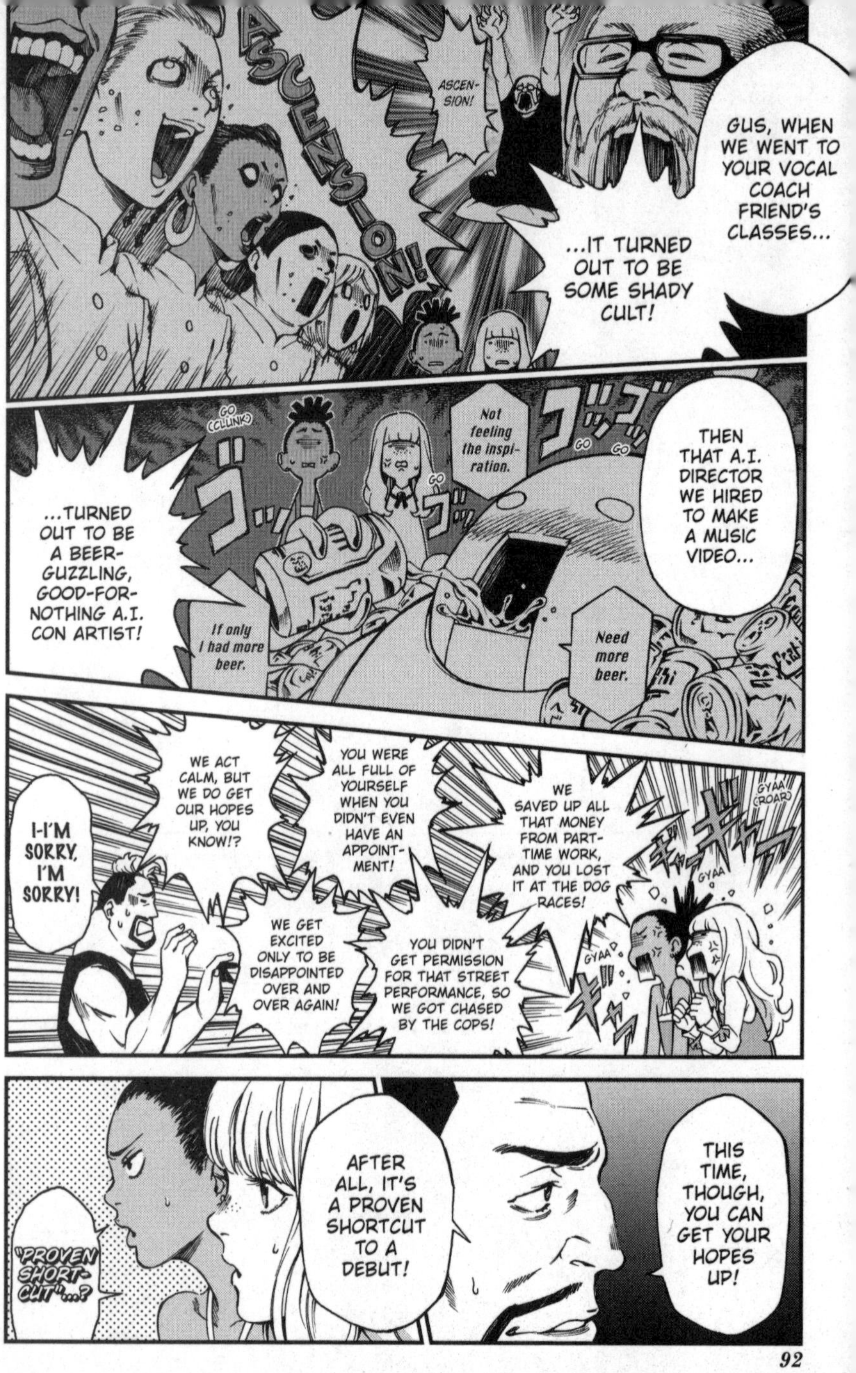

GUS, WHEN WE WENT TO YOUR VOCAL COACH FRIEND'S CLASSES...
...IT TURNED OUT TO BE SOME SHADY CULT!
ASCENSION!
ASCENSION!
THEN THAT A.I. DIRECTOR WE HIRED TO MAKE A MUSIC VIDEO...
GO GO
Need more beer.
Not feeling the inspiration.
GO
GO (CLUNK)
If only I had more beer.
...TURNED OUT TO BE A BEER-GUZZLING, GOOD-FOR-NOTHING A.I. CON ARTIST!
GYAA (ROAR)
WE SAVED UP ALL THAT MONEY FROM PART-TIME WORK, AND YOU LOST IT AT THE DOG RACES!
GYAA
GYAA
YOU DIDN'T GET PERMISSION FOR THAT STREET PERFORMANCE, SO WE GOT CHASED BY THE COPS!
YOU WERE ALL FULL OF YOURSELF WHEN YOU DIDN'T EVEN HAVE AN APPOINTMENT!
WE GET EXCITED ONLY TO BE DISAPPOINTED OVER AND OVER AGAIN!
WE ACT CALM, BUT WE DO GET OUR HOPES UP, YOU KNOW!?
I-I'M SORRY, I'M SORRY!
THIS TIME, THOUGH, YOU CAN GET YOUR HOPES UP!
AFTER ALL, IT'S A PROVEN SHORTCUT TO A DEBUT!
"PROVEN SHORTCUT"...?

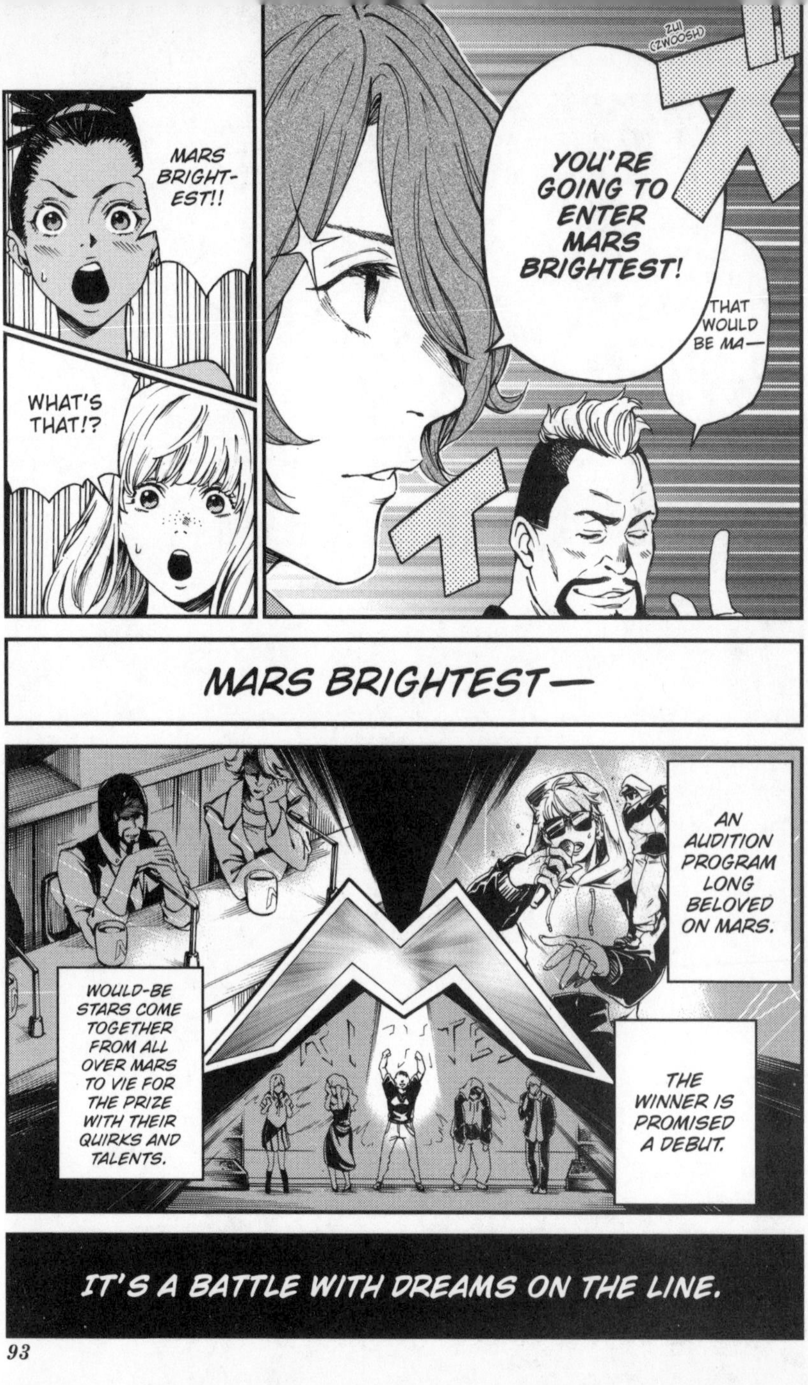
ZUI (ZWOOSH)
YOU'RE GOING TO ENTER MARS BRIGHTEST!
THAT WOULD BE MA—
MARS BRIGHT-EST!!
WHAT'S THAT!?
MARS BRIGHTEST—
AN AUDITION PROGRAM LONG BELOVED ON MARS.
WOULD-BE STARS COME TOGETHER FROM ALL OVER MARS TO VIE FOR THE PRIZE WITH THEIR QUIRKS AND TALENTS.
THE WINNER IS PROMISED A DEBUT.
IT'S A BATTLE WITH DREAMS ON THE LINE.

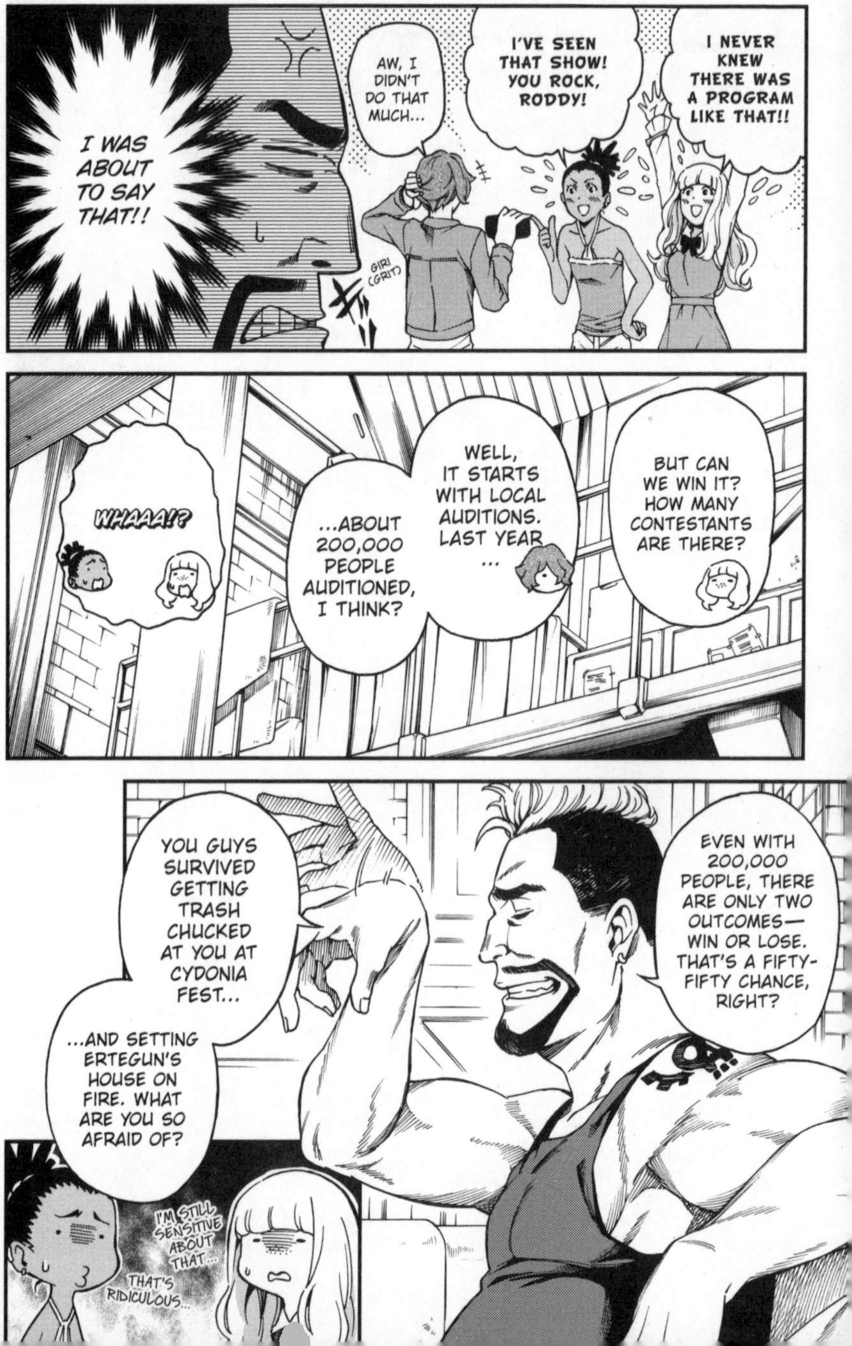
I NEVER KNEW THERE WAS A PROGRAM LIKE THAT!!
I'VE SEEN THAT SHOW! YOU ROCK, RODDY!
AW, I DIDN'T DO THAT MUCH...
GIRI (GRIT)
I WAS ABOUT TO SAY THAT!!
BUT CAN WE WIN IT? HOW MANY CONTESTANTS ARE THERE?
WELL, IT STARTS WITH LOCAL AUDITIONS. LAST YEAR ...
...ABOUT 200,000 PEOPLE AUDITIONED, I THINK?
WHAAA!?
EVEN WITH 200,000 PEOPLE, THERE ARE ONLY TWO OUTCOMES— WIN OR LOSE. THAT'S A FIFTY-FIFTY CHANCE, RIGHT?
YOU GUYS SURVIVED GETTING TRASH CHUCKED AT YOU AT CYDONIA FEST...
...AND SETTING ERTEGUN'S HOUSE ON FIRE. WHAT ARE YOU SO AFRAID OF?
I'M STILL SENSITIVE ABOUT THAT...
THAT'S RIDICULOUS...

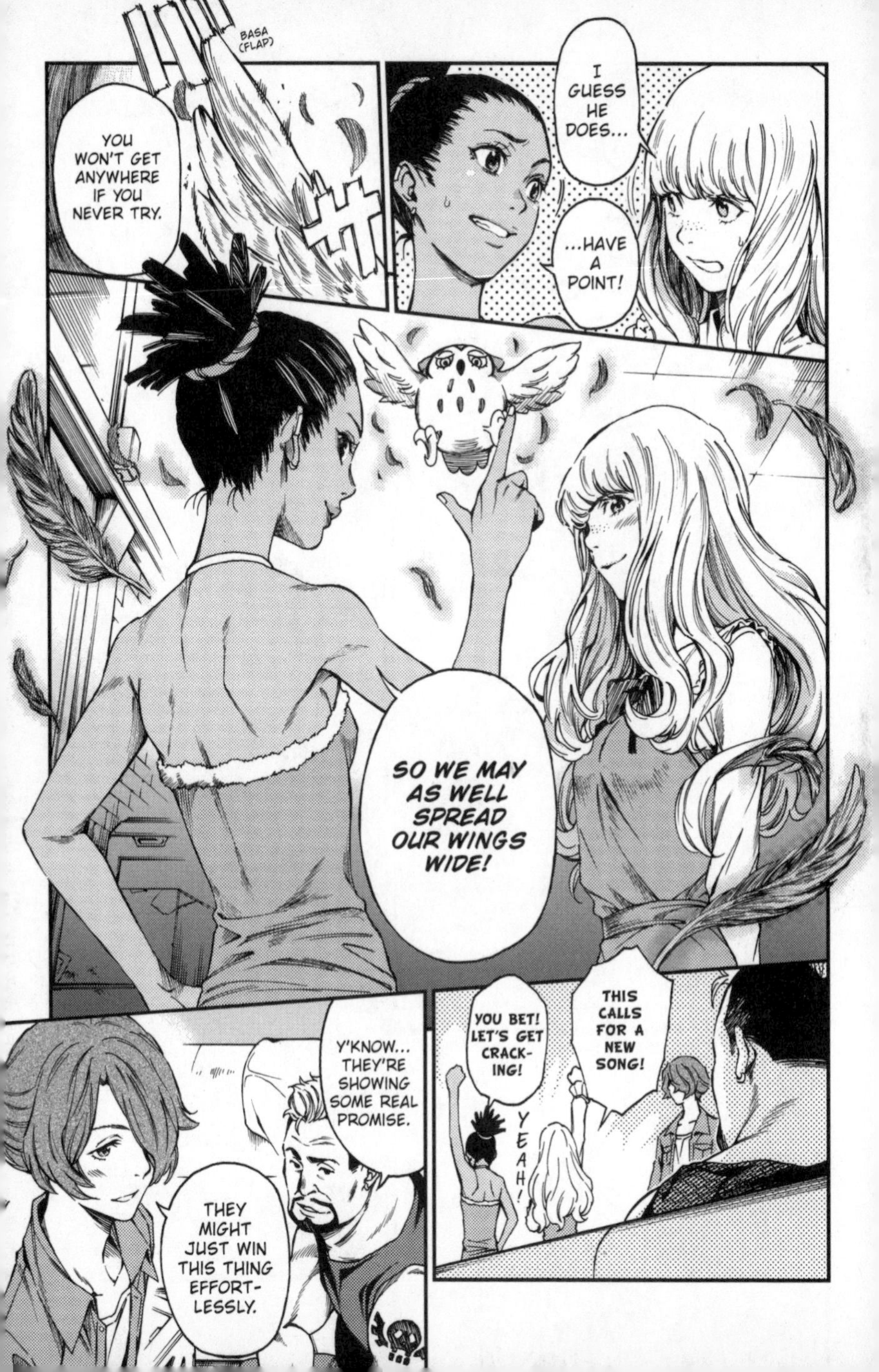
I GUESS HE DOES...
...HAVE A POINT!
BASA (FLAP)
YOU WON'T GET ANYWHERE IF YOU NEVER TRY.
SO WE MAY AS WELL SPREAD OUR WINGS WIDE!
THIS CALLS FOR A NEW SONG!
YOU BET! LET'S GET CRACKING!
YEAH!
Y'KNOW... THEY'RE SHOWING SOME REAL PROMISE.
THEY MIGHT JUST WIN THIS THING EFFORTLESSLY.

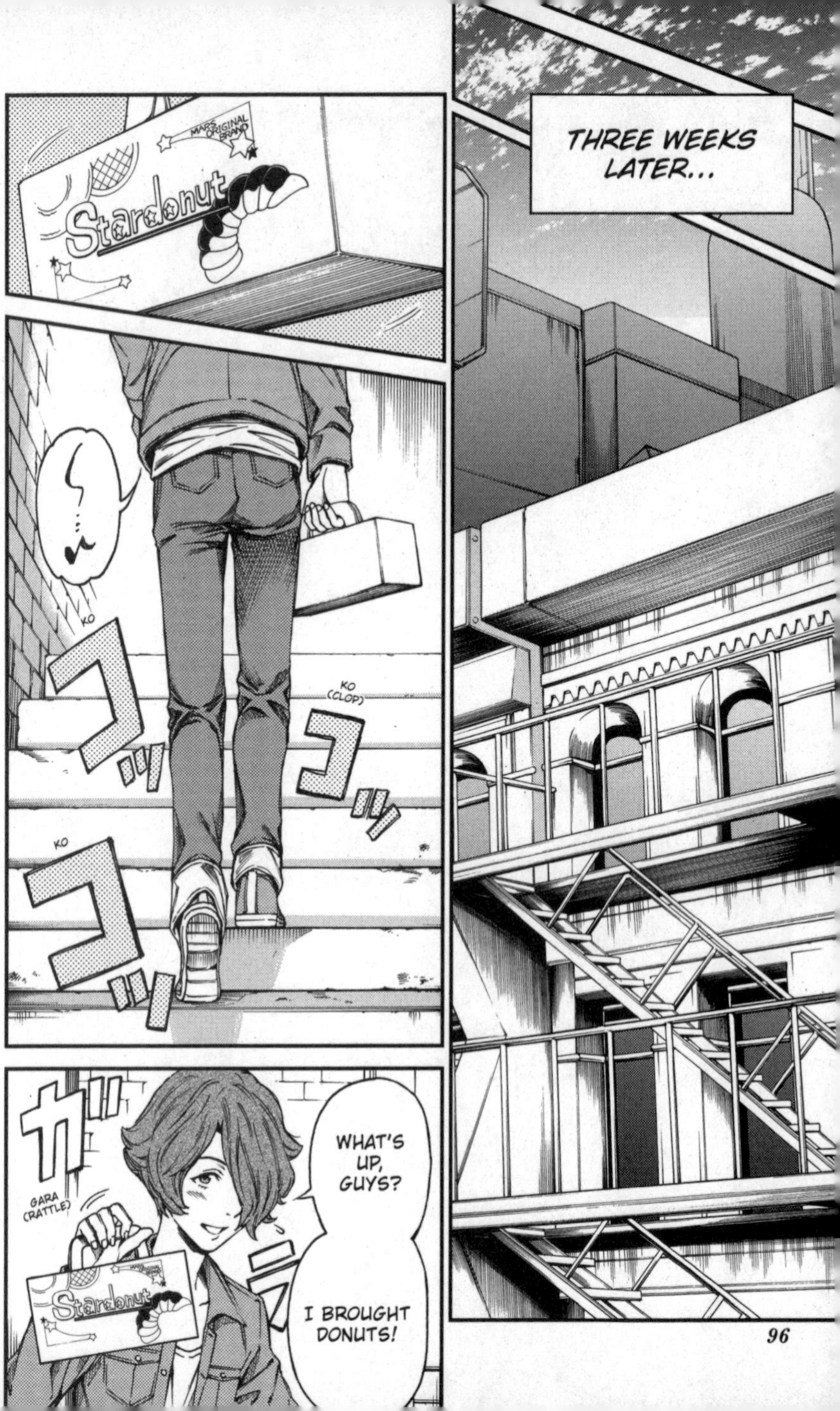
THREE WEEKS LATER...
MARS ORIGINAL BRAND
Stardonut
KO (CLOP)
KO
KO
GARA (RATTLE)
WHAT'S UP, GUYS?
I BROUGHT DONUTS!

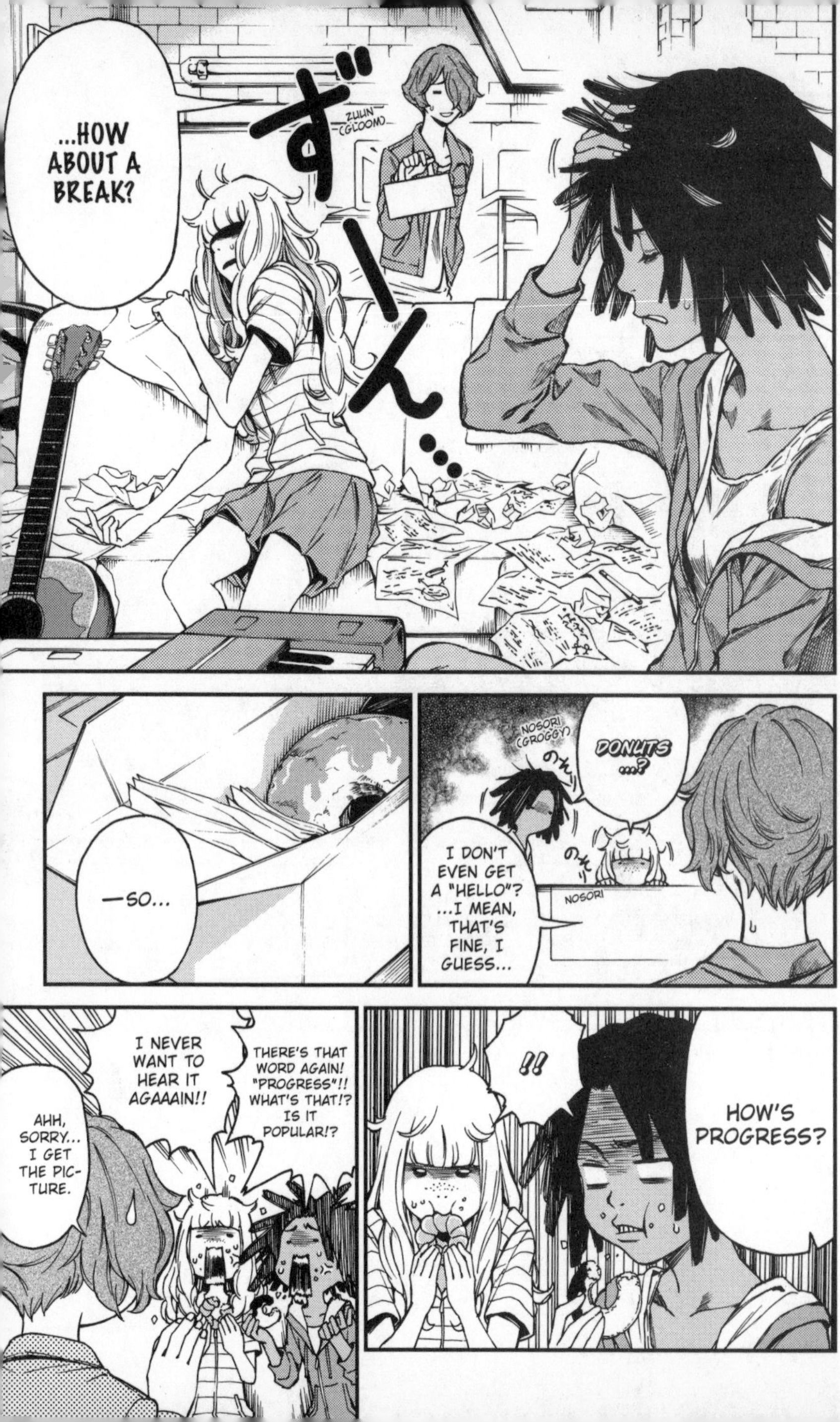
ずーん…
ZUUN (GLOOM)
...HOW ABOUT A BREAK?
NOSORI (GROGGY)
DONUTS ...?
NOSORI
I DON'T EVEN GET A "HELLO"? ...I MEAN, THAT'S FINE, I GUESS...
—SO...
HOW'S PROGRESS?
!!
THERE'S THAT WORD AGAIN! "PROGRESS"!! WHAT'S THAT!? IS IT POPULAR!?
I NEVER WANT TO HEAR IT AGAAAIN!!
AHH, SORRY... I GET THE PICTURE.

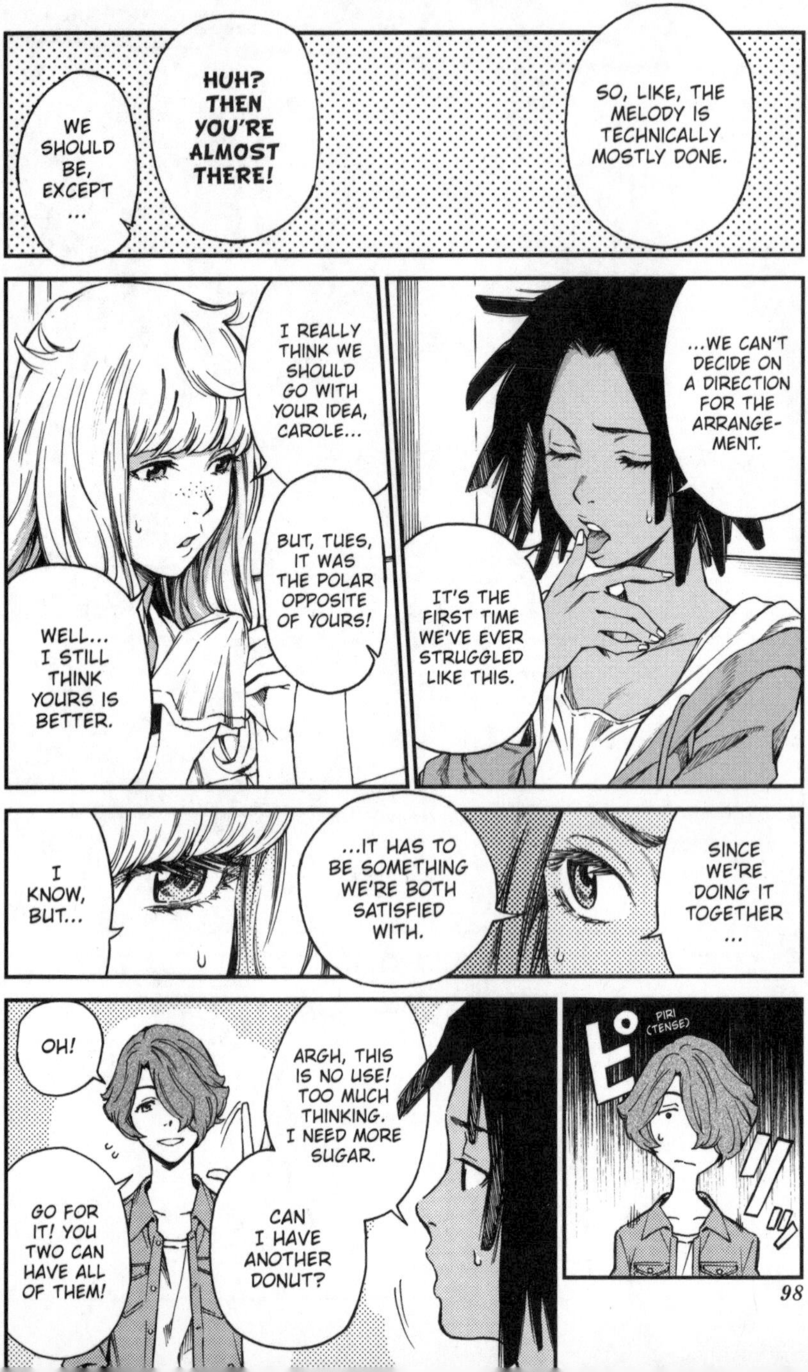
SO, LIKE, THE MELODY IS TECHNICALLY MOSTLY DONE.
HUH? THEN YOU'RE ALMOST THERE!
WE SHOULD BE, EXCEPT ...
...WE CAN'T DECIDE ON A DIRECTION FOR THE ARRANGE-MENT.
IT'S THE FIRST TIME WE'VE EVER STRUGGLED LIKE THIS.
I REALLY THINK WE SHOULD GO WITH YOUR IDEA, CAROLE...
BUT, TUES, IT WAS THE POLAR OPPOSITE OF YOURS!
WELL... I STILL THINK YOURS IS BETTER.
SINCE WE'RE DOING IT TOGETHER ...
...IT HAS TO BE SOMETHING WE'RE BOTH SATISFIED WITH.
I KNOW, BUT...
PIRI (TENSE)
ARGH, THIS IS NO USE! TOO MUCH THINKING. I NEED MORE SUGAR.
OH!
CAN I HAVE ANOTHER DONUT?
GO FOR IT! YOU TWO CAN HAVE ALL OF THEM!

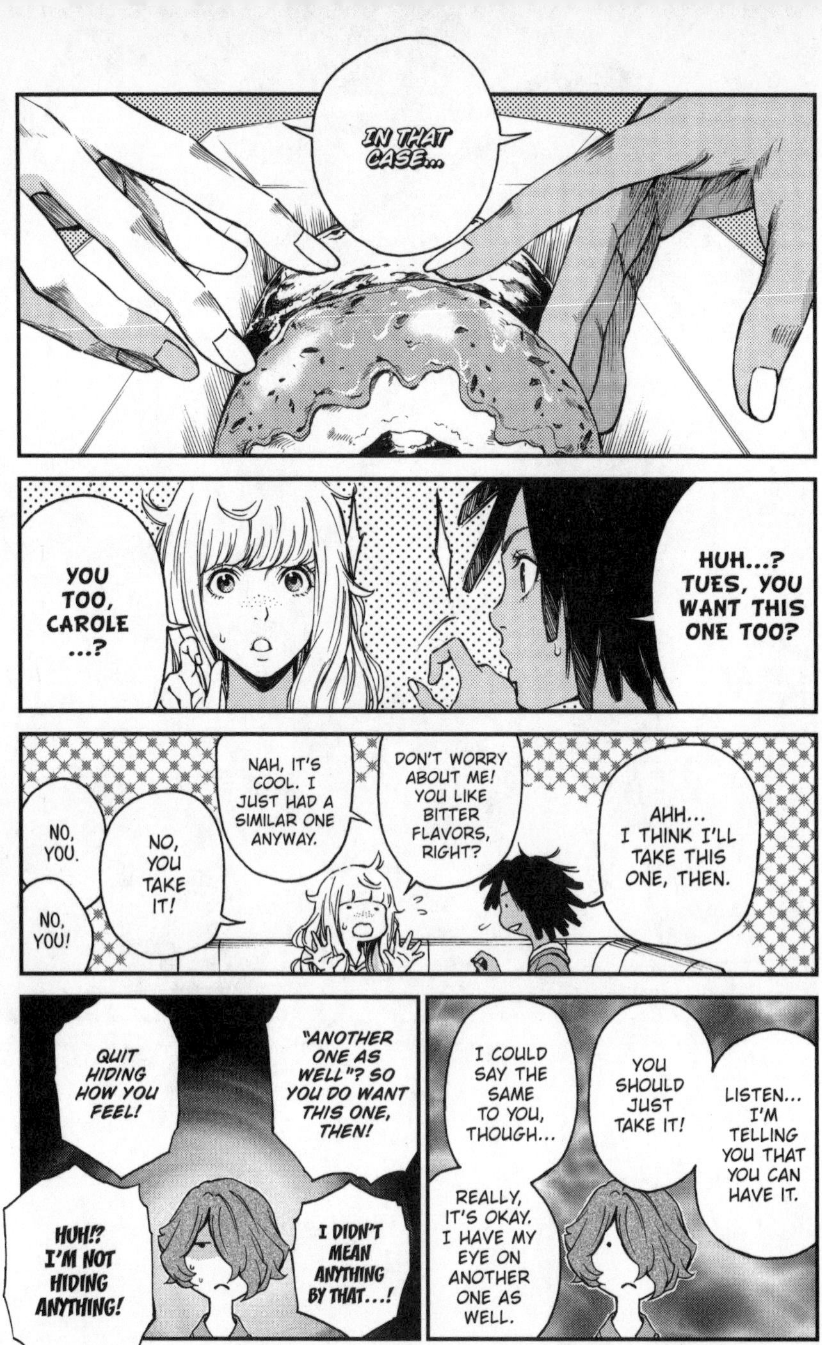
IN THAT CASE...
HUH...? TUES, YOU WANT THIS ONE TOO?
YOU TOO, CAROLE ...?
AHH... I THINK I'LL TAKE THIS ONE, THEN.
DON'T WORRY ABOUT ME! YOU LIKE BITTER FLAVORS, RIGHT?
NAH, IT'S COOL. I JUST HAD A SIMILAR ONE ANYWAY.
NO, YOU TAKE IT!
NO, YOU.
NO, YOU!
LISTEN... I'M TELLING YOU THAT YOU CAN HAVE IT.
YOU SHOULD JUST TAKE IT!
I COULD SAY THE SAME TO YOU, THOUGH...
REALLY, IT'S OKAY. I HAVE MY EYE ON ANOTHER ONE AS WELL.
"ANOTHER ONE AS WELL"? SO YOU DO WANT THIS ONE, THEN!
I DIDN'T MEAN ANYTHING BY THAT...!
QUIT HIDING HOW YOU FEEL!
HUH!? I'M NOT HIDING ANYTHING!

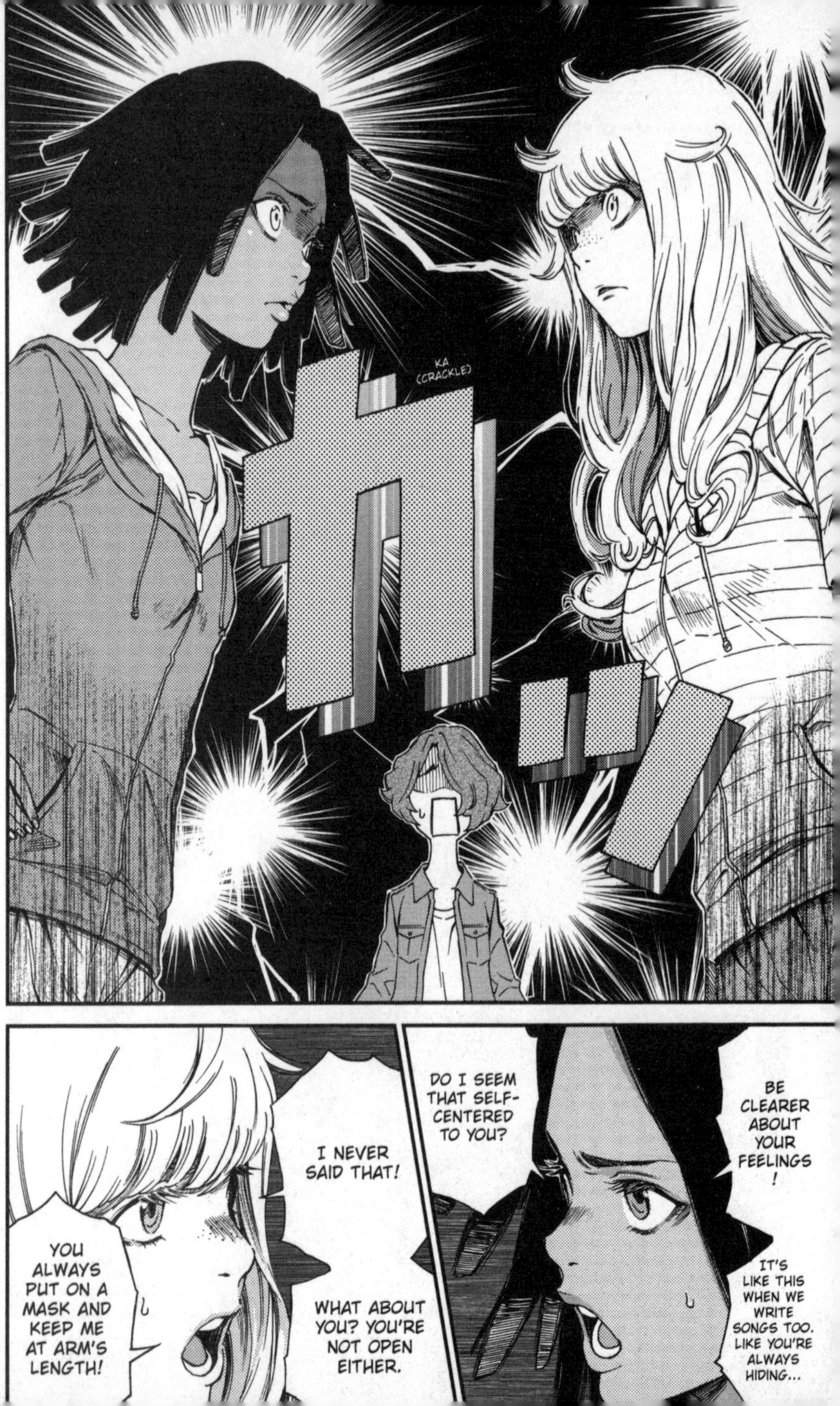

カッ
KA (CRACKLE)
BE CLEARER ABOUT YOUR FEELINGS!
DO I SEEM THAT SELF-CENTERED TO YOU?
IT'S LIKE THIS WHEN WE WRITE SONGS TOO. LIKE YOU'RE ALWAYS HIDING...
I NEVER SAID THAT!
WHAT ABOUT YOU? YOU'RE NOT OPEN EITHER.
YOU ALWAYS PUT ON A MASK AND KEEP ME AT ARM'S LENGTH!

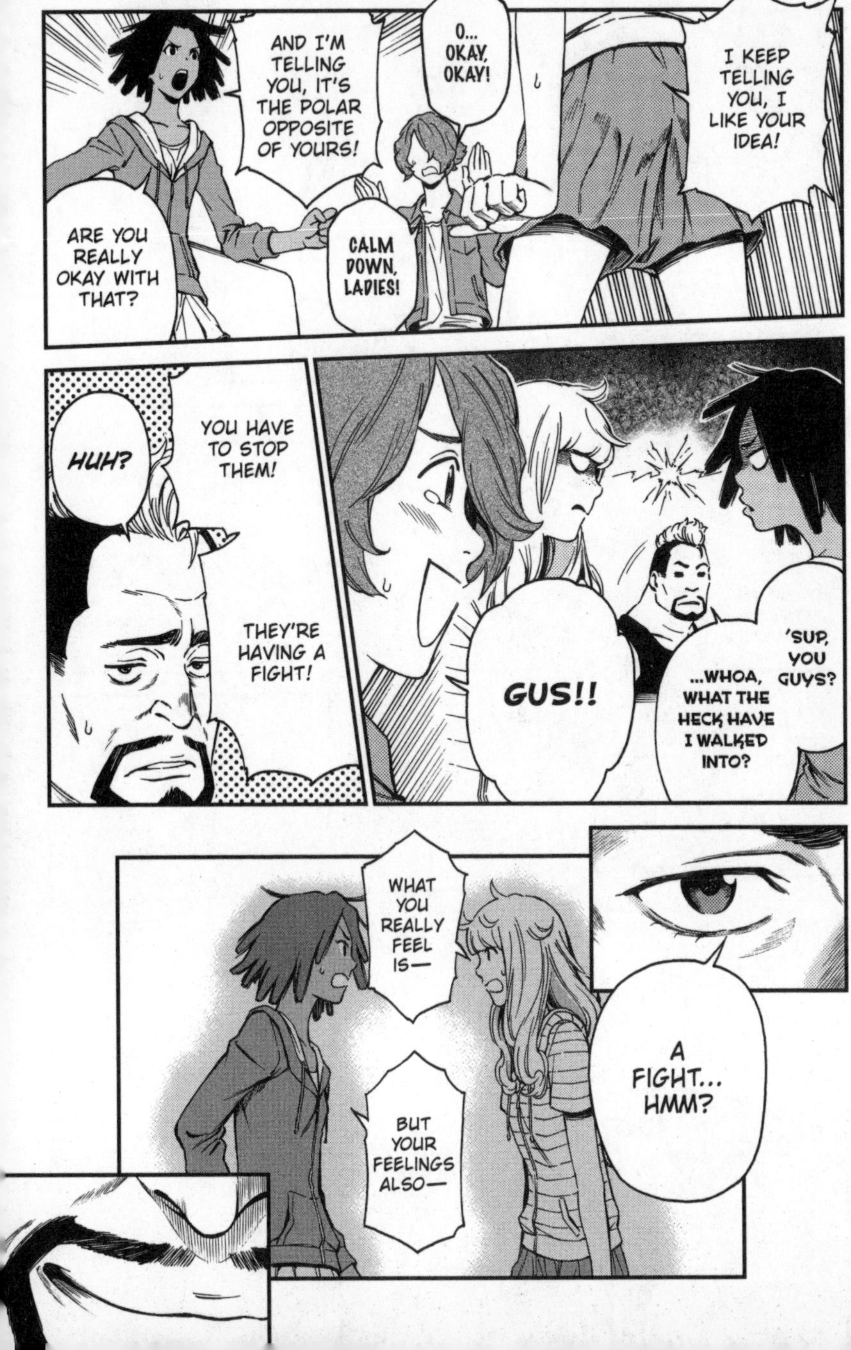
I KEEP TELLING YOU, I LIKE YOUR IDEA!
O... OKAY, OKAY!
AND I'M TELLING YOU, IT'S THE POLAR OPPOSITE OF YOURS!
CALM DOWN, LADIES!
ARE YOU REALLY OKAY WITH THAT?
'SUP, YOU GUYS?
...WHOA, WHAT THE HECK HAVE I WALKED INTO?
GUS!!
YOU HAVE TO STOP THEM!
HUH?
THEY'RE HAVING A FIGHT!
A FIGHT... HMM?
WHAT YOU REALLY FEEL IS—
BUT YOUR FEELINGS ALSO—

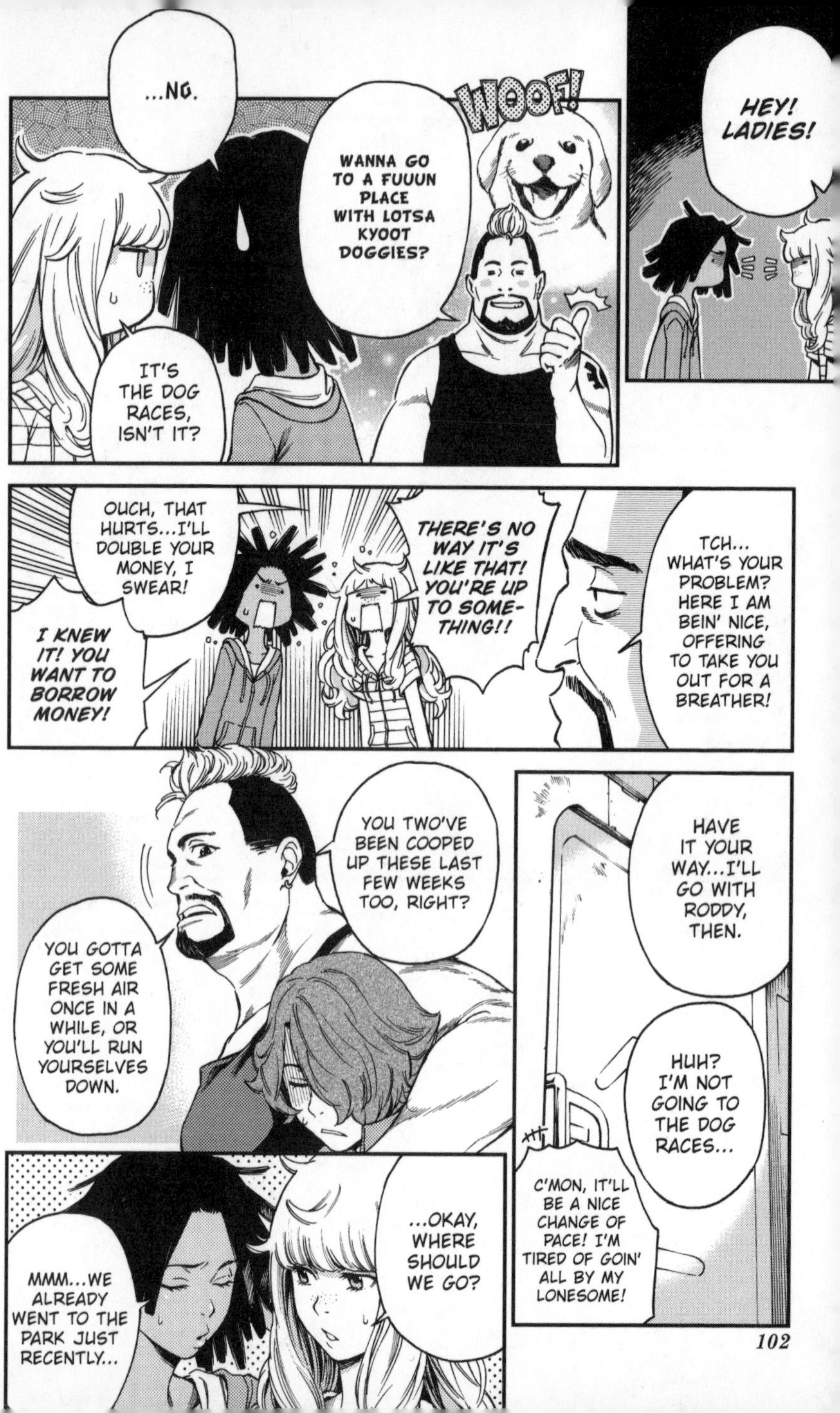
HEY! LADIES!
WOOF!
WANNA GO TO A FUUUN PLACE WITH LOTSA KYOOT DOGGIES?
...NG.
IT'S THE DOG RACES, ISN'T IT?
TCH... WHAT'S YOUR PROBLEM? HERE I AM BEIN' NICE, OFFERING TO TAKE YOU OUT FOR A BREATHER!
THERE'S NO WAY IT'S LIKE THAT! YOU'RE UP TO SOME-THING!!
OUCH, THAT HURTS...I'LL DOUBLE YOUR MONEY, I SWEAR!
I KNEW IT! YOU WANT TO BORROW MONEY!
HAVE IT YOUR WAY...I'LL GO WITH RODDY, THEN.
HUH? I'M NOT GOING TO THE DOG RACES...
C'MON, IT'LL BE A NICE CHANGE OF PACE! I'M TIRED OF GOIN' ALL BY MY LONESOME!
YOU TWO'VE BEEN COOPED UP THESE LAST FEW WEEKS TOO, RIGHT?
YOU GOTTA GET SOME FRESH AIR ONCE IN A WHILE, OR YOU'LL RUN YOURSELVES DOWN.
...OKAY, WHERE SHOULD WE GO?
MMM...WE ALREADY WENT TO THE PARK JUST RECENTLY...

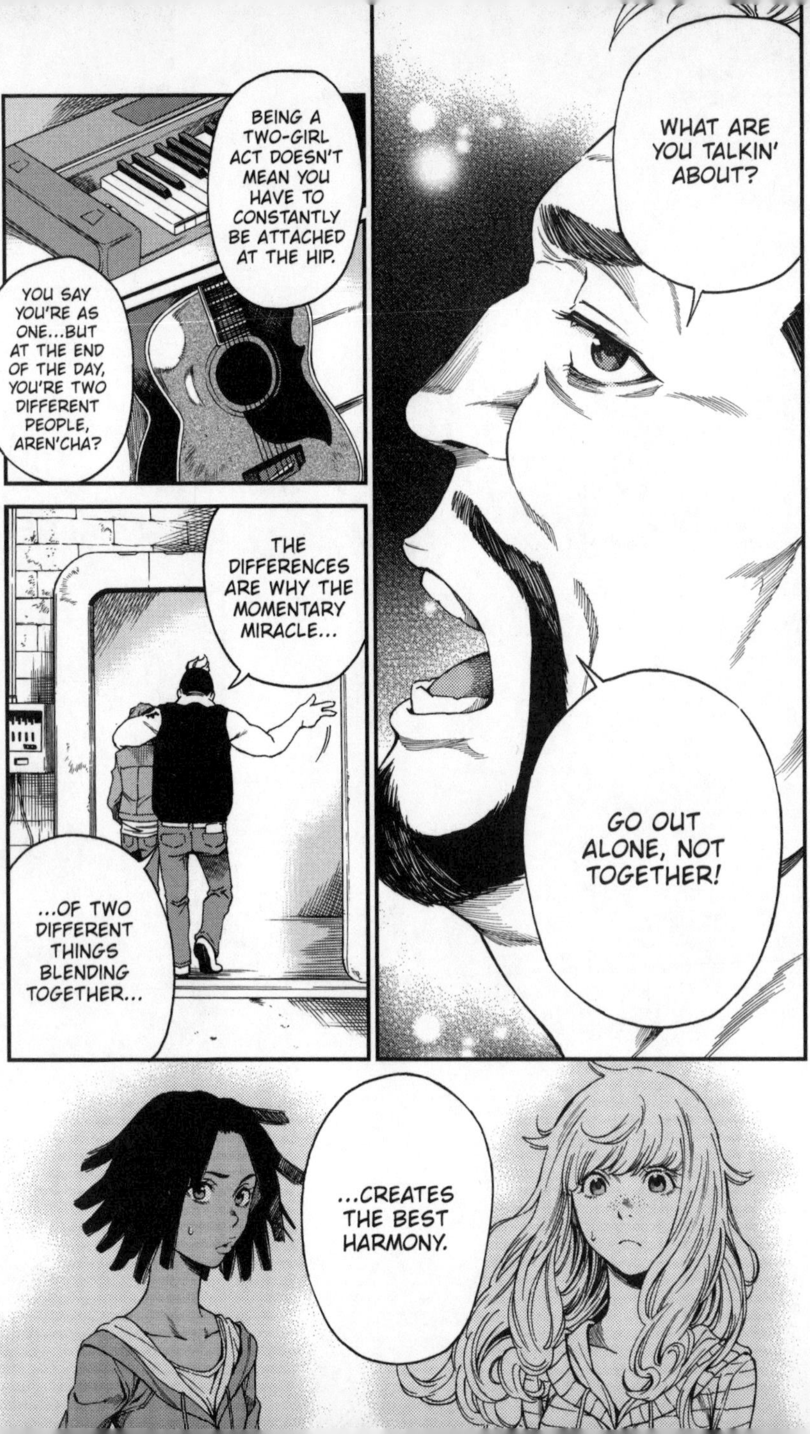
WHAT ARE YOU TALKIN' ABOUT?
GO OUT ALONE, NOT TOGETHER!
BEING A TWO-GIRL ACT DOESN'T MEAN YOU HAVE TO CONSTANTLY BE ATTACHED AT THE HIP.
YOU SAY YOU'RE AS ONE...BUT AT THE END OF THE DAY, YOU'RE TWO DIFFERENT PEOPLE, AREN'CHA?
THE DIFFERENCES ARE WHY THE MOMENTARY MIRACLE...
...OF TWO DIFFERENT THINGS BLENDING TOGETHER...
...CREATES THE BEST HARMONY.

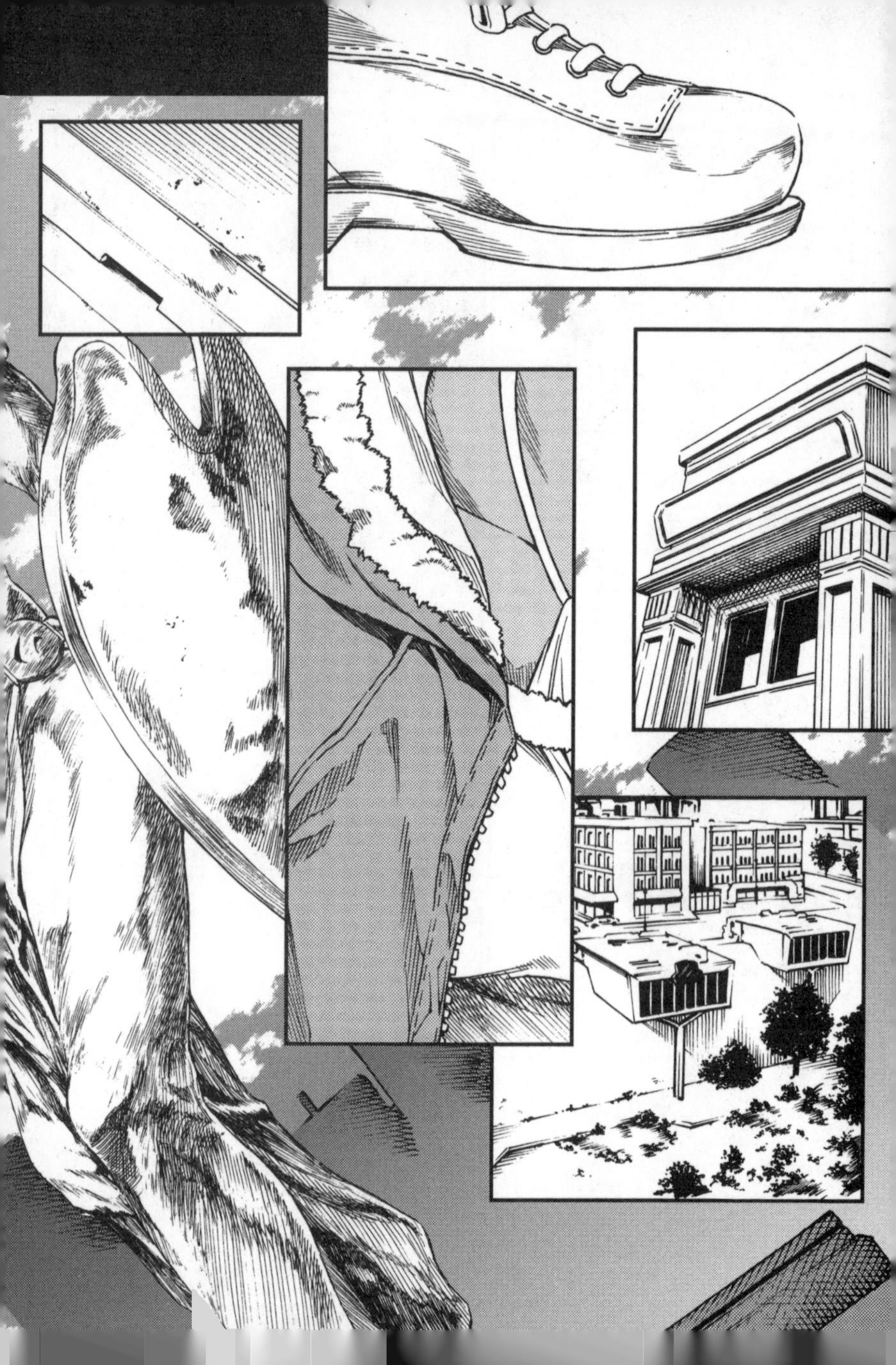

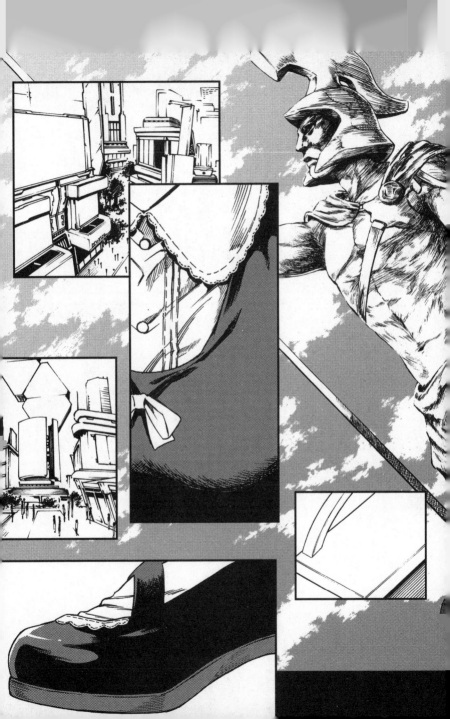

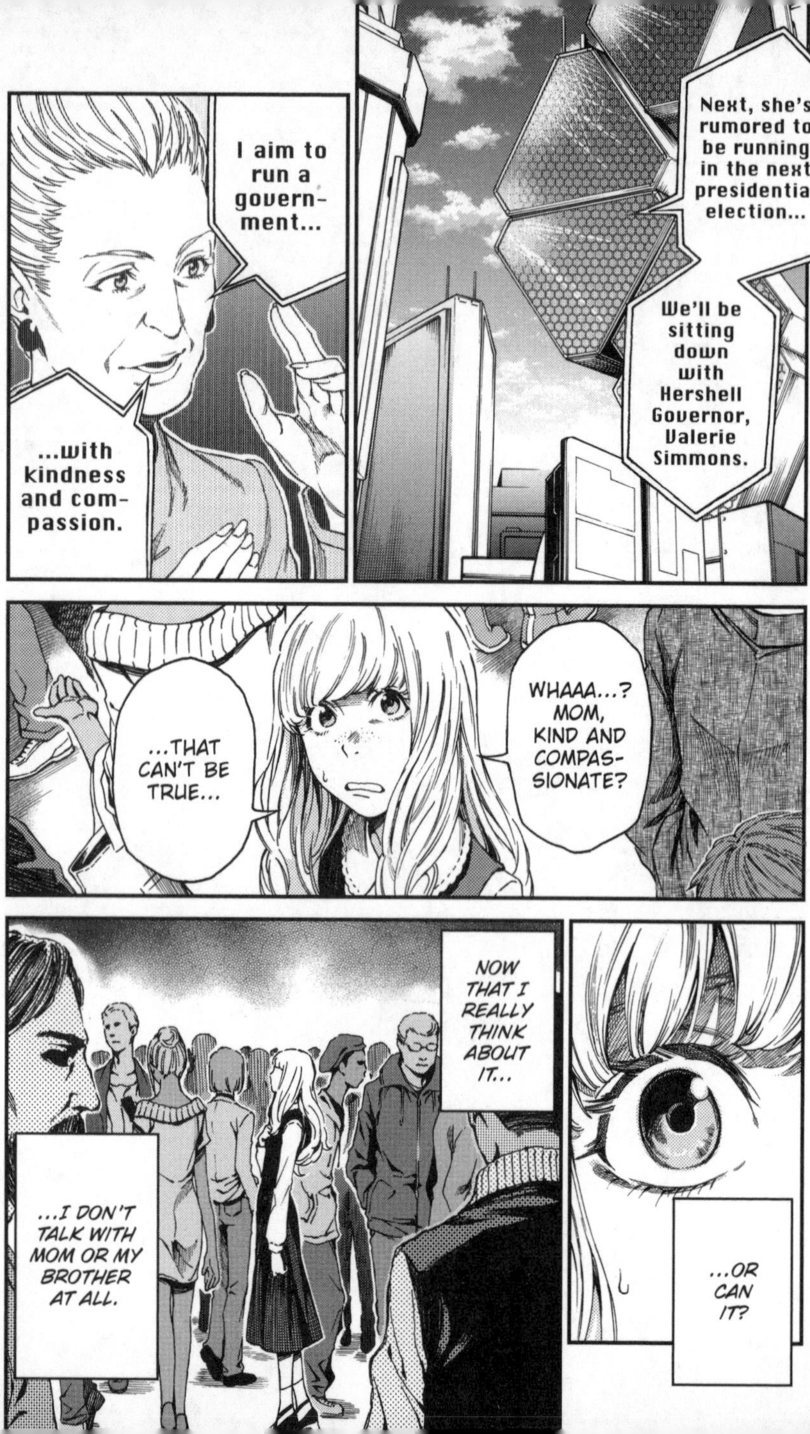
Next, she's rumored to be running in the next presidential election...
We'll be sitting down with Hershell Governor, Valerie Simmons.
I aim to run a govern-ment...
...with kindness and com-passion.
WHAAA...? MOM, KIND AND COMPAS-SIONATE?
...THAT CAN'T BE TRUE...
...OR CAN IT?
NOW THAT I REALLY THINK ABOUT IT...
...I DON'T TALK WITH MOM OR MY BROTHER AT ALL.

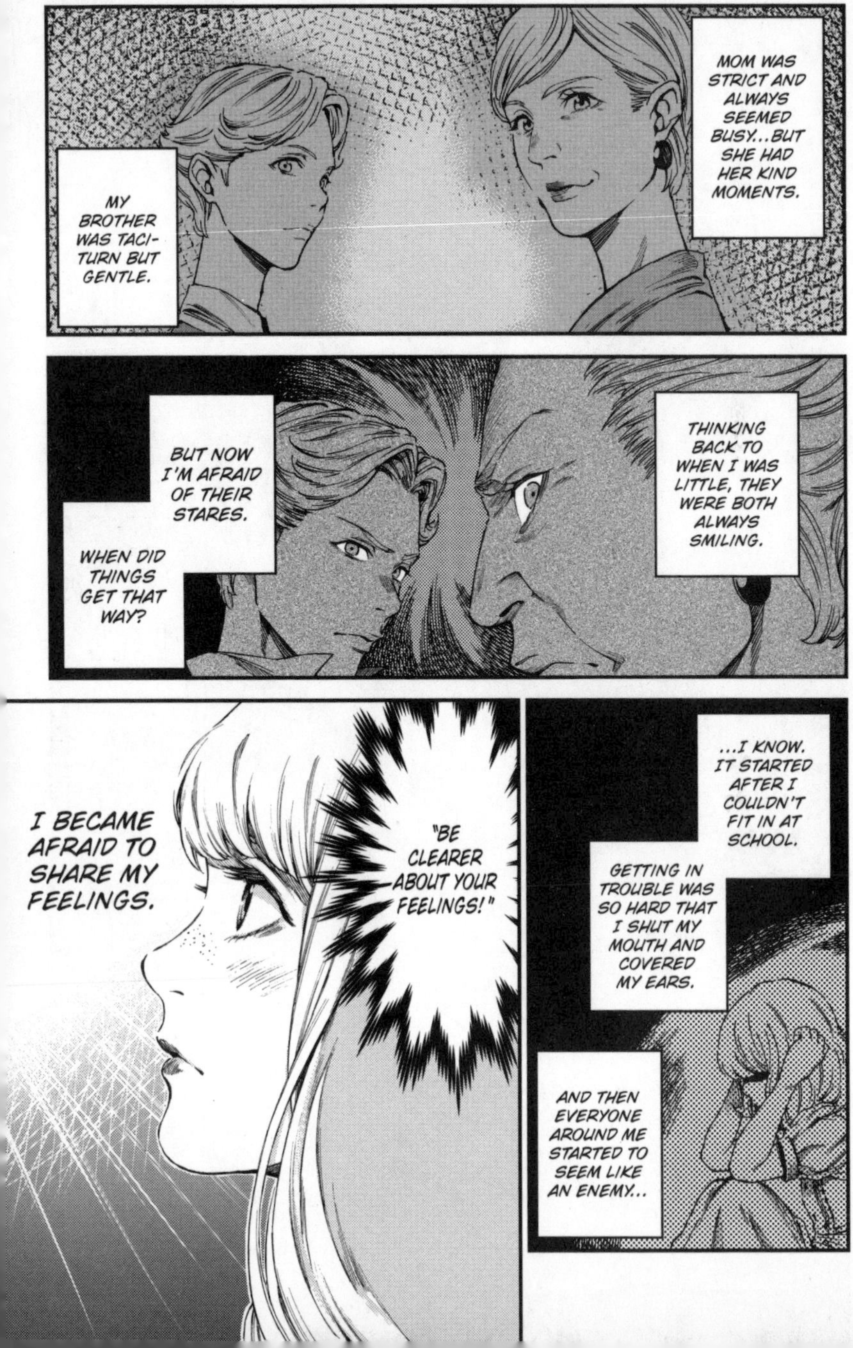
MOM WAS STRICT AND ALWAYS SEEMED BUSY...BUT SHE HAD HER KIND MOMENTS.
MY BROTHER WAS TACI-TURN BUT GENTLE.
THINKING BACK TO WHEN I WAS LITTLE, THEY WERE BOTH ALWAYS SMILING.
BUT NOW I'M AFRAID OF THEIR STARES.
WHEN DID THINGS GET THAT WAY?
...I KNOW. IT STARTED AFTER I COULDN'T FIT IN AT SCHOOL.
GETTING IN TROUBLE WAS SO HARD THAT I SHUT MY MOUTH AND COVERED MY EARS.
AND THEN EVERYONE AROUND ME STARTED TO SEEM LIKE AN ENEMY...
"BE CLEARER ABOUT YOUR FEELINGS!"
I BECAME AFRAID TO SHARE MY FEELINGS.

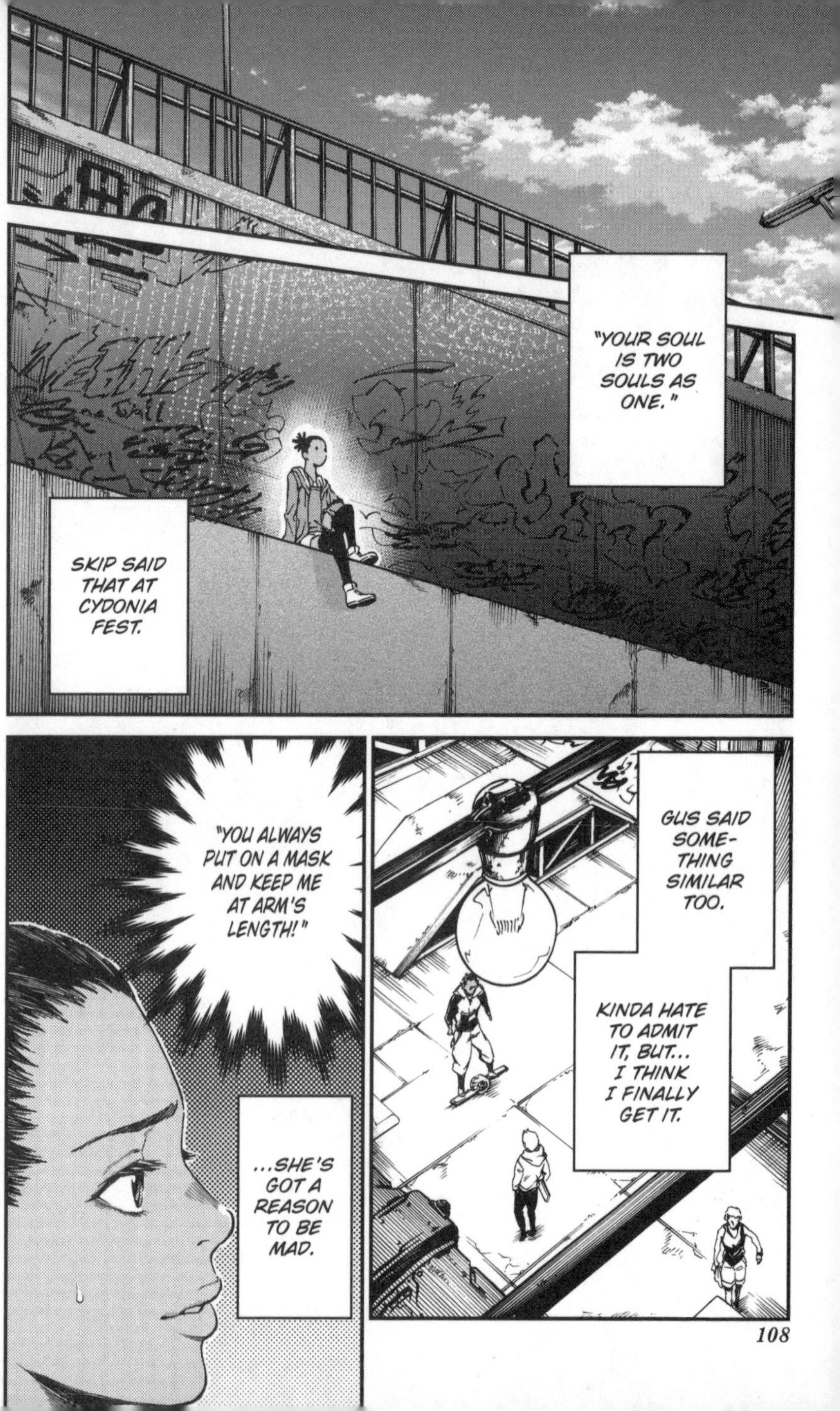
"YOUR SOUL IS TWO SOULS AS ONE."
SKIP SAID THAT AT CYDONIA FEST.
GUS SAID SOME-THING SIMILAR TOO.
KINDA HATE TO ADMIT IT, BUT... I THINK I FINALLY GET IT.
"YOU ALWAYS PUT ON A MASK AND KEEP ME AT ARM'S LENGTH!"
...SHE'S GOT A REASON TO BE MAD.

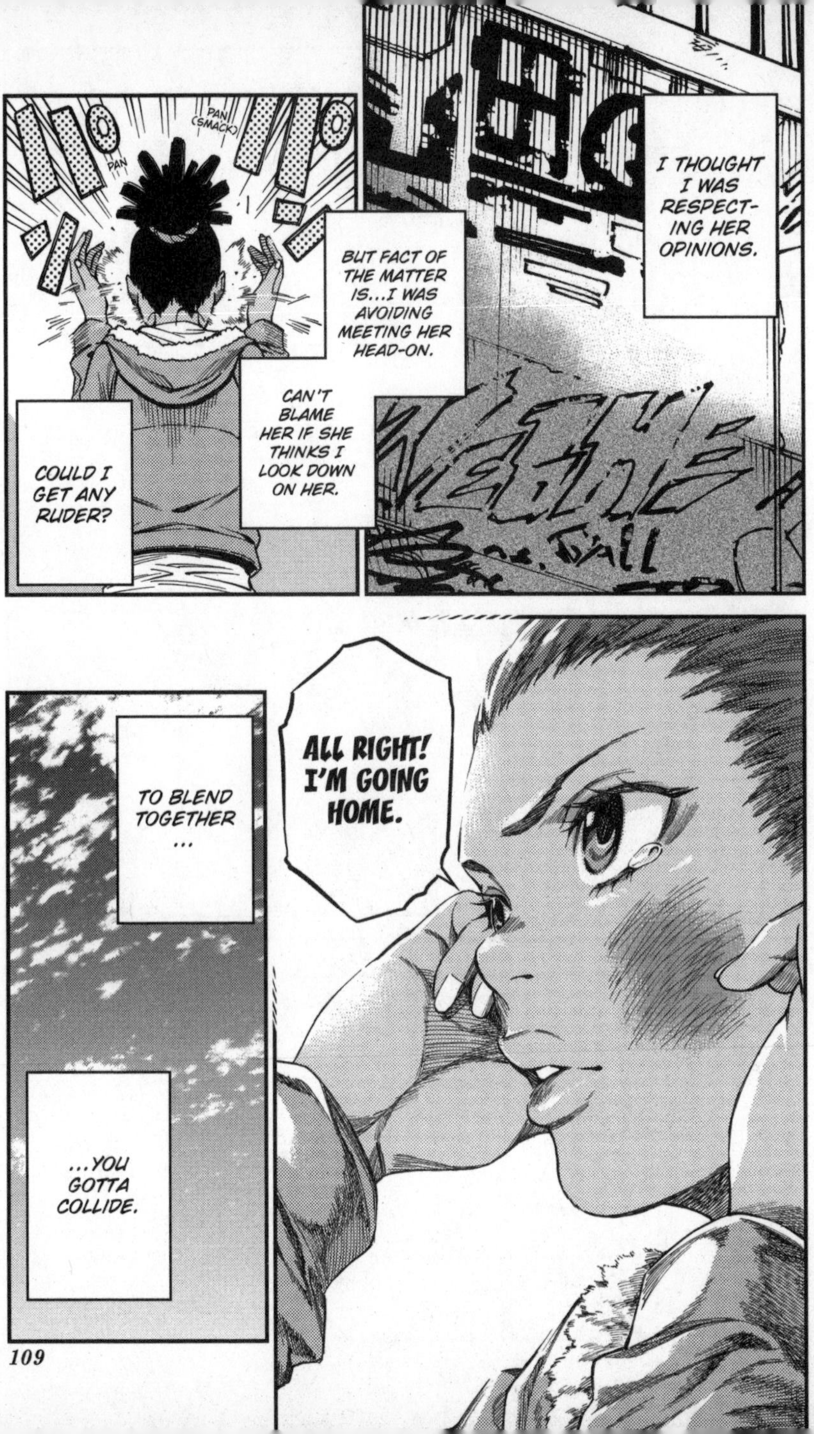
I THOUGHT I WAS RESPECT-ING HER OPINIONS.
PAN (SMACK)
PAN
BUT FACT OF THE MATTER IS...I WAS AVOIDING MEETING HER HEAD-ON.
CAN'T BLAME HER IF SHE THINKS I LOOK DOWN ON HER.
COULD I GET ANY RUDER?
ALL RIGHT! I'M GOING HOME.
TO BLEND TOGETHER ...
...YOU GOTTA COLLIDE.

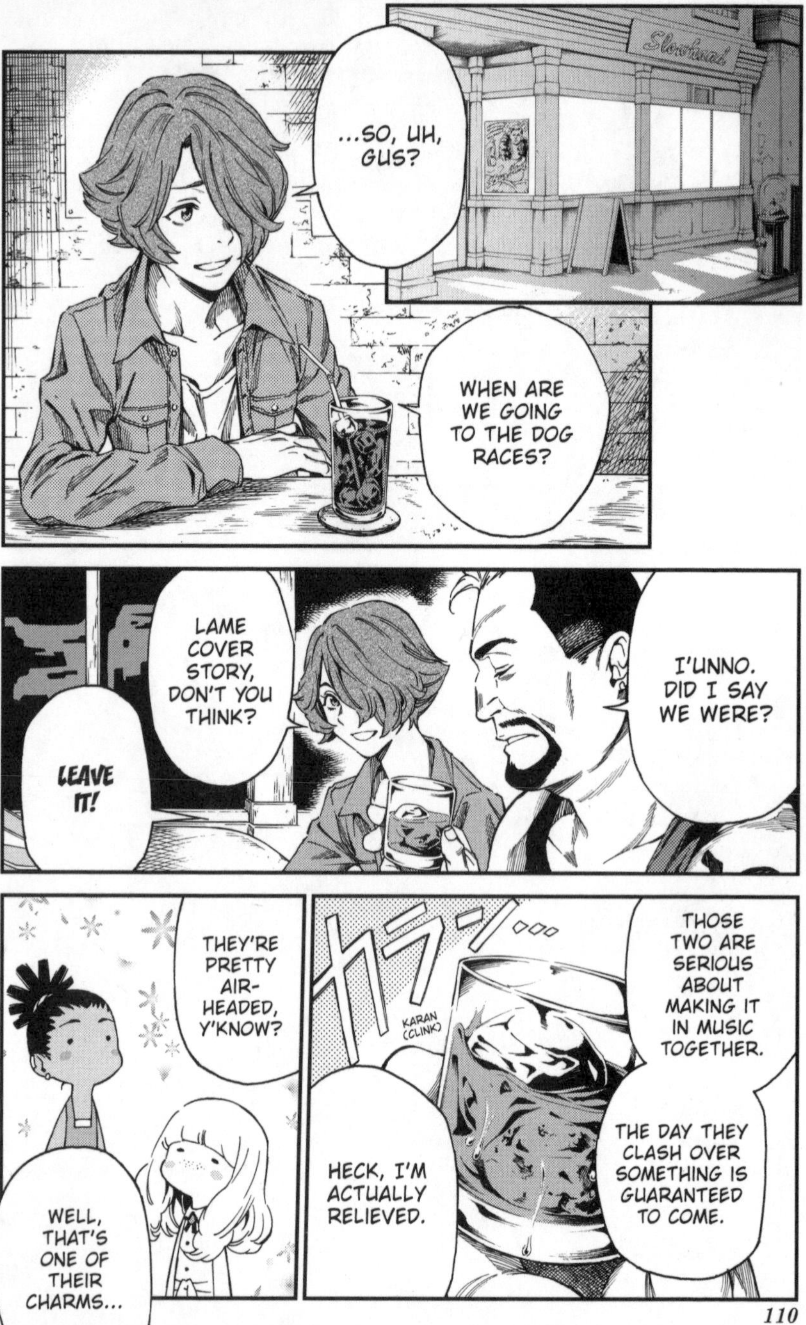
...SO, UH, GUS?
WHEN ARE WE GOING TO THE DOG RACES?
I'UNNO. DID I SAY WE WERE?
LAME COVER STORY, DON'T YOU THINK?
LEAVE IT!
THOSE TWO ARE SERIOUS ABOUT MAKING IT IN MUSIC TOGETHER.
THE DAY THEY CLASH OVER SOMETHING IS GUARANTEED TO COME.
カラーン
KARAN (CLINK)
HECK, I'M ACTUALLY RELIEVED.
THEY'RE PRETTY AIR-HEADED, Y'KNOW?
WELL, THAT'S ONE OF THEIR CHARMS...

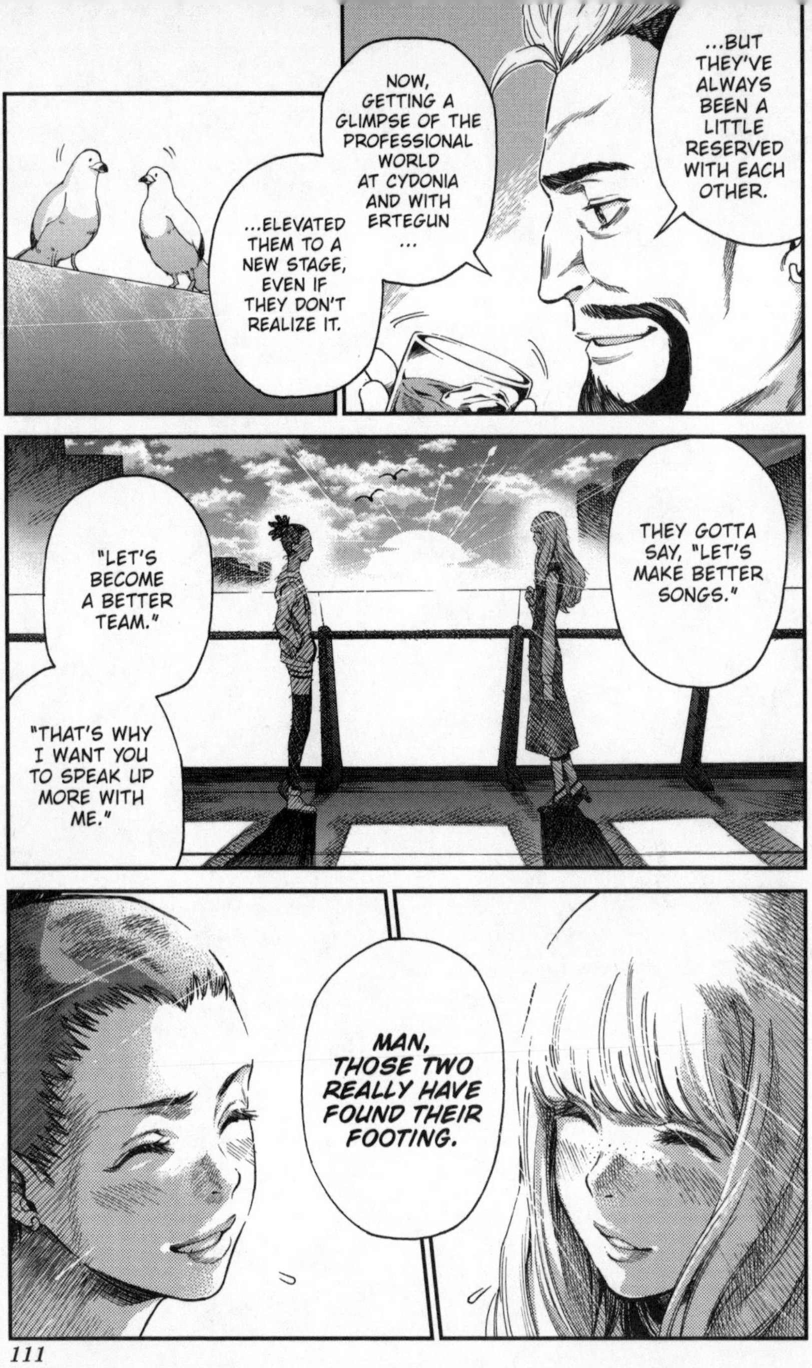
...BUT THEY'VE ALWAYS BEEN A LITTLE RESERVED WITH EACH OTHER.
NOW, GETTING A GLIMPSE OF THE PROFESSIONAL WORLD AT CYDONIA AND WITH ERTEGUN ...
...ELEVATED THEM TO A NEW STAGE, EVEN IF THEY DON'T REALIZE IT.
THEY GOTTA SAY, "LET'S MAKE BETTER SONGS."
"LET'S BECOME A BETTER TEAM."
"THAT'S WHY I WANT YOU TO SPEAK UP MORE WITH ME."
MAN, THOSE TWO REALLY HAVE FOUND THEIR FOOTING.

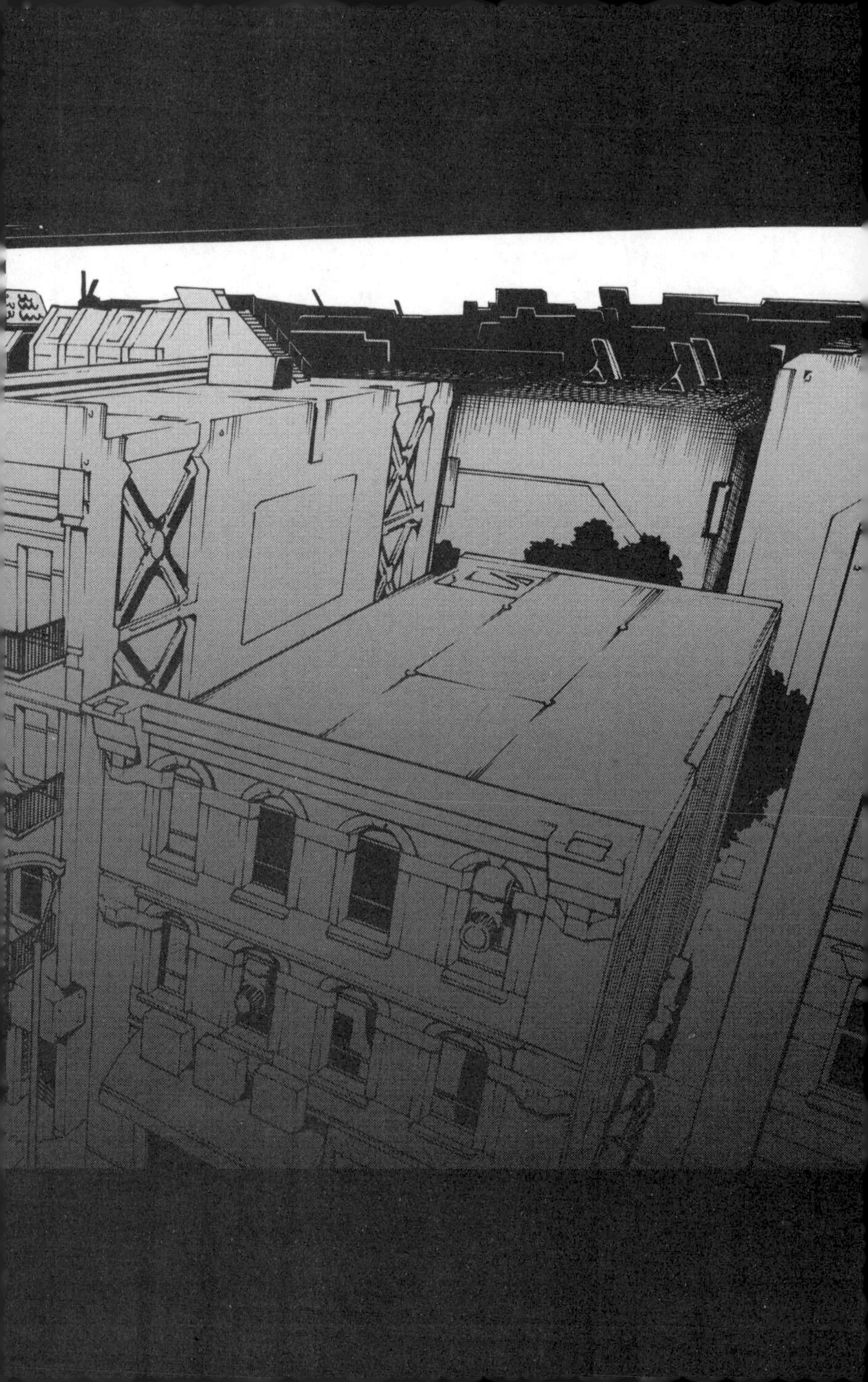

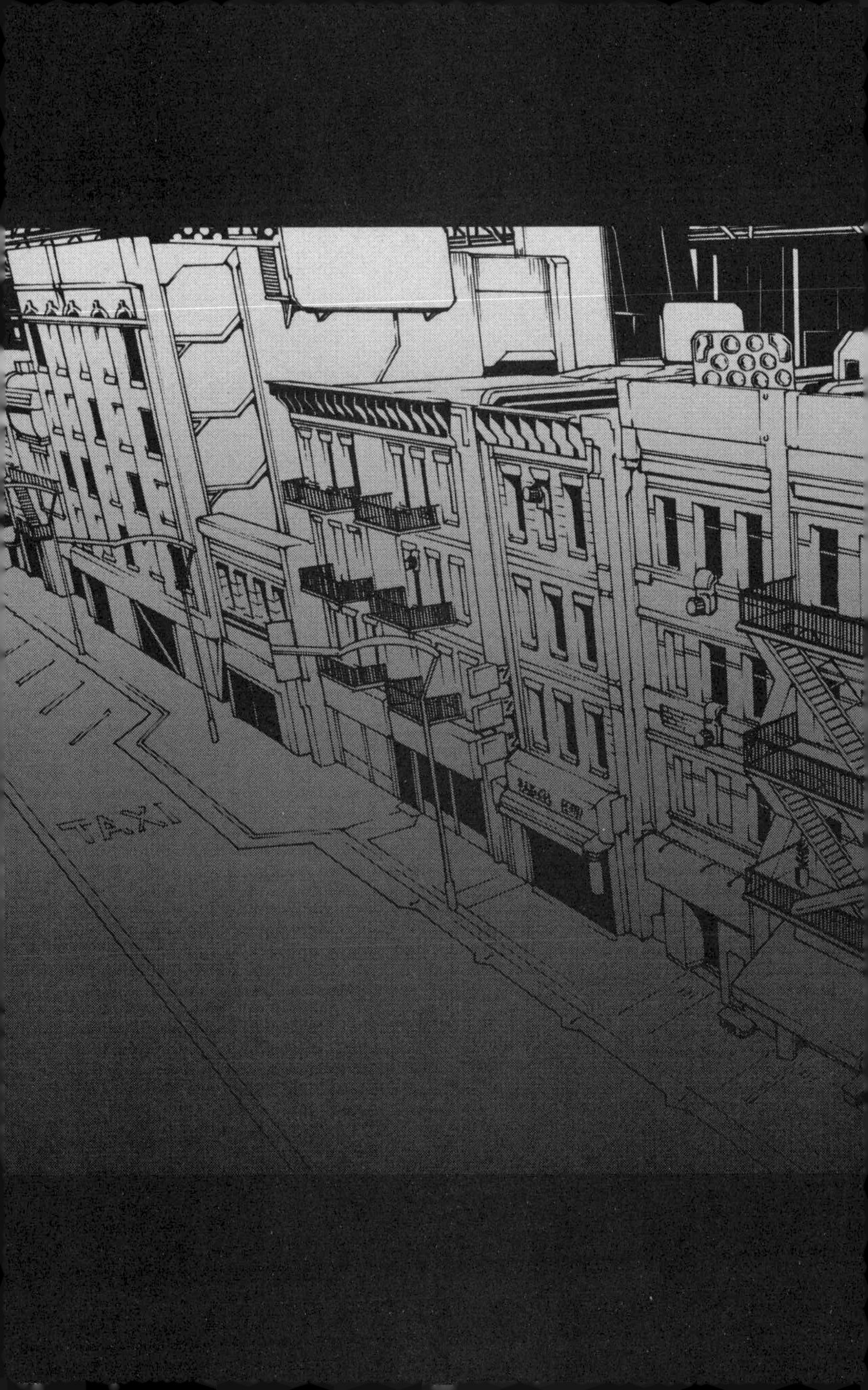
TAXI

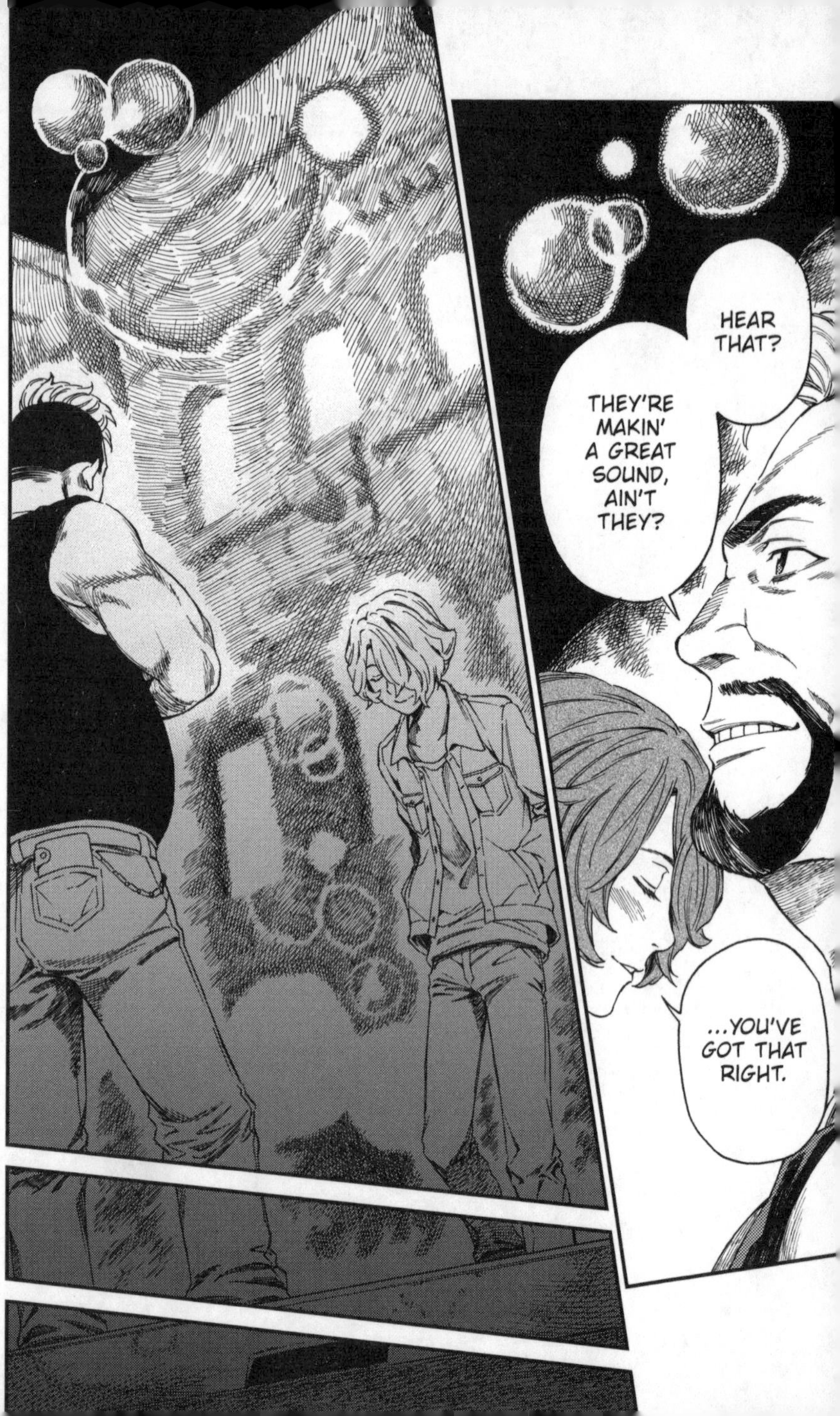
HEAR THAT?
THEY'RE MAKIN' A GREAT SOUND, AIN'T THEY?
...YOU'VE GOT THAT RIGHT.

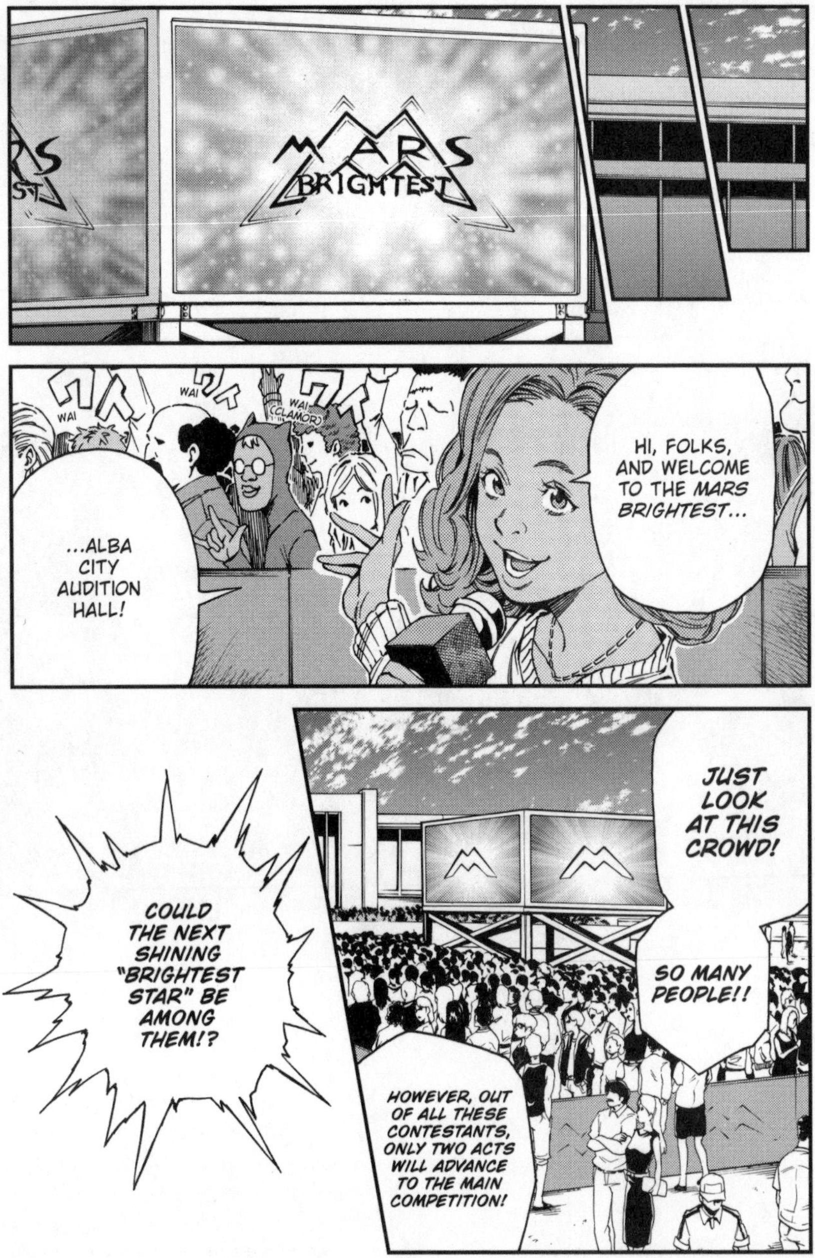
MARS BRIGHTEST
WAI
(CLAMOR)
WAI
WAI
HI, FOLKS, AND WELCOME TO THE *MARS BRIGHTEST*...
...ALBA CITY AUDITION HALL!
JUST LOOK AT THIS CROWD!
SO MANY PEOPLE!!
HOWEVER, OUT OF ALL THESE CONTESTANTS, ONLY TWO ACTS WILL ADVANCE TO THE MAIN COMPETITION!
COULD THE NEXT SHINING "BRIGHTEST STAR" BE AMONG THEM!?

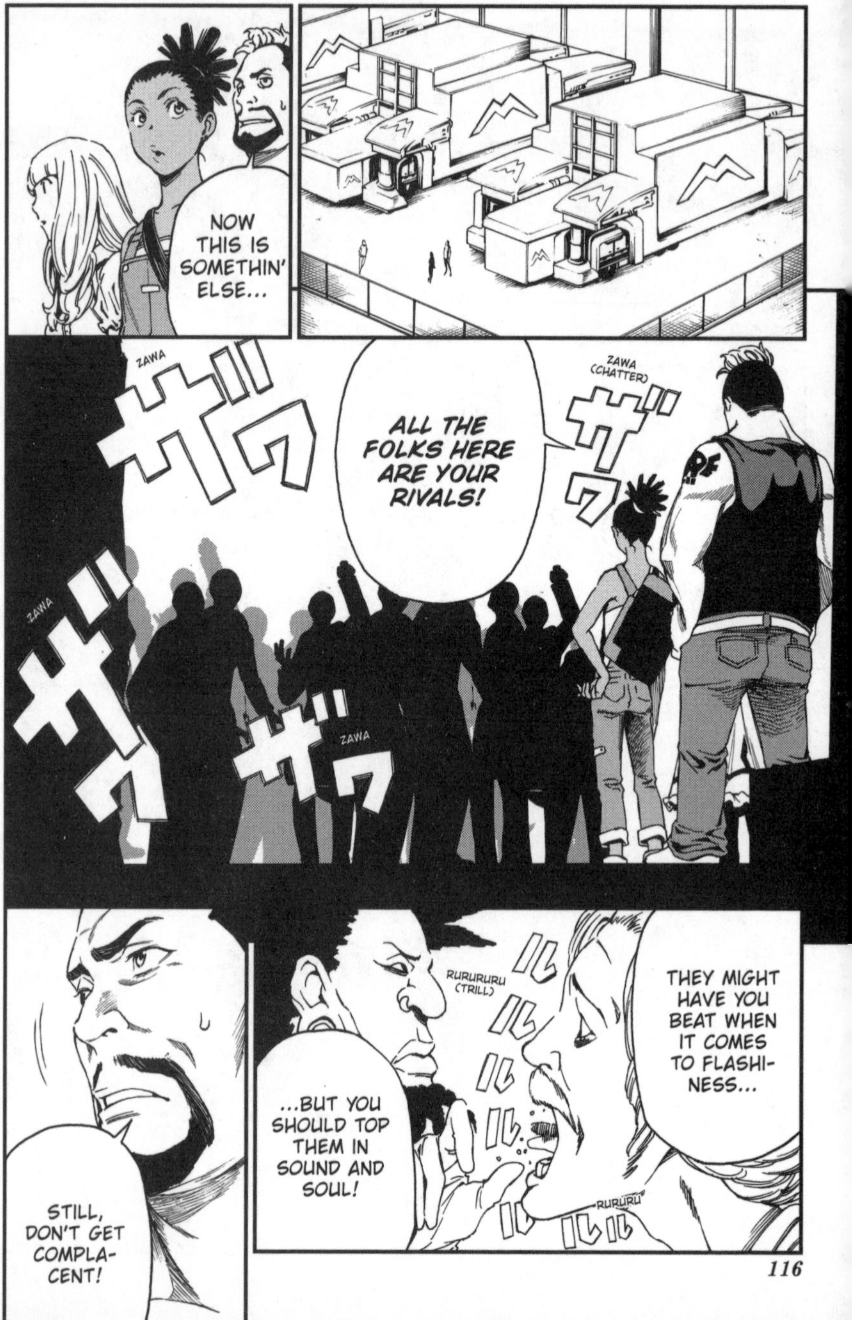
NOW THIS IS SOMETHIN' ELSE...
ZAWA (CHATTER)
ザワ
ALL THE FOLKS HERE ARE YOUR RIVALS!
ZAWA
ザワ
ZAWA
ザワ
ZAWA
ザワ
THEY MIGHT HAVE YOU BEAT WHEN IT COMES TO FLASHI-NESS...
RURURURU (TRILL)
ルルルル
...BUT YOU SHOULD TOP THEM IN SOUND AND SOUL!
RURURU
ルルル
STILL, DON'T GET COMPLA-CENT!

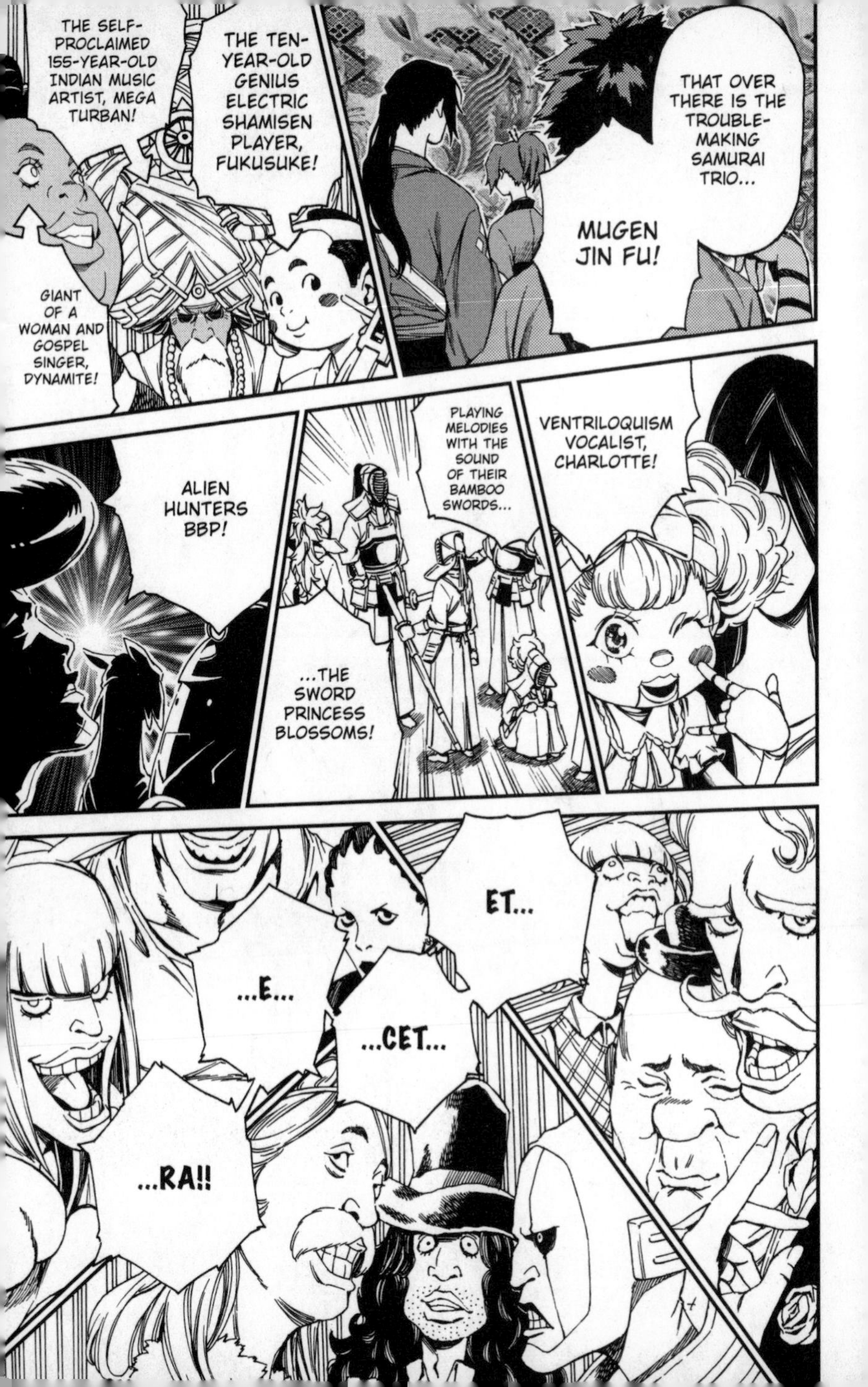
THAT OVER THERE IS THE TROUBLE-MAKING SAMURAI TRIO...
MUGEN JIN FU!
THE TEN-YEAR-OLD GENIUS ELECTRIC SHAMISEN PLAYER, FUKUSUKE!
THE SELF-PROCLAIMED 155-YEAR-OLD INDIAN MUSIC ARTIST, MEGA TURBAN!
GIANT OF A WOMAN AND GOSPEL SINGER, DYNAMITE!
VENTRILOQUISM VOCALIST, CHARLOTTE!
PLAYING MELODIES WITH THE SOUND OF THEIR BAMBOO SWORDS...
...THE SWORD PRINCESS BLOSSOMS!
ALIEN HUNTERS BBP!
ET...
...CET...
...E...
...RA!!

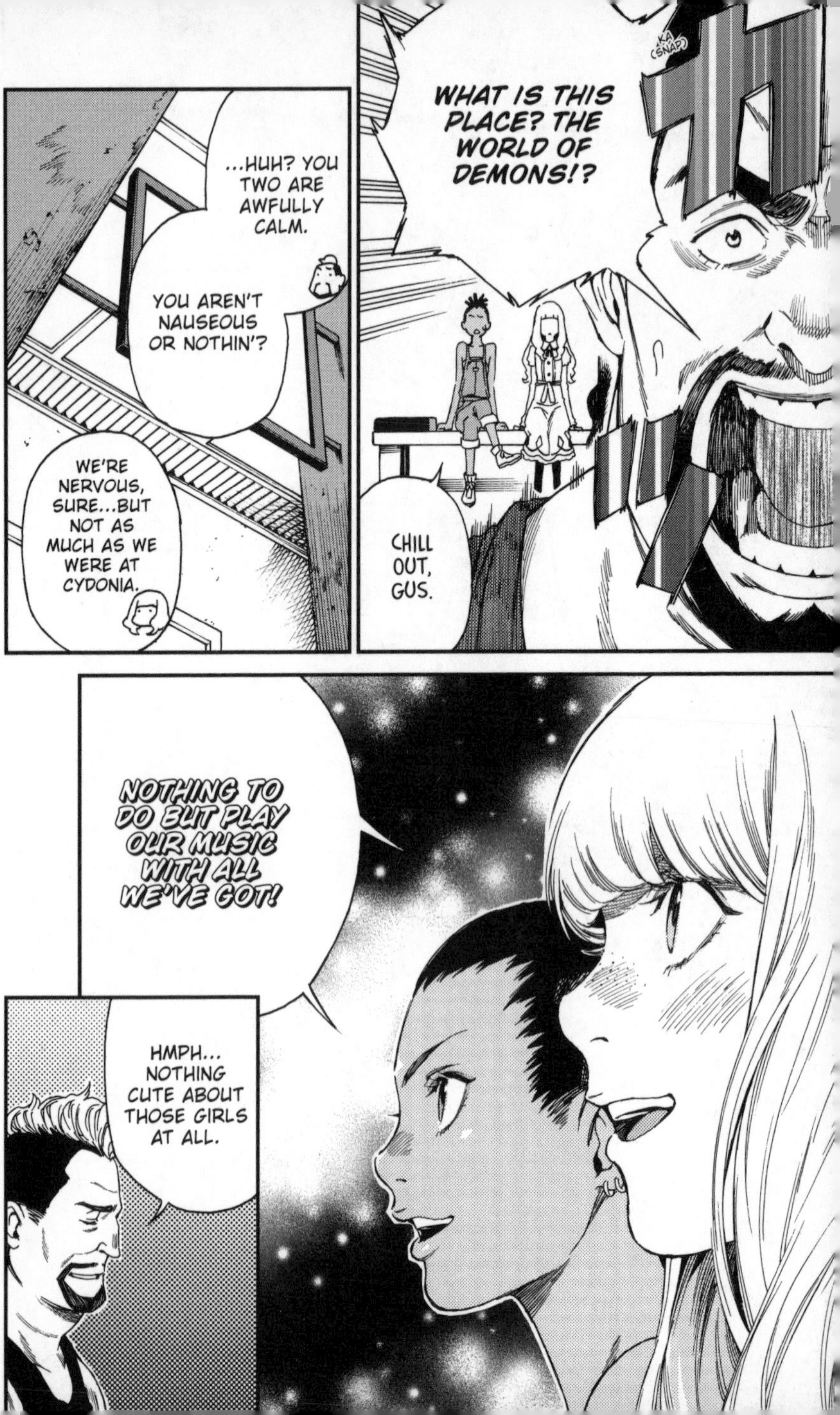
KA (SNAP)
WHAT IS THIS PLACE? THE WORLD OF DEMONS!?
CHILL OUT, GUS.
...HUH? YOU TWO ARE AWFULLY CALM.
YOU AREN'T NAUSEOUS OR NOTHIN'?
WE'RE NERVOUS, SURE...BUT NOT AS MUCH AS WE WERE AT CYDONIA.
NOTHING TO DO BUT PLAY OUR MUSIC WITH ALL WE'VE GOT!
HMPH... NOTHING CUTE ABOUT THOSE GIRLS AT ALL.

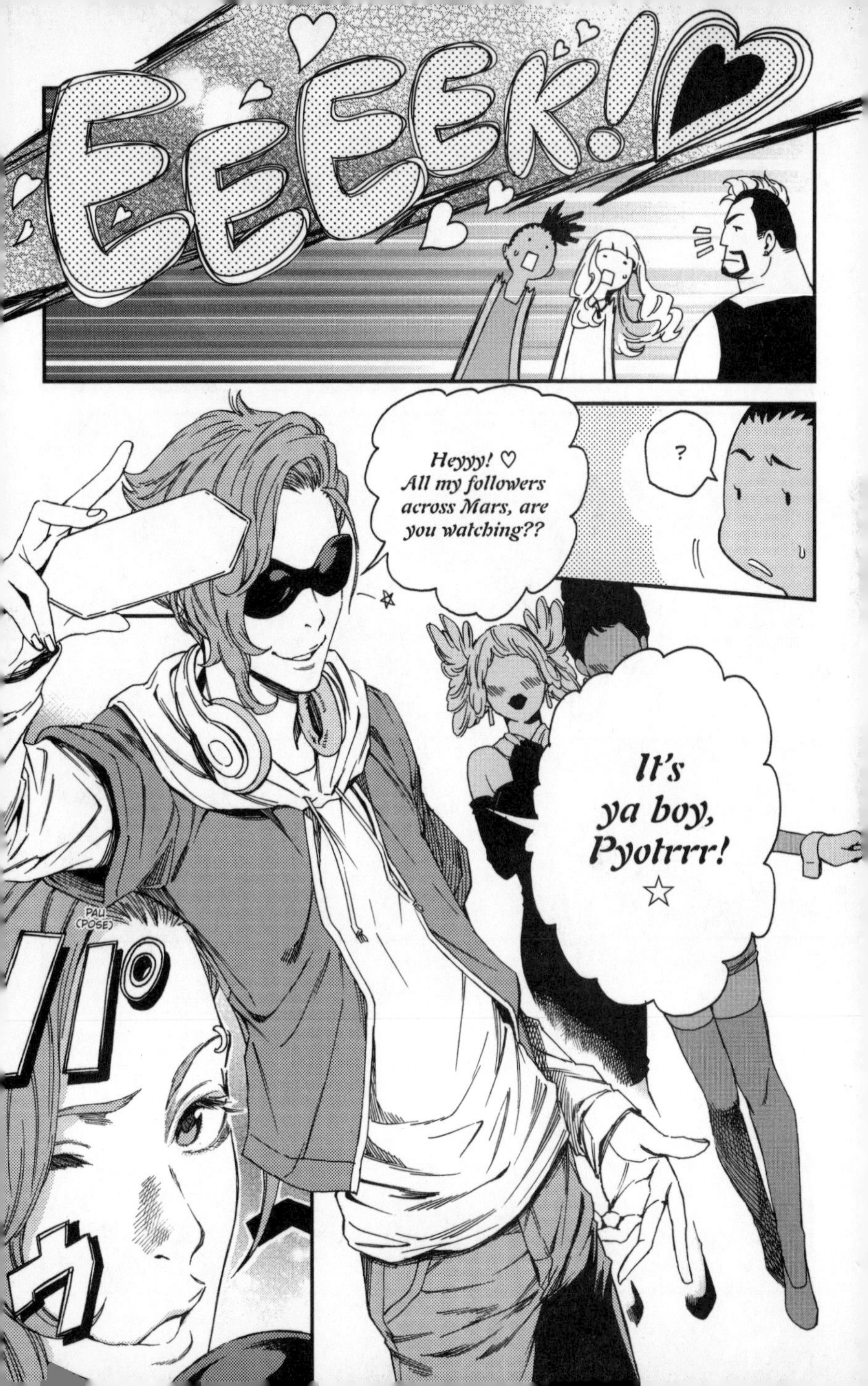
EEEEK!!♡
?
Heyyy! ♡ All my followers across Mars, are you watching??
It's ya boy, Pyotrrr! ☆
PAU (POSE)

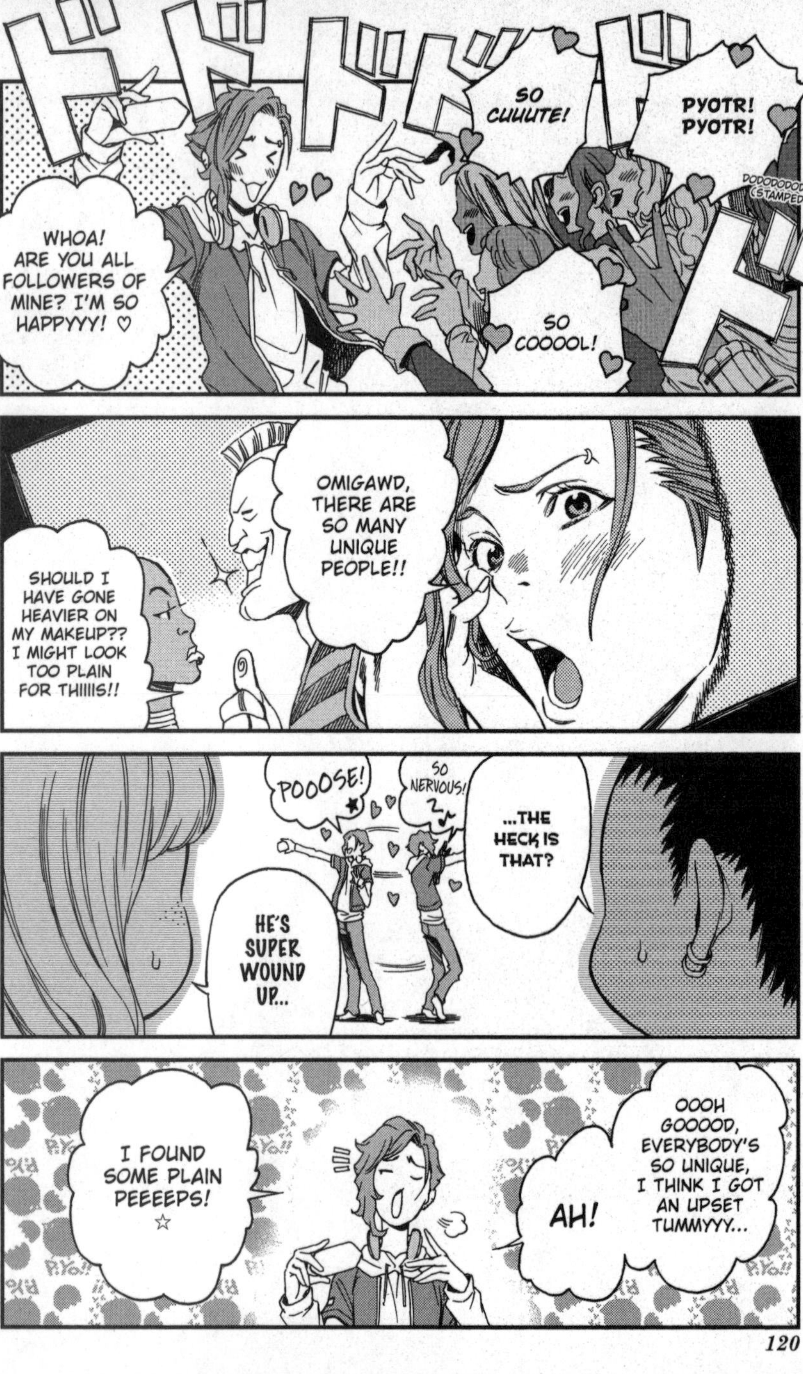
WHOA! ARE YOU ALL FOLLOWERS OF MINE? I'M SO HAPPYYY! ♡
SO CUUUTE!
PYOTR! PYOTR!
DODODODODODO (STAMPEDE)
SO COOOOL!
SHOULD I HAVE GONE HEAVIER ON MY MAKEUP?? I MIGHT LOOK TOO PLAIN FOR THIIIIS!!
OMIGAWD, THERE ARE SO MANY UNIQUE PEOPLE!!
POOOSE!
SO NERVOUS!
HE'S SUPER WOUND UP...
...THE HECK IS THAT?
I FOUND SOME PLAIN PEEEEPS! ☆
AH!
OOOH GOOOOD, EVERYBODY'S SO UNIQUE, I THINK I GOT AN UPSET TUMMYYY...

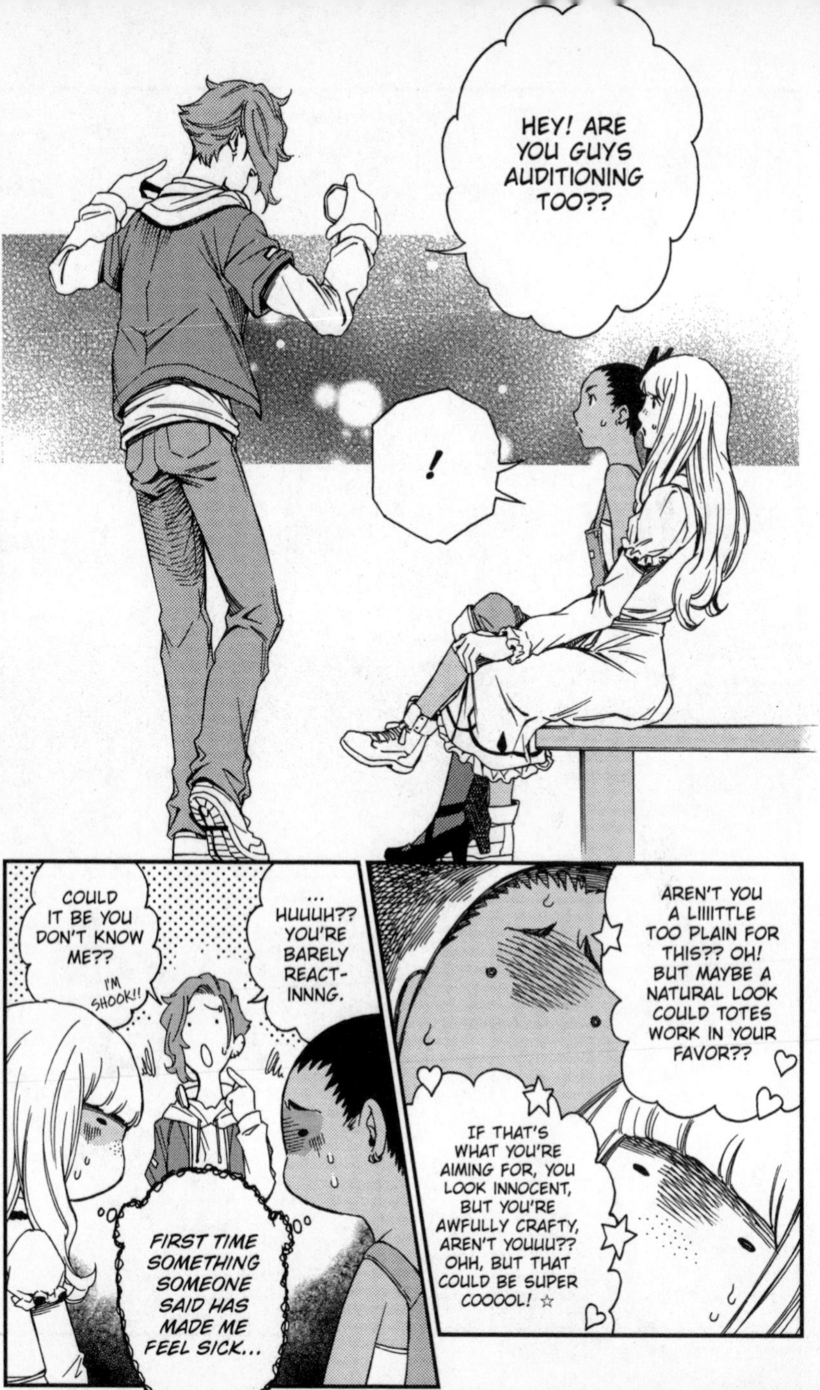
HEY! ARE YOU GUYS AUDITIONING TOO??
!
AREN'T YOU A LIIIITTLE TOO PLAIN FOR THIS?? OH! BUT MAYBE A NATURAL LOOK COULD TOTES WORK IN YOUR FAVOR??
IF THAT'S WHAT YOU'RE AIMING FOR, YOU LOOK INNOCENT, BUT YOU'RE AWFULLY CRAFTY, AREN'T YOUUU?? OHH, BUT THAT COULD BE SUPER COOOOL! ☆
... HUUUH?? YOU'RE BARELY REACT-INNNG.
COULD IT BE YOU DON'T KNOW ME??
I'M SHOOK!!
FIRST TIME SOMETHING SOMEONE SAID HAS MADE ME FEEL SICK...

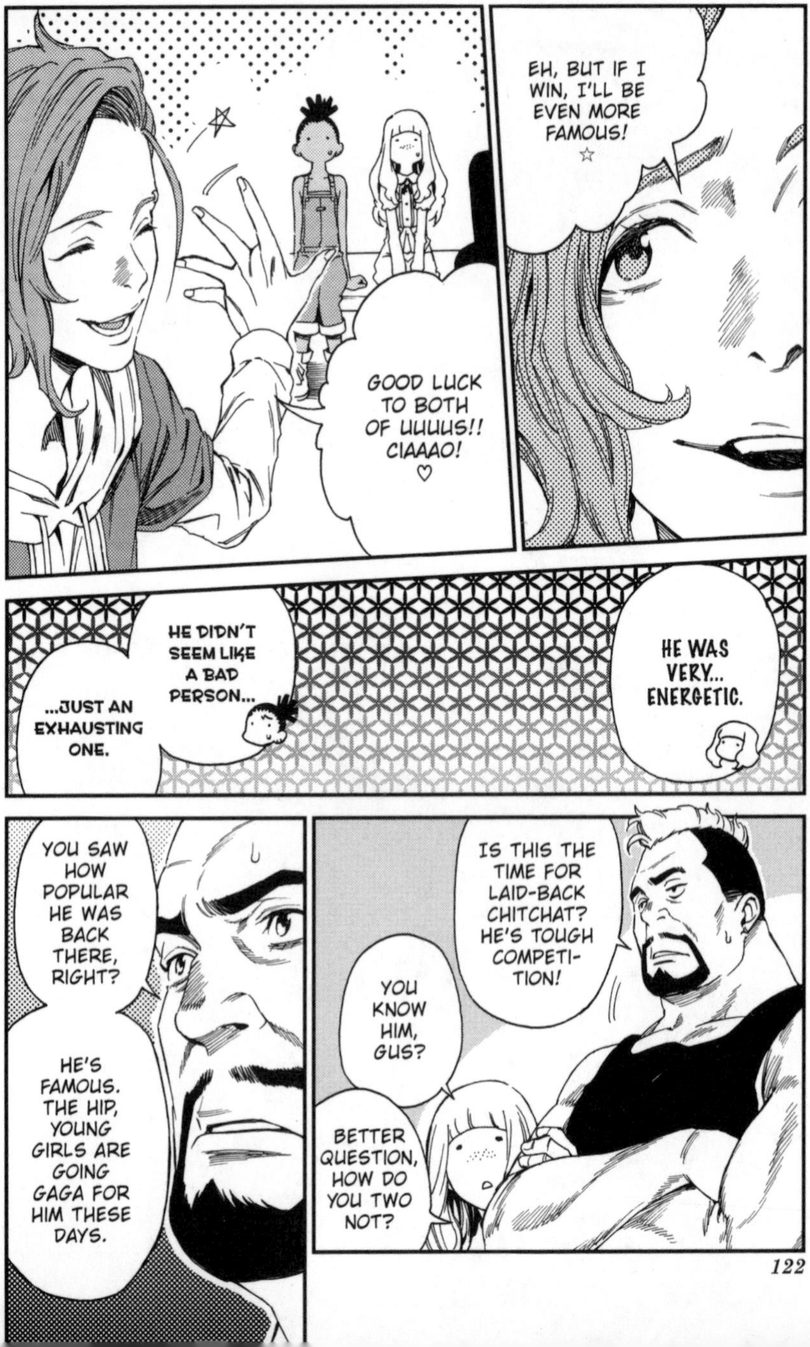
EH, BUT IF I WIN, I'LL BE EVEN MORE FAMOUS! ☆
GOOD LUCK TO BOTH OF UUUUS!! CIAAAO! ♡
HE WAS VERY... ENERGETIC.
HE DIDN'T SEEM LIKE A BAD PERSON...
...JUST AN EXHAUSTING ONE.
IS THIS THE TIME FOR LAID-BACK CHITCHAT? HE'S TOUGH COMPETITION!
YOU KNOW HIM, GUS?
BETTER QUESTION, HOW DO YOU TWO NOT?
YOU SAW HOW POPULAR HE WAS BACK THERE, RIGHT?
HE'S FAMOUS. THE HIP, YOUNG GIRLS ARE GOING GAGA FOR HIM THESE DAYS.

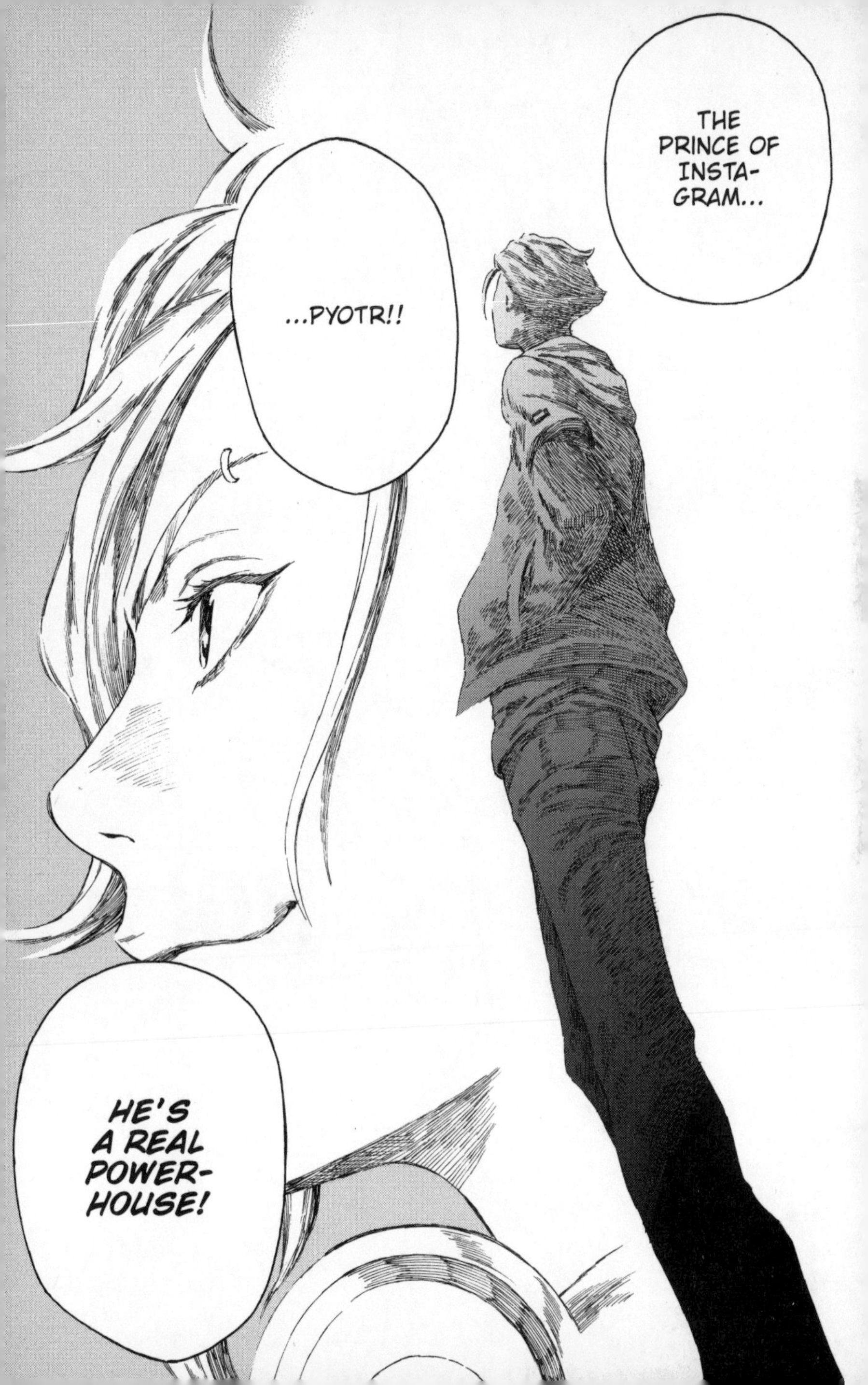
THE PRINCE OF INSTA-GRAM...
...PYOTR!!
HE'S A REAL POWER-HOUSE!

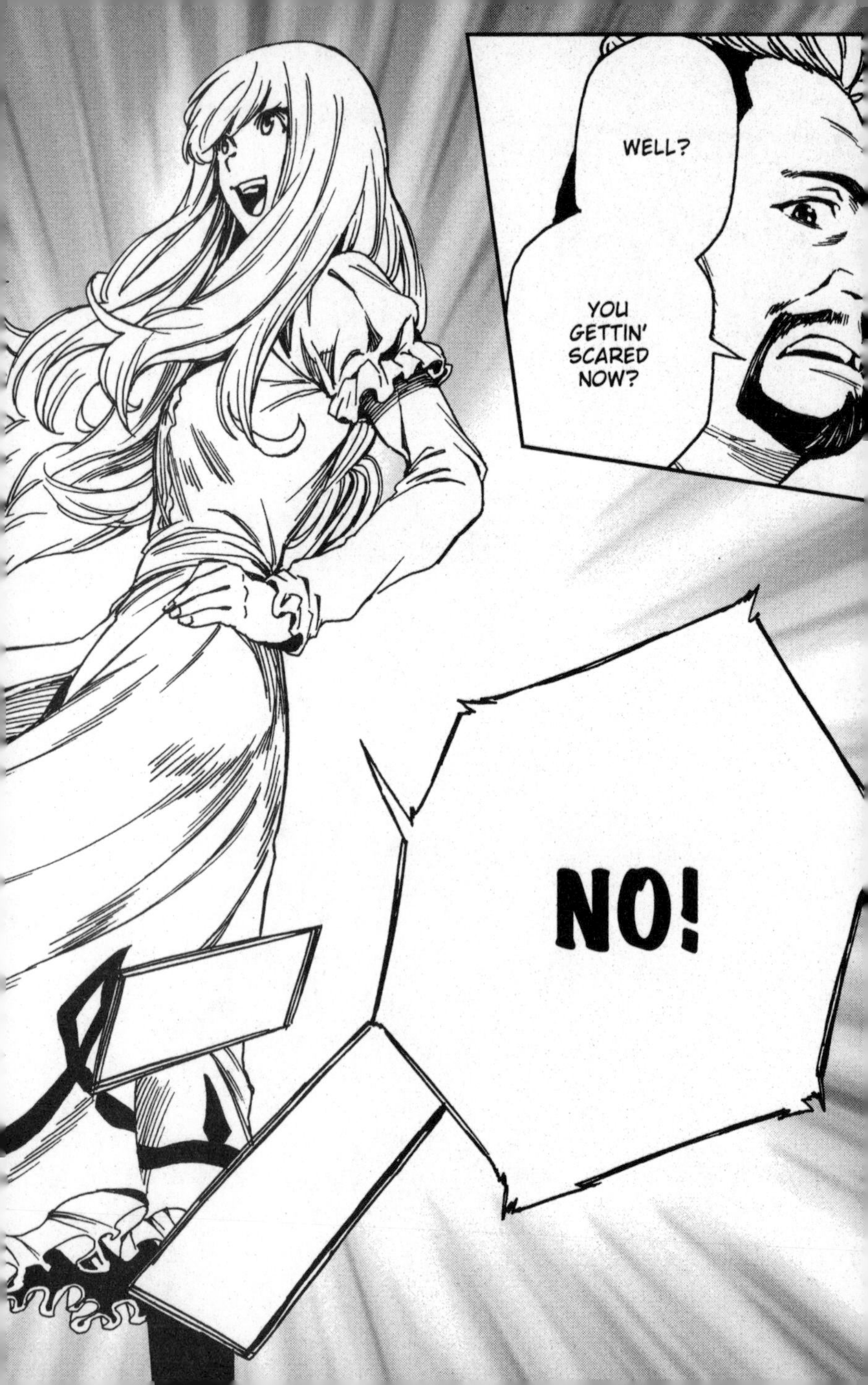
WELL?
YOU GETTIN' SCARED NOW?
NO!

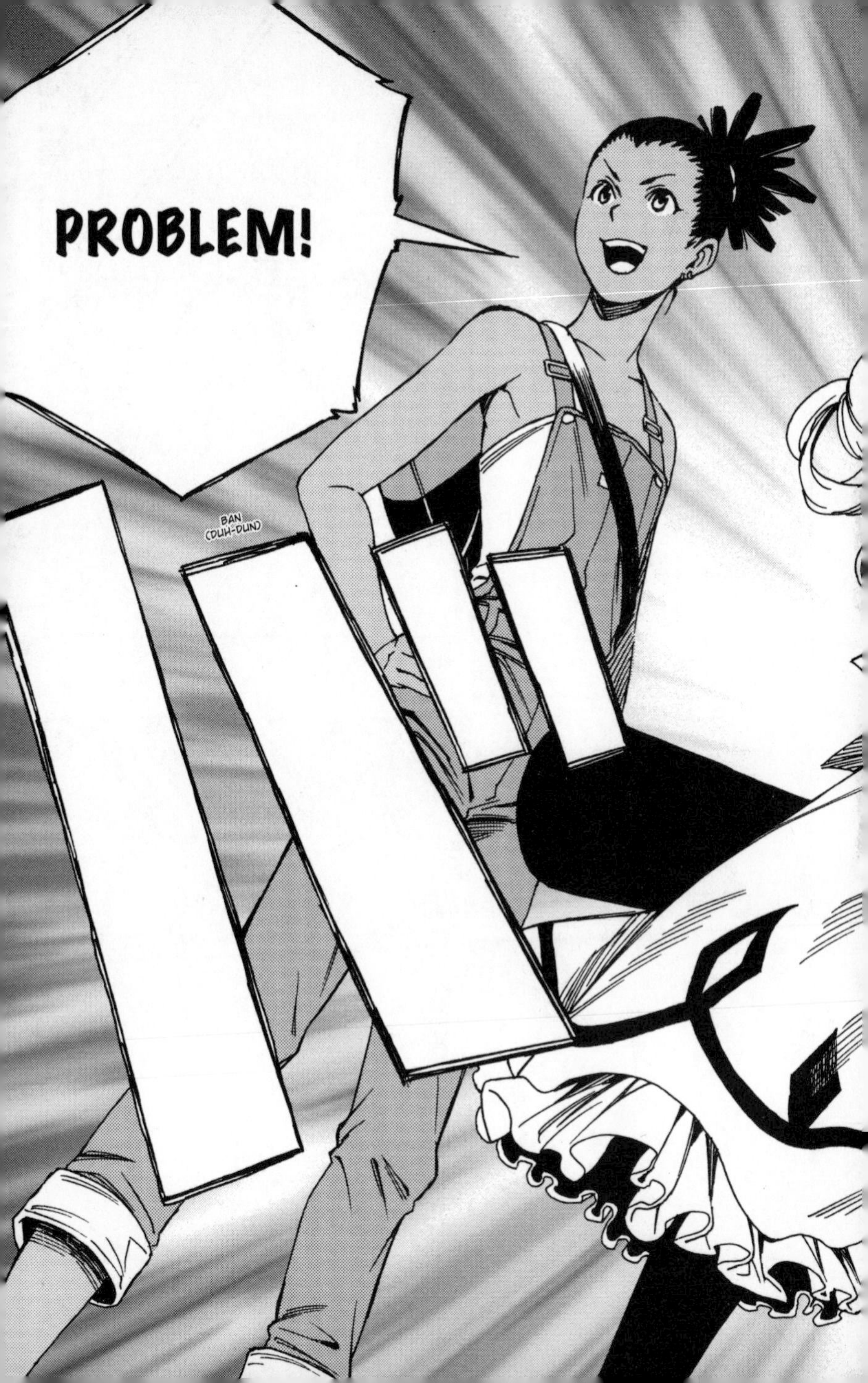
PROBLEM!
BAN
(DUH-DUN)

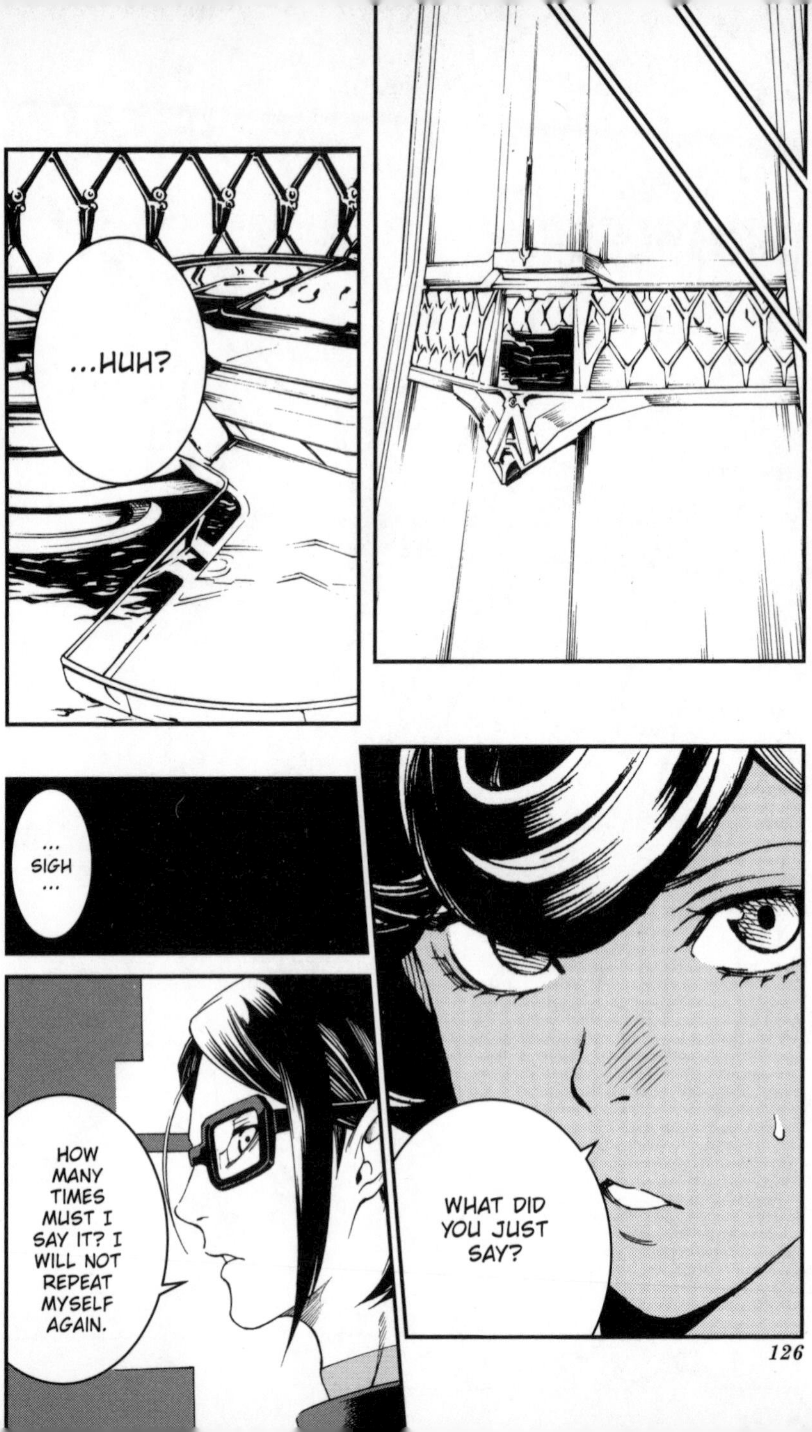
...HUH?
WHAT DID YOU JUST SAY?
... SIGH ...
HOW MANY TIMES MUST I SAY IT? I WILL NOT REPEAT MYSELF AGAIN.

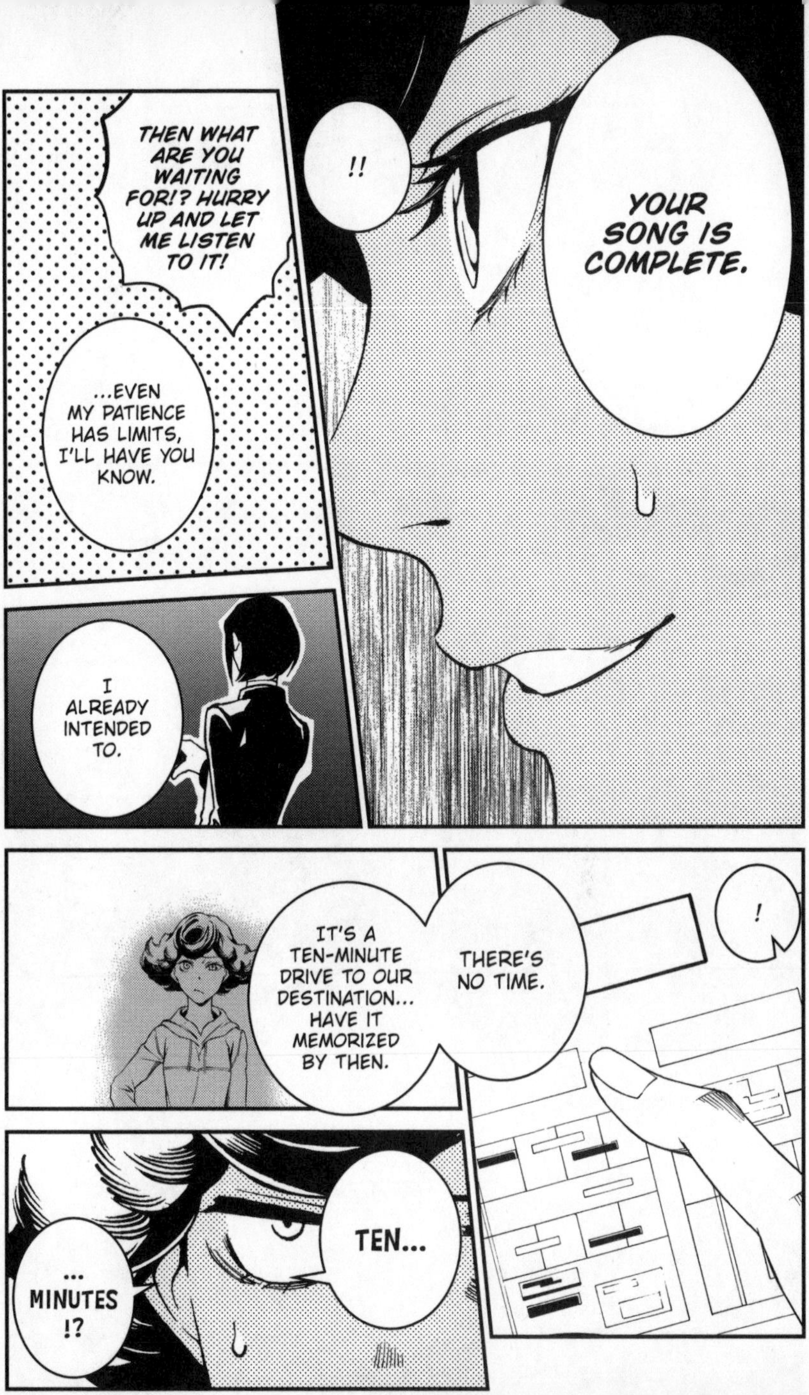
YOUR SONG IS COMPLETE.
!!
THEN WHAT ARE YOU WAITING FOR!? HURRY UP AND LET ME LISTEN TO IT!
...EVEN MY PATIENCE HAS LIMITS, I'LL HAVE YOU KNOW.
I ALREADY INTENDED TO.
!
THERE'S NO TIME.
IT'S A TEN-MINUTE DRIVE TO OUR DESTINATION... HAVE IT MEMORIZED BY THEN.
TEN...
...MINUTES!?

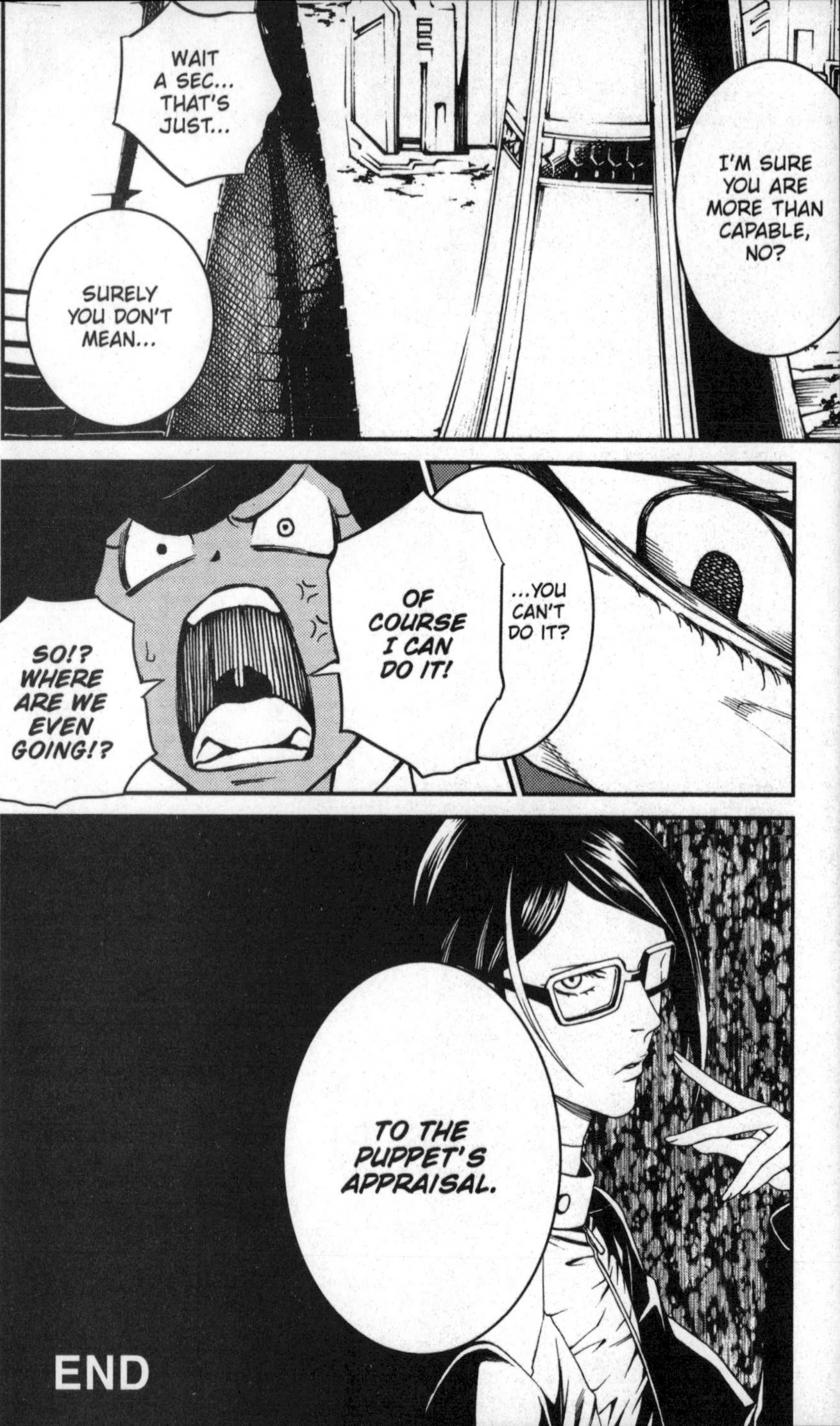
I'M SURE YOU ARE MORE THAN CAPABLE, NO?
WAIT A SEC... THAT'S JUST...
SURELY YOU DON'T MEAN...
...YOU CAN'T DO IT?
OF COURSE I CAN DO IT!
SO!? WHERE ARE WE EVEN GOING!?
TO THE PUPPET'S APPRAISAL.
END

CAROLE & TUESDAY

CAROLE
& TUES
DAY

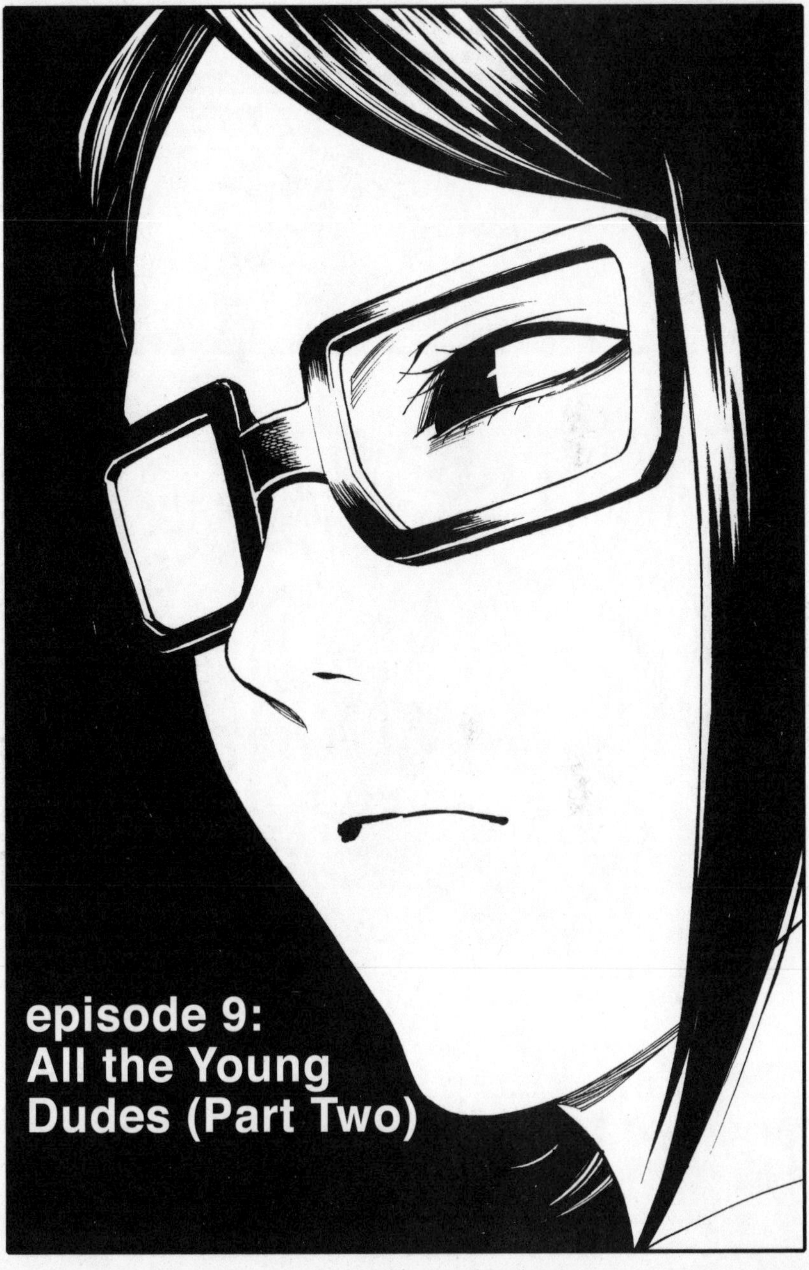
episode 9:
All the Young
Dudes (Part Two)

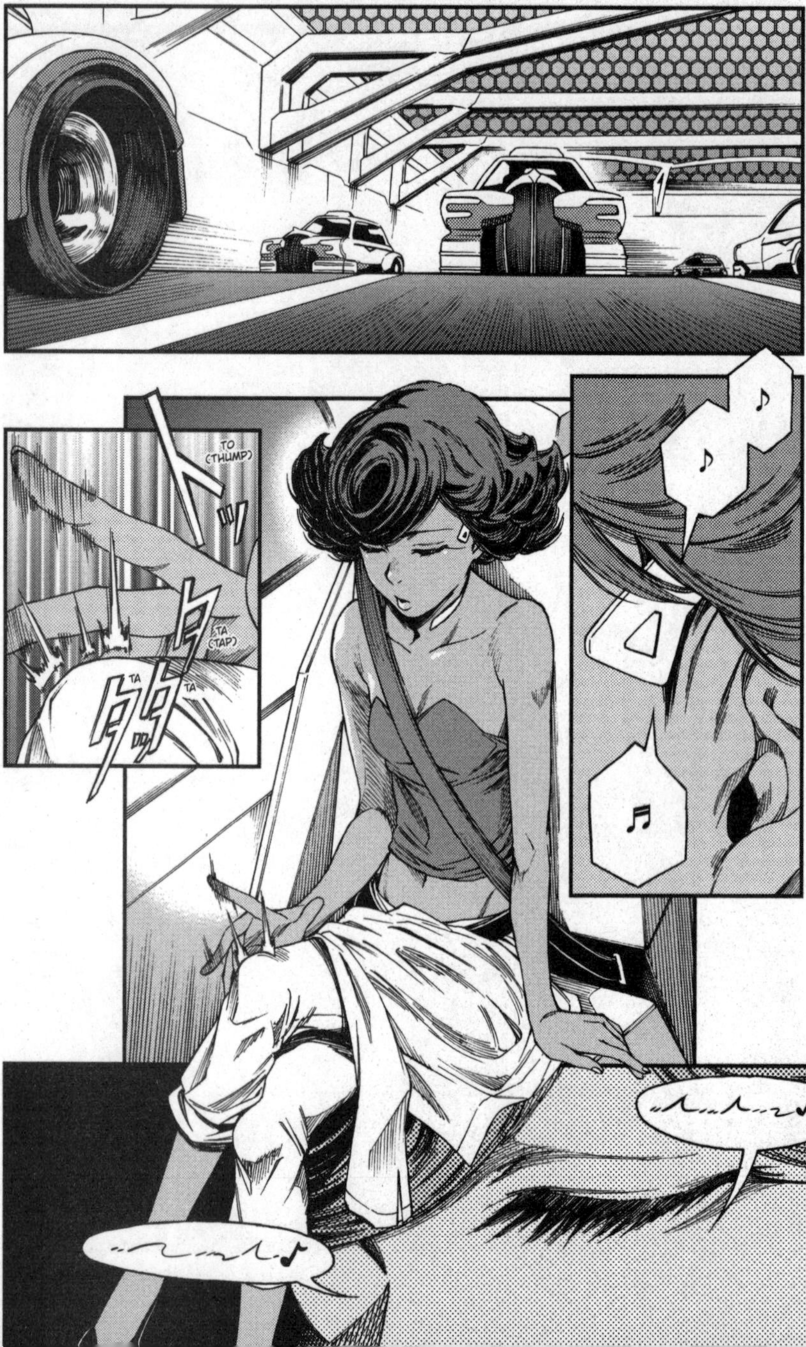
TO (THUMP)
TA (TAP)
TA
TA

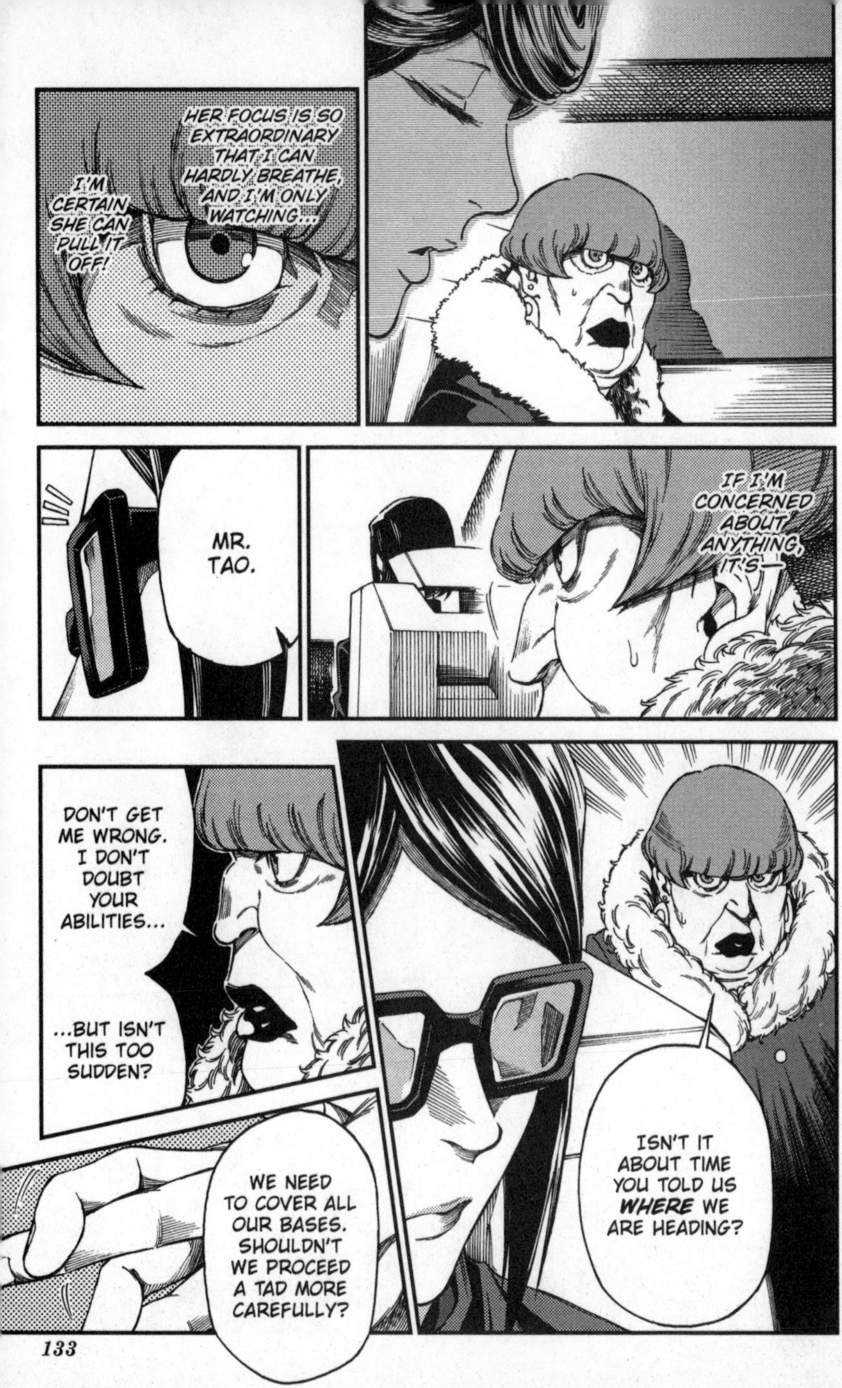
HER FOCUS IS SO EXTRAORDINARY THAT I CAN HARDLY BREATHE, AND I'M ONLY WATCHING...
I'M CERTAIN SHE CAN PULL IT OFF!
IF I'M CONCERNED ABOUT ANYTHING, IT'S—
MR. TAO.
ISN'T IT ABOUT TIME YOU TOLD US ***WHERE*** WE ARE HEADING?
DON'T GET ME WRONG. I DON'T DOUBT YOUR ABILITIES...
...BUT ISN'T THIS TOO SUDDEN?
WE NEED TO COVER ALL OUR BASES. SHOULDN'T WE PROCEED A TAD MORE CAREFULLY?

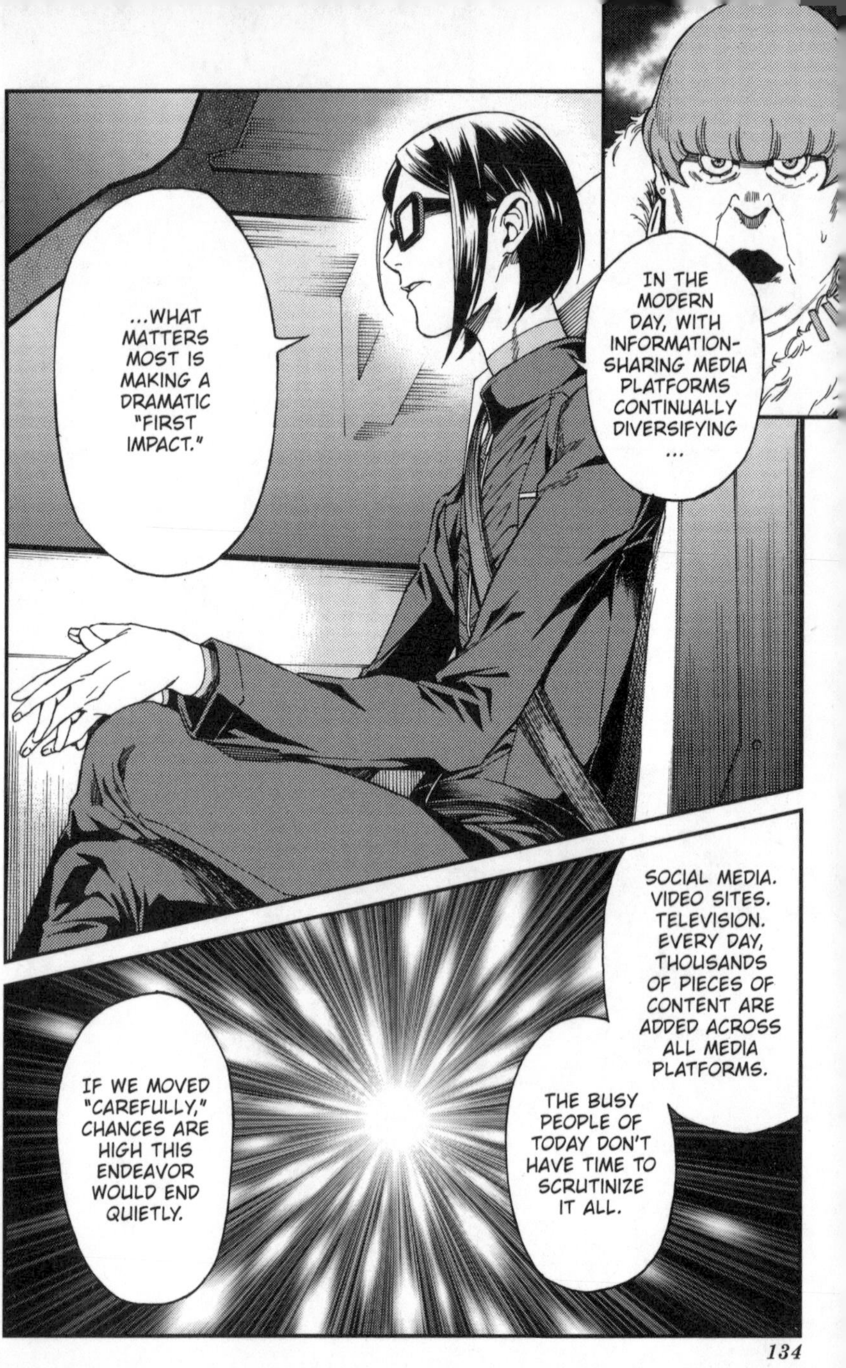
IN THE MODERN DAY, WITH INFORMATION-SHARING MEDIA PLATFORMS CONTINUALLY DIVERSIFYING ...
...WHAT MATTERS MOST IS MAKING A DRAMATIC "FIRST IMPACT."
SOCIAL MEDIA. VIDEO SITES. TELEVISION. EVERY DAY, THOUSANDS OF PIECES OF CONTENT ARE ADDED ACROSS ALL MEDIA PLATFORMS.
THE BUSY PEOPLE OF TODAY DON'T HAVE TIME TO SCRUTINIZE IT ALL.
IF WE MOVED "CAREFULLY," CHANCES ARE HIGH THIS ENDEAVOR WOULD END QUIETLY.

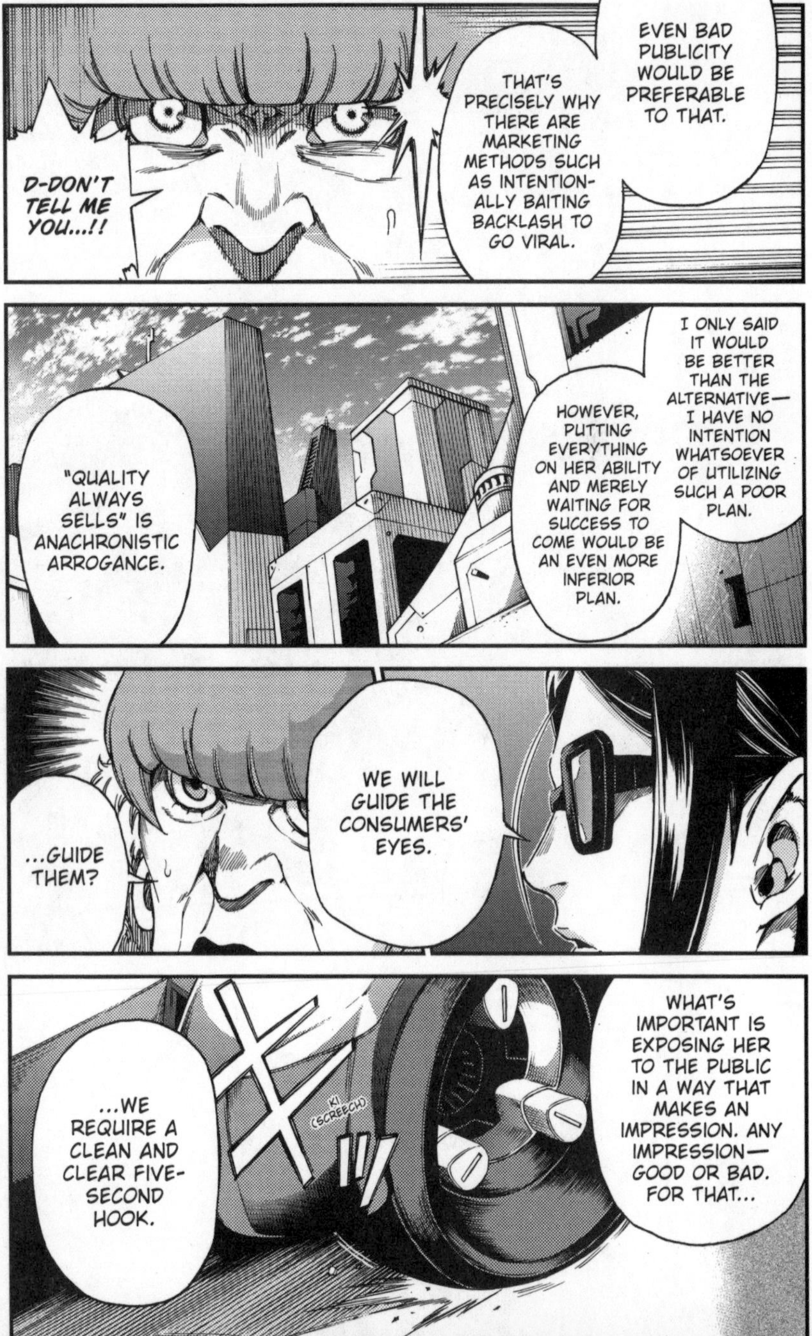
EVEN BAD PUBLICITY WOULD BE PREFERABLE TO THAT.
THAT'S PRECISELY WHY THERE ARE MARKETING METHODS SUCH AS INTENTION-ALLY BAITING BACKLASH TO GO VIRAL.
D-DON'T TELL ME YOU...!!
I ONLY SAID IT WOULD BE BETTER THAN THE ALTERNATIVE—I HAVE NO INTENTION WHATSOEVER OF UTILIZING SUCH A POOR PLAN.
HOWEVER, PUTTING EVERYTHING ON HER ABILITY AND MERELY WAITING FOR SUCCESS TO COME WOULD BE AN EVEN MORE INFERIOR PLAN.
"QUALITY ALWAYS SELLS" IS ANACHRONISTIC ARROGANCE.
WE WILL GUIDE THE CONSUMERS' EYES.
...GUIDE THEM?
WHAT'S IMPORTANT IS EXPOSING HER TO THE PUBLIC IN A WAY THAT MAKES AN IMPRESSION. ANY IMPRESSION—GOOD OR BAD. FOR THAT...
KI (SCREECH)
...WE REQUIRE A CLEAN AND CLEAR FIVE-SECOND HOOK.

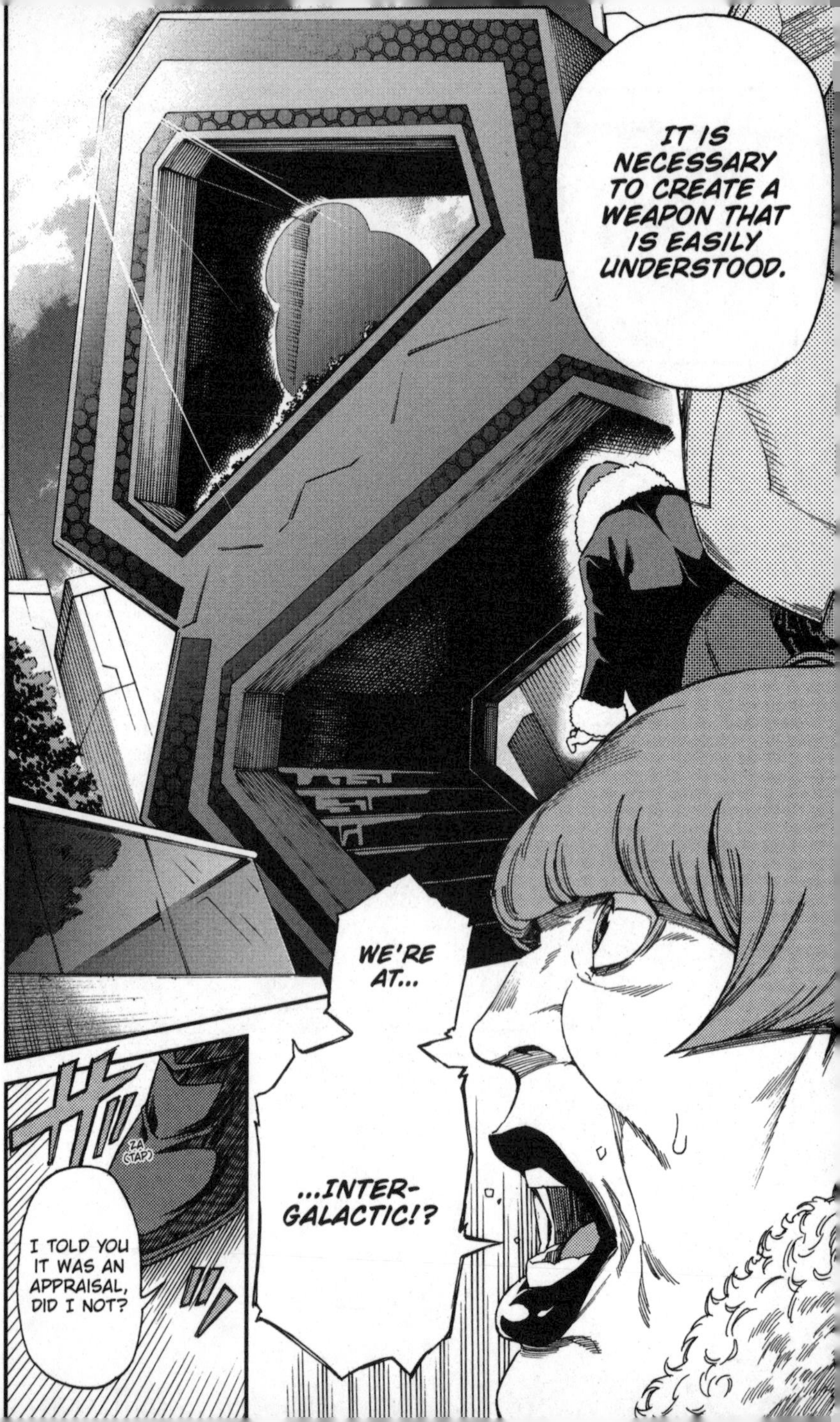
IT IS NECESSARY TO CREATE A WEAPON THAT IS EASILY UNDERSTOOD.
WE'RE AT...
...INTER-GALACTIC!?
ZA (STAP)
I TOLD YOU IT WAS AN APPRAISAL, DID I NOT?

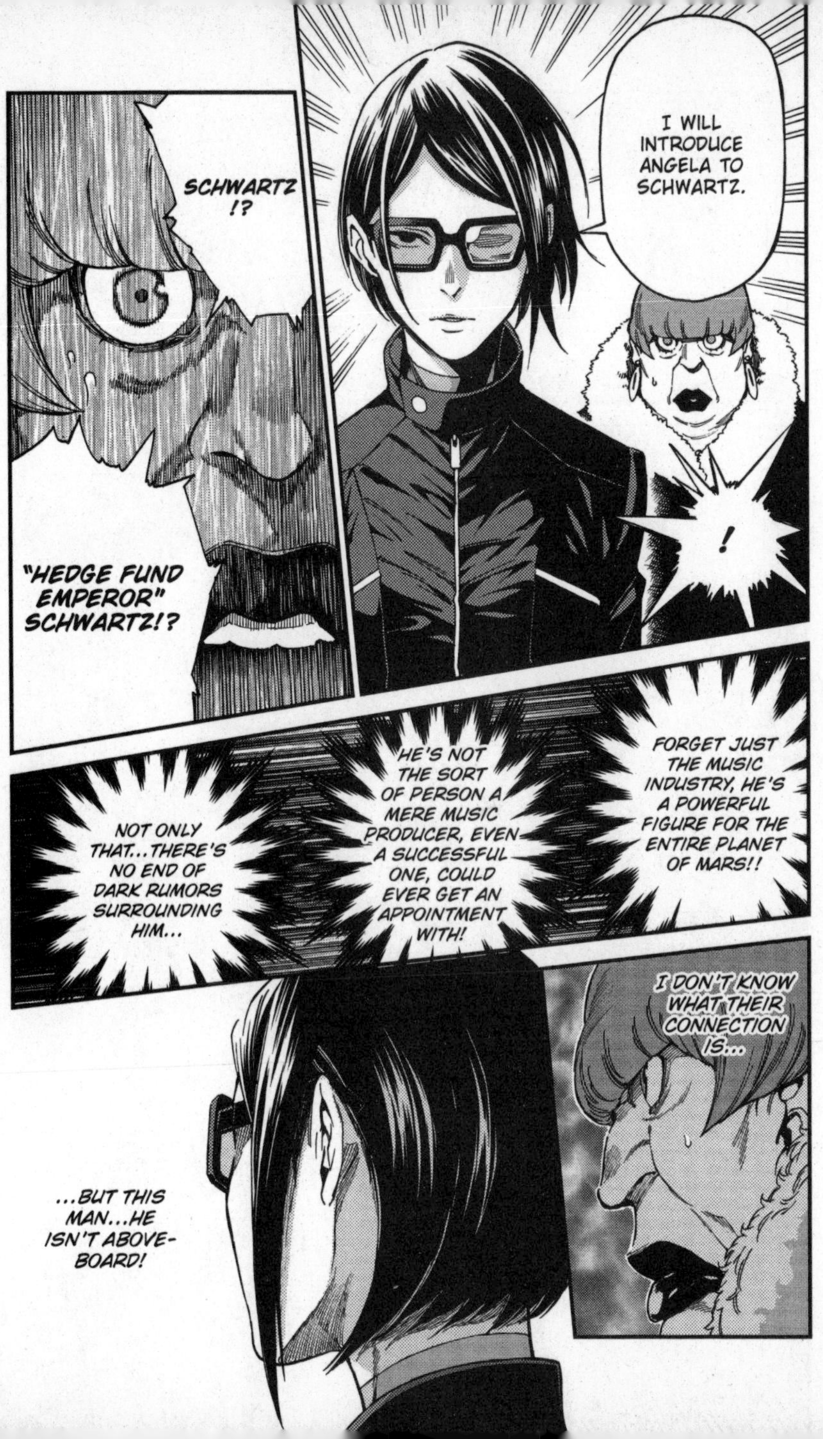
I WILL INTRODUCE ANGELA TO SCHWARTZ.
!
SCHWARTZ !?
"HEDGE FUND EMPEROR" SCHWARTZ!?
FORGET JUST THE MUSIC INDUSTRY, HE'S A POWERFUL FIGURE FOR THE ENTIRE PLANET OF MARS!!
HE'S NOT THE SORT OF PERSON A MERE MUSIC PRODUCER, EVEN A SUCCESSFUL ONE, COULD EVER GET AN APPOINTMENT WITH!
NOT ONLY THAT...THERE'S NO END OF DARK RUMORS SURROUNDING HIM...
I DON'T KNOW WHAT THEIR CONNECTION IS...
...BUT THIS MAN...HE ISN'T ABOVE-BOARD!

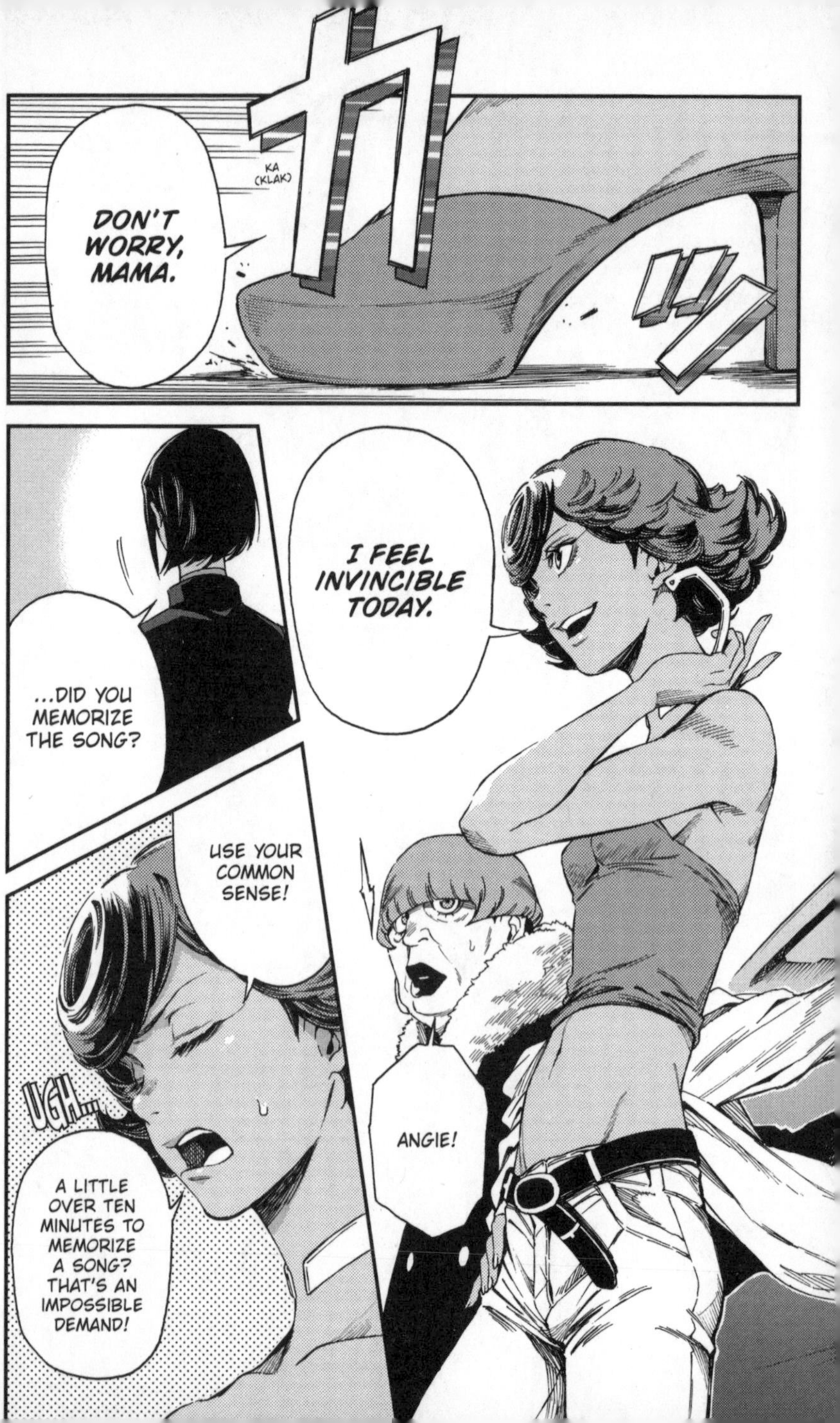
KA (KLAK)
DON'T WORRY, MAMA.
I FEEL INVINCIBLE TODAY.
ANGIE!
...DID YOU MEMORIZE THE SONG?
USE YOUR COMMON SENSE!
UGH...
A LITTLE OVER TEN MINUTES TO MEMORIZE A SONG? THAT'S AN IMPOSSIBLE DEMAND!

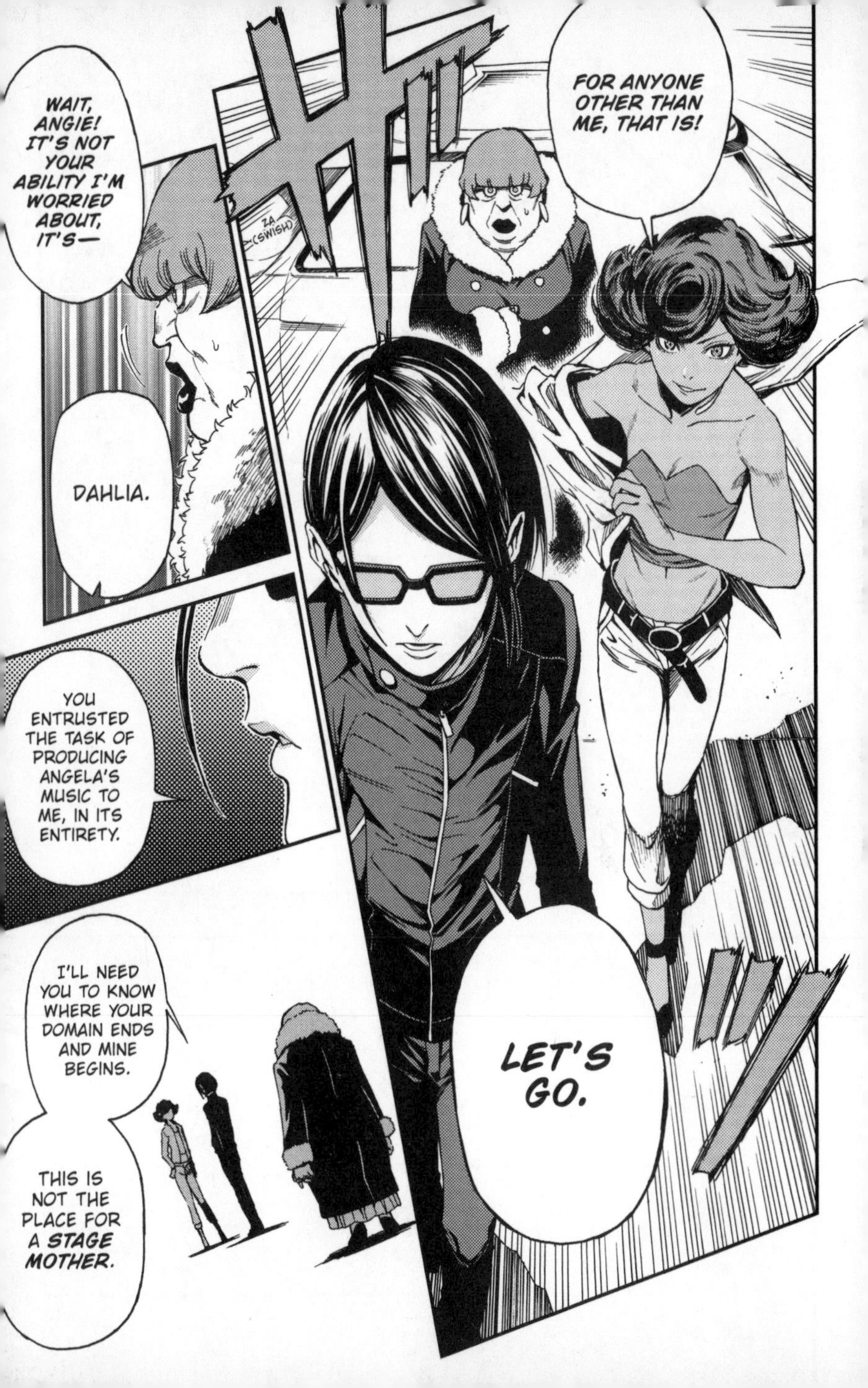
FOR ANYONE OTHER THAN ME, THAT IS!
ZA (SWISH)
WAIT, ANGIE! IT'S NOT YOUR ABILITY I'M WORRIED ABOUT, IT'S—
DAHLIA.
YOU ENTRUSTED THE TASK OF PRODUCING ANGELA'S MUSIC TO ME, IN ITS ENTIRETY.
I'LL NEED YOU TO KNOW WHERE YOUR DOMAIN ENDS AND MINE BEGINS.
THIS IS NOT THE PLACE FOR A STAGE MOTHER.
LET'S GO.

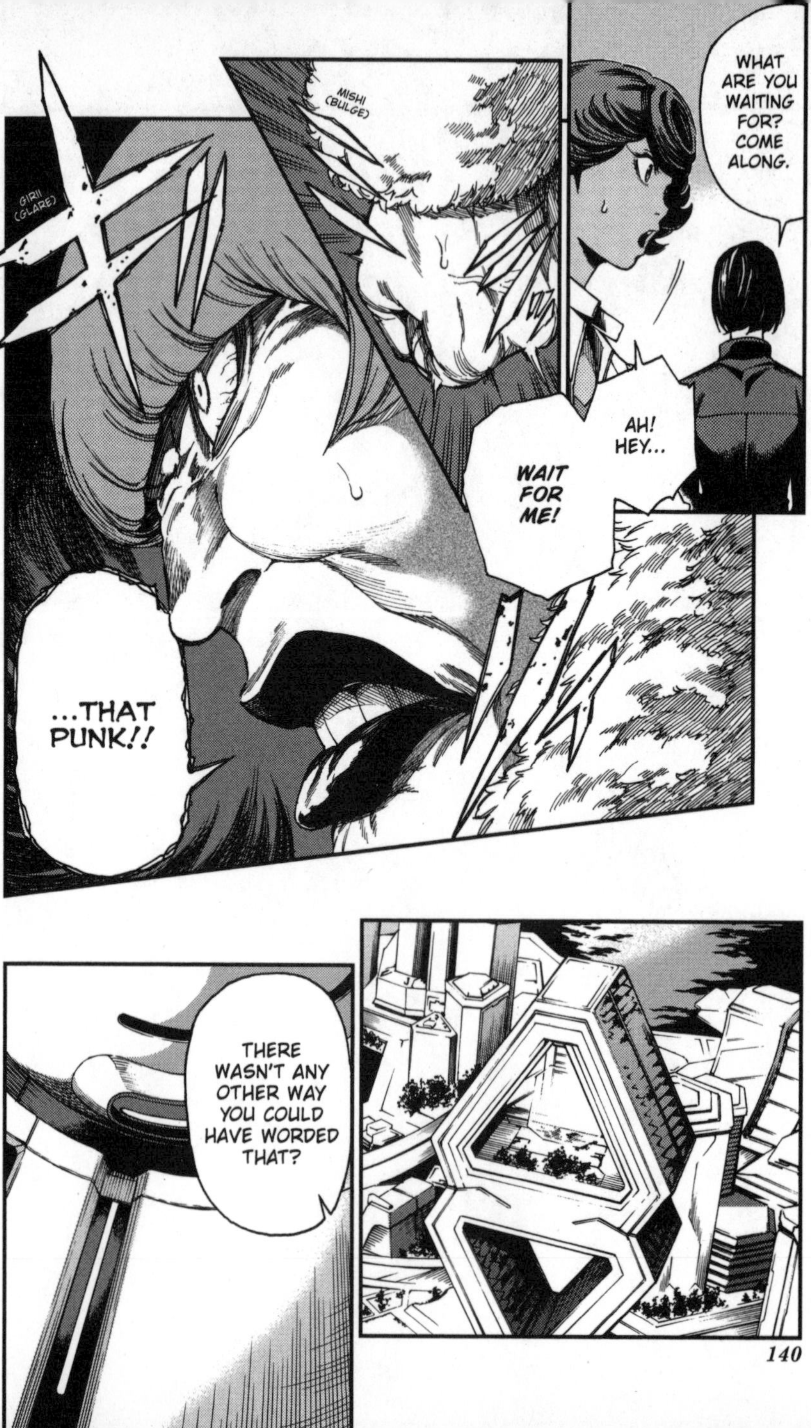
WHAT ARE YOU WAITING FOR? COME ALONG.
AH! HEY...
WAIT FOR ME!
MISHI (BULGE)
GIRII (GLARE)
...THAT PUNK!!
THERE WASN'T ANY OTHER WAY YOU COULD HAVE WORDED THAT?

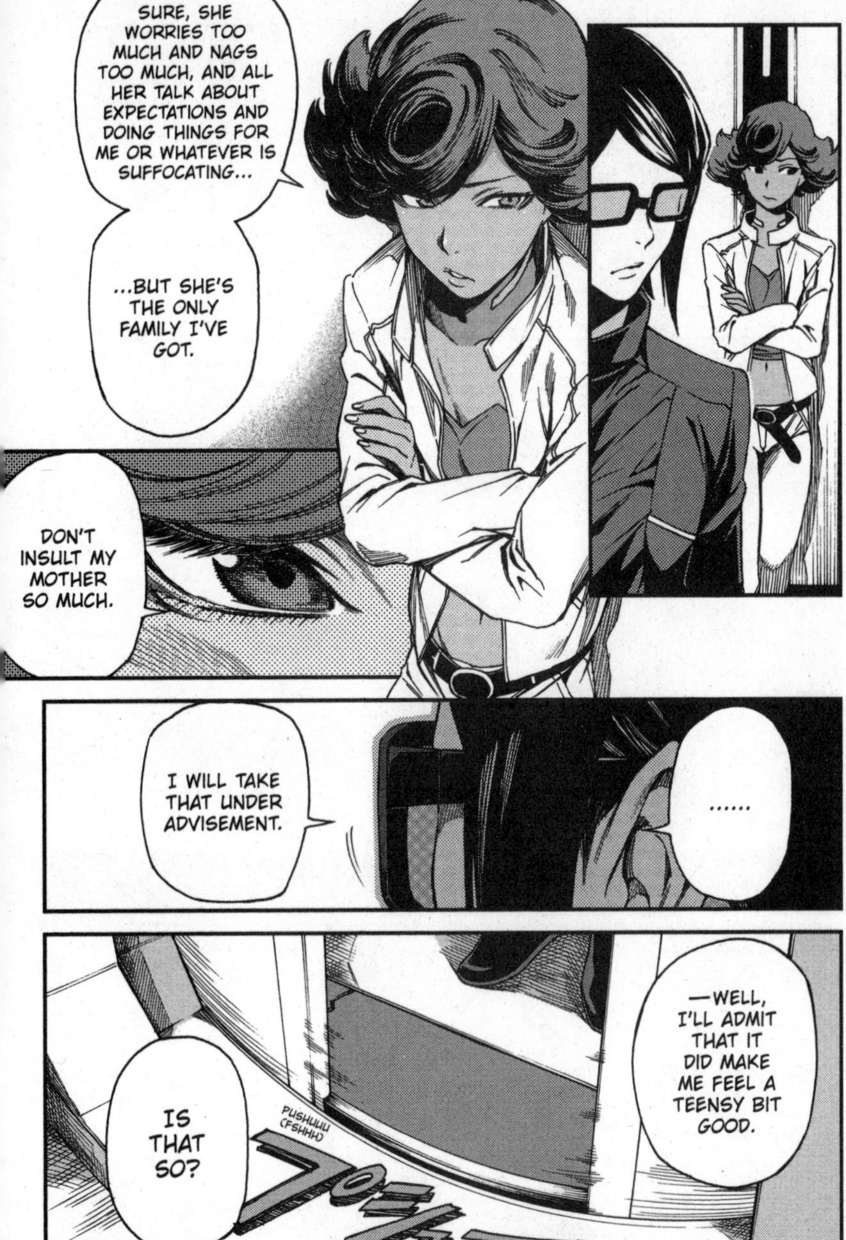
SURE, SHE WORRIES TOO MUCH AND NAGS TOO MUCH, AND ALL HER TALK ABOUT EXPECTATIONS AND DOING THINGS FOR ME OR WHATEVER IS SUFFOCATING...
...BUT SHE'S THE ONLY FAMILY I'VE GOT.
DON'T INSULT MY MOTHER SO MUCH.
......
I WILL TAKE THAT UNDER ADVISEMENT.
—WELL, I'LL ADMIT THAT IT DID MAKE ME FEEL A TEENSY BIT GOOD.
PUSHUUU (FSHHH)
IS THAT SO?

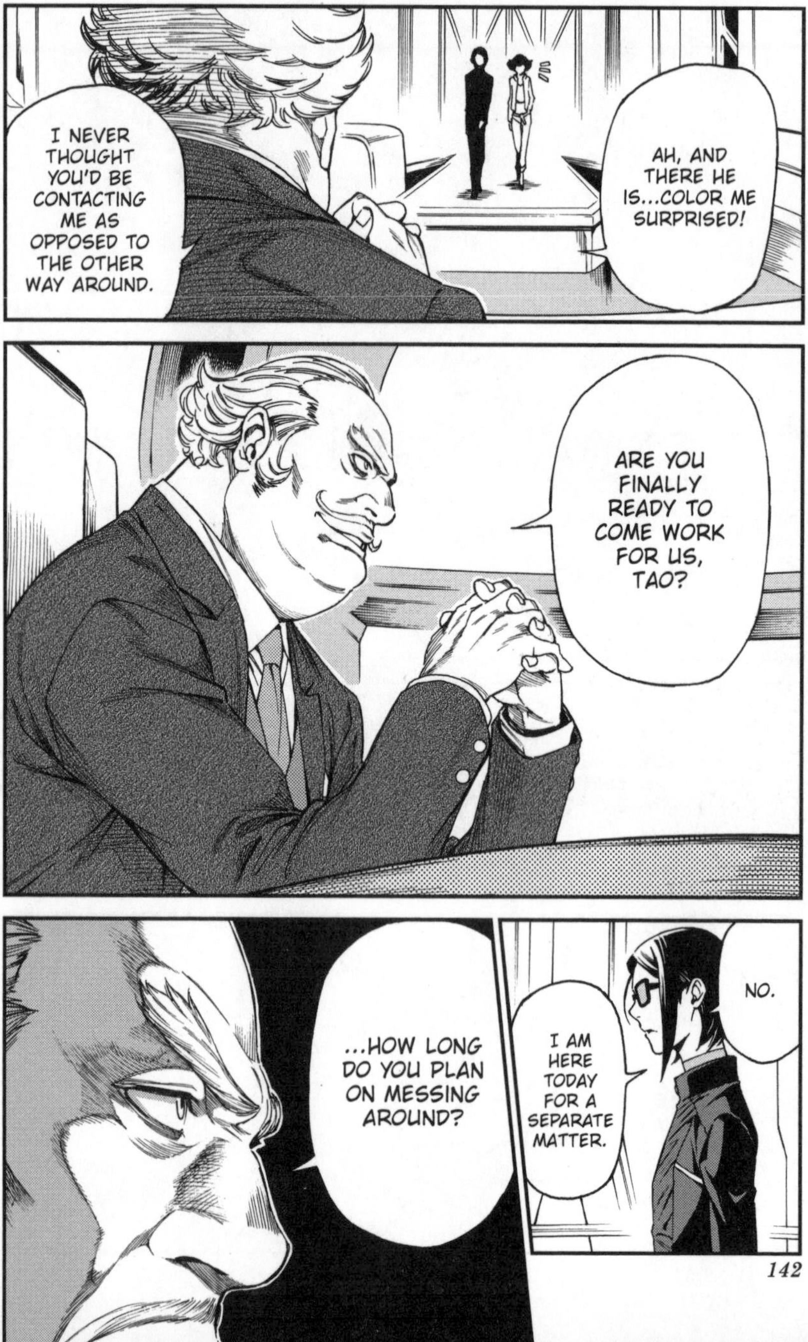
AH, AND THERE HE IS...COLOR ME SURPRISED!
I NEVER THOUGHT YOU'D BE CONTACTING ME AS OPPOSED TO THE OTHER WAY AROUND.
ARE YOU FINALLY READY TO COME WORK FOR US, TAO?
NO.
I AM HERE TODAY FOR A SEPARATE MATTER.
...HOW LONG DO YOU PLAN ON MESSING AROUND?

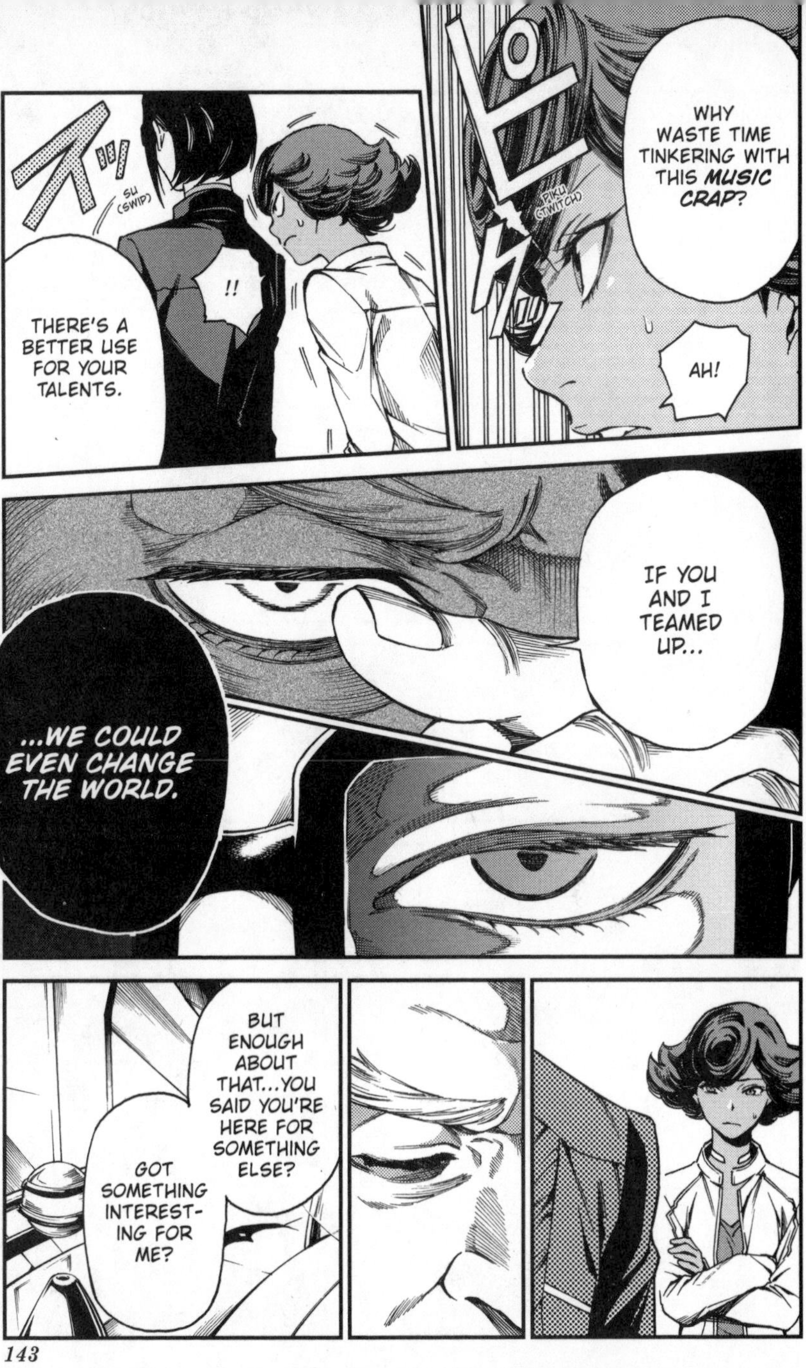
WHY WASTE TIME TINKERING WITH THIS MUSIC CRAP?
PIKU (TWITCH)
AH!
SU (SWIP)
!!
THERE'S A BETTER USE FOR YOUR TALENTS.
IF YOU AND I TEAMED UP...
...WE COULD EVEN CHANGE THE WORLD.
BUT ENOUGH ABOUT THAT...YOU SAID YOU'RE HERE FOR SOMETHING ELSE?
GOT SOMETHING INTERESTING FOR ME?

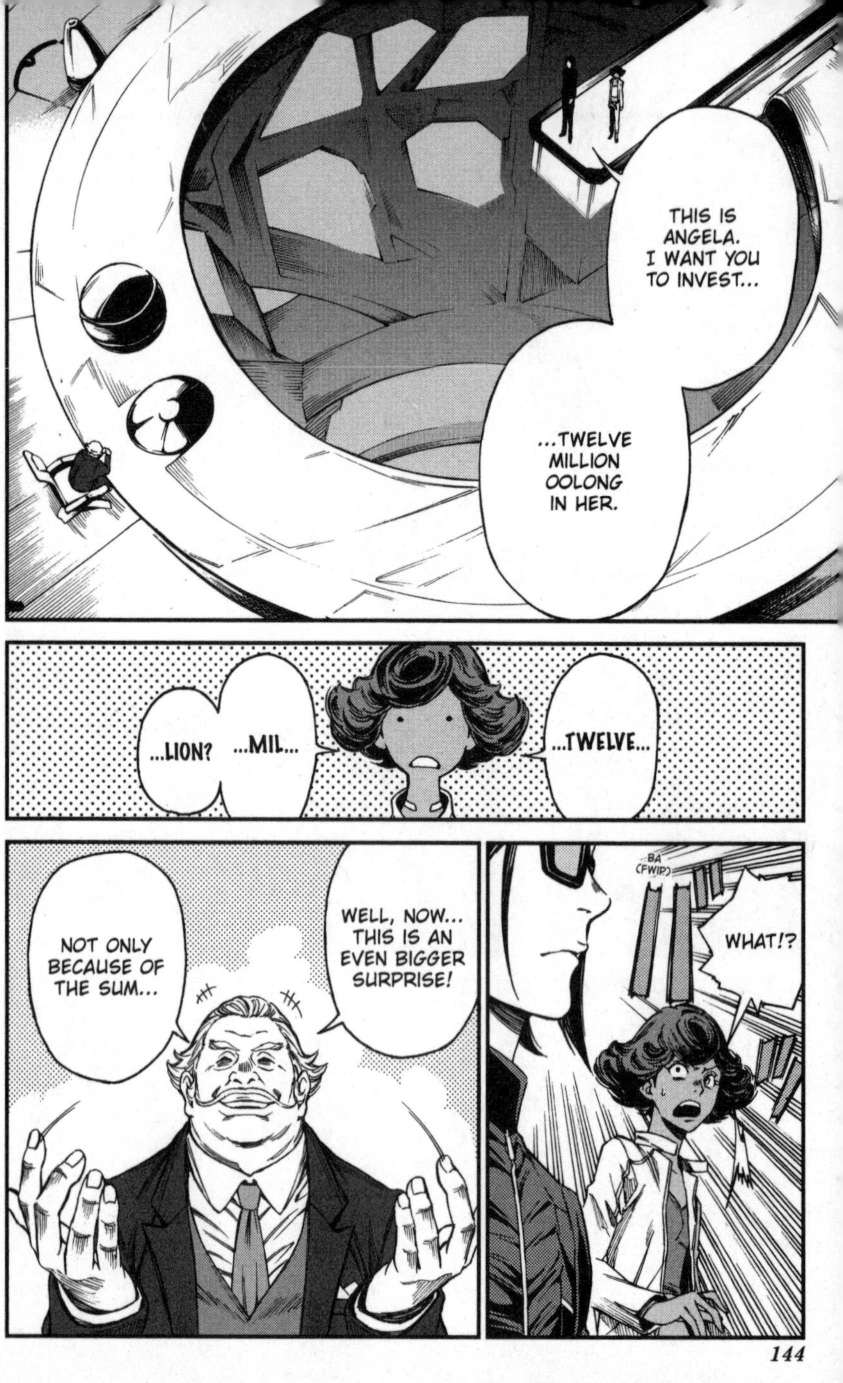
THIS IS ANGELA. I WANT YOU TO INVEST...
...TWELVE MILLION OOLONG IN HER.
...TWELVE...
...MIL...
...LION?
BA (FWIP)
WHAT!?
WELL, NOW... THIS IS AN EVEN BIGGER SURPRISE!
NOT ONLY BECAUSE OF THE SUM...

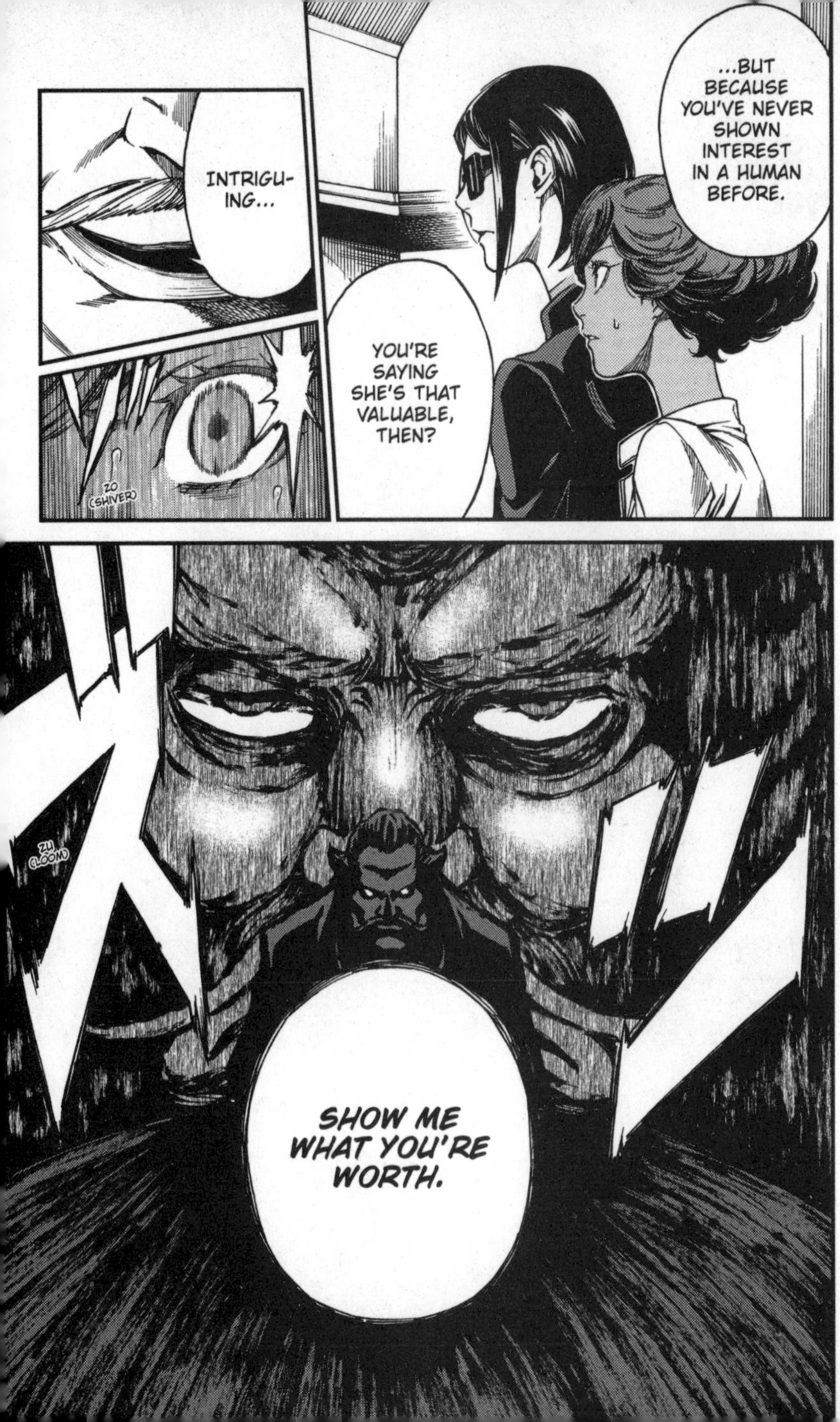
...BUT BECAUSE YOU'VE NEVER SHOWN INTEREST IN A HUMAN BEFORE.
YOU'RE SAYING SHE'S THAT VALUABLE, THEN?
INTRIGU-ING...
ZO (SHIVER)
ZU (LOOM)
SHOW ME WHAT YOU'RE WORTH.

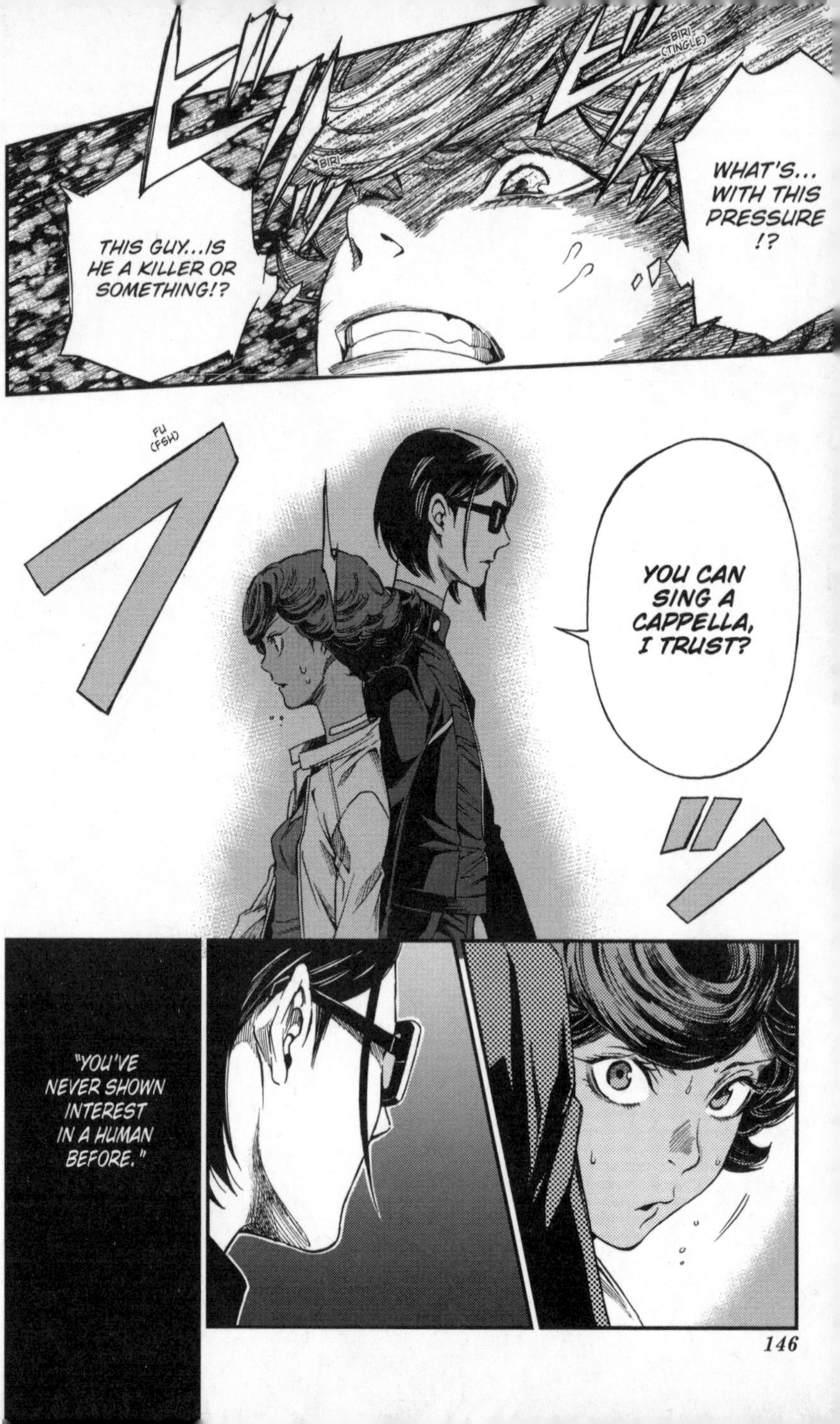
BIRI (TINGLE)
WHAT'S... WITH THIS PRESSURE !?
BIRI
THIS GUY...IS HE A KILLER OR SOMETHING!?
YOU CAN SING A CAPPELLA, I TRUST?
FU (FSH)
"YOU'VE NEVER SHOWN INTEREST IN A HUMAN BEFORE."

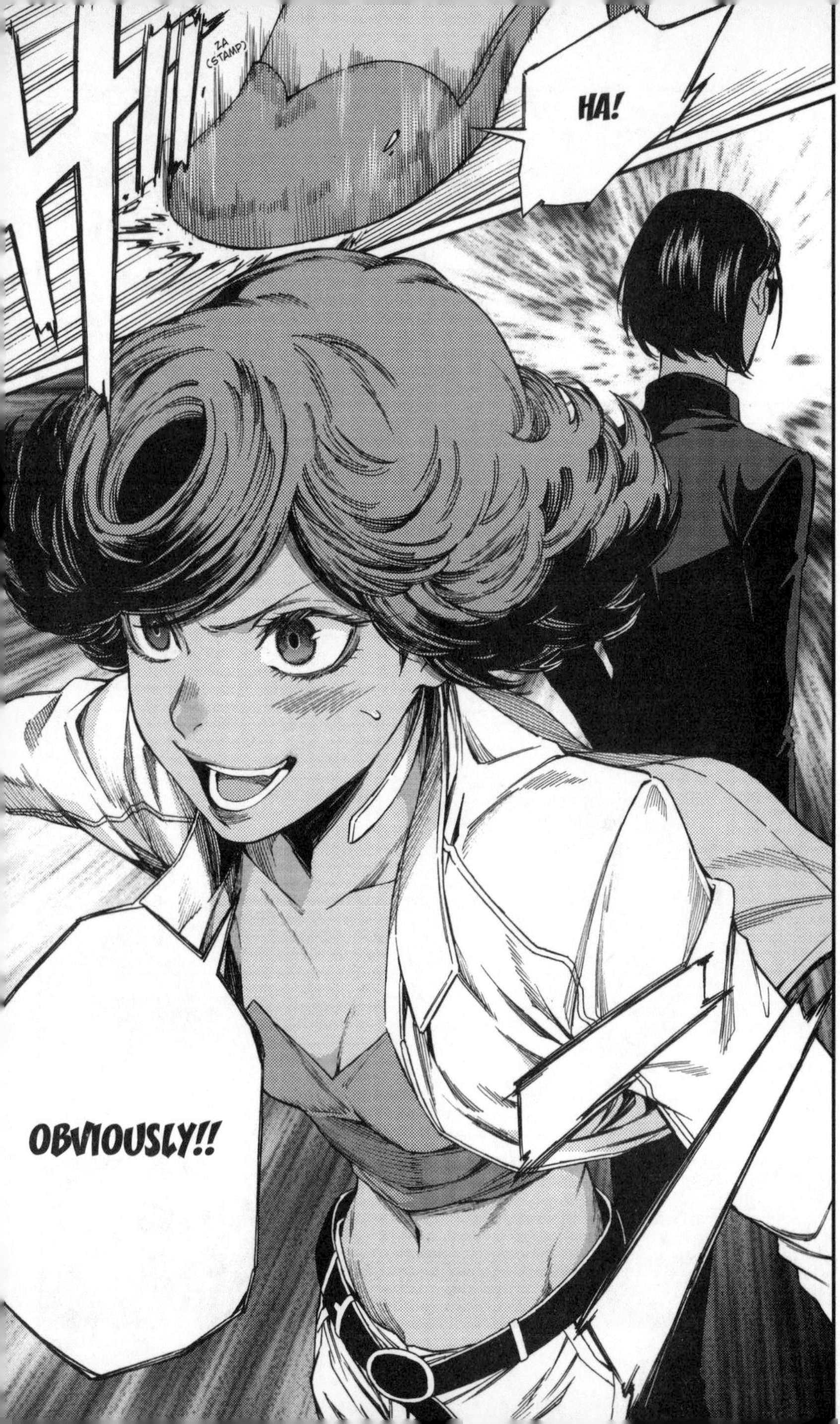
HA!
ZA (STAMP)
OBVIOUSLY!!

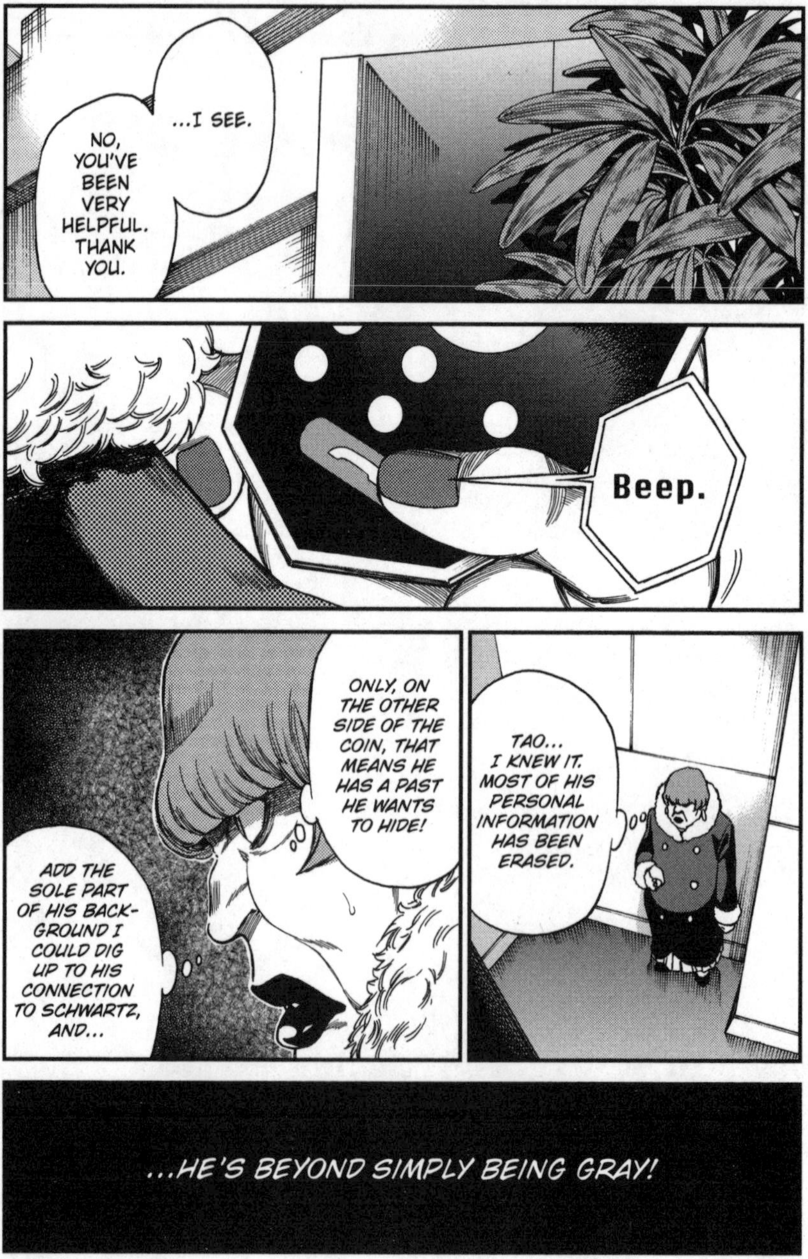
...I SEE.
NO, YOU'VE BEEN VERY HELPFUL. THANK YOU.
Beep.
TAO... I KNEW IT. MOST OF HIS PERSONAL INFORMATION HAS BEEN ERASED.
ONLY, ON THE OTHER SIDE OF THE COIN, THAT MEANS HE HAS A PAST HE WANTS TO HIDE!
ADD THE SOLE PART OF HIS BACK-GROUND I COULD DIG UP TO HIS CONNECTION TO SCHWARTZ, AND...
...HE'S BEYOND SIMPLY BEING GRAY!

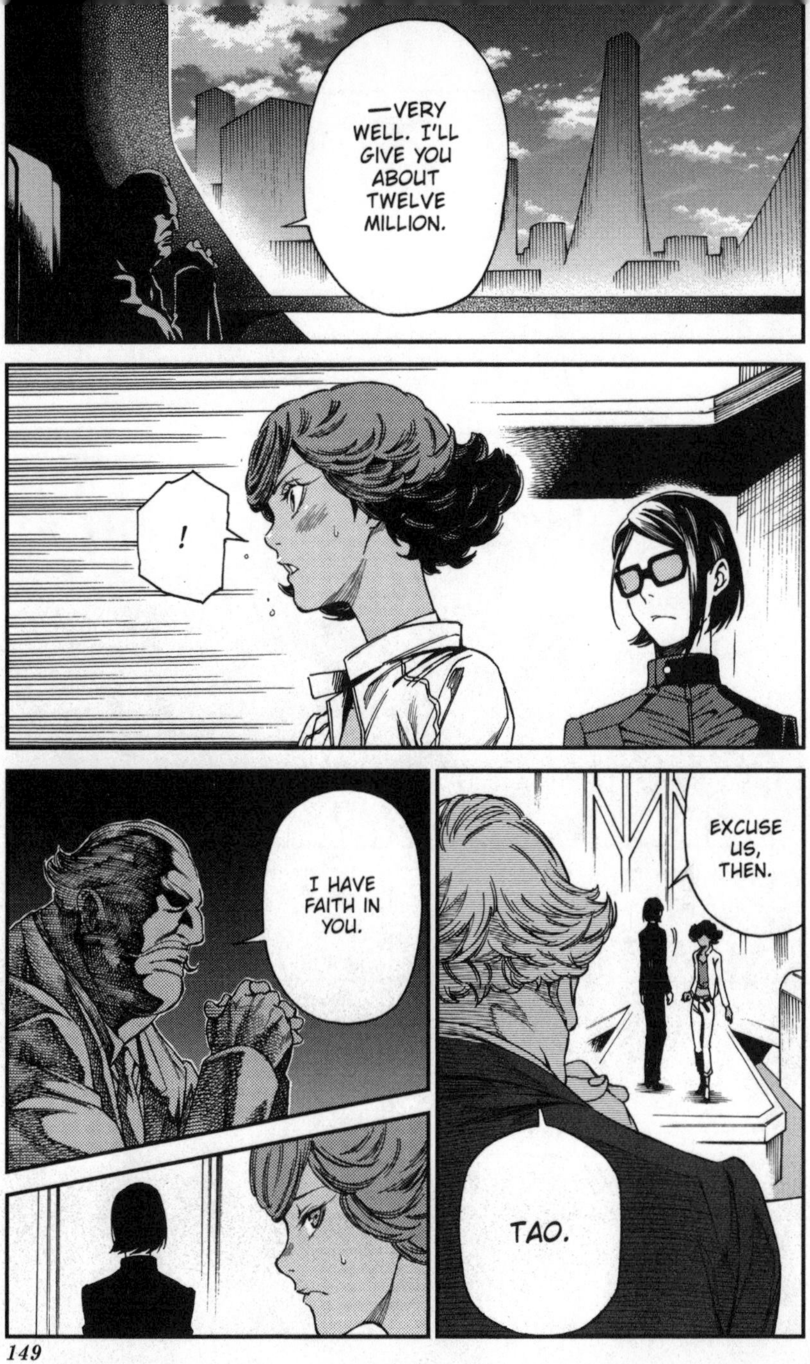
—VERY WELL. I'LL GIVE YOU ABOUT TWELVE MILLION.
!
EXCUSE US, THEN.
TAO.
I HAVE FAITH IN YOU.

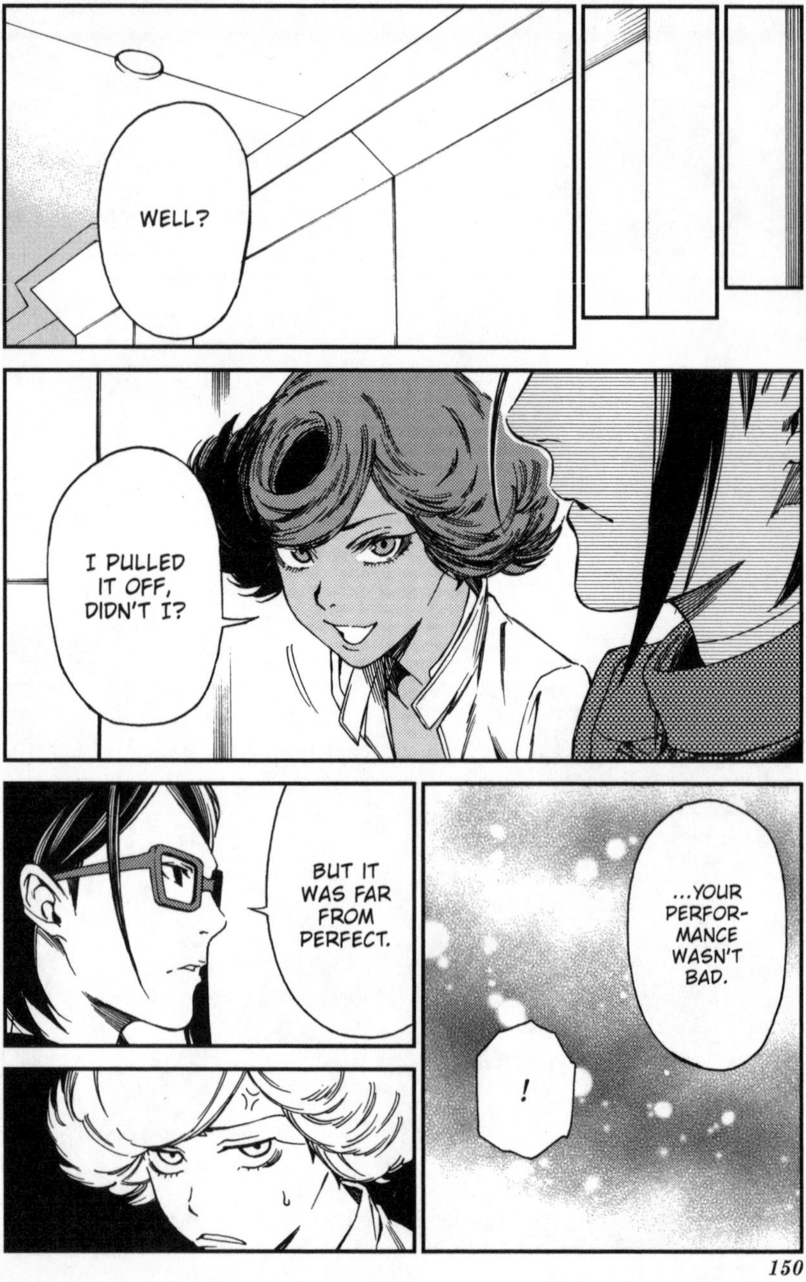
WELL?
I PULLED IT OFF, DIDN'T I?
...YOUR PERFORMANCE WASN'T BAD.
!
BUT IT WAS FAR FROM PERFECT.

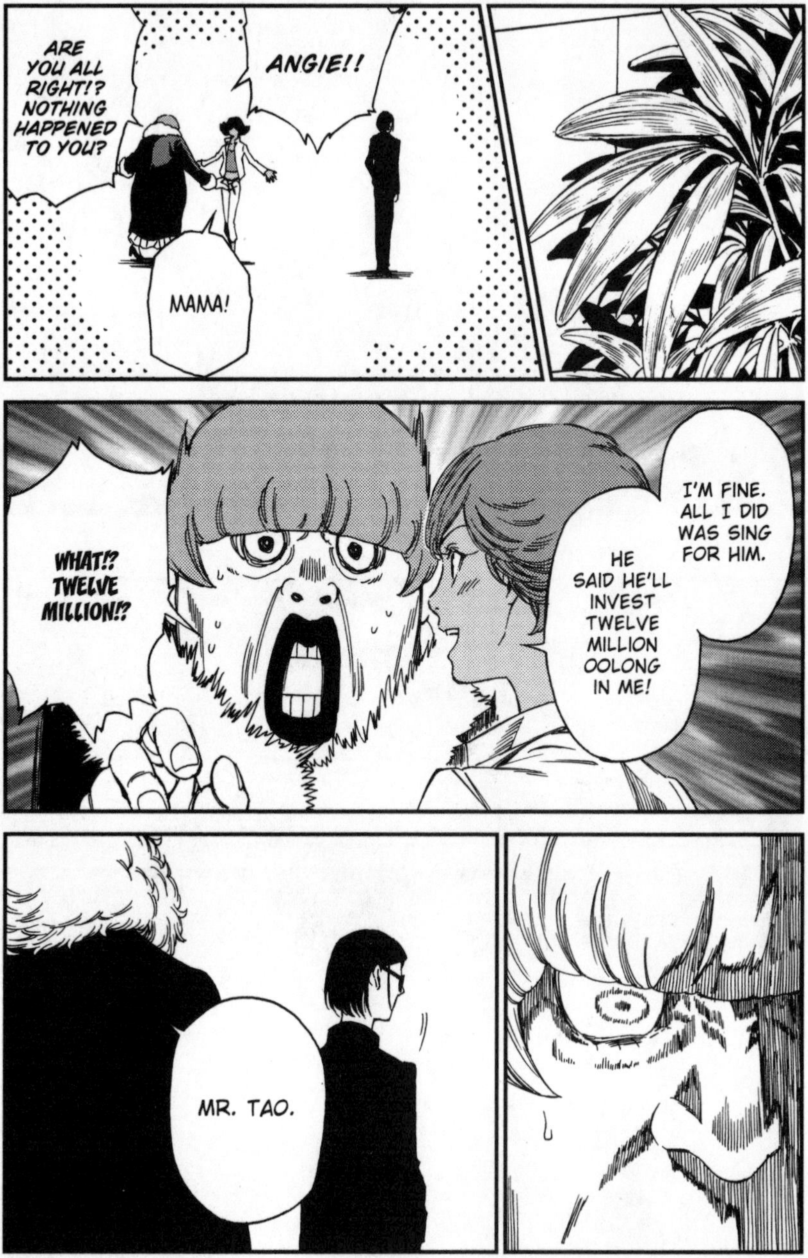
ANGIE!!
ARE YOU ALL RIGHT!? NOTHING HAPPENED TO YOU?
MAMA!
I'M FINE. ALL I DID WAS SING FOR HIM.
HE SAID HE'LL INVEST TWELVE MILLION OOLONG IN ME!
WHAT!? TWELVE MILLION!?
MR. TAO.

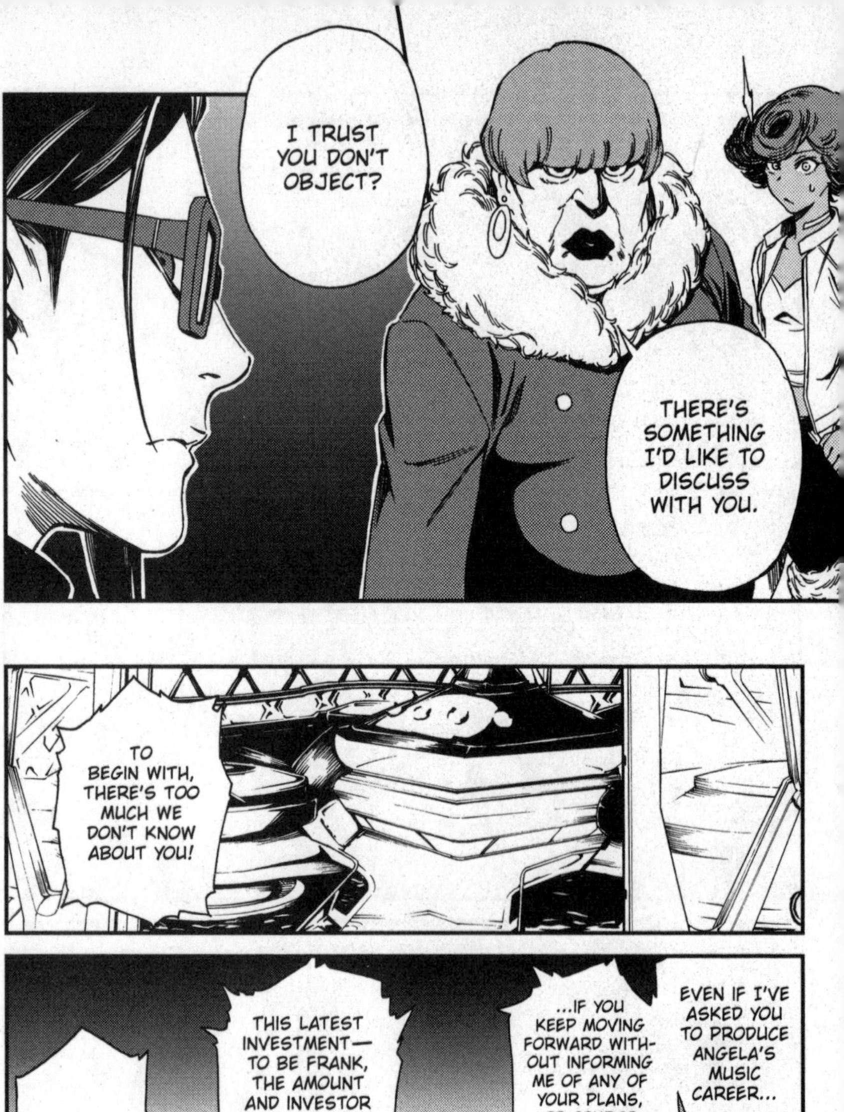
THERE'S SOMETHING I'D LIKE TO DISCUSS WITH YOU.
I TRUST YOU DON'T OBJECT?
TO BEGIN WITH, THERE'S TOO MUCH WE DON'T KNOW ABOUT YOU!
EVEN IF I'VE ASKED YOU TO PRODUCE ANGELA'S MUSIC CAREER...
...IF YOU KEEP MOVING FORWARD WITH-OUT INFORMING ME OF ANY OF YOUR PLANS, OF COURSE I'LL HAVE CONCERNS!
THIS LATEST INVESTMENT— TO BE FRANK, THE AMOUNT AND INVESTOR ARE BOTH TOO UNUSUAL!
IT'S SUSPI-CIOUS!

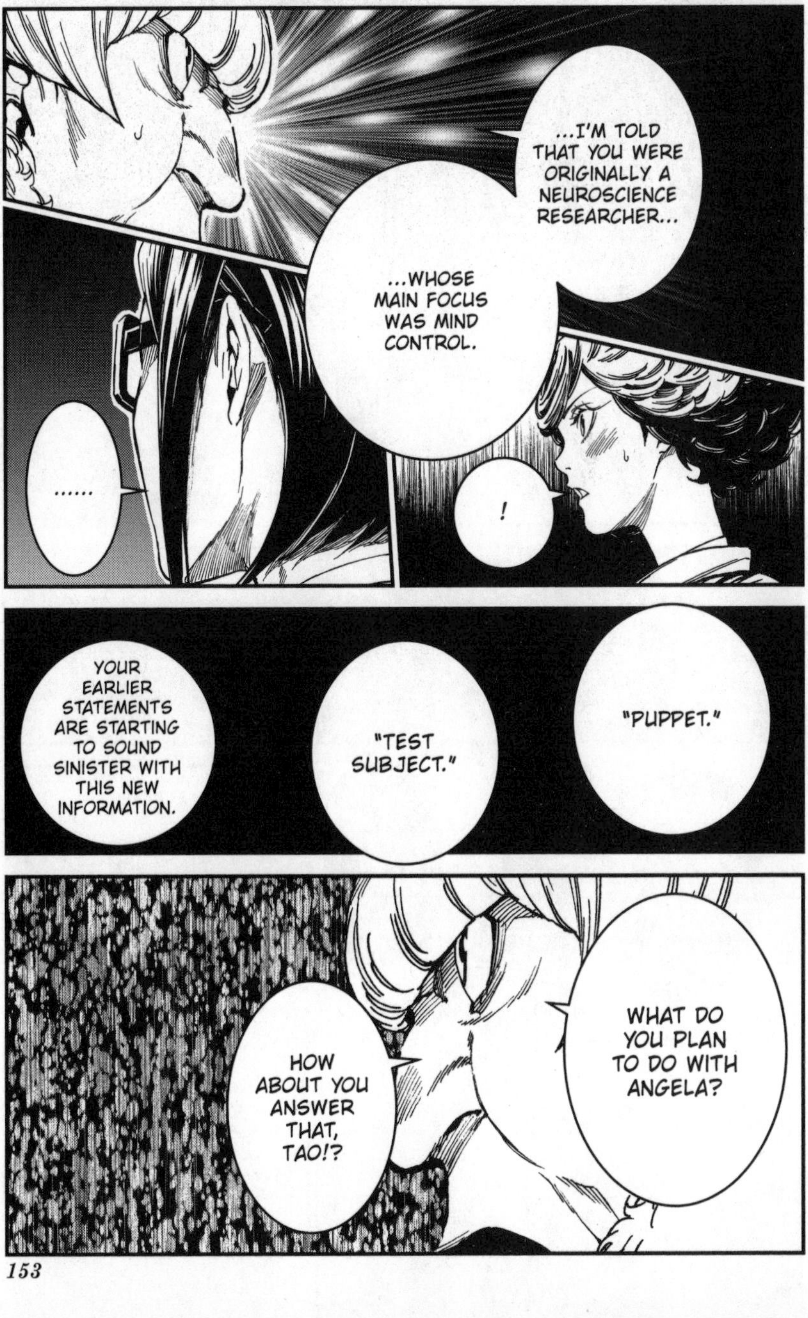
...I'M TOLD THAT YOU WERE ORIGINALLY A NEUROSCIENCE RESEARCHER...
...WHOSE MAIN FOCUS WAS MIND CONTROL.
!
......
"PUPPET."
"TEST SUBJECT."
YOUR EARLIER STATEMENTS ARE STARTING TO SOUND SINISTER WITH THIS NEW INFORMATION.
WHAT DO YOU PLAN TO DO WITH ANGELA?
HOW ABOUT YOU ANSWER THAT, TAO!?

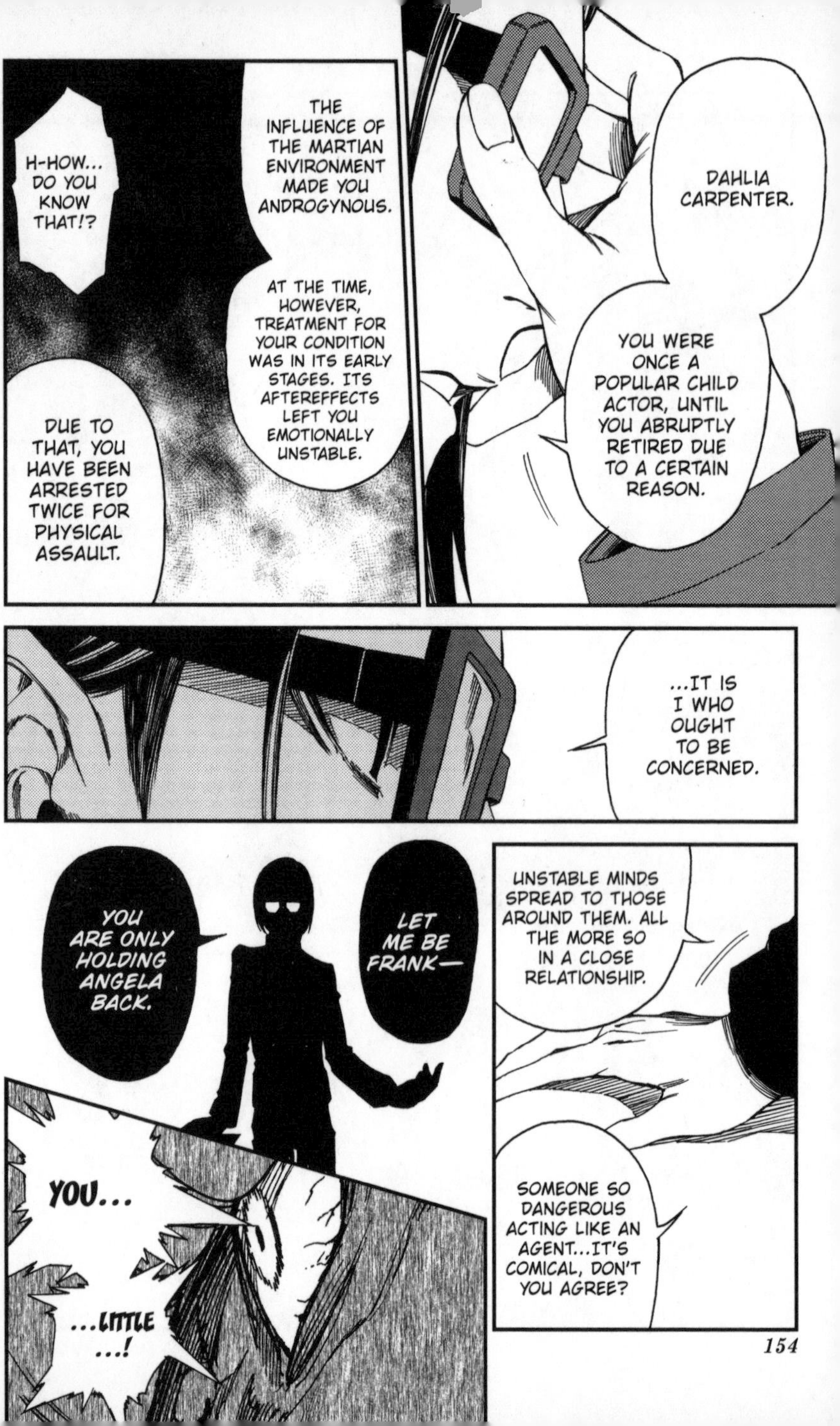
DAHLIA CARPENTER.
YOU WERE ONCE A POPULAR CHILD ACTOR, UNTIL YOU ABRUPTLY RETIRED DUE TO A CERTAIN REASON.
THE INFLUENCE OF THE MARTIAN ENVIRONMENT MADE YOU ANDROGYNOUS.
AT THE TIME, HOWEVER, TREATMENT FOR YOUR CONDITION WAS IN ITS EARLY STAGES. ITS AFTEREFFECTS LEFT YOU EMOTIONALLY UNSTABLE.
DUE TO THAT, YOU HAVE BEEN ARRESTED TWICE FOR PHYSICAL ASSAULT.
H-HOW... DO YOU KNOW THAT!?
...IT IS I WHO OUGHT TO BE CONCERNED.
UNSTABLE MINDS SPREAD TO THOSE AROUND THEM. ALL THE MORE SO IN A CLOSE RELATIONSHIP.
SOMEONE SO DANGEROUS ACTING LIKE AN AGENT...IT'S COMICAL, DON'T YOU AGREE?
LET ME BE FRANK—
YOU ARE ONLY HOLDING ANGELA BACK.
YOU...
...LITTLE ...!

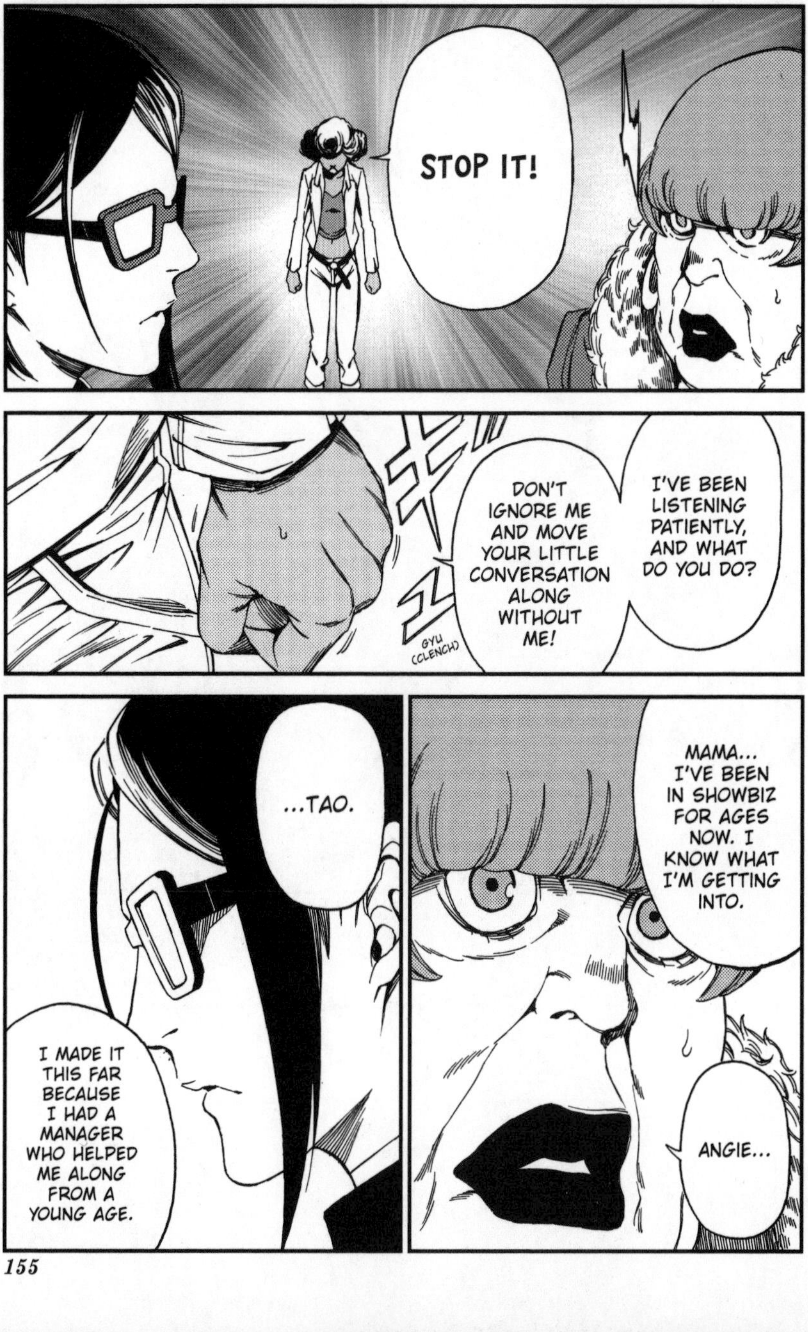
STOP IT!
I'VE BEEN LISTENING PATIENTLY, AND WHAT DO YOU DO?
DON'T IGNORE ME AND MOVE YOUR LITTLE CONVERSATION ALONG WITHOUT ME!
GYU (CLENCH)
MAMA... I'VE BEEN IN SHOWBIZ FOR AGES NOW. I KNOW WHAT I'M GETTING INTO.
ANGIE...
...TAO.
I MADE IT THIS FAR BECAUSE I HAD A MANAGER WHO HELPED ME ALONG FROM A YOUNG AGE.

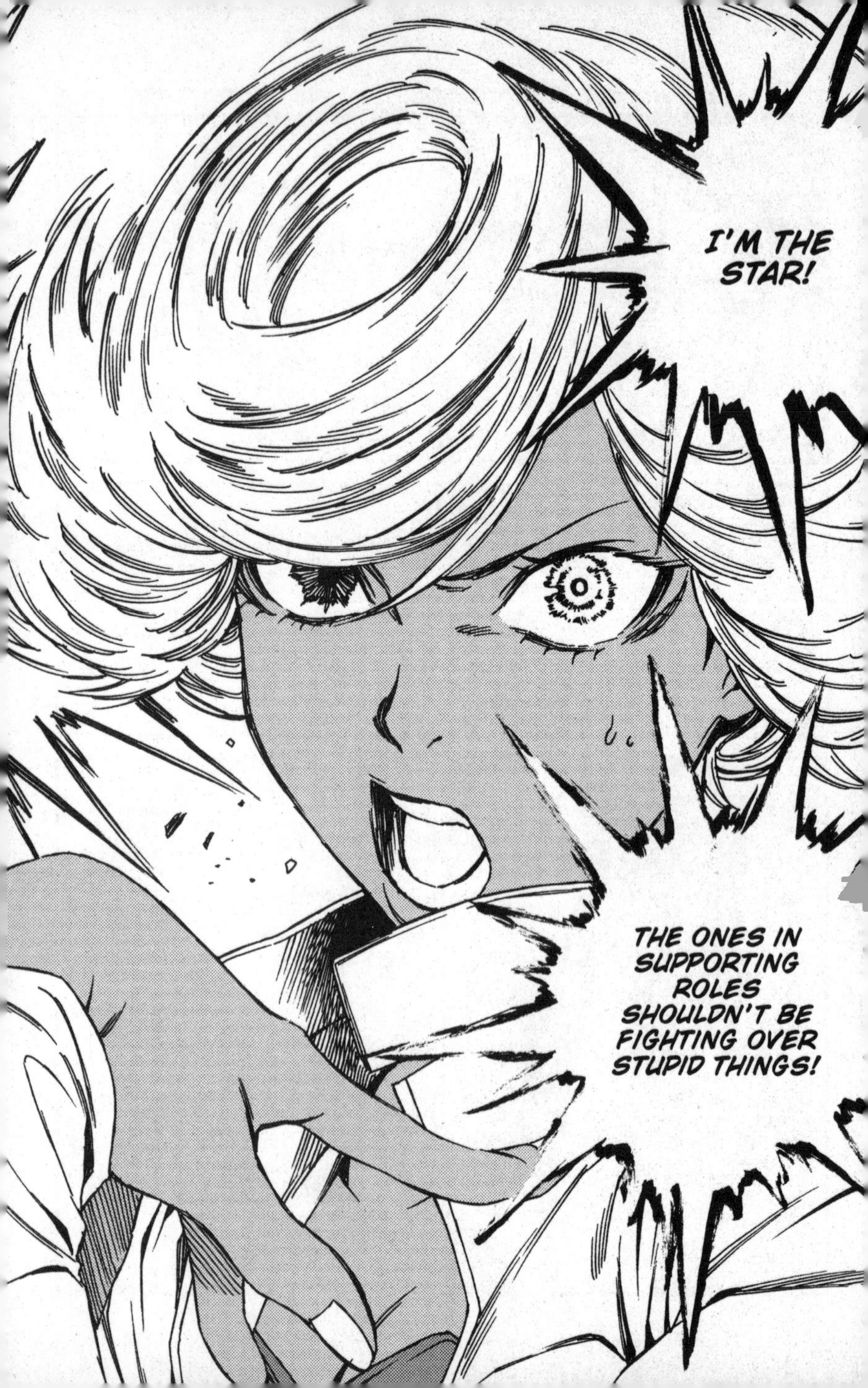
I'M THE STAR!
THE ONES IN SUPPORTING ROLES SHOULDN'T BE FIGHTING OVER STUPID THINGS!

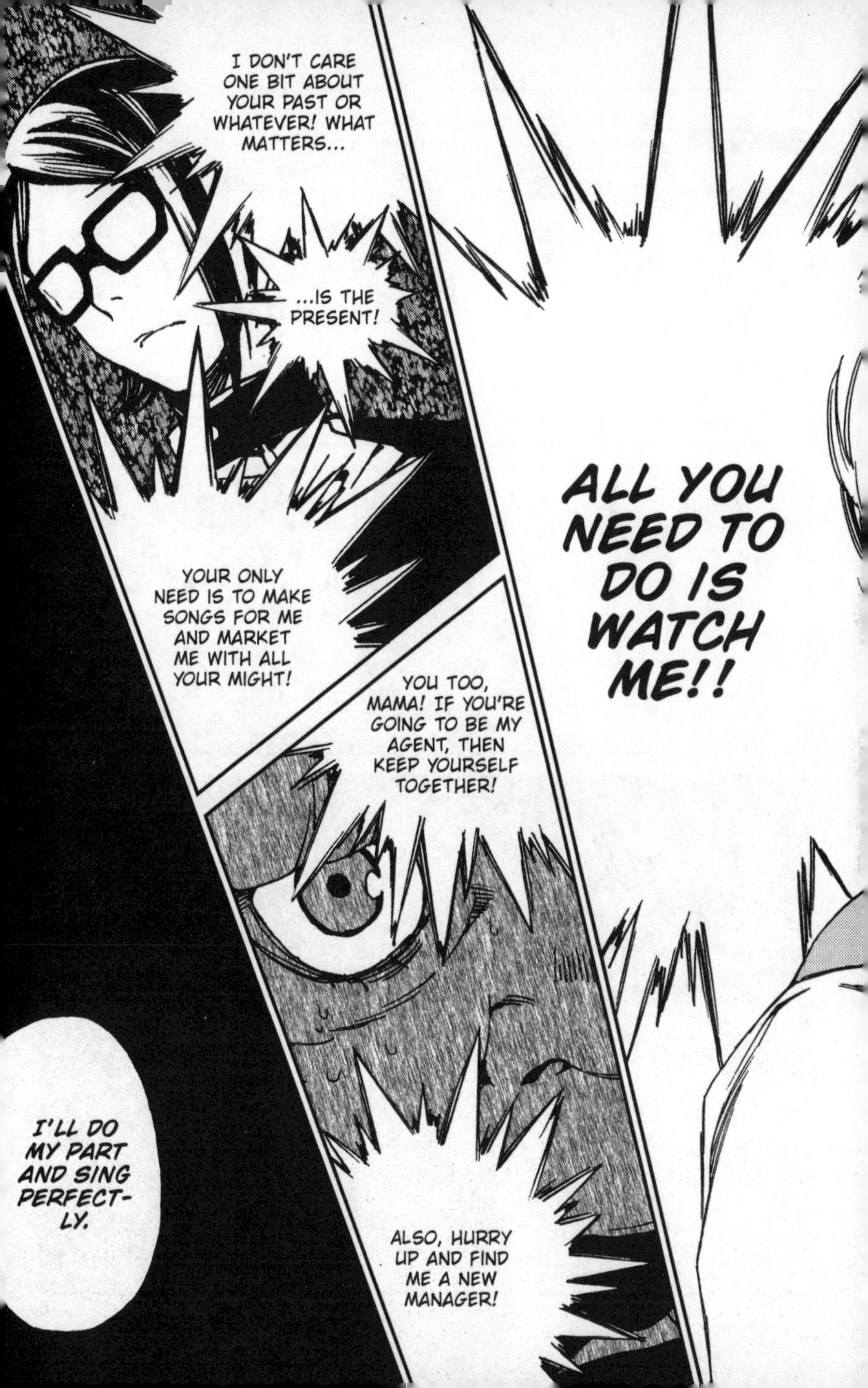
I DON'T CARE ONE BIT ABOUT YOUR PAST OR WHATEVER! WHAT MATTERS...
...IS THE PRESENT!
YOUR ONLY NEED IS TO MAKE SONGS FOR ME AND MARKET ME WITH ALL YOUR MIGHT!
YOU TOO, MAMA! IF YOU'RE GOING TO BE MY AGENT, THEN KEEP YOURSELF TOGETHER!
ALSO, HURRY UP AND FIND ME A NEW MANAGER!
I'LL DO MY PART AND SING PERFECTLY.
ALL YOU NEED TO DO IS WATCH ME!!

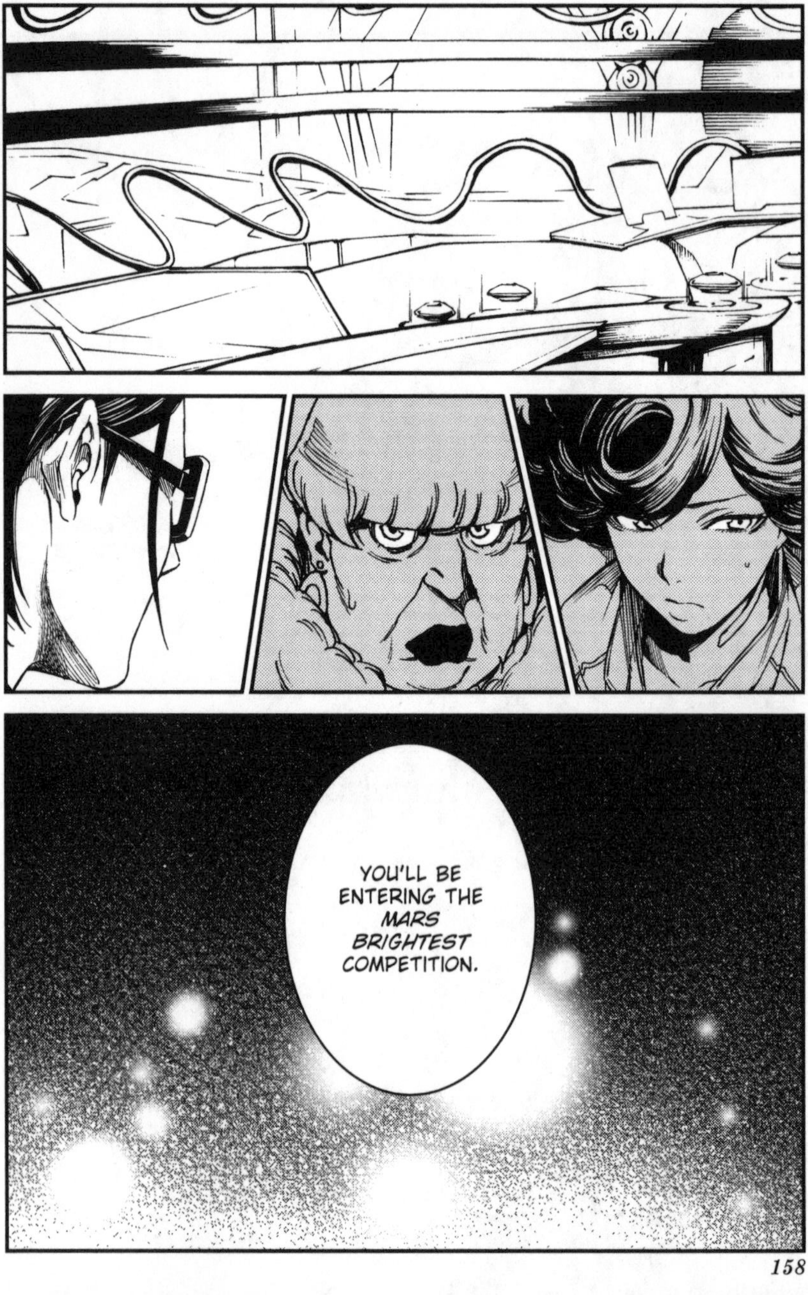
YOU'LL BE ENTERING THE MARS BRIGHTEST COMPETITION.

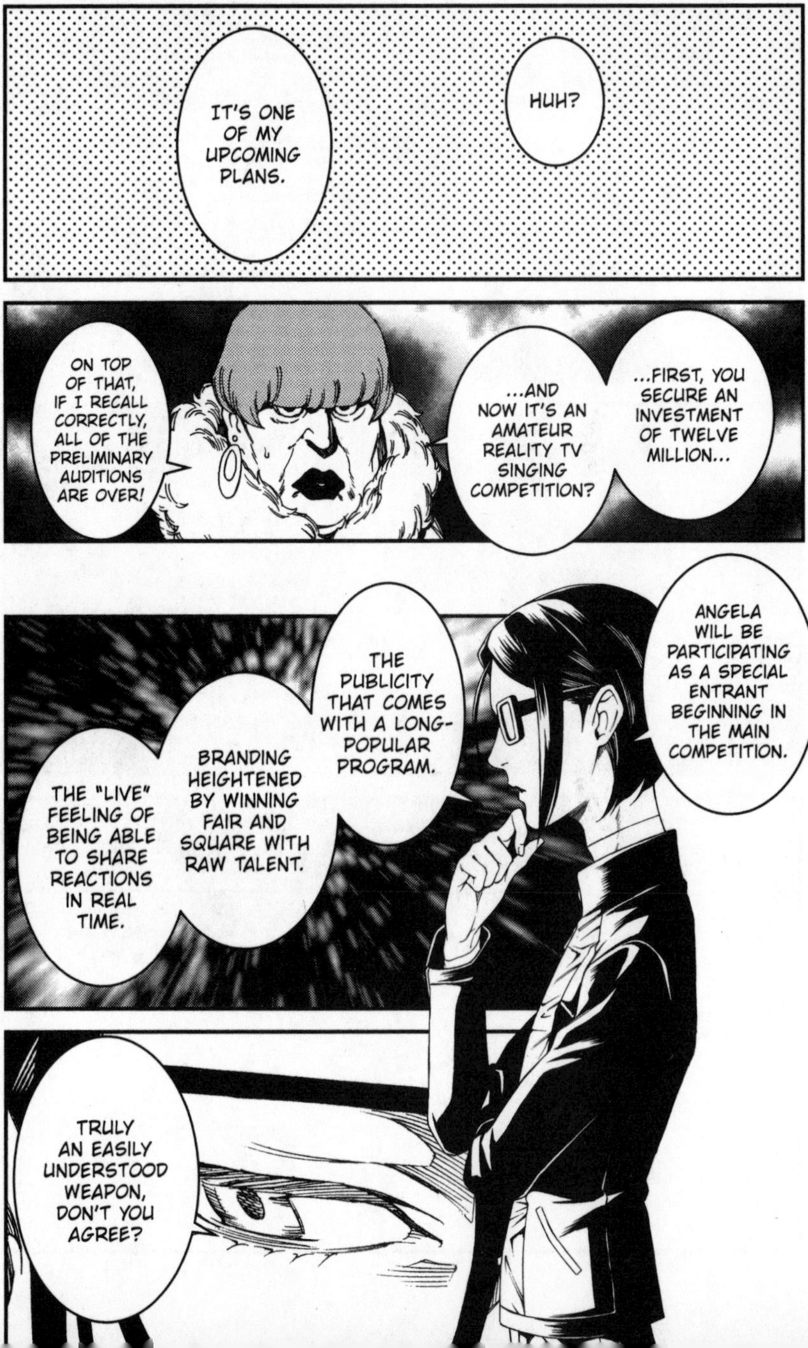
HUH?
IT'S ONE OF MY UPCOMING PLANS.
...FIRST, YOU SECURE AN INVESTMENT OF TWELVE MILLION...
...AND NOW IT'S AN AMATEUR REALITY TV SINGING COMPETITION?
ON TOP OF THAT, IF I RECALL CORRECTLY, ALL OF THE PRELIMINARY AUDITIONS ARE OVER!
ANGELA WILL BE PARTICIPATING AS A SPECIAL ENTRANT BEGINNING IN THE MAIN COMPETITION.
THE PUBLICITY THAT COMES WITH A LONG-POPULAR PROGRAM.
BRANDING HEIGHTENED BY WINNING FAIR AND SQUARE WITH RAW TALENT.
THE "LIVE" FEELING OF BEING ABLE TO SHARE REACTIONS IN REAL TIME.
TRULY AN EASILY UNDERSTOOD WEAPON, DON'T YOU AGREE?

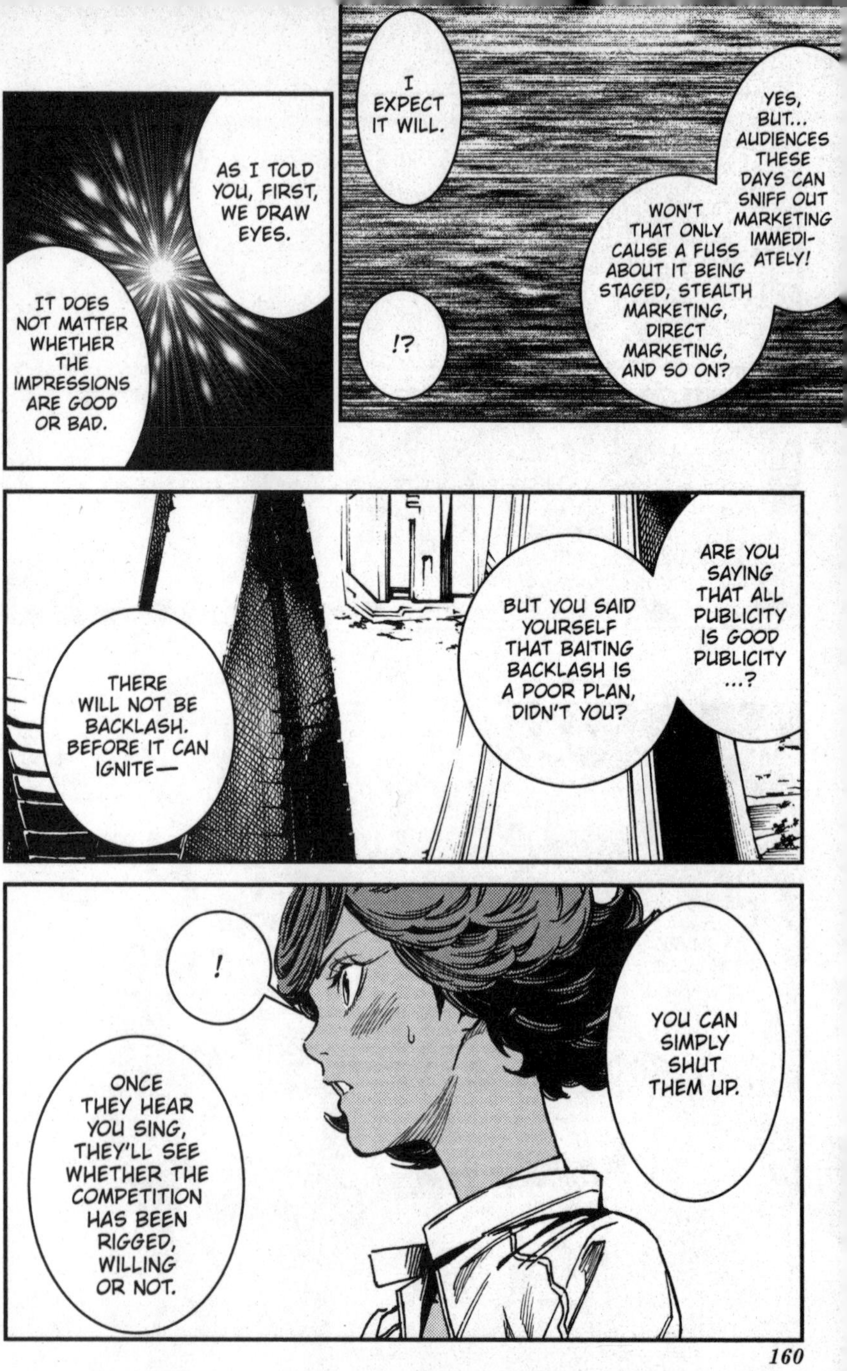
YES, BUT... AUDIENCES THESE DAYS CAN SNIFF OUT MARKETING IMMEDI-ATELY!
WON'T THAT ONLY CAUSE A FUSS ABOUT IT BEING STAGED, STEALTH MARKETING, DIRECT MARKETING, AND SO ON?
I EXPECT IT WILL.
!?
AS I TOLD YOU, FIRST, WE DRAW EYES.
IT DOES NOT MATTER WHETHER THE IMPRESSIONS ARE GOOD OR BAD.
ARE YOU SAYING THAT ALL PUBLICITY IS GOOD PUBLICITY ...?
BUT YOU SAID YOURSELF THAT BAITING BACKLASH IS A POOR PLAN, DIDN'T YOU?
THERE WILL NOT BE BACKLASH. BEFORE IT CAN IGNITE—
YOU CAN SIMPLY SHUT THEM UP.
!
ONCE THEY HEAR YOU SING, THEY'LL SEE WHETHER THE COMPETITION HAS BEEN RIGGED, WILLING OR NOT.

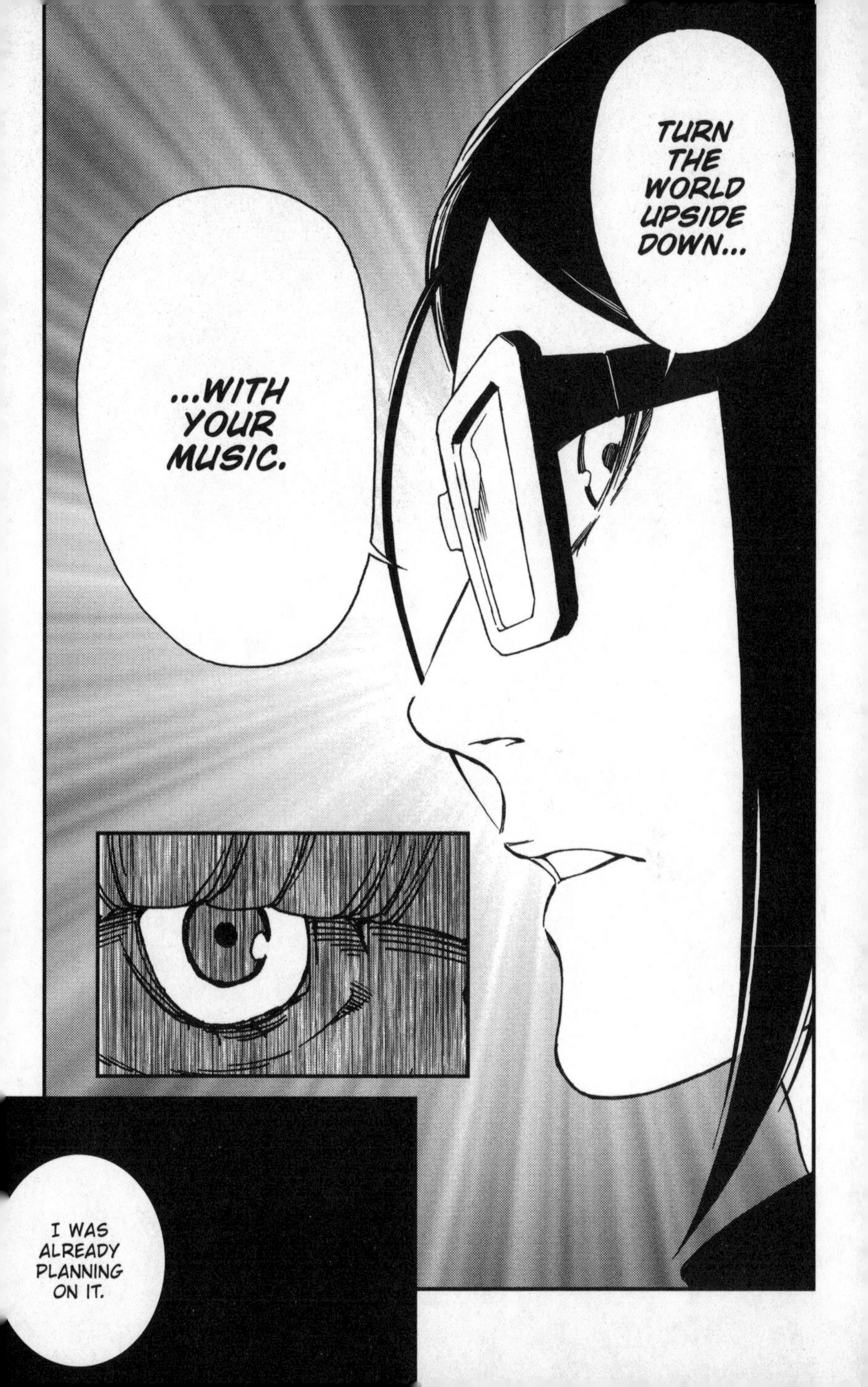
TURN THE WORLD UPSIDE DOWN...
...WITH YOUR MUSIC.
I WAS ALREADY PLANNING ON IT.

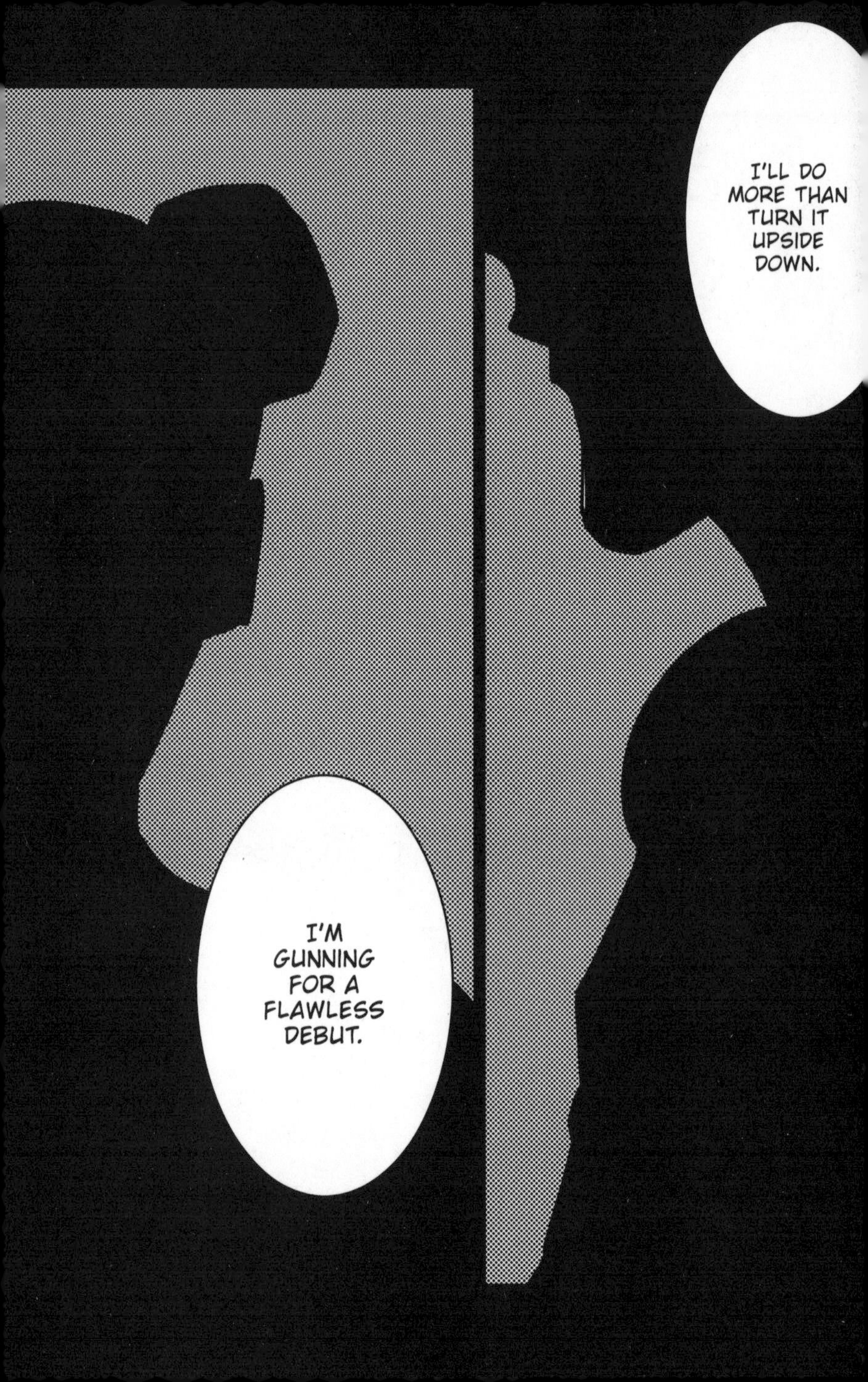
I'LL DO MORE THAN TURN IT UPSIDE DOWN.
I'M GUNNING FOR A FLAWLESS DEBUT.

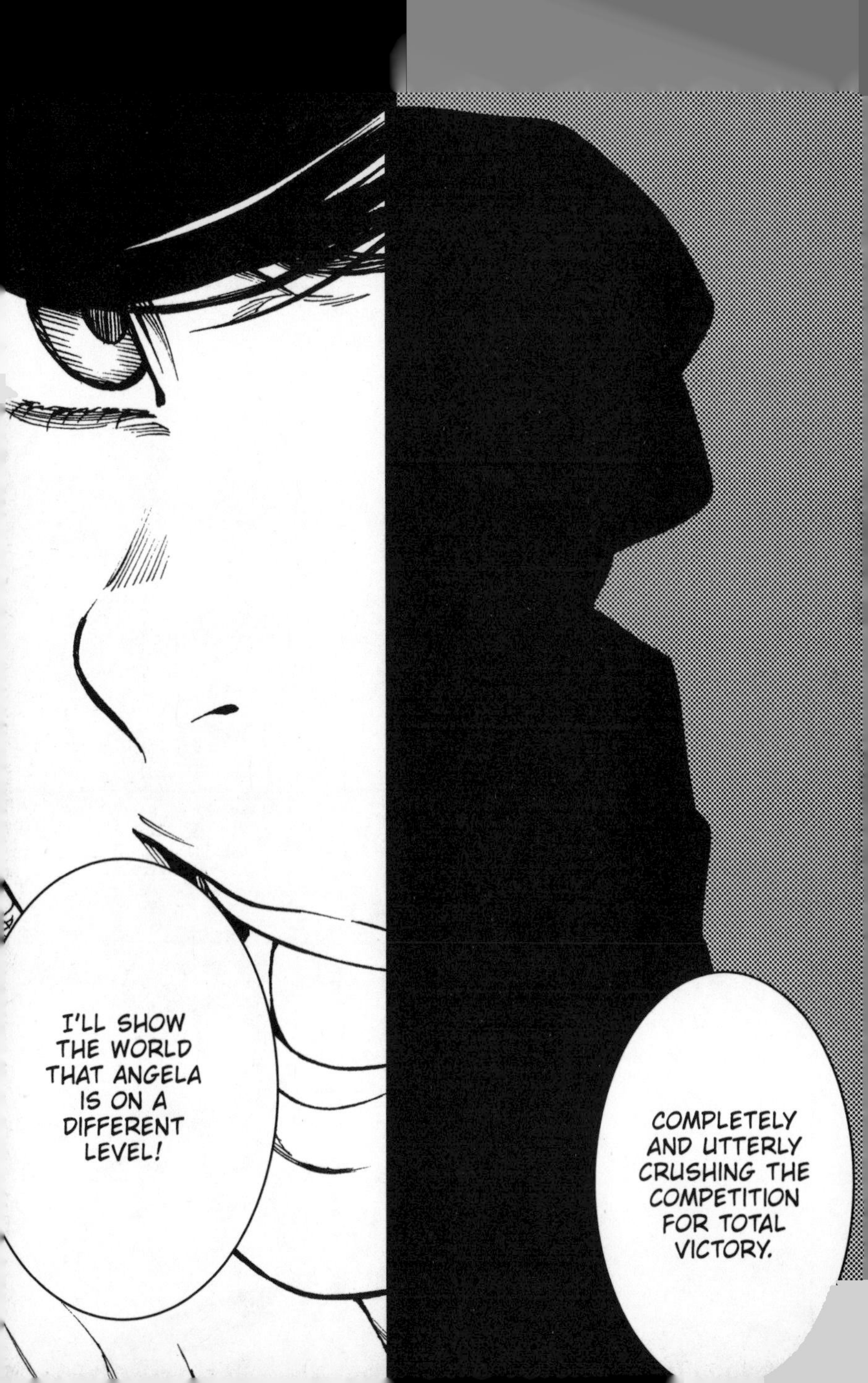
COMPLETELY AND UTTERLY CRUSHING THE COMPETITION FOR TOTAL VICTORY.
I'LL SHOW THE WORLD THAT ANGELA IS ON A DIFFERENT LEVEL!

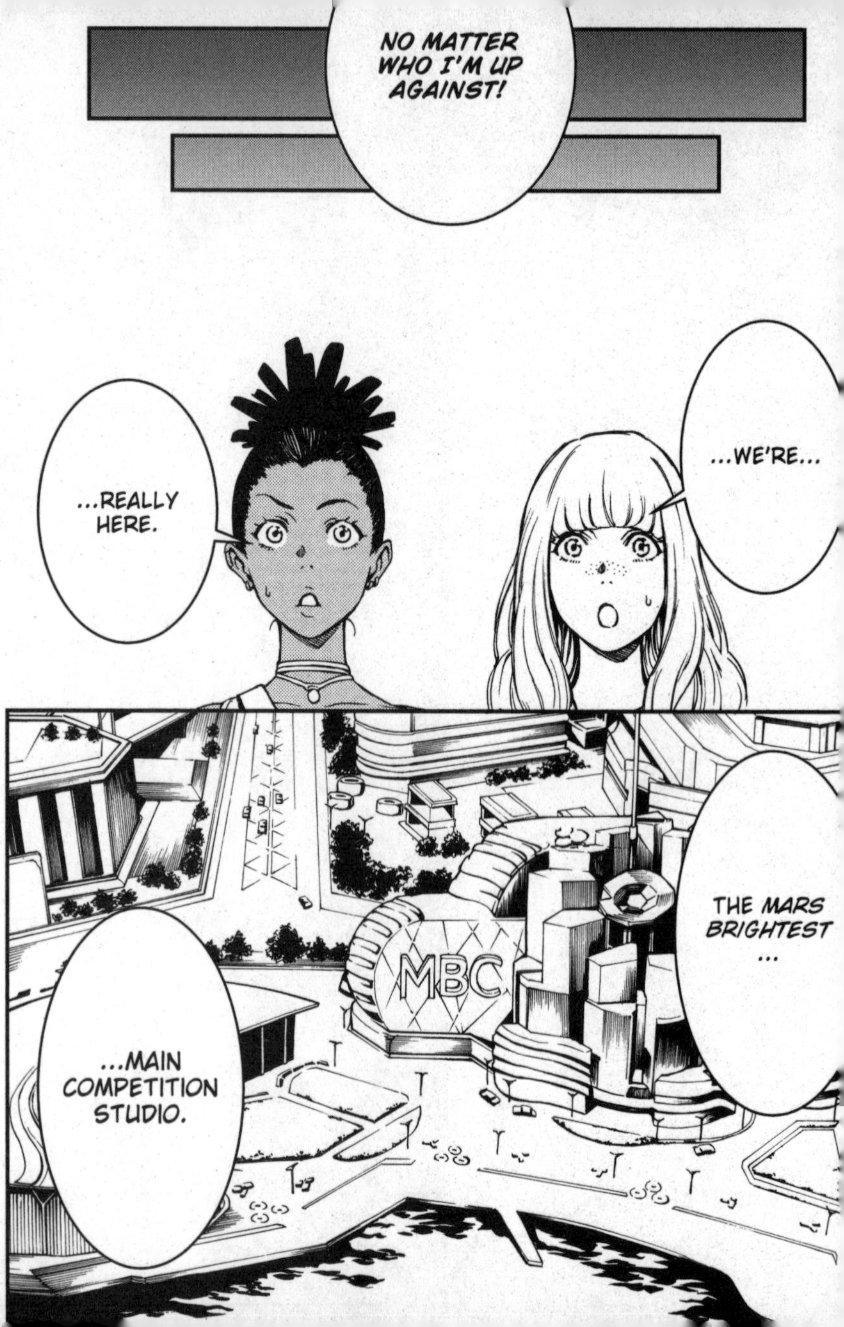
NO MATTER WHO I'M UP AGAINST!
...WE'RE...
...REALLY HERE.
THE MARS BRIGHTEST ...
MBC
...MAIN COMPETITION STUDIO.

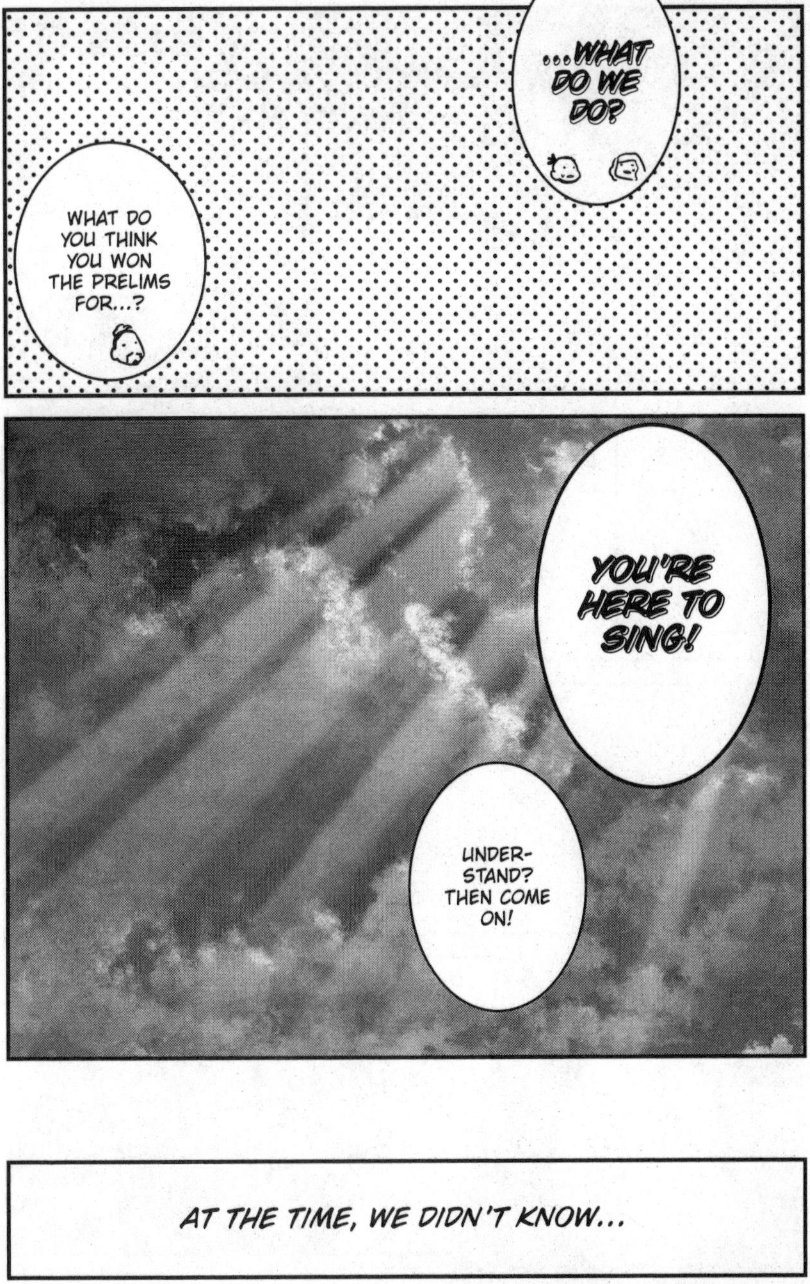
...WHAT DO WE DO?
WHAT DO YOU THINK YOU WON THE PRELIMS FOR...?
YOU'RE HERE TO SING!
UNDER-STAND? THEN COME ON!
AT THE TIME, WE DIDN'T KNOW...

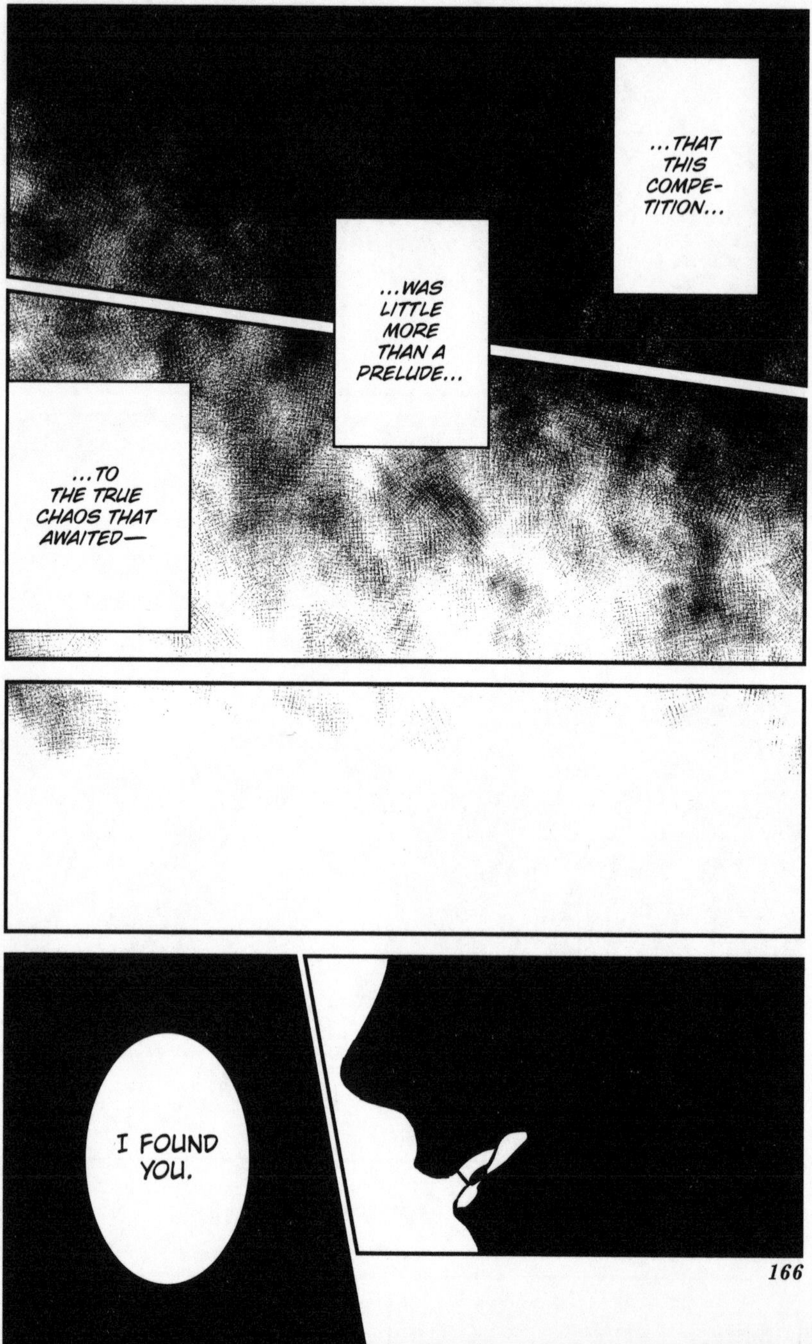
...THAT THIS COMPE- TITION...
...WAS LITTLE MORE THAN A PRELUDE...
...TO THE TRUE CHAOS THAT AWAITED—
I FOUND YOU.

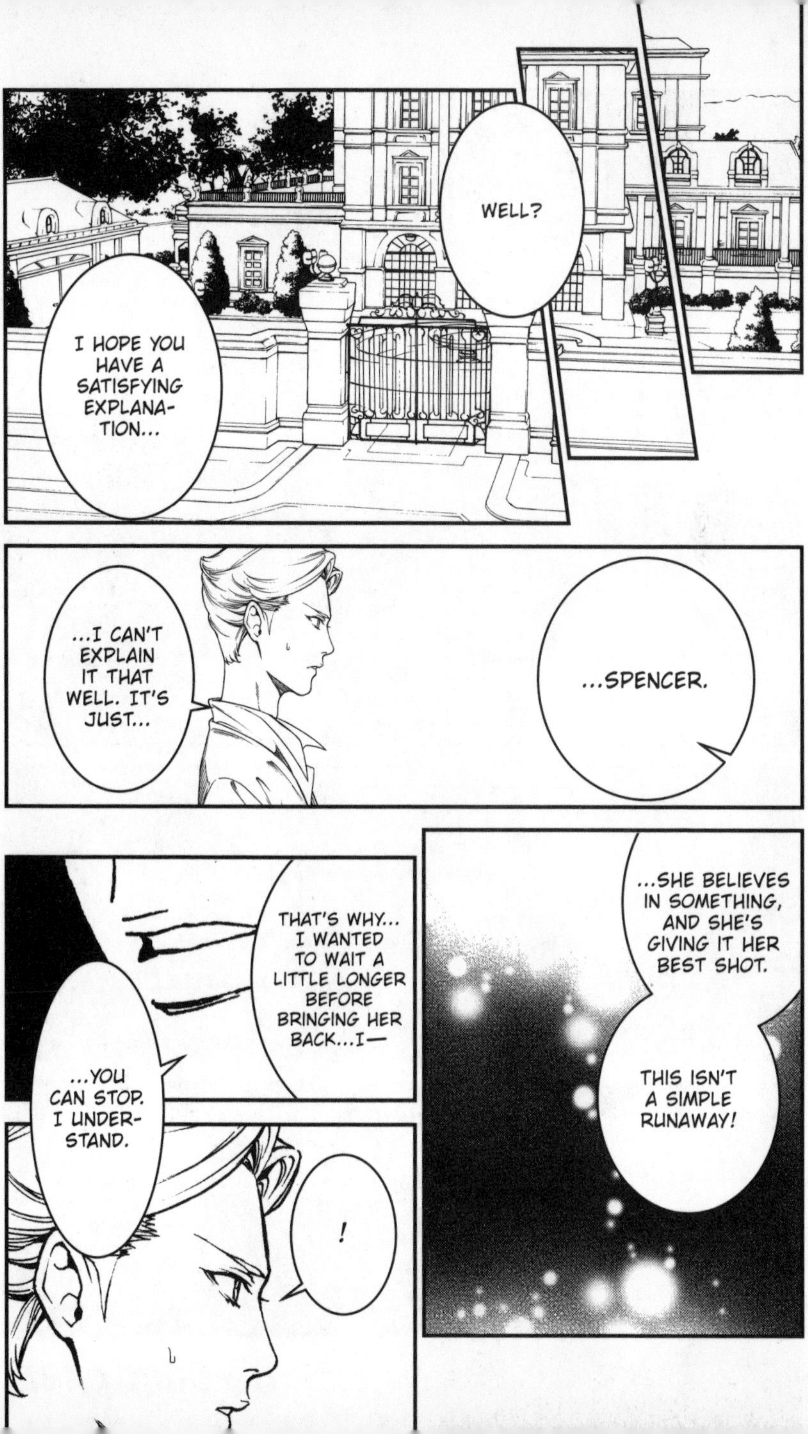
WELL?
I HOPE YOU HAVE A SATISFYING EXPLANA-TION...
...SPENCER.
...I CAN'T EXPLAIN IT THAT WELL. IT'S JUST...
...SHE BELIEVES IN SOMETHING, AND SHE'S GIVING IT HER BEST SHOT.
THIS ISN'T A SIMPLE RUNAWAY!
THAT'S WHY... I WANTED TO WAIT A LITTLE LONGER BEFORE BRINGING HER BACK...I—
...YOU CAN STOP. I UNDER-STAND.
!

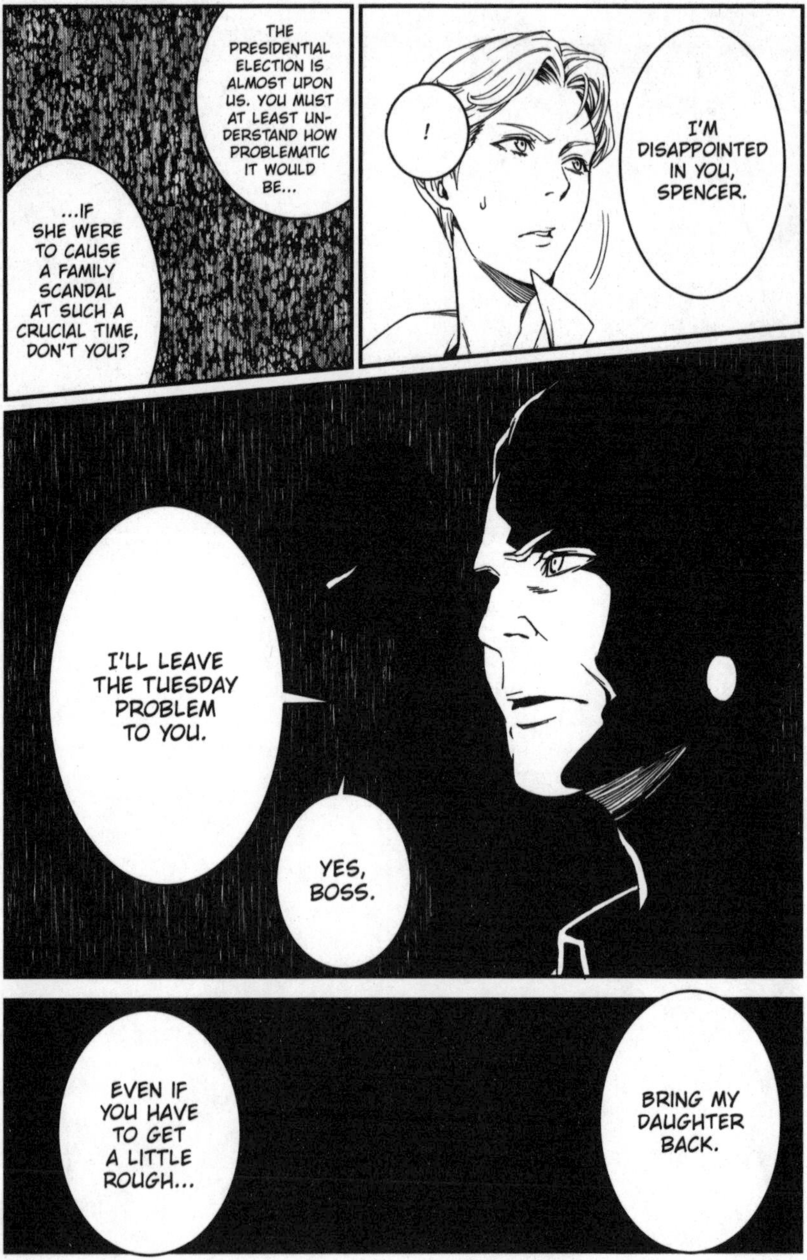
I'M DISAPPOINTED IN YOU, SPENCER.
!
THE PRESIDENTIAL ELECTION IS ALMOST UPON US. YOU MUST AT LEAST UNDERSTAND HOW PROBLEMATIC IT WOULD BE...
...IF SHE WERE TO CAUSE A FAMILY SCANDAL AT SUCH A CRUCIAL TIME, DON'T YOU?
I'LL LEAVE THE TUESDAY PROBLEM TO YOU.
YES, BOSS.
BRING MY DAUGHTER BACK.
EVEN IF YOU HAVE TO GET A LITTLE ROUGH...

...To Be Continued.

CAROLE & TUESDAY

THE LONELIEST CAROLE

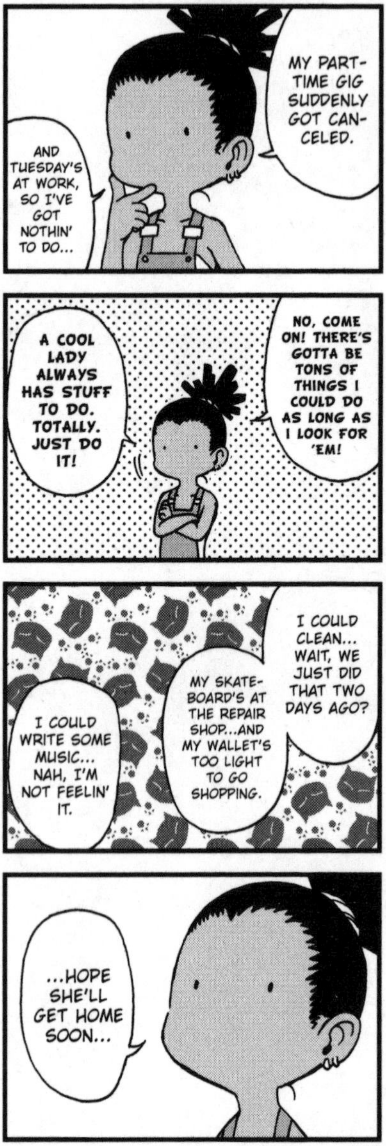
MY PART-TIME GIG SUDDENLY GOT CANCELED.
AND TUESDAY'S AT WORK, SO I'VE GOT NOTHIN' TO DO...
NO, COME ON! THERE'S GOTTA BE TONS OF THINGS I COULD DO AS LONG AS I LOOK FOR 'EM!
A COOL LADY ALWAYS HAS STUFF TO DO. TOTALLY. JUST DO IT!
I COULD CLEAN... WAIT, WE JUST DID THAT TWO DAYS AGO?
MY SKATEBOARD'S AT THE REPAIR SHOP...AND MY WALLET'S TOO LIGHT TO GO SHOPPING.
I COULD WRITE SOME MUSIC... NAH, I'M NOT FEELIN' IT.
...HOPE SHE'LL GET HOME SOON...

WHISPERING TUESDAY

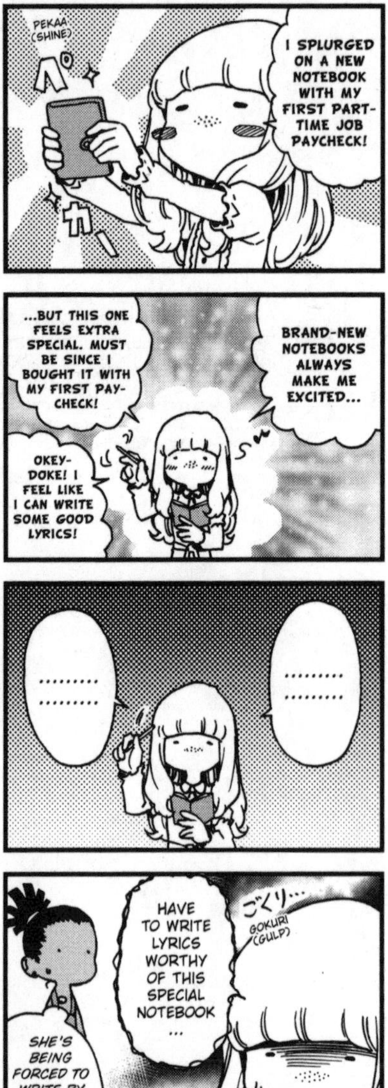
I SPLURGED ON A NEW NOTEBOOK WITH MY FIRST PART-TIME JOB PAYCHECK!
PEKAA (SHINE)
BRAND-NEW NOTEBOOKS ALWAYS MAKE ME EXCITED...
...BUT THIS ONE FEELS EXTRA SPECIAL. MUST BE SINCE I BOUGHT IT WITH MY FIRST PAYCHECK!
OKEY-DOKE! I FEEL LIKE I CAN WRITE SOME GOOD LYRICS!
....
....
....
....
ごくり…
GOKURI (GULP)
HAVE TO WRITE LYRICS WORTHY OF THIS SPECIAL NOTEBOOK...
SHE'S BEING FORCED TO WRITE BY THE NOTEBOOK...

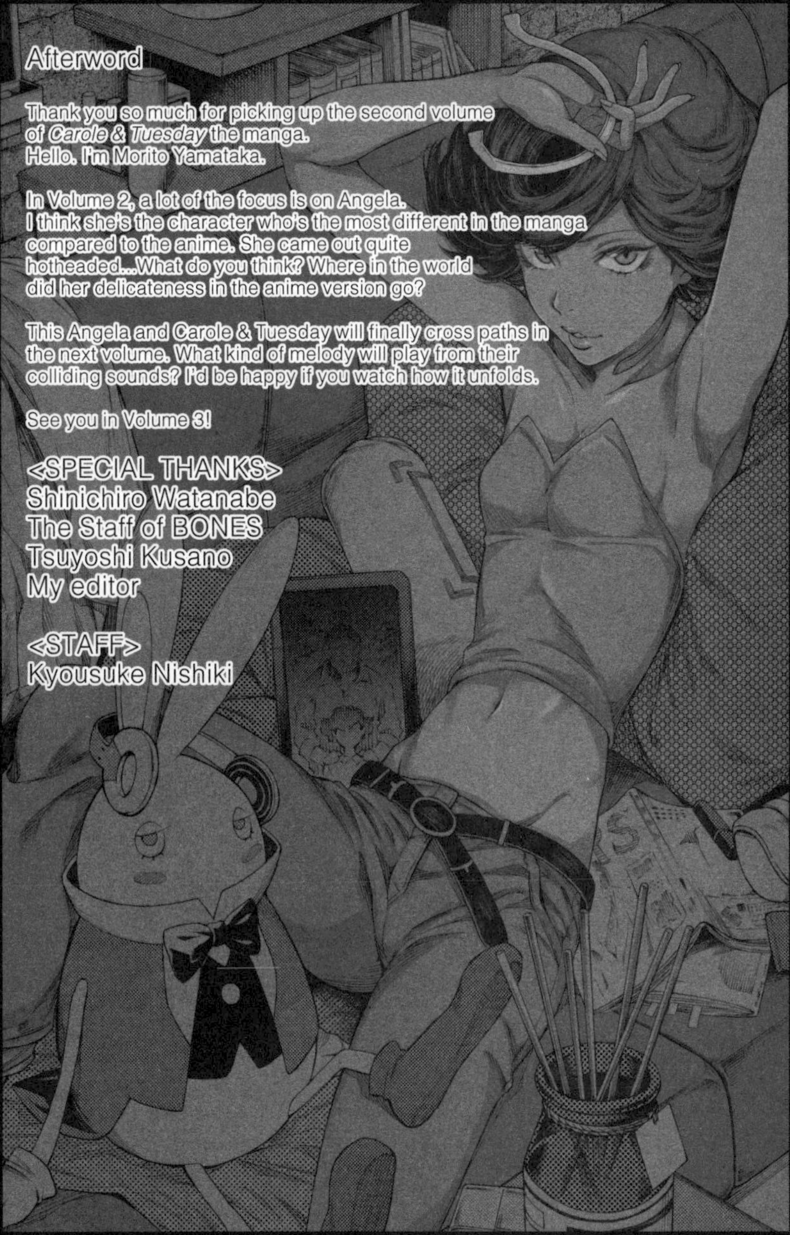

Afterword

Thank you so much for picking up the second volume of *Carole & Tuesday* the manga.
Hello. I'm Morito Yamataka.

In Volume 2, a lot of the focus is on Angela.
I think she's the character who's the most different in the manga compared to the anime. She came out quite hotheaded...What do you think? Where in the world did her delicateness in the anime version go?

This Angela and Carole & Tuesday will finally cross paths in the next volume. What kind of melody will play from their colliding sounds? I'd be happy if you watch how it unfolds.

See you in Volume 3!

<SPECIAL THANKS>
Shinichiro Watanabe
The Staff of BONES
Tsuyoshi Kusano
My editor

<STAFF>
Kyousuke Nishiki

Translation Notes

PAGE 117

The band Mugen Jin Fu consists of the main characters from the Shinichiro Watanabe and BONES anime *Samurai Champloo* (2004). The band BBP is a cameo of the main characters from another Watanabe and BONES anime, *Space Dandy* (2014).

The *shamisen* is a three-stringed traditional Japanese instrument.

CAROLE & TUESDAY

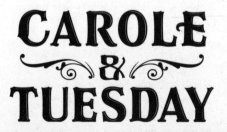

Two girls, a new school, and the beginning of a beautiful friendship.

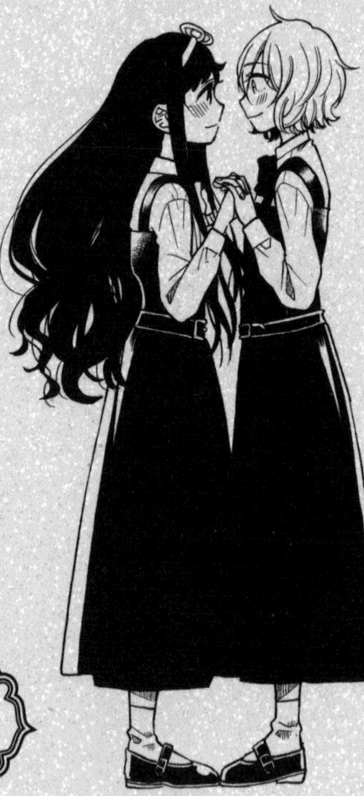

Complete series available now!

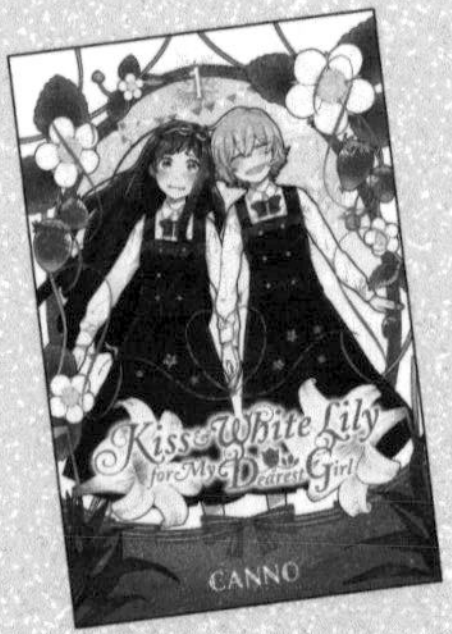
Kiss & White Lily for My Dearest Girl
CANNO

Kiss & White Lily for My Dearest Girl

In middle school, Ayaka Shiramine was the perfect student: hard-working, with excellent grades and a great personality to match. As Ayaka enters high school she expects to still be on top, but one thing she didn't account for is her new classmate, the lazy yet genuine genius Yurine Kurosawa. What's in store for Ayaka and Yurine as they go through high school...together?

Yen Press

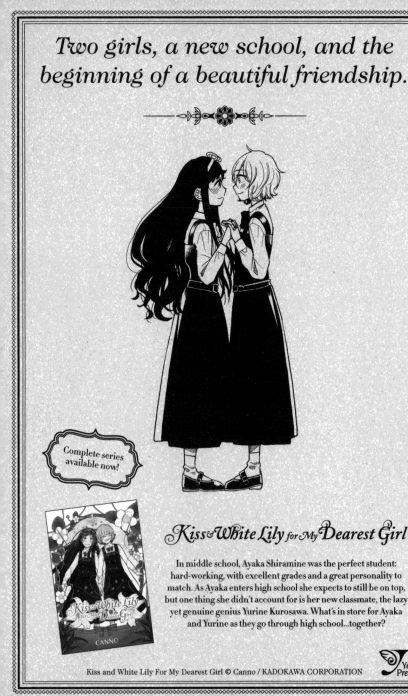

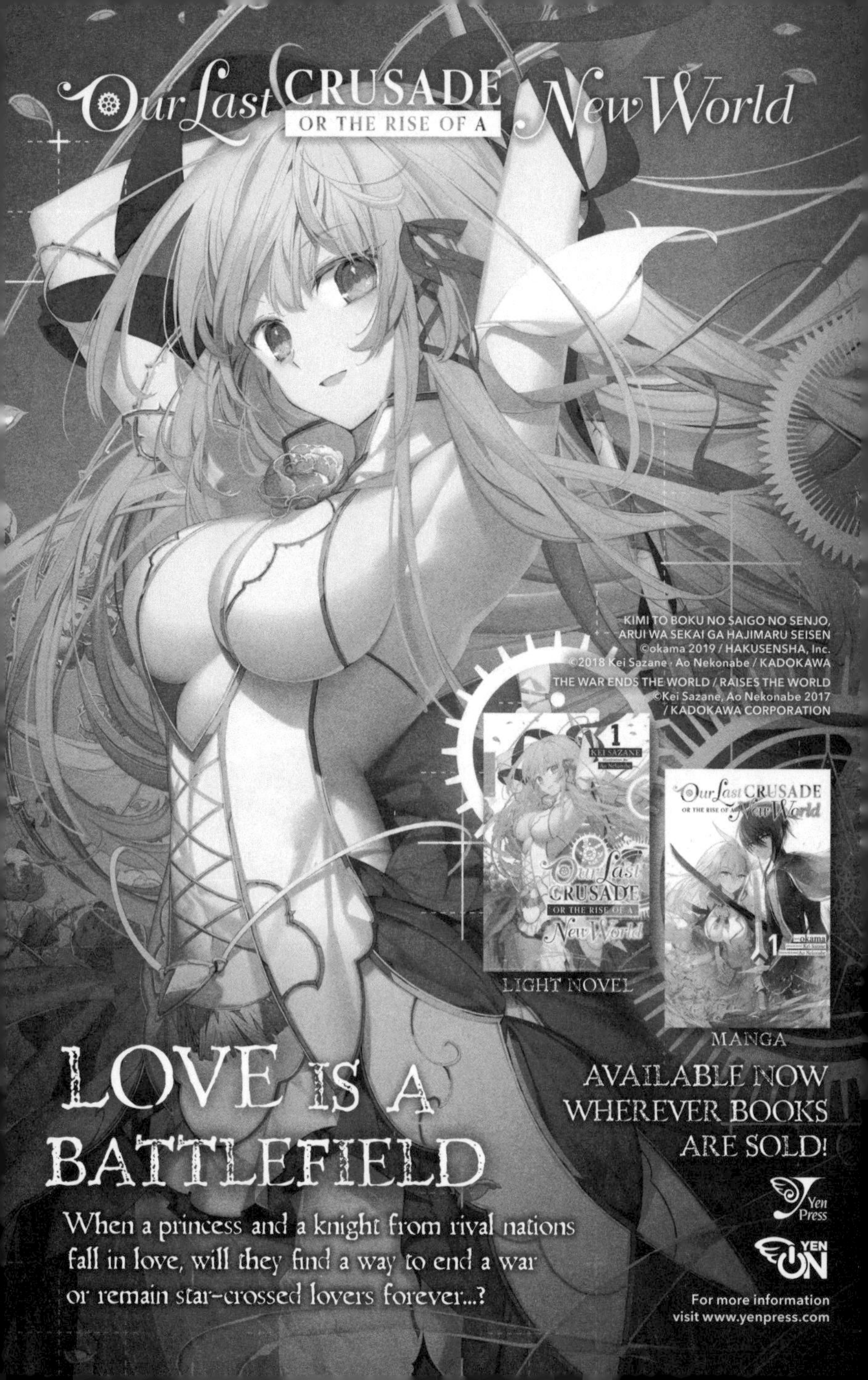
Our Last CRUSADE OR THE RISE OF A New World
KIMI TO BOKU NO SAIGO NO SENJO,
ARUI WA SEKAI GA HAJIMARU SEISEN
©okama 2019 / HAKUSENSHA, Inc.
©2018 Kei Sazane · Ao Nekonabe / KADOKAWA
THE WAR ENDS THE WORLD / RAISES THE WORLD
©Kei Sazane, Ao Nekonabe 2017
/ KADOKAWA CORPORATION
LIGHT NOVEL
MANGA
LOVE IS A BATTLEFIELD
When a princess and a knight from rival nations fall in love, will they find a way to end a war or remain star-crossed lovers forever...?
AVAILABLE NOW WHEREVER BOOKS ARE SOLD!
Yen Press
YEN ON
For more information visit www.yenpress.com

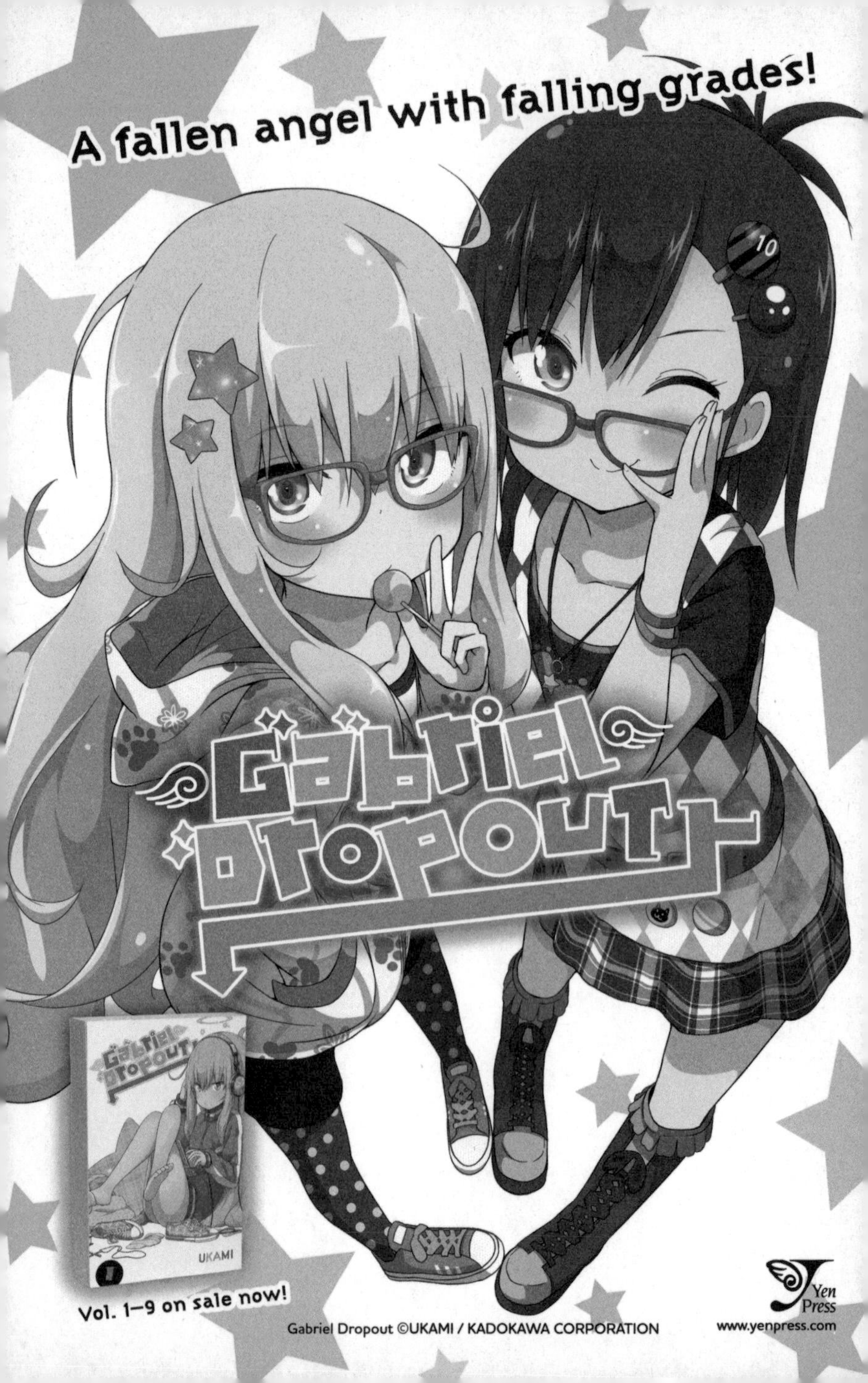

A fallen angel with falling grades!
Gabriel Dropout
Gabriel Dropout
UKAMI
Vol. 1–9 on sale now!
Gabriel Dropout ©UKAMI / KADOKAWA CORPORATION
Yen Press
www.yenpress.com

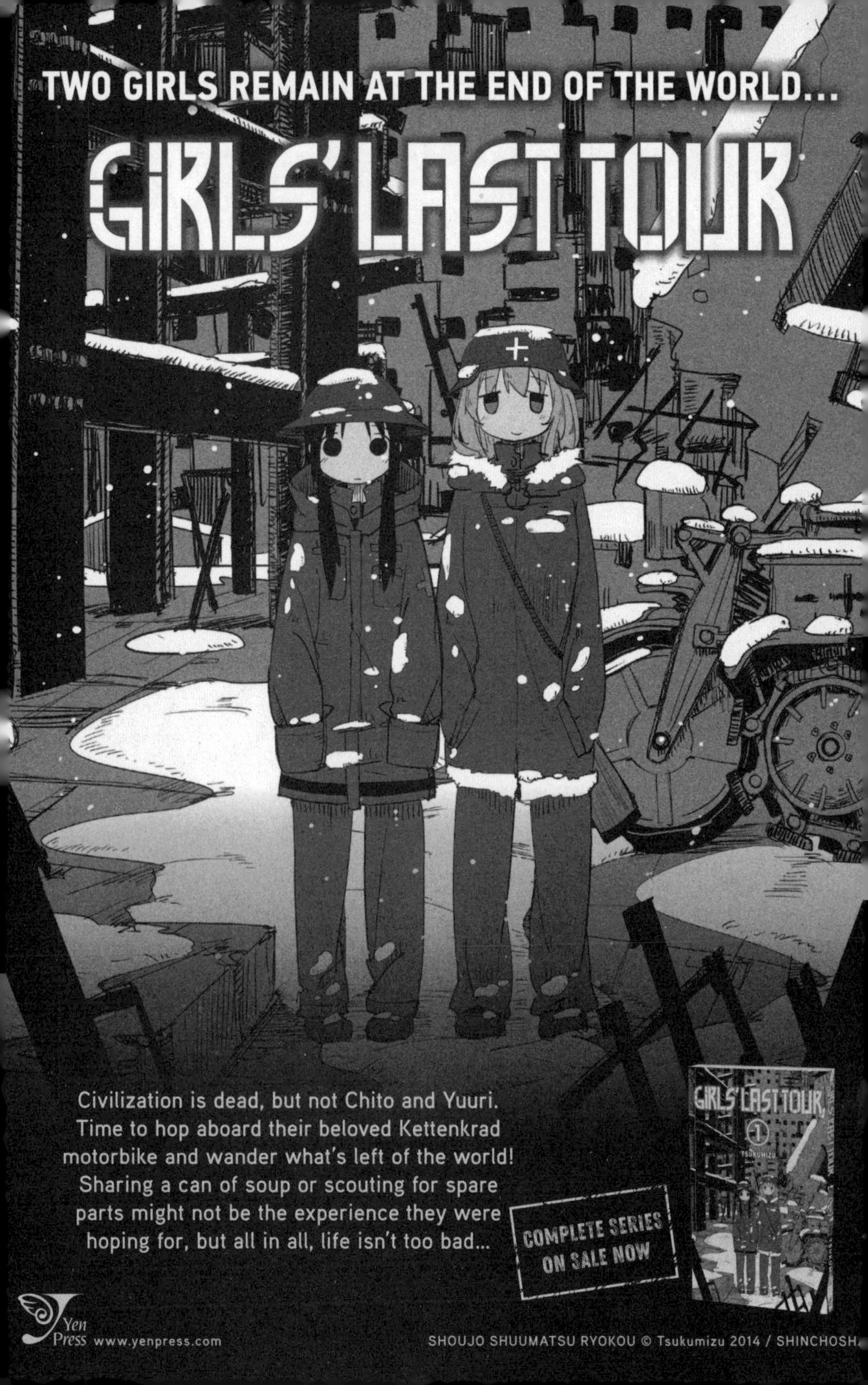
TWO GIRLS REMAIN AT THE END OF THE WORLD...
GIRLS' LAST TOUR
Civilization is dead, but not Chito and Yuuri. Time to hop aboard their beloved Kettenkrad motorbike and wander what's left of the world! Sharing a can of soup or scouting for spare parts might not be the experience they were hoping for, but all in all, life isn't too bad...
COMPLETE SERIES ON SALE NOW
GIRLS' LAST TOUR
1
TSUKUMIZU
Yen Press www.yenpress.com
SHOUJO SHUUMATSU RYOKOU © Tsukumizu 2014 / SHINCHOSHA

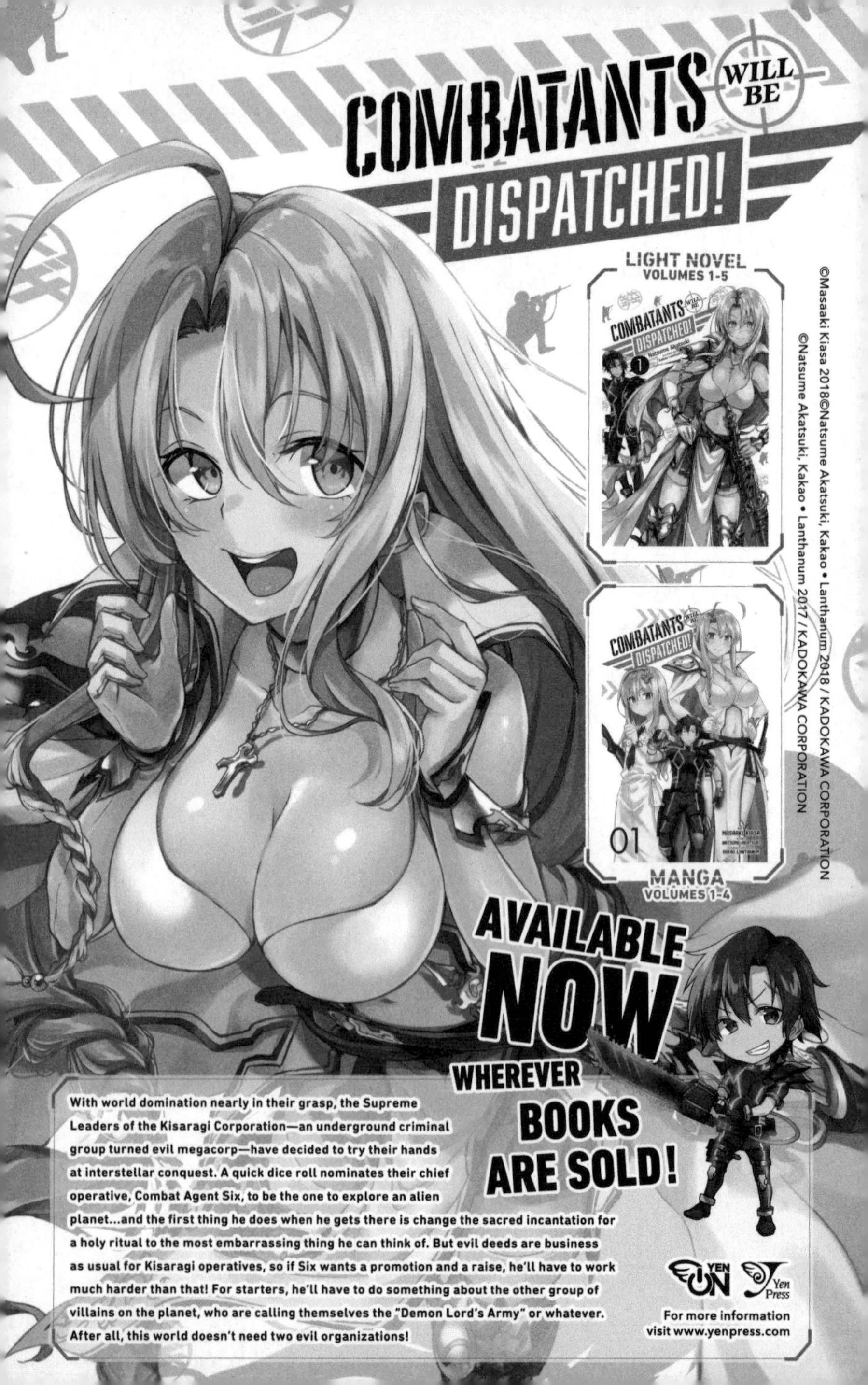
COMBATANTS WILL BE DISPATCHED!
LIGHT NOVEL
VOLUMES 1-5
MANGA
VOLUMES 1-4
AVAILABLE NOW WHEREVER BOOKS ARE SOLD!
With world domination nearly in their grasp, the Supreme Leaders of the Kisaragi Corporation—an underground criminal group turned evil megacorp—have decided to try their hands at interstellar conquest. A quick dice roll nominates their chief operative, Combat Agent Six, to be the one to explore an alien planet...and the first thing he does when he gets there is change the sacred incantation for a holy ritual to the most embarrassing thing he can think of. But evil deeds are business as usual for Kisaragi operatives, so if Six wants a promotion and a raise, he'll have to work much harder than that! For starters, he'll have to do something about the other group of villains on the planet, who are calling themselves the "Demon Lord's Army" or whatever. After all, this world doesn't need two evil organizations!
YEN ON
Yen Press
For more information
visit www.yenpress.com